THE NORMAL:

OR

METHODS OF TEACHING

THE COMMON BRANCHES,

ORTHOEPY, ORTHOGRAPHY, GRAMMAR, GEOGRAPHY
ARITHMETIC AND ELOCUTION;

INCLUDING

THE OUTLINES, TECHNICALITIES, EXPLANATIONS, DEMONSTRATIONS,
DEFINITIONS AND METHODS,
INTRODUCTORY AND PECULIAR TO EACH BRANCH.

By ALFRED HOLBROOK,
PRINCIPAL OF NORMAL SCHOOL, LEBANON, OHIO.

FOURTH EDITION.

A. S. BARNES & COMPANY,
NEW YORK AND CHICAGO.

PREFACE.

Multitudes of *growing* teachers spend money by tens or hundreds every year, in *visiting schools*, in order, that by witnessing the operations of teachers of acknowledged ability, they may improve or remodel their own systems. This volume is designed to take a working school on a visit to teachers. It presents to its readers in succession, classes in the several grades of the common branches in actual operation, and the teachers pursuing such methods as have proved abundantly successful with large numbers who have tried them.

The Normal has been undertaken as a matter of necessity for training classes of Teachers. All books hitherto written for teachers, being designed only as reference books, are too general to be used as text books. If Teaching is a science, it can be taught as a science; and text books can be used with as much advantage as in other sciences. As the work has progressed, the different PARTS have been brought to the test in Classes of Teachers, and have been found greatly to facilitate the peculiar duties and labors of the Normal School.

The different PARTS, as they have appeared from time to time, have been used by many hundreds of teachers as Guide-books in their school-room duties, being consulted, more or less, daily, for hints and aids in the management of the several classes. From many such teachers, in the different grades of schools, both public and private, the author has received encouraging assurances of the utility, the necessity of the work. In numerous instances teachers, aided by its directions and suggestions, have remodeled their entire operations, and from very indifferent materials, as they had supposed, have been able to reconstruct and build up an efficient and successful system.

The PARTS on Geography, Grammar, and Arithmetic, are used by pupils as well as teachers, for reference books in the preparation of their lessons; the classifications and demonstrations affording aid in the thorough investigation of each of these branches.

The Second and Sixth Parts are designed to be used as text books in Reading and Speaking; though prepared for Teachers' Classes in the Normal School, they will be found none the less suitable for classes in Reading and Speaking in any school.

Though the special methods of only the branches mentioned on the title page are given in this volume, the General Method described in connection with teaching advanced classes in Grammar in Part III, is equally applicable to the Higher Branches.

Fellow Teachers, should any one of you make a panorama of the school under your special charge, or the system of schools under your general supervision, painted on successive pages in word pictures, as I have endeavored to do, please let me know; I shall wish to obtain a sight of it.

I have already been amply compensated for the labor and expense bestowed in the preparation and publication of the Normal; and should the bound volume meet with the same cordial reception from my brethren, which has greeted the several Parts as they have successively appeared, I shall surely have abundant reason to feel that "my labor has not been in vain." A. H.

SOUTH-WESTERN NORMAL SCHOOL,
Lebanon, O., Jan. 1859.

PART I.

CLASSIFIED KNOWLEDGE: OR, SCIENCE.

INTRODUCTION.

Knowledge is that which is already known by the individual, or which he may certainly know by study. In a more general sense, it is that which is already known by any one of the human species; and hence may be known by many others.

All else is *mystery*. The limits of knowledge are constantly enlarging, but mystery, instead of diminishing, becomes still more enlarged. Mysterious, unanswerable problems rise on every side. For every new fact that is acquired by accident or investigation, many new mysteries present themselves to the inquirer. This will be found to be true in every direction. The man of few thoughts has few difficulties or doubts; the idiot, none. But as the boundaries of thought increase by its own activity, innumerable queries spring up on every side, some of which are generalized with previous queries and their answers, and are thus solved or explained; others, however, are retained for generalization and solution till a sufficient number of other truths of similar kind are clustered or classified together to form a law or general principle. He who is most successful in classifying isolated facts, in perceiving identities, similarities, and relations in truths, will most speedily arrive at a satisfactory knowledge of things. Again, he who has the most truth already classified has every advantage over him whose knowledge, such as it, lies in chaos; in bare, isolated, unconnected facts, or semblances of facts, retained in the memory on the principle of locality or association. Again, it is not always borne in mind that truth generalized or systematized is just as mysterious after all. The reference of a new fact to a general principle is commonly taken for a satisfactory solution of the why and wherefore connected with it; while to the thinker the mystery remains just as much unsolved as before; nay, much enhanced by the consideration.

Take, for example, the great Newtonian theory of the law of gravitation. "Why," said NEWTON, as thousands had said before, "does this apple fall to the ground?" The thousands had generalized the fact by saying, "All bodies fall to the earth." NEWTON asked again, "Why do all bodies fall to the earth?" The matter remained just as much a mystery after that generalization as before. In solving the mystery he discovered and demonstrated the wider generalization, "All matter attracts all other, directly as the weight of the masses and inversely as the square of the distance."

Thinkers are now left in more profound mystery than before NEWTON. For, why does matter exert this power in this manner? Non-thinker replies, "God has imparted this property to matter;" just as Non-thinker before the days of Newton, said, "God has established this law, 'All things fall towards the earth.'"

Who will then explain the law of gravitation? that is, generalize it with other facts known or unknown, and, perhaps, subvert this law, as NEWTON dissipated the notion that bodies fall because the direction is downward.

It has been well remarked, that there is but one idea in the mind of God, *i. e.*, all facts are generalized or comprehended under one law, universal and eternal. Is that law simply his will? or is it the inevitable relation of things over which a God of truth exerts no control, but with which all his acts harmonize, and with which he would have the acts of all his creatures coincide? Who will answer?

That which is unknown, we call *mystery*. But that which is known and not generalized may take different names according to circumstances. It may be called *information*, *intelligence*, or *crude undigested knowledge*, which is but a slight remove from ignorance. A man possessing much knowledge in this unsystematized state, may be said, possibly, to be *intelligent*, but surely no one would call him *scientific*. Whereas, another, whose general knowledge was incomparably less, who had mastered the principles of one subject, as of chemistry or botany, might justly be called a *man of science*.

In *systematizing knowledge* as it now exists, in other words, converting it into *Science*, it will be found that there are no very well defined lines of division. Ideas may be grouped, facts gathered in clusters and crystallized into sub-systems, but we shall discover before any group is complete and well arranged in itself, that we have numerous truths that are required just as necessarily to complete the arrangement in another group. We may find, indeed, that some sciences, as generally received, may be entirely absorbed by others, either in a mass or by being divided, according to the respective claims of the several others.

In a General Classification of Knowledge, then, like the one presented, there will arise numerous difficulties, from the first division, down through the location of the various branches, according to their natural relations. No two persons, even though equally well disciplined, would probably agree in the details of an arrangement of this kind.

With regard to the first division of *Knowledge*, viz: Literature, the Sciences, and the Arts; it is that *generally* recognized. The nature of things demands this division, and general assent corroborates it. The division of the Ancients was Physics, Metaphysics, and the Arts. The division of the Moderns is, Mind, Matter, and its inseparable concomitants, power and quantity; lastly, the Arts. The difficulty, then, is not in the grand division as aforesaid, but in locating the several departments; much more in locating the various branches. One might claim, for instance, that Ethics belongs more properly in Phrenics, another would place it in Epistatics, as connected inseparably with human governments. We have placed it in Theotics, as being more closely associated with relations to the Deity: the moral nature being the image of God implanted in the soul.

CLASSIFIED KNOWLEEGE: OR, SCIENCE.

- Literature.
- The Sciences.
- The Arts.

DEPARTMENTS AND BRANCHES OF LITERATURE

- **Phrenics,**
  - Psychology,
  - Phrenology,
  - Grammar,
  - Elocution,
  - Rhetoric,
  - Logic,
  - Didactics.
- **Theotics,**
  - Theology,
    - Theism,
    - Deism,
    - Pantheism,
    - Polytheism,
    - Atheism.
  - Religion,
    - Christianity,
    - Judaism,
    - Mohammedanism,
    - Paganism,
    - Infidelity,
    - Ethics,
- **Chronics,**
  - History,
    - True,
      - Sacred,
      - Profane.
    - Fictitious.
  - Chronology,
  - Biography,
    - True,
    - False—Novels.
  - Travels,
  - Poems,
    - Epic.
  - Archæology,
- **Epistatics,**
  - Law,
    - Natural,
    - Civil,
      - Common,
      - Statute.
    - International,
    - Ecclesiastical.
  - Government,
    - Patriarchal,
    - Monarchical,
      - Absolute,
      - Limited.
    - Democratic,
      - Pure,
      - Representative.

CLASSIFIED KNOWLEDGE: OR, SCIENCE.

{ LITERATURE
THE SCIENCES
THE ARTS.

DEPARTMENTS AND BRANCHES OF THE SCIENCES.

GEOTICS, { Geography, Geology, Mineralogy, Chemistry, Botany, Zoology.

MATHEMATICS, { Abstract, { Arithmetic, Geometry, Analysis, Algebra, An. Geometry, Calculus.
Applied, { Book-Keeping, Mensuration, Surveying, Navigation, Astronomy.

THERAPEUTICS, { Anatomy, Physiology, Pathology, Hygiene, Medicine, { Physopathy, Allopathy, Homœopathy, Hydropathy, Electropathy.

PHYSICS, { Mechanics, Hydrostatics, Hydraulics, Pneumatics, Acoustics, Pyronomics, Optics, Electrics, Physical Astronomy.

CLASSIFIED KNOWLEDGE: or, SCIENCE.

- Literature.
- The Sciences
- The Arts.

DEPARTMENTS AND BRANCHES OF THE ARTS.

Technics,
- Agriculture,
- Horticulture,
- Pomology,
- Manufactures,
- Printing.

Graphics,
- Drafting,
  - Linear,
  - Mathematical,
  - Perspective,
  - Isometrical,
  - Shades and Shadows.
- Architecture,
- Navitecture,
- Civil Engineering.

Polemics,
- Strategy,
  - Infantry,
  - Cavalry,
  - Artillery,
  - Naval.
- Tactics,
- Military Engineering.

Cosmics,
- Painting,
  - Pencilling,
  - Photography,
  - Engraving.
- Sculpture,
- Music,
- Poetry,
- Dancing.

DEFINITIONS.

PRELIMINARY TERMS.

1

Knowledge. That which is known.

Mystery. That which is not known.

2.

Science. Knowledge systematized and explained.

Empiricism. Knowledge not systematized or explained.

Dogmatism. Opinions asserted as knowledge.

3.

Conjecture. A supposition assumed without satisfactory data.

Hypothesis. A supposition assumed to account for a fact.

Theory. A supposition sustained by several facts, which it generalizes and explains.

4.

Theory, The systematic arrangement of laws and principles.

Practice. The application of such laws and principles to useful purposes.

5.

Discovery. The act of finding out that which previously existed.

Invention. The act of contriving and producing that which did not previously exist.

6.

GRAND DIVISIONS OF KNOWLEDGE.

LITERATURE. That grand division of knowledge which comprises all those branches treating of the mind, its nature and communications; also, the responsibilities, history and government of man.

THE SCIENCES. That grand division of knowledge which comprises all those branches which treat of matter and quantity.

THE ARTS. That grand division of knowledge which comprises all those branches which treat of the improvement or embellishment of matter.

7.

DEPARTMENTS OF LITERATURE.

PHRENICS. That department of knowledge which comprises all those branches which treat of the nature of mind, and the communication of thought.

THEOTICS. That department of knowledge which comprises all those branches which treat of God, and the obligations of men to the Deity and to each other.

CHRONICS. That department of knowledge which comprises all those branches which involve the lapse of time as a necessary element.

EPISTATICS. That department of knowledge which comprises all those branches which treat of human laws and government.

8.

DEPARTMENTS OF THE SCIENCES.

GEOTICS. That department of the sciences which comprises all those branches which treat of the material world, its surface, structure, materials and inhabitants.

THERAPEUTICS. That department of the sciences which comprises all those branches necessary to the preservation and restoration of health.

PHYSICS. That department of the sciences which comprises all those branches which treat of matter in the mass; also, of force and motion.

MATHEMATICS. That department of the sciences which comprises all those branches which treat of quantity, and its applications to substance, time and space.

9.

DEPARTMENTS OF THE ARTS.

TECHNICS. That department of the arts which comprises all those branches which contribute to the necessities and comfort of man and beast.

GRAPHICS. That department of the arts which comprises all those useful branches in which mathematical drafting is a necessary element.

POLEMICS. That department of the arts which comprises all those branches which treat of war and fortification.

COSMICS. That department of the arts which comprises all those branches which contribute to the pleasures of the taste and imagination; usually called the Fine Arts.

10.

BRANCHES OF PHRENICS.

PSYCHOLOGY. That branch of knowledge which treats of the mind, its nature, powers and relations.

Phrenology. That branch which treats of the mind, as manifested by the form of the skull.

Grammar. That branch which treats of language, and its correct use, in the communication of thought.

Elocution. That branch which treats of vocal delivery, in reading and speaking.

Rhetoric. That branch which treats of clearness, force, and elegance, in the use of language; also, of the invention, development, and arrangement of ideas.

Logic. That branch which treats of thinking and reasoning correctly.

Didactics. That branch which treats of the means and methods of imparting instruction; also, of school arrangements and school discipline.

11.

DIVISIONS OF THEOTICS.

Theology. That division of knowledge which treats of the existence, nature, and attributes of God.

Religion. That division of knowledge which treats of the obligations of men to God, and to each other.

12.

BRANCHES OF THEOLOGY.

Theism. That branch which treats of God, as having given a revelation of his will to man.

Deism. That branch which treats of God as xisting, but denies a revelation.

Pantheism. That branch which treats of God as being all things, and of all things as being God.

Polytheism. That branch which treats of many gods, with distinct and conflicting natures.

Atheism. That branch which treats of natural law as controlling all things, and denies the existence of a Supreme Intelligence.

13.

BRANCHES OF RELIGION.

Christianity. That branch which treats of the religion of Jesus Christ, which recognizes the Old and New Testaments as a divine revelation.

Judaism. That branch which treats of the religion of the Jews, which recognizes only the Old Testament as a divine revelation.

Mohammedanism. That branch which treats of the religion established by Mahomet, and which recognizes the Koran as a divine revelation.

Paganism. That branch which treats of the various beliefs of the heathen, or polytheists.

Infidelity. That branch which treats of the doctrine of sceptics; or those who do not believe in a divine revelation.

Ethics. That branch which treats of morality, or the obligations of men to each other; usually called Moral Philosophy.

14.

BRANCHES OF CHRONICS.

History. That branch which treats of the rise and progress of nations and communities; giving a narration of events pertaining to each, in order of their occurrence, with their causes and consequences.

Sacred History. That given by the writers of the Old and New Testaments.

Profane History. That derived from any other source than the Bible.

CHRONOLOGY. That branch which treats of the various divisions and periods of time, and the methods of reckoning the dates of past events.

BIOGRAPHY. That branch which treats of the lives and characters of individuals.

ARCHÆOLOGY. That branch which treats of the Ancients, their knowledge, manners, customs, etc.

TRAVELS. That branch which treats of adventures in journeys; also, of the manners, customs, curiosities, and productions of foreign countries or states.

15.

BRANCHES OF EPISTATICS.

Law—A rule of action.

NATURAL LAW. That branch which treats of law as existing in the social relations, prior to any positive precept or enactment.

CIVIL LAW. That branch which treats of law established in society, by general usage or positive enactment.

STATUTE LAW. That form of civil law established by legislative power; also, recorded and published as law.

COMMON LAW. That form of civil law established by general usage, and recognized by the decisions of courts.

INTERNATIONAL LAW. That branch which treats of the regulation of the intercourse of nations.

ECCLESIASTICAL LAW. That branch which treats of the laws established for the government of a church.

Government.—A method of administering law.

PATRIARCHAL GOVERNMENT. That in which the law is administered by the head of the family or tribe, called a Patriarch, Chief, Sheik, etc.

ABSOLUTE MONARCHY. That form of government in which the will of the sovereign is unrestrained by legislative enactment.

LIMITED MONARCHY. That form of government in which the power of the sovereign is restrained by a constitution and laws.

DEMOCRACY. That form of government in which the people choose their own rulers, and make their own laws.

REPUBLIC. That form of government in which the people choose their own rulers; also, representatives to make their laws. It is also called a Representative Democracy.

16.

BRANCHES OF GEOTICS.

GEOGRAPHY. That branch which treats of the Earth's surface; also, of the phenomena of land, water, and atmosphere.

GEOLOGY. That branch which treats of the structure of the earth and the causes of the existing arrangement of the mineral masses in the earth's crust.

MINERALOGY. That branch which treats of the inorganic materials of the earth; their composition, properties, relations and classification; also, of the means of determining them.

CHEMISTRY. That branch which treats of the elements of matter; their nature and properties; their laws of combination and decomposition; also, of the means of combining and separating them.

BOTANY. That branch which treats of plants; their habits, habitations, uses, and classification; also, of the means of determining them.

ZOOLOGY. That branch which treats of animals, their structure, habits, habitations and classification; also, of the succession and distribution of the various classes, orders, genera, and species of the earth.

17.

BRANCHES OF THERAPEUTICS.

ANATOMY. That branch which treats of the different parts of organized bodies; their composition, construction, and arrangement.

PHYSIOLOGY. That branch which treats of the functions and properties of the different parts of organized bodies; also, of vital phenomena, their causes, methods, and aims.

PATHOLOGY. That branch which treats of diseases, their nature, symptoms and causes.

HYGIENE. That branch which treats of the preservation of health.

MEDICINE. That branch which treats of the cure or alleviation of disease.

PHYSOPATHY. The cure of disease by attending to the demands of the system, as indicated to the patient himself by his feelings and desires.

Allopathy. The cure of disease by inducing a condition of the system opposite to, or incompatible with that essential to the disease.

Homœopathy. The cure of disease by inducing in the patient affections similar to the disease. It is accomplished chiefly by minute doses of medicine.

Hydropathy. The cure of disease by the internal or external application of water.

Electropathy. The cure of disease by the application of electrical currents to the system, or part affected.

Motorpathy. The cure of disease by rubbing or kneading the parts affected.

18.

DIVISIONS OF MATHEMATICS.

Pure, or Abstract Mathematics. That division of the subject which considers quantity, apart from any particular substance, time, or space.

Mixed, or Applied Mathematics. That division of the subject which considers magnitude or number, as applied to some definite substance, time, or space.

19

BRANCHES OF PURE MATHEMATICS.

Arithmetic. That branch which treats of Numbers; their properties, laws, proportions; also, of the processes involved in their applications.

Geometry. That branch which treats of space, in all its varied forms, portions, and relations; also, of the processes involved in determining magnitudes in known units.

Analysis. That branch which treats of Quantity, and makes use of letters of the alphabet to express numbers, and of signs to express operations.

Algebra. The application of Analysis to Arithmetic.

Analytical Geometry. The application of Analysis to Geometry.

Calculus—Differential and Integral. That branch of Mathematics, in which infinitesimal differences are used as a means of investigation and calculation.

20.

BRANCHES OF MIXED MATHEMATICS.

Book-Keeping, or Commercial Arithmetic. That branch which treats of the application of Arithmetic, to all transactions of trade; and of such a record of transactions, as enables a person to ascertain the true state of his business, at any time.

Mensuration. That branch which treats of the means of ascertaining the exact quantity of surface or solidity, contained on or in the different forms and portions of matter.

Surveying. That division of Mensuration which treats of determining the limits, and area of land; also, of dividing lands proportionally.

Navigation. That branch which treats of the means of directing and measuring the course of ships, by the application of geometrical principles, or by astronomical observations.

Astronomy. That branch which treats of the

celestial bodies; their magnitudes, motions, distances, periods of revolution, and eclipses.

21.

BRANCHES OF PHYSICS.

MECHANICS. That branch which treats of force and motion; their properties, laws and applications, either directly or through machinery.

HYDROSTATICS. That division of Mechanics which treats of the equilibrium and pressure of fluids at rest, and of their properties and laws.

HYDRAULICS. That division of Mechanics which treats of the motions, and forces of elastic fluids, as air and steam.

ACOUSTICS. That branch which treats of sound; its cause, nature, laws, and phenomena.

PYRONOMICS. That branch which treats of heat, its causes, nature, laws, phenomena, and applications.

OPTICS. That branch which treats of light, and vision; their causes, nature, laws, and phenomena; also, of the construction and use of instruments, designed to modify light, or aid vision. Such instruments are always constructed on mathematical principles.

ELECTRICS. That branch which treats of Electricity; its development, nature, laws, phenomena, and applications; also, of the construction and use of the various instruments designed for the development and application of the agent, or the elucidation of the principles involved.

PHYSICAL ASTRONOMY. That branch which treats of the celestial bodies; their nature, their phenomena, the laws by which their motions are governed, the forces by which their motions are maintained, and their influence on each other.

22.

BRANCHES OF TECHNICS.

AGRICULTURE. That branch which treats of the cultivation of fields for the purpose of producing roots, fruits, and grains, for the use of man and beast; also, the raising and feeding of animals useful for food or labor.

HORTICULTURE. That branch which treats of the cultivation of gardens, for the purpose of producing vegetables, for immediate home consumption; also, ornamental and medicinal plants.

POMOLOGY. That branch which treats of the cultivation of fruits; also, of their preservation, and preparation for market.

MANUFACTURES. That branch which treats of working, by hand or machinery, any raw material, as obtained from the earth, the agriculturist, or the miner into any form more suitable for use.

23.

BRANCHES OF GRAPHICS.

DRAFTING. That branch which treats of representing objects by lines, with mathematical precision; such representations being used as guides by mechanics in construction.

ARCHITECTURE. That branch which treats of the construction of houses, and other buildings, for purposes of civil life.

NAVITECTURE. That branch which treats of the construction of ships, other vessels, and boats, for navigation, or home purposes.

CIVIL ENGINEERING. That branch which treats of the construction of railroads, canals, docks, bridges, roads, and other public works. It is distinguished from Military Engineering, which treats of matters pertaining to war.

24.

BRANCHES OF POLEMICS.

STRATEGY. That branch which treats of the management of an army, in such a manner as to diminish or destroy an enemy's forces.

TACTICS. That branch which treats of the management and drill of different portions of an army —as the fleet, artillery, cavalry, and infantry.

MILITARY ENGINEERING. That branch which treats of the construction of camps and fortifications; also, of the means of conducting a siege or blockade.

GUNNERY. That branch which treats of the management of ordnance, and other fire-arms.

FENCING. That branch which treats of the sword, its use in attack or defence.

25.

BRANCHES OF COSMICS; OR THE FINE ARTS.

PAINTING. That branch which treats of representing objects on surfaces, by the proper application and arrangement of light, shade, and colors.

PHOTOGRAPHY. That branch which treats of representing objects on surfaces by the chemical action of light, on various substances. It is divided into various sub-branches; as daguerreotyping, ambrotyping, petroleotyping, etc., depending on the material of the surface on which the picture is taken.

ENGRAVING. That branch which treats of producing letters, figures, designs, or pictures, on some hard substance, for the purpose of being subsequently printed on paper.

SCULPTURE. That branch which treats of carving, cutting, or hewing wood, stone, or metal, into images, to represent real or imaginary objects.

MUSIC. That branch which treats of the production and combination of agreeable sounds, in such a manner as to constitute melody or harmony; also, of the properties of sounds, and their relation to each other.

POETRY. "The music of the soul." That branch which treats of the production of such thought, and the use of such metrical language, as will excite the imagination, and gratify the taste.

DANCING. "The poetry of motion." That branch which treats of the motion of the human form, in measured and graceful steps, curves, gyrations, and figures, usually in harmony with music, and regulated by it.

METHOD

OF USING THE GENERAL CLASSIFICATION OF KNOWLEDGE IN TEACHING.

This Classification is an introduction to every branch taught in every grade of school; District School, Seminary, or College. No teacher should commence any subject, at least with scholars who are able to read fluently, and intelligently, without pointing out the relation of that branch to other branches, and its location in the circle of the Sciences. Knowledge exists too much in eddies, and detached parcels, in most minds, even of our better class of teachers. The relations, scope, and symmetry of the various branches, are almost entirely neglected, and they are studied as they are taught, as having no connection with each other; and not unfrequently, without teacher or scholar perceiving any relations existing between his subject, and any existing object in heaven, or earth, save the text-book, and an examination day.

The true teacher may lay a broad foundation for every subject, outside of his text-book, in the presentation of this, or some similar outline of his subject with its related subjects.

In opening a school, or in commencing a term, when scholars have no lessons prepared to recite, this General Classification of Knowledge, in part, or entire, forms a very appropriate and interesting introduction to all the branches to be taught in the school. Scholars, especially the younger classes, should not be required to copy it all, but only such parts as are more directly connected with the branches they are designing to pursue.

The student of Grammar, for instance, when somewhat advanced in the study, will find new light and interest, in discovering its relations with the other branches of Phrenics, and the other departments of Literature. The grand division, Literature, with its four Departments, and the Branches of Phrenics, might be copied into his Note Book or Copy Book. The definitions should also be copied, (unless scholars supply themselves with the printed classification,) and committed to memory.

Again; the student of Arithmetic, especially if reviewing, should acquaint himself with the various divisions of Mathematics; and should take a comprehensive view of the whole field, by means of that Department of the general classification and the definitions, given in *The Normal;* and the explanations which any competent teacher could add.

So in other branches. Teachers and students should, in the commencement, and in the reviews, bring up the Department in which the Branch is located, and give on the blackboard, all the sister branches, with their definitions. Should any branch be taken up, which is not found in the General Classification, it will probably find its place as a division of one of the branches given. Conchology, for instance, is a division of Zoology; Meteorology is a subdivision of Geography; Uranography is a division of Physical Astronomy.

PART II.

ORTHOEPY

AND

ORTHOGRAPHY.

ACKNOWLEDGEMENT.

THE EDITOR takes pleasure in acknowledging the important aid afforded by Mr. C. S. Royce, Agent of the Ohio State Phonetic Association, in the preparation of this part on Orthoepy and Orthography. It is confidently believed that through him the most approved views of Phoneticians have been made subservient to a more systematic and useful presentation of the principles involved in the connection of the written and spoken elements of our language than in any work that has hitherto appeared.

INTRODUCTION.

LOCATION AND BEARINGS.

IN commencing every subject of instruction, it is the first business of the Teacher to direct his own attention to the place that subject holds in the Grand Circle of the Sciences. He may aid himself, by consulting the General Classification of knowledge, contained in Part I. If his pupils are sufficiently advanced, they should be required to copy his presentation of so much of that classification as he may think desirable, on the black-board; and having learned the definitions, they should reproduce it from memory on the board, and give the definitions.

In this manner, both teacher and scholar will discover the true location and bearing of whatever subject they undertake.

Primary and secondary scholars, however, in reading and spelling, would hardly be profited by a consideration of the General Classification; but all scholars more advanced would do well to ascertain what BRANCH they are studying while they are learning to spell.

A presentation of PHRENICS and the definitions of the branches it includes. place this matter in its proper light.

THE NATURAL ORDER OF THE BRANCHES.

The first study of the child is the voice of its mother. Almost instinctively it recognizes it, and gathers much meaning from its varied tones and accents. At a very early period the child is able to distinguish, also, many articulate sounds, and their signification. No sooner does it do this, than it endeavors to reproduce these sounds in the expression of its desires and feelings.

Orthoepy, then, being the first study by nature; it is proper that art should fall in with the plan. There is no advantage, however, in beginning any course of instruction till children are able to communicate and receive ideas readily by means of spoken language. When instruction does commence, let it be so much in accordance with nature, with the child's nature, that he shall not conceive a repugnance for knowledge, that years will not eradicate.

Orthoepy is but an introduction to Orthography. Then, Orthography serves as an introduction to Reading and Composition; and these are indispensable in the pursuit of all other branches.

METHODS OF TEACHING THE ALPHABET.

The common or a-b-c method of teaching the alphabet is as serious an obstacle as can well be devised, in the way of the child, to hinder his progress, and render instruction repulsive; yet millions have lived through it, in spite of all the horrors of the passage. It is not to be wondered, however, that so many ever after hate their books and persist in ignorance and vice.

To show the absurdity of the plan: the child is compelled to call twenty-six shapeless characters by their meaningless names, until he learns them. After he has learned them, he is worse off than before, so far as their use is concerned. These names only mislead the child as to the true power of the letters, and are constantly in his way in finding out the sound of any of them in any of their combinations.

Take, for instance, *a* in hat, or hall; *e* in met, or hate. What idea of the *sound* of these letters in these words is obtained from their names? If any, a false idea, which the teacher has to correct by long drilling.

The sounds or powers of letters unincumbered with these delusive names, can be obtained with great rapidity, if letters are so used as to be reliable. The Phonotypic alphabet presents letters of a reliable character to children; and when they learn a letter, it has not to be unlearned or learned over again from two to five times, involving every word in which it occurs in almost impenetrable obscurity.

But the objector says, "The child has to learn the common alphabet after all, even after he has learned the Phonotypic with its forty-three characters." I answer, that is true, but he learns it without effort on the part of the teacher. Having got the scent of ideas in words of Phonotypic letters, he will search them out in the Romanic, and will thread their mazes with an avidity so keen that he will compel his mother to aid him, rather than be himself compelled by his teacher, against a repugnance that is continually increasing.

The use of the Romanic Alphabet may be learned by means of the Phonotypic, in one-tenth of the time, and with one-fiftieth of the labor bestowed by the teacher in the common method.

TEACHING SPELLING.

The charge is brought against our modern schools, that "children do not learn to spell." It is further urged that they are crowded through the higher branches, while they cannot write a friendly letter without misspelling half of the words. Our teachers should be so *trained*, as to leave no ground for this charge; hence, much space is given in this number to the various methods of teaching Spelling or Orthography.

ORTHOGRAPHIC PARSING.

The subject of Orthography is beginning to assume its proper place in our County Examinations of teachers. Many Boards are adopting the practice of testing the knowledge of candidates by some plan of orthographic parsing.

A complete system is developed in this work, which reaches all that is desirable to be known in the analysis of spoken and written words. Not only is a form given for the purpose, with explanations, but a great variety of words is analyzed by the form. So that if a teacher carefully study these examples, he never can be at loss for the proper method of disposing of any class of words or combinations of sounds, or letters.

GENERAL OUTLINE OF GRAMMAR.

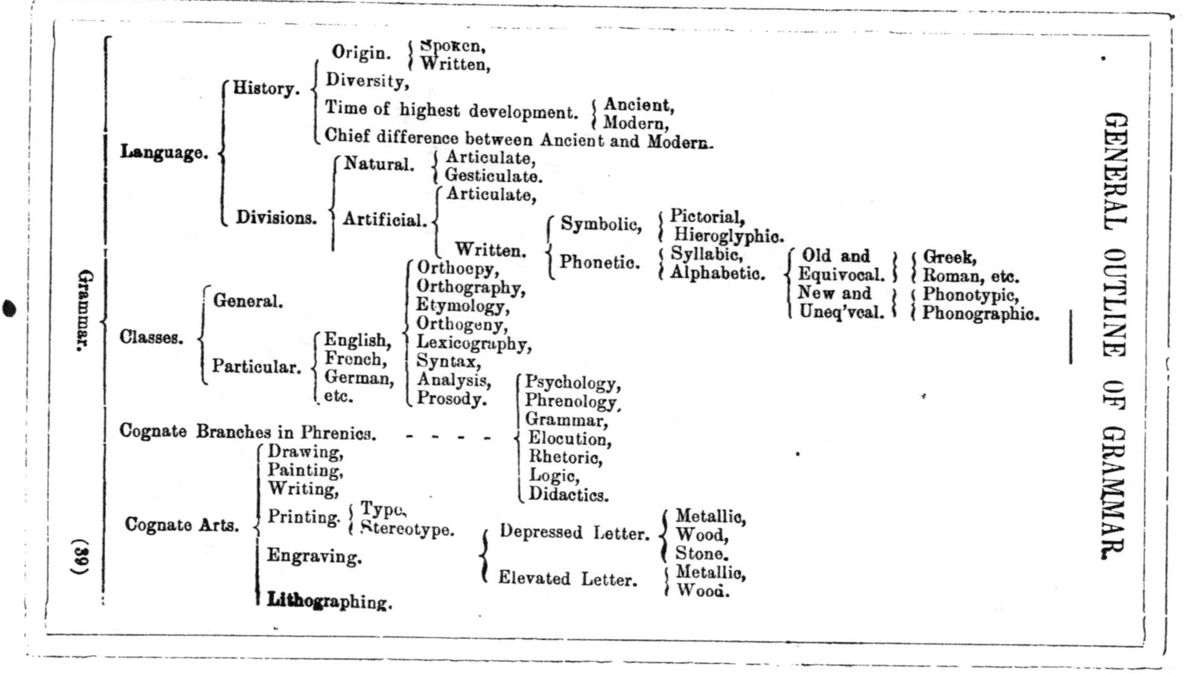

LANGUAGE.

HISTORY.

1

ORIGIN OF SPOKEN LANGUAGE.

LANGUAGE was a divine gift. Spoken Language was used undoubtedly by our first parents. Adam gave names to all cattle, and to fowls of the air, and to every beast of the field, before there was a helpmeet for him; so says the Bible. He is also represented as talking directly with that Being, from whom he derived the faculty of speech, and who trained him in its use.

Let us, Teachers, remember who was the first of our profession; and not only so, but that no profession has been more highly honored.

2

ORIGIN OF WRITTEN LANGUAGE.

The first account we have of Written Language, is the writing of the decalogue on the tablets of stone. It is remarked that all the Hebrew characters except one or two unimportant marks, which have since been added to the language, are found in the Ten Commandments.

Before Written Language, Pictures, Monuments, and Medals were used to commemorate events, and to some slight extent to communicate ideas between those of the same age. These forms, however, represented *things*, and not *sounds* used in words. The Romanic letters, which we use, are evidently derived from the Greek letters; while the Greek letters, according to their historians, were brought by Cadmus from Phenicia, B. C., 1493. The Phenician alphabet is similar, in some respects, to the Hebrew, as is also the Greek.

Mr. Pitman, in forming his Phonographic Alphabet, seems to have imitated the Hebrew more nearly than any other, especially in his vowel system. Thus we have in the latest and most improved form of Written Language, a restoration of the original characters to some extent, as taught to Moses on Mount Sinai.

3

DIVERSITY OF LANGUAGES.

Profane History assigns no reason for the multiplicity of languages. Sacred History gives us an account of the "confusion of tongues," at the Tower of Babel, and the consequent dispersion of mankind. This may account for the existing number and variety of languages; or, if, as many commentators suppose, the "confusion of tongues" refers to a disagreement of the builders in their plans, and the consequent irreconcilable quarrels, which drove these early inhabitants into diverse parts of the earth, then the changes which take place in the pronunciation and signification of many words in a few years in modern society, even though language is fixed by written characters, and the diversity of pronunciation in different localities in the same country, where there is much and frequent intercourse, will show that when tribes have wandered far from each other, with no written language, with no intercourse, their language, though originally the same, will, in a few generations, become so changed as to become entirely unintelligible to others than the tribe or tribes in more immediate proximity. The great diversity of languages ceases to be a wonder, then, even though men were originally of one blood, used one language, and no miracle inter posed to confound their language.

4

TIME OF HIGHEST DEVELOPMENT.

Both Greece and Rome, at the time of their highest political power, enjoyed the greatest refinement in the arts and sciences. Language is no exception to the rule. Gradual improvement may be traced in the style of their authors from the earliest historical dawn of those nations to the period of their highest glory respectively. This improvement may be noticed in all the qualities which constitute excellence of language; some of which are precision, euphony, flexibility, and susceptibility of nice shades of difference in expressing thought or feeling.

At the present time, the several spoken languages have attained a higher degree of polish and power than at any previous period. Among these modern languages, the German is highly cultivated for the expression of thought, and the Italian for the exhibition of the emotions; while the English yields to no other in its strength, flexibility, and delicacy of expression for both thought and feeling.

5

CHIEF DIFFERENCE BETWEEN ANCIENT AND MODERN LANGUAGES.

This lies in the more highly mechanical structure of their verbs and nouns; the nouns of the ancient languages having more methods of declension, and each declension more terminations than any of the modern nouns. This variety of termination gives equal precision, with much greater latitude of arrangement. The cases of modern nouns are determined to some extent by their position with relation to the verb. The cases of ancient nouns depend entirely on their termination, and not in the least on their position in the sentence. Hence the ancient languages give a better opportunity for securing harmony in the arrangement than the modern.

The verbs of the ancient languages are much more complete in their terminations, and of course make use of less auxiliary verbs. None are necessary save that denoting *being*, which is used only in the passive voice.

6

DEFINITIONS, EXPLANATIONS, AND REMARKS.

1. LANGUAGE. Any method of communicating thought or feeling.

2. NATURAL LANGUAGE. Instinctive methods of communicating thought or feeling.

Remark. Brute animals possess their own instinctive forms of language; many of which forms are understood by other species than those which use them.

Artificial Language. That which must be learned before it can be used.

Vocal Language. That produced by the organs of speech.

7

Written Language. Any method of communicating thought by visible characters, depicted on a surface.

Symbolic Language. That form of written language in which the characters are designed to represent ideas and not sounds.

Phonetic Language. That form of written language in which the characters are designed to represent sounds.

Pictorial Language. That form of symbolic language in which the ideas are plainly represented.

Hieroglyphic Language. That form of symbolic language in which the ideas are so obscurely represented as to need an interpreter.

Syllabic Language. That form of phonetic language in which the characters represent syllables.

Alphabetic Language. That form of phonetic language in which the characters represent separate articulate sounds.

Equivocal Alphabetic Languages. Those in which a letter represents more than one sound, and in which a sound is represented by more than one letter.

The Unequivocal Alphabetic Languages, are those in which the number of letters equals the number of separate articulate sounds—giving but one sound to each letter, and but one letter for each sound.

GESTICULATE LANGUAGE. Any method of communicating or impressing thought or feeling, by motions, postures, or appearances of the animal form, not producing or representing articulated sounds or written characters.

8

GENERAL OR UNIVERSAL GRAMMAR. That form of grammar which treats of all those principles and usages which are common to all languages.

PARTICULAR GRAMMAR. That form of grammar which treats of all those principles, usages, characters, and sounds, comprised in any particular language.

ENGLISH GRAMMAR. That branch which treats of the English language.

9

ORTHOEPY. That division of grammar which treats of articulate sounds, and of their correct use in pronunciation.

ORTHOGRAPHY. That division of grammar which treats of letters, words, and spelling.

ETYMOLOGY. That division of grammar which treats of the derivation and formation of words.

ORTHOGENY. That division of grammar which treats of the classification of words according to their uses.

LEXICOGRAPHY. That division of grammar which treats of the signification of words.

SYNTAX. That division of grammar which treats of the arrangement of words in sentences

Analysis. That division of grammar, which treats of the separation of sentences into their elements.

Prosody. That division of grammar, which treats of versification and punctuation.

General Remark. The definitions of Cognate Branches in Phrenics, including Grammar, will be found in Part I, pages 16 and 17, Section 10.

ORTHOEPY.

Sound.
- Nature,
- Limit of Vibration,
- Rate of progress.

Organs.
- Articulatory,
- Vocal.
- Respiratory.

Articulate sounds.
- See Chart No. 1.

Pronunciation.
- Divisions.
  - Articulation,
  - Accent.
    - Common,
    - Discriminative,
    - Emphatic,
    - Poetic.
- Rules.
  - 1st.,
  - 2nd.

Methods of Teaching.
1. Drill in articulate sounds.
2. Drill in notation of Dictionaries
3. Spell words Phonetically.
4. Parse words Orthographically.

ORTHOEPY.

10

DEFINITIONS, EXPLANATIONS, AND REMARKS.

ORTHOEPY. That division of grammar, which treats of articulate sounds, and their correct use in pronunciation.

SOUND. A sensation produced on the auditory nerve by the rapid vibratory motion of air or other elastic substance.

Remark 1. The vibration that produces the sound is often called sound, as, we say "sound travels," &c.

Remark 2. *Limit of Vibrations.* The least number of vibrations in a second, that can yield a sound to human ear, is 32. The highest number is 30,000; though other animals may perceive vibrations more or less rapid than these limits.

Remark 3. *Rate of Progress.* Sound travels through air at the rate of seven hundred sixty-three miles per hour, or eleven hundred twenty feet per second; through liquids and solids at a rate many times greater.

11

ORGANS OF SPEECH. All those distinct parts of the human system, which are necessarily used in producing the sounds of language.

Articulatory Organs. Those organs of speech which are used in modifying or obstructing sound as produced by the other organs.

They are labia, (lips,) dentes, (teeth,) palatum, (hard palate,) uvula, (soft palate,) nasal fossæ, (cavities of the nose,) larynx, with its cartilages and muscles.

Vocal Organs. Chordæ Vocales, (vocal chords.) These are two pair of membranes, extending backwards and forwards, opposite to each other, through the larynx. They are attached by their two ends and one side, to the walls of the larynx, leaving an open space between them, through which air is drawn in and forced out by the respiratory organs

Voice or Vocal Sound. That sound produced by the vocal chords.

Remark. The vibration of these chords during the emission of vocal sound, may be perceived by placing the fingers on the larynx, externally, at the projection of Adam's apple. The vibration can be detected at no other time.

Respiratory Organs. Those organs of speech used in forcing air through the other organs. They are trachea, (windpipe,) bronchi, (bronchial tubes,) pulmo, (lungs,) diaphragm, and the intercostal, dorsal, and abdominal muscles.

12

Articulate Sound. That made by the organs of speech, and used in language.

Voiced Sound, or Voice. A sound made by the vibration of the vocal chords.

Vocal Sound, or Vocal. A voiced sound,

modified but not obstructed by the articulatory organs.

SIMPLE VOCAL. A vocal, made without a change in the position of the articulatory organs during its emission.

COMPOUND VOCAL. A vocal, made by a change in the position of the articulatory organs, from that required by one simple vocal to that required by another, during its emission.

Remark. This change commences with the emission of the sound, and continues until the close; hence the elements of the compounds are not heard in their purity.

COALESCENT. An articulate sound, that always precedes, and unites with, a vocal.

13

SUBVOCAL SOUND, OR SUBVOCAL. A voiced sound modified and obstructed by the articulatory organs.

ASPIRATED SOUND OR ASPIRATE. An articulate sound made without the vibration of the vocal chords.

PURE ASPIRATE. An aspirate, modified but not obstructed by the articulatory organs.

OBSTRUCTED ASPIRATE. An aspirate, modified and obstructed by the articulatory organs.

14

LABIAL. An articulate sound, modified or obstructed at the lips.

Remark. The vocals and pure aspirates are *modified* only, while the subvocals and the other aspirates are obstructed also.

DENTAL. An articulate sound modified or obstructed at the teeth or gums.

Palatal. An articulate sound, modified or obstructed at the hard palate.

Guttural. An articulate sound, modified or obstructed at the soft palate.

Remark 1*st*. Sounds are obstructed at the lips by the lips alone, or by the teeth and lips.

Remark 2*d*. Sounds are obstructed at the teeth, gums, or hard palate, by the tip of the tongue; and at the soft palate, by the root of the tongue.

15

Abrupt, (also called Explodent and Mute.) An articulate sound, made by such a *perfect contact* of the organs as entirely prevents the escape of air externally.

Continuant, (also called Subvocal.) An articulate sound, made by such *partial contact* of the organs, as to admit of escape of air externally.

Liquid. A continuant, susceptible of simultaneous combination with other obstructed sounds. The liquids are *l* and *r*.

Nasal. A continuant, made by the escape of air through the cavities of the nose only.

Cognate Sounds. Those sounds made by the articulatory organs, in the same positions, and differing only in the vibrations of the vocal chords.

16

Pronunciation. The enunciation of the sounds of a word with correct articulation and accent.

Articulation, (joining.) The distinct enunciation of the sounds in words.

Accent. The greater stress given to one syllable of a word than to others; also, the greater force given to long syllables in poetry.

Common Accent. That given in the ordinary pronunciation of a word, without reference to any other word.

Discriminative Accent. That given to words of the same articulation to distinguish different parts of speech.

EXAMPLES.

1. *Nouns from Verbs.* Ac′cent, accent′; con′cert, concert′; in′sult, insult′, etc.

2. *Adjectives from Verbs.* Ab′sent absent′; com′-pound, compound′; fre′quent, frequent′, etc.

Emphatic Accent. That in which the stress is transferred from the ordinary syllable to another, for the purpose of giving antithetic emphasis more distinctly.

Poetic Accent. That which is placed on long syllables of a poetic foot; even though those syllables should be monosyllabic words.

17
METHODS OF TEACHING PRONUNCIATION.

DRILL IN ARTICULATE SOUNDS.

Commence with vocals as given in Chart No. 1.

1. Repeat each long sound twice in order.

2. Direct the class to do the same in concert with yourself.

3. Direct the class to do the same without your aid. Continue this process until the large majority make the sounds correctly, and in the order of the chart.

4. Drill individuals failing, before the class, in groups, or singly, till each pupil masters all the difficulties.

Chart No. 1.

A Physiological Classification of the Articulate Sounds of the English Language, with the Phonotypic, Websterian, and Worcesterian Notation

					MODIFIED AT THE			
				Producing	Lips. Labials.	Teeth, or Gums. Dentals.	Hard Palate. Palatals.	Soft Palate. Gutturals.
Voiced	Unobstructed Voiced, or Vocals.	Simple.	Long. Notation	Phonotypic,	ɷ ɷ	ɛ ȩ	a ą	ɋ ɵ
				Webster's,	ö, oo ō	ē, ï e	â e̱	ä a̤
				Worcester's	ô, oo ō	ē, ī ë	â a, ai, ea	ä â
			Medial. Notation	Phonotypic, Webster's, Worcester's,				ɑ ȧ
			Short. Notation	Phonotypic,	ɯ	i	e u a	ɵ
				Webster's, Worcester's,	u̦, o̤, o̤o̤ û	i ĭ	e u a ĕ ŭ ă	o̧ ŏ
		Compound.	Open. Notation	Phonotypic,				ȣ ɵ
				Webster's,				ou, ow oi, oy
				Worcester's,				öû, öw öĭ, öy
			Close. Notation	Phonotypic, Webster's, Worcester's,		ų ū ū		ɨ ī ī
		Coalescents, or Continuants.	Notation	Phonotypic, Webster's, Worcester's	w w w	y y y		

OBSTRUCTED AT THE

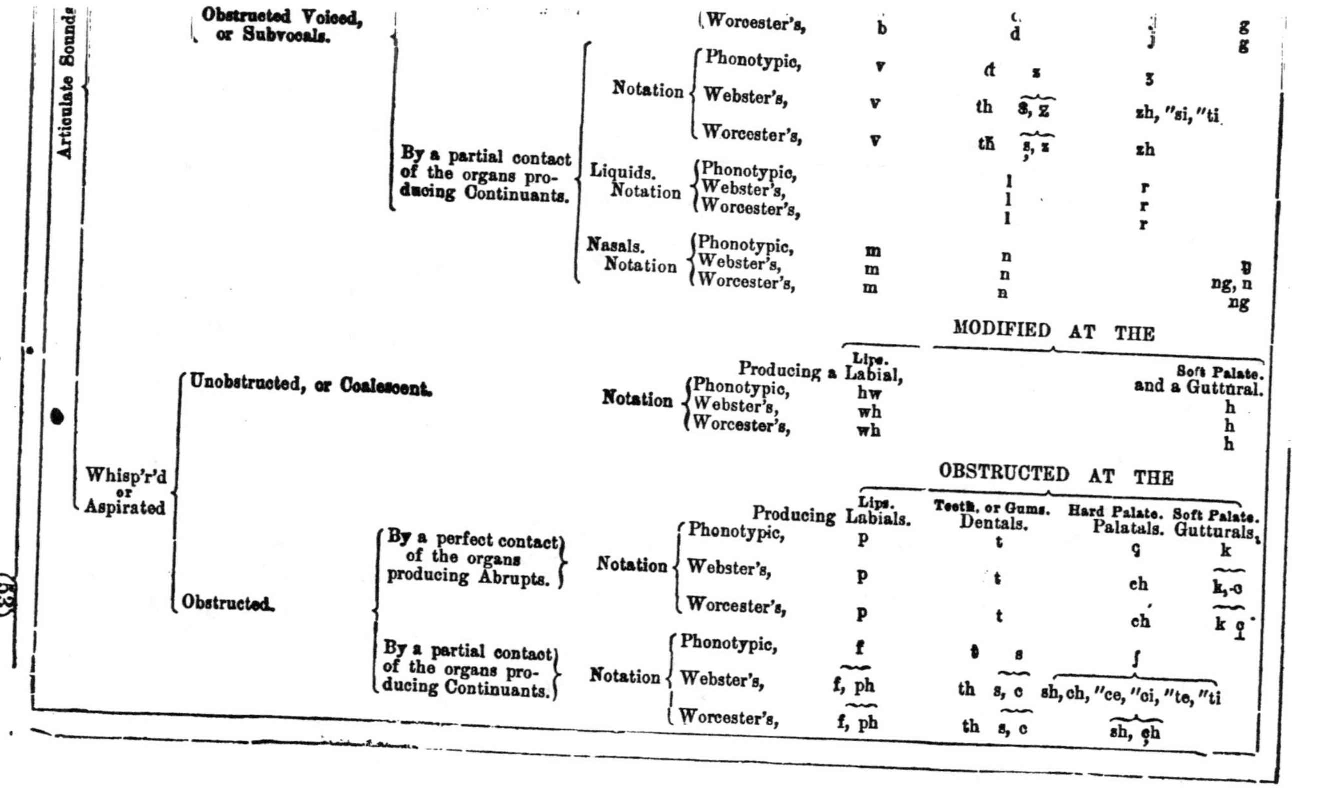

					Lips. Labials.	Teeth, or Gums. Dentals.		Hard Palate. Palatals.	Soft Palate. Gutturals.
Articulate Sounds	Obstructed Voiced, or Subvocals.			Worcester's,	b		d	j	g g
		By a partial contact of the organs producing Continuants.	Notation	Phonotypic,	v	d	z	ʒ	
				Webster's,	v	th	s, z	zh, "si, "ti	
				Worcester's,	v	th	s, z	zh	
			Liquids. Notation	Phonotypic,			l	r	
				Webster's,			l	r	
				Worcester's,			l	r	
			Nasals. Notation	Phonotypic,	m		n		ŋ
				Webster's,	m		n		ng, n
				Worcester's,	m		n		ng
					MODIFIED AT THE				
	Whisp'r'd or Aspirated	Unobstructed, or Coalescent.		Producing a	Lips. Labial,				Soft Palate. and a Guttural.
			Notation	Phonotypic,	hw				h
				Webster's,	wh				h
				Worcester's,	wh				h
					OBSTRUCTED AT THE				
		Obstructed.		Producing	Lips. Labials.	Teeth, or Gums. Dentals.		Hard Palate. Palatals.	Soft Palate. Gutturals.
		By a perfect contact of the organs producing Abrupts.	Notation	Phonotypic,	p	t		ç	k
				Webster's,	p	t		ch	k, c
				Worcester's,	p	t		ch	k c
		By a partial contact of the organs producing Continuants.	Notation	Phonotypic,	f	θ	s	ʃ	
				Webster's,	f, ph	th	s, c	sh, ch, "ce, "ci, "te, "ti	
				Worcester's,	f, ph	th	s, c	sh, çh	

COGNATES.

Chart No. 2.

A. S. E. L.			Labials.	Dentals.	Palatals.	Gutturals
Vocals.	Long,		ꝏ ɷ	ɛ ẹ	a * ą	q ɵ
	Medial,					
	Short,		ɯ *	i *	ɵ u a	ɑ o *
Coalescents.	Vocals,		w	y		
	Aspirates.		hw	*		h
Abrupts.	Subvocals,		b	d	ȷ	g
	Aspirates.		p	t	ç	k
Continuants.	Subvocals,		v	đ z	ʒ	
	Aspirates,		f	ŧ s	ʃ	
	Subvocals,	Liquids.		l	r	
				*	*	
	Subvocals,	Nasals.	m	n		ŋ
			*	*		*

*These sounds are wanting in our language.

5. Pursue the same course with the short vocals.

6. Alternate the cognate vocals on Chart No. 2 and in case a cognate is wanting, say "wanting."

7. Repeat and vary these drills until every scholar can *go through* the vocals long and short, and name the organ at which the sound is modified.

9. Pursue a similar course with the obstructed sounds beginning with the aspirates and following with the subvocals on Chart No. 1; then with cognate sounds, on Chart No. 2.

18

DRILL IN THE NOTATION OF DICTIONARIES.

Take Chart No. 3, and go over in concert, the names of sounds as given, with the sounds following, and the notation of any dictionary used in school.

Thus: Long *a*—a, notation ā, with a short horizontal mark over it.

Short *a*—a, notation ă, with a curved line over it.
Broad *a*—ɵ, notation â, with a circumflex over it.
Italian *a*—q, notation ä, with a diæresis over it.
Medial *a*—ą, wanting in Webster's dictionary.

This will be sufficient to show the drill on the notations It need be followed no further in this form.

2. Require the scholars to look out words in their dictionary, and describe the marks to signify the irregular sounds of the consonants, as city, cane. off, of, church, chaise, etc.

19

SPELLING WORDS PHONETICALLY.

1. This should be practiced more or less in connection with every exercise, in concert, the Teacher accompanying; next, the class in concert without his aid, lastly, individual scholars, always giving opportunity for the members of the class to criticise the spelling of the individuals,—they first raising their hands for permission to do so.

2. Let the Teacher select such phonotypic characters in order, from Chart No. 1 or No. 2, as shall form words. The class will pronounce each sound, as its representative is touched with the pointer, until the elements of a word are thus separately pronunced, then, a signal given, they are expected to pronounce the word together. This exercise should begin with monosyllables, and from these proceed to the most complicated and difficult words.

20

CRITICISM ON PRONUNCIATION.

In recitation of all studies, opportunity should be given the classes for mutual criticism on pronunciation, as well as in other particulars.

This matter of criticism is managed thus.

The teacher asks, "Are there any errors in pronunciation?"

Pupils who have noticed errors, raise their hands.

The teacher calls upon such a scholar as is least in the habit of criticism, to mention the error.

The scholar does it in this form: "Mr. A. B. pronounced 'heard' 'heerd.' He should have given the close sound of e rather than the long." The scholar continues, "he pronounced 'demonstrate' 'demonstrate,' accenting the first syllable instead of the second."

In case of doubt in the mind of any one, either pupil or teacher, a scholar is requested to examine the authorities, Worcester's or Webster's dictionary, which should always be on the teacher's table, and in the pupil's desk.

ORTHOGRAPHY.

Chart No. 3.

						Compound.			
	Simple.					Digraphs.		Trigraphs.	
Vowels.	Species	Notations. Web.	Notations. Wor.	Power.	Example.	Conjoined.	Disjoined.	Conjoined.	Disjoined.
a	Long	ā	ā	a	ate	ai ay ea ei ey	a-e		a-ue
a	Short	a	ă	a	at	aa ai	a-e		
a	Long before *r*	*	á	a	air	aa ai ea ei	a-e		
a	Italian	ä	ä	ɑ	arm	ea ua			
a	Medial	*	a	ɑ	ask				
a	Broad.	a	â	ɵ	all	au aw oa		awe	au-e
e	Long	ē	ē	ɛ	eel	ea ee ei eo ey ie oe	e-e		ea-e ei-e
e	Short	e	ĕ	e	ell	ai ea ei ie oe ue			
e	Close	*	ë	ẹ	ərr				
i	Long	ī	ī	qɛ=ị	isle	ei ie ui uy	i-e		
i	Short	i	ĭ	i	it	ee ei ia ie ui			
o	Long	ō	ō	ω	own	au eo ew oa oe oo ou ow	o-e	eau owe	o-ue
o	Short	o	ŏ	o	on	au ow			
o	Long close	ö	ô	ɷ	move	oe oo ou	o-e		ou-e
o	Short close	o	û	ɯ	wolf	oo ou			
u	Long	ū	ū	ɛɷ=ụ	few	eu ew ue ui	u-e	eau ieu iew	
u	Short	u	ŭ	u	up	eo oe oo ou		eou iou	
w	used only in combinations.								
y	is used as a substitute, or in combinations.								

Diphthongs.

Consonants.	c	soft	c	ç	s	cease		qɛ=i̧	ī ī	eye
	d		d	d	d	did	dd	ɵi=ơ	oi oy öĭ öў	
	f		f	f	f	fife	ff gh ph	qɷ=ɤ	ou ow öu öw	
	g	hard	g	g	g	gig	gg	ɛɷ=ɥ	ħ ū	
		soft	g	g	j	gem				
	h		h	h	h	him				
	j		j	j	j	judge	dg			
	k		k	k	k	kick	ch			
	l		l	l	l	lull	ll			
	m		m	m	m	maim				
	n		n	n	n	nine	nn			
	p		p	p	p	pipe	pp			
	q		q	q	k	quick				
	r		r	r	r	roar	rr			
	s		s	s	s	sauce	ss			
	t		t	t	t	tight				
	v		v	v	v	valve				
	w		w	w	w	way				
			x	x	ks	wax				
	x	sub. for	x	x	gz	exact				
			x	x	z	Xenia				
	Digraphs representing simple sounds.									
	ch		ch	ch	ç	church				
	th	subvocal	th	th	đ	then				
		aspirate	th	th	ŧ	thin				
Aphthongs.	sh		sh	sh	ʃ	shire				
	zh		zh	zh	ʒ	azure				
	ng		ng	ng	ŋ	sing				
	Vowel,									
	Consonant.									

ORTHOGRAPHY.

- **Letters.**
  - **Forms.**
    - **Typical.**
      - *Script,*
      - *Italic.*
      - Roman.
      - Old English.
      - German Text.
      - ORNAMENTAL.
    - **Grammatical.**
      - Capital,
      - Small.
      - Classes.
        - Large,
        - Small.
      - Rules.
    - **Rhetorical.**
      - *Italic.*
      - SMALL CAP.
      - LARGE CAP.
      - **Bold Faced.**
  - **Sizes.**
    - Diamond.
    - Agate,
    - Pearl.
    - Nonpareil,
    - Minion,
    - Brevier,
    - Bourgeois,
    - Long Primer,
    - Small Pica,
    - Pica,
    - English,
    - Great Primer,
  - **Arrangement in Classes, Genera, Species, etc.** — See Chart No. 3.
- **Representation.**
  - By proper representatives,
  - By substitutes.

ORTHOGRAPHY.—Continued.

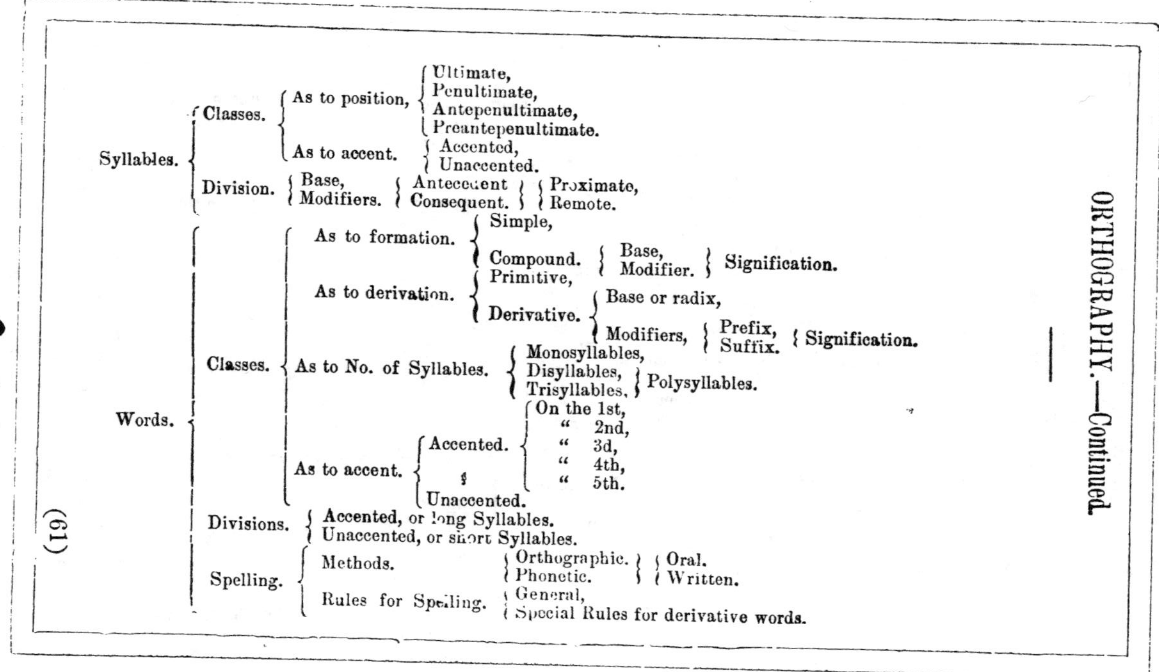

- Syllables.
  - Classes.
    - As to position,
      - Ultimate,
      - Penultimate,
      - Antepenultimate,
      - Preantepenultimate.
    - As to accent.
      - Accented,
      - Unaccented.
  - Division.
    - Base,
    - Modifiers.
      - Antecedent
      - Consequent.
        - Proximate,
        - Remote.
- Words.
  - Classes.
    - As to formation.
      - Simple,
      - Compound.
        - Base,
        - Modifier.
          - Signification.
    - As to derivation.
      - Primitive,
      - Derivative.
        - Base or radix,
        - Modifiers,
          - Prefix,
          - Suffix.
            - Signification.
    - As to No. of Syllables.
      - Monosyllables,
      - Disyllables,
      - Trisyllables,
        - Polysyllables.
    - As to accent.
      - Accented.
        - On the 1st,
        - " 2nd,
        - " 3d,
        - " 4th,
        - " 5th.
      - Unaccented.
  - Divisions.
    - Accented, or long Syllables.
    - Unaccented, or short Syllables.
  - Spelling.
    - Methods.
      - Orthographic.
      - Phonetic.
        - Oral.
        - Written.
    - Rules for Spelling.
      - General,
      - Special Rules for derivative words.

ORTHOGRAPHY.—Continued.

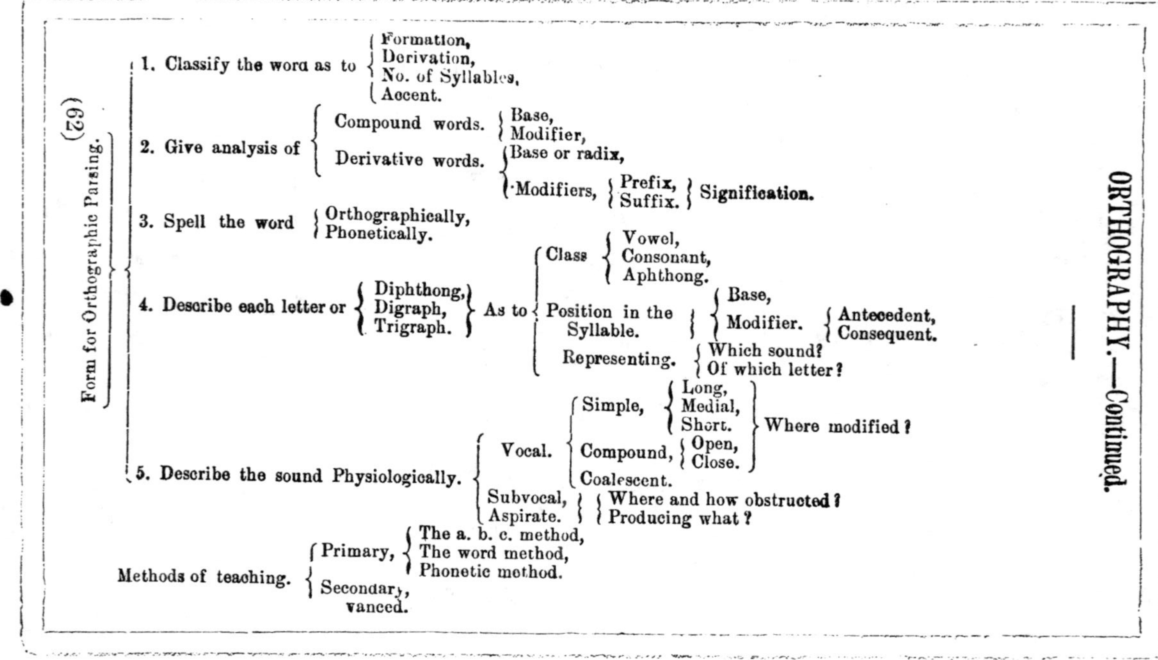

Form for Orthographic Parsing.

1. Classify the word as to
   - Formation,
   - Derivation,
   - No. of Syllables,
   - Accent.
2. Give analysis of
   - Compound words.
     - Base,
     - Modifier,
   - Derivative words.
     - Base or radix,
     - Modifiers,
       - Prefix,
       - Suffix.
         - Signification.
3. Spell the word
   - Orthographically,
   - Phonetically.
4. Describe each letter or
   - Diphthong,
   - Digraph,
   - Trigraph.
   - As to
     - Class
       - Vowel,
       - Consonant,
       - Aphthong.
     - Position in the Syllable.
       - Base,
       - Modifier.
         - Antecedent,
         - Consequent.
     - Representing.
       - Which sound?
       - Of which letter?
5. Describe the sound Physiologically.
   - Vocal.
     - Simple,
       - Long,
       - Medial,
       - Short.
     - Compound,
       - Open,
       - Close.
       - Where modified?
     - Coalescent.
   - Subvocal,
   - Aspirate.
     - Where and how obstructed?
     - Producing what?

Methods of teaching.
- Primary,
  - The a. b. c. method,
  - The word method,
  - Phonetic method.
- Secondary,
  vanced.

ORTHOGRAPHY

21

ORTHOGRAPHY. That division of grammar which treats of letters, syllables, words, and spelling.

LETTER. A visible character, representing by itself, or with one or more besides, an articulate sound; also used to determine signification.

TYPICAL FORMS. These are given in the names that distinguish them in the classification. There are many ornamental forms in use, not given.

GRAMMATICAL FORMS. These are used for em-emphasis or other rhetorical distinction.

POWER OF A LETTER. The sound which a letter represents in a word; also the influence which one letter exerts upon the representative character of another.

22

VOWEL. A letter used to represent a vocal sound; the basis of a syllable.

CONSONANT. A letter used to represent a sub-vocal or aspirate sound, modifying the basis of a syllable.

Remark. Phonographers write many syllables without a vowel as a basis, contending that a sub-vocal is often the basis of a syllable. *e.g.* apple, often. They claim that there is no vocal heard in the second syllable, and that they should be written apl, oftn, or ofn. It seems to me, however, more in accordance with the principles of our orthography to consider a vocal, accented or unaccented, plain or obscure, as the basis of *every* syllable.

APHTHONG, OR SILENT LETTER. A letter which represents no sound, but is used either to modify the representative character of another, or merely to determine signification.

Remark. An aphthong may be a vowel or a consonant aphthong, according to the more common use of the letter.

Explanation. *E*, in the word lade, changes the sound of *a* from short to long; also *g*, in sign, changes the sound of *i* short to long; also *w* in write, determines the signification of the word, and distinguishes it from that of rite; also, *b* in dumb, determines signification, since dum has no signification.

23

DIPHTHONG. One or two vowels, representing a combination of two vocal sounds.

Explanation. The diphthong *i* represents a combination of Italian *a* and long *e*.

The diphthong long *u* represents a combination of long *e* and close *o*.

The diphthong *oi* represents a combination of broad *a* and short *i*.

The diphthong *ou* represents a combination of Italian *a* and close *o*.

These are all the proper diphthongs in the English Language.

24

A Vowel Digraph, or improper diphthong, is a combination of two vowels, in which only one receives a sound, the other being a modifier.

A Conjoined Vowel Digraph is one in which the two vowels are not separated by a consonant.

A Disjoined Vowel Digraph is one in which the two vowels are separated by one or more consonants.

A Consonant Digraph is a combination of two consonants, one or both of which are required to represent a sound.

Remark. A consonant not required to represent a sound of the word, is an aphthong, whether modifying the representative character of a letter or not. Thus, in the consonant digraph *gn*, in the word condign, the *g* modifies the sound of *i*, but is not necessary for the representation of the final sound, and hence is an aphthong.

A Combined Digraph is a combination of a consonant and a vowel to represent a subvocal or an aspirate sound.

Explanation. The consonant *t*, and the vowel *i* are used in the terminal syllable *tion*, to represent the aspirate sound of *sh* or *ch*. *Ci*, *ce*, and *si*, are used in a similar manner.

Vowel Trigraph. A combination of three vowels, representing one or two sounds.

Remark. *Eau* in *beau*, represents one sound; in *beauty*, it represents two combined.

Disjoined Trigraph. One in which a consonant occurs between two of the vowels.

25

SYLLABLE. One or more sounds uttered at one impulse of the breath; also, the letters representing any sound or sounds so uttered.

ULTIMATE SYLLABLE. The last syllable in a word.

PENULTIMATE SYLLABLE, OR PENULT. The last syllable but one in a word.

ANTEPENULTIMATE SYLLABLE. The last syllable but two in a word.

PREANTEPENULTIMATE SYLLABLE. The last syl-syllable but three in a word.

Remark. The syllables of a word are also described in their numerical order, commencing at the left, as first, second, third, &c.

BASE OF A SYLLABLE. The vocal or vowel used in its formation.

MODIFIER. Any sound preceding or succeeding the base of a syllable, or letter or digraph representing such sound.

ANTECEDENT. Any sound preceding the base of a syllable; or letter or digraph representing such sound.

CONSEQUENT. Any sound succeeding the base of a syllable; or letter or digraph representing such sound.

Remark. A letter representing a sound, preceding another, is parsed as an antecedent, though the order of the letter should differ from that of the sounds represented by them.

26

Word. The received sign of an idea, expressed in one or more articulate sounds, or in visible characters representing such sounds.

Simple Word. One which cannot be divided into separate words without radically altering the signification.

Compound Word. One which can be divided into separate words without radically altering their signification.

Primitive Word. One which cannot be reduced to a simpler form, without radically altering its signification.

Derivative Word. One which can be reduced to a simpler form, without radically altering its signification.

Remark. A compound word is considered primitive, if all its parts are primitive, otherwise a derivative. A derivative is considered simple, unless it plainly comes under the definition of a compound.

The Base of a Compound Word is that word representing the fundamental idea.

The Modifier in a Compound Word is that word which describes the other.

The Base of a Derivative Word is the primitive word from which it is derived.

The Modifiers in a Derivative Word are the prefixes or suffixes, or both.

Prefix. One or more syllables, not used as a word of similar meaning in the English language, but placed before words to modify their signification.

Suffix. One or more syllables, not used as a word of similar meaning in the English language, but placed after words to modify their signification.

27

Monosyllable. A word of one syllable.

Dissyllable. A word of two syllables.

Trisyllable. A word of three syllables.

Accented Syllable. One that is pronounced with more force than others in the same word.

Remark 1. Accent may be primary when it is greater than that received by some other syllable in the same word; or secondary, when it is less than that received by some other syllable in the same word.

Remark 2. In prosody, an accented syllable is long in quantity, an unaccented syllable, short in quantity, *i. e.* of time taken to pronounce it.

28

Spelling. A distinct expression of the letters or sounds of a word, in their proper order.

Orthographic Spelling. The expression of the letters, of which a written word is composed, and in their proper order, according to the received authority.

Phonetic Spelling. The separate expression of the elementary sounds of which a word is composed, and in their proper order, according to established usage.

GENERAL RULES FOR SPELLING.

Rule 1. Write no word unless sure of its orthography and signification.

Rule 2. Consult the dictionary in case of doubt.

Rule 3. Apply the rules for derivatives.

Remark. The *special rules* for spelling are to be found in every good grammar, and spelling-book, and need *special attention.* All grades, except primary, should be thoroughly *drilled* in their use. It is not enough *to memorize* them. More than one-half the bad spelling found in school exercises, as well as in business operations, may be justly charged to ignorance of these special rules.

TEACHING THE ALPHABET.

29

TEACHER'S PREPARATION.

The preparation necessary for the successful teaching of Phonotypy, the all-important preparation, I might say, is a thorough practical knowledge of the articulate sounds of our language: an ability to enunciate them distinctly, either separately or in combinations, and to give such directions to others as will, when followed, enable them to do the same.

30

PREPARATION OF PUPILS.

The only preparation necessary for the pupils, is, that they should be of a proper school age, that the school should be properly organized, and that the teacher should so gain the confidence of his young pupils by a pleasant conversation, or other means, as to lead them to speak and act with the freedom of children in a well-regulated home. I very much prefer that they should know nothing of any alphabet.

31

TEACHING THE ARTICULATE SOUNDS.

The first effort in imparting instruction should be to give them some knowledge of articulate sounds. In doing this, avoid the use of technicalities. Select a few such words as *saw*, *say*, *so*, *see*, and taking one of them, as *saw*, call upon the pupils to speak it carefully a few times. The teacher should now resolve it into its elements; enunciating them at first, with a long pause, as, s - - - - - -ө, then with less and less pause, as, s - - - - - ө, s - - - - ө, s - - - ө, s - - ө, s - ө, leading them, if possible, to perceive that those sounds, if enunciated by one impulse of the voice, would constitute the word *saw*, without his thus uttering them. But if this can not be done, the teacher may pronounce the word; after which, he should separate it into its elements, and proceed as before.

Now he should take the elements of another word, as, *say*, without calling their attention to the word by pronouncing it, and enunciate their elements, as in the other case; asking after each enunciation, what the word would be if the sounds were spoken together. Generally, if this is skilfully managed, there will be a corrcet response; after which the sounds should be uttered more and more rapidly, to show them clearly that they were right.

Now, take another word, as, *see*, using special care that they shall perceive from the separate elements, what word they constitute.

32

TEACHING TO READ.

If we have succeeded thus far in cultivating our pupils' powers of observing sound, there will be little trouble in teaching them the letters that represent those sounds.

Calling their attention to the first sound in "*see,*" let us print upon the blackboard the letter "s" as the representative, the "*picture*" of that sound. We should now cultivate their powers of observation, by calling upon them to find a similar letter on the charts; of which there should be at least two suspended before the class: also, among the tablets. (*These are pieces of card-board with a letter upon each.*) As each child finds the letter on a chart or on a tablet, he should enunciate the sound represented.

The *name* of the letter should not be taught them. If any of them, already knowing the name, should call the letter "*Es,*" say "Yes, that is its name, but what sound does it represent? What sound are you to make when you see it?

33

LESSON SECOND.

Review the first lesson, calling their attention, as before, to the analysis of "*saw, say, so, see,*" and to "s" as the representative of the initial sound of those words. Now teach them "ε" as the representative of the final sound in "*see.*"

34

COMBINING LETTERS TO REPRESENT WORDS.

The pupils have already discovered that sounds combined form spoken words; and they now know the representatives of two sounds. The combining of these representatives may now be taught them. Print those letters on the black board thus:

s — — — — — — — ε

s — — — — — ε

s — — ε

sε

Now call upon them to enunciate those sounds as you point to the letters. Pass the index slowly from one letter to the other in the upper line, and more rapidly as you descend, until they blend the two sounds, and pronounce the word "see."

Printed cards, with the lessons on them, should also be used, but they should not supersede the use of the black-board.

35

SUBSEQUENT LESSONS.

Proceed in a similar manner to teach them the letters a, ɵ, m, and w; and they will read several words and a few sentences. They should now be taught to spell by sound all the words they can read; after which they may learn other letters, always using each new letter in combination with familiar ones.

The Phonetic Primer should be given to the children at this stage, and they should be permitted to read from it in connection with the black-board and charts. Some teachers succeed finely with the black-board and Primer, without charts or tablets.

36

WORDS OF THREE LETTERS.

When they are to be taught words of three letters, familiar words of two letters, followed by a third letter also familiar, may be presented on the black-board thus:

hɤ – – – s

hɤ – s

hɤs.

The class should pronounce the word hɤ, and then enunciate the sound represented by s, as the teacher points from the one to the other, moving his index more and more rapidly, until unconsciously they find themselves pronouncing the word hɤs. Other words, as mɛt, mat, tam, should be taught by similar means.

Now take the tablets, and show them a similar word, as mɛ, and after they have pronounced it, drop the hand that holds the word, and with the other hand present a tablet having the letter t on it. The class will enunciate it: when the other hand should be raised and the tablets held so as to form the word mɛt.

Then, with the right hand, present the m only, and after the enunciation of the sound, remove that hand, and present the word ɛt with the other. After they pronounce the word ɛt, prefix the m to it, and they will pronounce the word mɛt. If they fail to pronounce the word at the first trial, make another effort. By no means pronounce the word for them. Manage skilfully, and the pronunciation of the word will come from the class.

TRANSITION TO ROMANIC READING

38

I must caution the young teacher against permitting his pupil to make the transition too soon. Children sometimes make the transition successfully, after having barely read the Phonetic Primer, but sometimes they find it very difficult. But by waiting, as I have suggested, nothing is necessary but to permit them to read in the Second Reader of any series, and it will be found that they will need much less instruction than children reading in the same book that were taught in the common way, and they need no *special* instruction. They may be taught as others are.

39

SPELLING.

Without the direct aid of the teacher, they will now have learned the names of the Roman letters, and they may be taught the common orthography as other children are; and it will be found that they will by far excel children taught in the common way, not only in *articulation*, but in *spelling* also.

40

EMPLOYMENT FOR THE CHILDREN.

What has been written refers only to class in-

TRANSITION TO ROMANIC READING

38

I must caution the young teacher against permitting his pupil to make the transition too soon. Children sometimes make the transition successfully, after having barely read the Phonetic Primer, but sometimes they find it very difficult. But by waiting, as I have suggested, nothing is necessary but to permit them to read in the Second Reader of any series, and it will be found that they will need much less instruction than children reading in the same book that were taught in the common way, and they need no *special* instruction. They may be taught as others are.

39

SPELLING.

Without the direct aid of the teacher, they will now have learned the names of the Roman letters, and they may be taught the common orthography as other children are; and it will be found that they will by far excel children taught in the common way, not only in *articulation*, but in *spelling* also.

40

EMPLOYMENT FOR THE CHILDREN.

What has been written refers only to class instruction. For employment between recitations, the children should be *permitted* and *encouraged*, not *required* and *compelled*, to print on slates all the exercises they read, copying them from the exercises placed on the black-board by the teacher, or from cards suspended before them, or from their Primers.

41

TEACHING ORTHOGRAPHY TO PRIMARY CLASSES.

Many teachers use no other Spelling Book than the Reading Books; thus teaching their pupils to spell the words they are daily using in their lessons. In this way they have, or should have, a correct idea of the meaning of the words of their spelling lessons, though they may not, at this early age, be able to define them.

42

STUDYING SPELLING LESSONS.

While making, and after having made, the transition from the Phonetic print, children should be required to *study* spelling lessons. The best way to do this is to *print* them on their slates, until they learn the script form of letters; when they should use that form, or write their lessons. The practice of requiring pupils to study their lessons a given number of times, only teaches them to hurry *over their study*, and not to study to any purpose. It is not the *number* of times a lesson has been studied that should be considered the mark of success, but the ability to *spell every word* in the lesson.

43

MANNER OF CONDUCTING RECITATIONS IN SPELLING

We cannot vary the mode of conducting spelling recitations as much as with the more advanced classes. One very good method, and perhaps the best one, is to require them to read the lesson from their slates; each one pronouncing a word, and then spelling it and again pronouncing it.

Every pupil should give notice of any mistake observed, by raising the hand. In this way, the teacher can ascertain whether they have studied their lessons aright. The side of the slates, containing the lesson, should be held up to the teacher for criticisms: and the criticisms should embrace, not only the size and appearance of the letters, but the proper arrangement of the words in columns.

The slate should now be laid down on the recitation seat or on the floor, with the side containing the lessons *from* the pupils, and the words pronounced for them once, *and only once;* and a pupil should be permitted to try to spell the word once, and *only once.* If he cannot spell it on the first trial, he has not learned his lesson; and he is now on the floor to be examined in reference to that matter, and not to learn his lesson.

It is a good plan, frequently, to call upon some pupil in the class to pronounce the words for the class, under the eye and ear of the teacher. If a word is misspelled, it should be made a part of the next lesson.

44

SECURING THE ATTENTION.

Pronouncing a word but once, will go far towards securing the attention of every pupil; but in addition to this, when a word is misspelled, another pupil should be called upon to spell it without being spoken to. A movement of the eye, or hand, or some other sign, is all the notice that is necessary, if the pupils are giving their attention; and a failure on the part of the pupil to receive this notice, should be considered as much a failure as the misspelling of a word.

45

KEEPING UP AN INTEREST.

A variety of methods may be resorted to, though not as great a variety as with older pupils.

The class may commence all standing, as each one spells he may sit down, until all are seated. The class may then rise in order as they spell, until all are up. The practice of having a head and foot to a class is often resorted to, and with good effect, if properly managed. If this practice is found to discourage any in the class, it should be abandoned.

A better method is for the teacher to call on the scholars at the close of the recitation for the number each one has missed, which should be recorded, and have a bearing on the grade of the tickets given them to take home weekly.

The respelling of misspelled words by those who misspelled them, and then by the class in concert, is another method.

46

SPELLING WITH OTHER RECITATIONS.

In reading exercises, if a word is mispronounced, attention should be called to its orthography. In their exercises in Mental Arithmetic, words that *they* use, and other words, should occasionally be spelled by the pupils, and so in other studies.

TEACHING SPELLING TO SECONDARY CLASSES.

47

Remarks.—I make use of no spelling book, but assign a definite part of a reading lesson as a spelling lesson. The advantage of this is, that scholars learn the forms of words in connection with their use in sentences, and associate their forms rather with their signification than with their places on the page of the spelling book.

What teacher has not seen instances, in which a scholar could spell every word in the Spelling book, perhaps, without any one to "put out the words;" while, if called upon to write an essay, or a letter, that same scholar would misspell the most common words? Such words, as, *there their*, *are air*, *two too to*, *plain plane*, are almost certainly misspelled in writing by spelling book spellers.

48

ORAL METHOD.

Let the class stand in a line, in order of their numbers as determined at the close of the last spelling exercise; save that No. 1 takes his place at the foot of the class.

Pronounce a word for No. 2, who now stands at the head. He spells it. All in the class who think he spelled it wrong, will raise the hand. If the word was spelled right, those who raised their hands go below those who did not: all the scholars of each kind keeping their relative places with those of the same kind; but *all* the scholars who were mistaken will take their places below *all* who were right in their opinion of the spelling as given by scholar No. 2.

If the scholar misspelled the word, then the first scholar in order who raised his hand is called upon to spell the word, then the next, and so on till all who thought the word mispelled are tested. Those who are thus tested and fail, then take their places below with those who indicated that they thought the word spelled correctly, by not raising their hands.

This method never fails to secure the attention of *all* in the class, and involves no confusion or disorder, if the teacher follow the direction of keeping every scholar of each kind in his place relatively with others of his own kind. The two kinds being: first, those who spell correctly or indicate correctly by raising their hands or not raising them; and second, those who spell incorrectly or indicate incorrectly, it being understood that *all* who show that they were mistaken take their places below all who show that they were right.

Successive scholars are called upon to spell words, and the same indications taken and the same course pursued, till the time allotted for the exercise is exhausted.

At the close of the exercise, the teacher calls upon each member of the class, as he has him enrolled in his class book, for the number of times he was mistaken in his opinion of the spelling, and he is graded accordingly.

The class is then dismissed in order, No. 1 speaking his number and going to his seat; No. 2 following in the same manner. So of all the rest.

Short sentences, or phrases, containing as many words as the class can well recollect, may be pronounced at once, instead of single words. This method has the advantage of more distinctly impressing the meaning of words in connection with their spelling

49

TEACHING SPELLING TO SECONDARY CLASSES BY USE OF SLATES.

Words or sentences, which have been studied, are dictated to a class of scholars sitting on a recitation seat or at their desks, till perhaps they have written twenty words, each, on their slates. Slates are then exchanged. Some scholar is then called upon to give orally the spelling of the first word written on the slates. Teacher says, "How many agree?" All who think his spelling right, raise the hand. Teacher says, "How many disagree?" All such raise the hand. Teacher notes those who are wrong. Teacher then says, "How many slates are wrong?" All who have slates with the word incorrectly spelled, raise their slates to a vertical position on their knees, or on their desks. They are then called on in order, to give the correct spelling; or, to save time, the teacher says, after one has given an incorrect spelling, "How many slates have that spelling?" He thus continues with the word till he gets all the false spellings and determines also the bad spellers.

The next word is then taken up and treated in a similar manner.

It takes much time to describe this method, but it is really the most expeditious and thorough method of getting at the knowledge of a class, and makes a more durable impression, perhaps, of the correct spelling and of the evil of bad spelling than any other method that has ever been devised for secondary scholars.

50

ANOTHER METHOD WITH SLATES.

Let the teacher write one or more sentences, which the scholars have studied, on the black-board, with many of the words misspelled, involving such errors as the class would be most likely to fall into.

The scholars sitting at their desks are required to copy the matter on the black-board, and to correct the errors in spelling and capitals. The teacher afterwards examines their slates or papers, and grades them according to the accuracy, or want of it.

ORTHOGRAPHY TO ADVANCED CLASSES.

51

1. Criticism of Reports Written on the Black-board.—The criticism of spelling comes next in order after the criticism of pronunciation. It is done by the class in the usual way by raising the hand at the instance of the teacher.

Illustration.—A scholar in an advanced class in Grammar has had the subject of the noun assigned to him, on which to give a report before the class. Having had a day for preparation, he writes out the classification of his subject on the black-board *from memory*, without referring to notes or book. He then gives, in the order of his classification, all necessary explanations, definitions, and illustrations of the subject, orally. When the pupil has gone through with his report, the teacher calls on the class for criticisms ; first, in pronunciation; second, in spelling ; and so proceeds with the other items till the subject is thoroughly sifted.

52

2. Criticism of Compositions.—The teacher notes words misspelled in compositions, by drawing a lead mark under them. The scholar is required to go to his dictionary and obtain the correct spelling of these words, and to make a rec-

ord of them in the two forms in a blank book, which he keeps for this purpose, called The Spelling Book. Every advanced scholar, who is not an accurate speller, should have such a book.

These spelling books are arranged with two columns on each page, one headed with the name of the pupil, the other with the name of the author of the Dictionary which he consults. In the column under his own name, he writes his bad spelling. In the other column, he writes the correct spelling according to his authority.

Scarcely will a scholar fall into a second blunder with regard to the spelling of a word, after having made such a record of his error.

Teachers must, of course, have a regular and definite time for examining these spelling books, or they will soon fall into neglect. Without them, the criticisms on bad spelling in compositions will not amount to much.

ADVANCED METHODS OF TEACHING.

53

TEACHING ORTHOGRAPHY BY CHARTS.

The methods of using the charts are explained in articles 21 to 28.

These charts can be copied in an enlarged form by the teacher, or by scholars, on to one or more large sheets of printing paper, with a crayon. Charts of orthography are sold frequently for two dollars. Such a chart would cost the teacher not over a half dime, including paper and crayon, and will serve as good a purpose as the most expensive. If scholars are permitted to make such charts, they have the advantage of learning them by the process, and of cultivating their taste in drawing and writing,

54

TEACHING ORTHOGRAPHY BY DERIVATIVES.

It is an excellent practice to give spelling lessons in the derivatives. Let the teacher propose two or three roots for a lesson: as, *press*, *act*, etc. The scholars, at the recitation, are required to write as many derivatives as they have been able to obtain; either on their slates, or on the blackboard. They should, of course, be provided with dictionaries in the preparation of such a lesson. They can also make use of tables of prefixes and suffixes. They will also bring into use the SPECIAL RULES for spelling derivatives.

The definitions of the derivatives should be required as a part of the exercise. Many teachers make use of Mc Elligott's, or Town's analysis. The exercise can be made very profitable without them, with the use of a dictionary and the tables of prefixes and suffixes defined.

These tables can be copied from Mc Elligott on to large sheets of paper and into the "spelling books" of the pupils, as described in article 52.

55

Examples in formation of derivatives, with the rules for spelling, according to Goold Brown.

WITH SUFFIXES.

ACT. A primitive word, signifying to do or to make.

ACTOR. The person who acts.
ACTRESS. The female who acts.
ACTION. The result or process of acting.
ACTS. Does act.
ACTEST. Dost act.
ACTETH. Does act.
ACTED. Did act.
ACTING. Continuing to act.
ACTIONABLE. Admitting of an action.
ACTIONABLY. By admitting an action.
ACTIONARY. } A person who has a share in an
ACTIONIST. } action.
ACTIVE. Inclined to act.

ACTIVITY. Rule VI. } The state or quality of being active.
ACTIVENESS. Rule VII.
ACTIVELY. Rule VII. In an active manner.
ACTUAL. Real in acting or being.
ACTUALITY. } The state of being actual.
ACTUALNESS.
ACTUALLY. In an actual manner.
ACTUATE. To cause to act.

WITH PREFIXES AND SUFFIXES.

COACT. To act together with force.
COACTION. The process of coacting.
COACTIVE. Inclining to coact.
COUNTERACT. To act against.
COUNTERACTION. The process of acting against.
ENACT. To act in making a law.
ENACTMENT. The process or result of enacting.
INACTIVE. Without action.
INACTION. An inactive state.
INACTIVELY. Rule VII. In an inactive manner.
INACTIVITY. Rule VI. An inactive state.
EXACT.—*Verb.* To act in forcing out of.
EXACTING. Continuing to exact.
EXACTION. The process or result of exacting.
EXACTOR. The person who exacts.
EXACT.—*Adjective.* Acting from rule. Accurate.
EXACTLY. In an exact manner.
EXACTNESS. } The state of being exact.
EXACTITUDE.
REACT. To act again. To act back.
REACTING. Continuing to react.
REACTION. The process of reacting.

REACTIVE. Inclining to react.

REACTIVELY. Rule VII. In a reactive manner

SUBACTION. The process of acting to place under.

56

PEL. An inseparable radical word, signifying to drive or force. From *Pello*, *Pulsus*. With the only suffix—

PULSION. The act of driving.

With prefixes and suffixes—

COMPEL. COMPELLED, Rule III. COMPELLING, Rule III. COMPULSION. COMPULSIVE. COMPULSIVELY, Rule VII. COMPULSIVENESS, Rule VII. COMPULSORY, etc.

57

From the root *Press*, nearly two hundred derivatives can be obtained. From the inseparable root *Gress*, a long list can be formed.

These two examples, *Act* and *Pel*, will be sufficient to illustrate the method of spelling by the use of prefixes and suffixes in forming derivatives from separable and inseparable primitives.

58

DRILLING ON THE SPECIAL RULES FOR SPELLING.

The class should be required to memorize these as they are given in the grammar used, with the exceptions and remarks. They should so memorize them, that they can give them as they are called for by the teacher promiscuously. They should then be required to write, or spell orally, words as they are dictated, or pronounced from the examples contained in the grammar, under each rule, in order, until every scholar shows that he is able to apply the rules correctly.

Sentences may then be dictated for writing, containing derivative words coming under the rules promiscuously.

Sentences may be written on the board by the teacher in which these rules are violated. The scholars are expected to rewrite the sentences on slates or paper, with references by number to the rules which were violated.

This course should be pursued day after day, for weeks, until the scholars have formed the habit of noticing the application of these rules in spelling.

We find that the larger part of misspelling in the compositions of advanced scholars, is in violation of these rules, until they have been thoroughly drilled in them.

ORTHOGRAPHIC PARSING.

EXERCISES IN ORTHOGRAPHIC PARSING.

The following lists of words are selected with the design of bringing in as large a variety of combinations both of syllables and letters as possible. It is presumed that the teacher, by carefully examining the methods by which these words and the letters and sounds of which they are composed, are disposed of, under the **Form of Orthographic Parsing**, given on page 62, will be able to parse any words, letters or sounds in the language.

List of words analyzed :—

Pin, Called, Through, Ewe, Manlike, Inkstand, Condition.

List of words whose letters and sounds are analyzed :—

Sound, Chaise, Xenophon, Rough, Lough, Phthisic, Motion, Filial.

List of words parsed orthographically in full :—

Impossibility.

In commencing to teach Orthographic Parsing, it is well to divide the subject, and, at first, drill the class on words, including spelling, afterward upon letters and sounds, and finally combine the two.

DRILL ON WORDS INCLUDING SPELLING.

Pin is a simple, primitive, monosyllable, spelled orthographically (naming the letters) p, i, n, and phonetically (enunciating the sounds) p, i, n.

Called is a simple, derivative monosyllable, except in poetry, where it is sometimes a dissyllable, accented on the first. As a derivative, its base is *call*, modified by the simple suffix, ed, signifying did. The signification of called is, did name, summons, invite, &c. Spelled orthographically, c, a, ll, e, d, phonetically, k, ȯ, l, d.

Through is a simple, primitive monosyllable. Spelled, orthographically, t, h, r, o, u, g, h ; phonetically, ŧ, r, ꝏ.

Ewe is a simple, primitive monosyllable. Spelled, orthographically, e, w, e, phonetically, y, ų.

Manlike is a compound, primitive dissyllable, accented (slightly) on the first. Spelled, orthographically, m, a, n, l, i, k, e, phonetically, m, a, n, l, į, k. The base of the word is *man* ; which is modified by the word like, signifying resembling in manner, or appearance. The signification of the word is, resembling a man.

Inkstand is a compound, primitive dissyllable, accented on the first. Spelled, orthographically, i, n, k, s, t, a, n, d, phonetically, i, ŋ, k, s, t, a, n, d. The base of the word is *stand*, modified by the word *ink*, signifying (here,) a fluid for writing. The word signifies a vessel for holding the fluid.

Condition is a simple, primitive trisyllable, accented on the second; spelled, orthographically, c, o, n, d, i, t, i, o, n, phonetically k, o, n, d, i, ʃ, o, n.

DRILL ON LETTERS AND SOUNDS.

Sound. S is a consonant, antecedent to the base of the syllable, ou, and represents its own proper sound, s; (*enunciate the sound,*) which is an aspirate, obstructed at the gums by a partial contact of the organs: producing a dental and a continuant.

Ou, the base of the syllable, is a diphthong, representing its own proper sound, ȣ; (*enunciate,*) which is an open, compound vocal, modified (in the commencement of the sound,) at the soft palate, and at the conclusion at the lips.

N is a consonant, and the immediate consequent of the base of the syllable, representing its own proper sound, n; (*enunciate,*) which is a subvocal, obstructed at the hard palate by a contact made perfect there, but with an opening of the nasal cavities, through which there is an escape of air externally, and, hence, obstructed by a partial contact of the organs; producing a palatal, a continuant, and a nasal.

D is a consonant, and the remote consequent of the base of the syllable, representing its own proper sound, d; (*enunciate,*) which is a subvocal, obstructed at the teeth or gums, (at the teeth by some, and at the gums by others,) by a perfect contact of the organs, producing an abrupt, and a dental.

Chaise. Ch is a consonant digraph, the antecedent of the base of the syllable, ai, final e, and represents the sound of sh, ʃ; (*enunciate,*) which is an aspirate, obstructed at the hard palate, by a partial contact of the organs; producing a palatal and a continuant.

Ai—e, the base of the syllable, is a disjoined trigraph, representing the long sound of a, a; (*enunciate,*) which is a long, simple vocal, modified at the hard palate.

S is a consonant, having its position between the parts of the disjoined trigraph, which forms the base of the syllable, and represents the sound of z, z; (*enunciate,*) which is a subvocal, obstructed at the gums by a partial contact of the organs; producing a dental and a continuant.

Xenophon. X is a consonant, antecedent to the base of the first syllable, e, and represents the sound of z, z; (*enunciate,*) which is a subvocal, obstructed at the gums, by a partial contact of the organs; producing a dental and a continuant.

E, the base of the first syllable, is a vowel, representing the short sound of e, e; (*enunciate,*) which is a short, simple vocal, modified at the hard palate.

N is a consonant, the consequent of the base of the first syllable, and represents its own proper sound, n; (*enunciate,*) which is a subvocal, obstructed at the hard palate by a partial contact of the organs; producing a palatal, a continuant, and a nasal.

O, the base of the second syllable, is a vowel, representing its own long sound, ꞷ; (*enunciate,*) which is a long, simple vocal modified at the lips.

Ph is a consonant digraph, antecedent to the base of the third syllable, o, and represents the sound of f, f; (*enunciate,*) which is an aspirate, obstructed at the lips by a partial contact of the organs, producing a labial and a continuant.

O, the base of the third syllable, is a vowel, representing its own short sound, o; (*enunciate,*) which is a short, simple vocal, modified at the short palate.

N is a consonant, the consequent of the base of the third syllable, and represents its own proper sound, n; (*enunciate,*) which is a subvocal, and is obstructed at the hard palate, by a partial contact of the organs; producing a palatal, a continuant, and a nasal.

Rough. R is a consonant and is antecedent to the base of the syllable, ou; representing its own proper sound, r; (*enunciate,*) which is a subvocal, obstructed at the hard palate, by a partial contact of the organs, producing a palatal, a continuant and a liquid.

Ou, the base of the syllable, is a conjoined vowel digraph, representing the short sound of u, u; (*enunciate,*) which is a short, simple vocal, modified at the hard palate.

Gh is a consonant digraph, and the consequent of the base of the syllable, representing the sound of f, f; (*enunciate,*) which is an aspirate, obstructed at the lips by a partial contact of the organs; producing a labial and a continuant.

Lough. L is a consonant, and the antecedent of the base of the syllable, ou; representing its own proper sound, l; (*enunciate,*) which is a subvocal, obstructed at the hard palate, by a partial contact of the organs, producing a palatal, a continuant and a liquid.

Ou, the base of the syllable, is a vowel digraph, representing the sound of short o, o; (*enunciate,*) which is a short, simple vocal, modified at the soft palate.

Gh is a consonant digraph, and the consequent of the base of the syllable, representing the sound of k, k; (*enunciate,*) which is an aspirate, obstructed at the soft palate, by a perfect contact of the organs; producing a guttural and an abrupt.

Phthisic. Ph are two aphthongs and remote antecedents of the base of the first syllable, i, and are used to modify the representative character of the digraph th, and to determine the signification of the word.

Th is a consonant digraph, and the immediate antecedent of i, the base of the first syllable, representing the sound of t, t; (*enunciate,*) which is an aspirate, obstructed at the teeth or gums, by a perfect contact of the organs, producing an abrupt and a dental.

I, the base of the first syllable, is a vowel representing its own short sound, i; (*enunciate,*) which is a short, simple vocal, modified at the teeth.

S is a consonant, the consequent of the base of the syllable and represents the sound of z, z; (*enunciate,*) which is a subvocal, obstructed at the gums, by a partial contact of the organs, producing a dental and a continuant.

I, the base of the second syllable, is a vowel, representing its own short sound, i; (*enunciate,*) which is a short, simple vocal, modified at the teeth.

C is a consonant, and the consequent of the base of the syllable; representing the sound of k, k; (*enunciate,*) which is an aspirate, obstructed at the soft palate, by a perfect contact of the organs; producing a guttural and an abrupt.

Motion. M is a consonant, and the antecedent of o, the base of the first syllable; representing its own proper sound, m (*enunciate,*) which is a subvocal, obstructed at the lips, by a partial contact of the organs; producing a labial, a continuant, and a nasal.

O, the base of the first syllable, is a vowel, representing its own long sound, ω; (*enunciate,*) which is a long, simple vocal modified at the lips.

Ti is a combined digraph, and the antecedent of o, the base of the second syllable; representing the sound of sh, ʃ; (*enunciate,*) which is an aspirate, obstructed at the hard palate, by a partial contact of the organs; producing a palatal and a continuant.

O, the base of the second syllable, is a vowel, representing the sound of short u, u; (*enunciate,*) which is a short, simple vocal, modified at the hard palate.

N is a consonant, and the consequent of the base of the syllable, representing its own proper sound, n; (*enunciate,*) which is a subvocal, obstructed at the hard palate, by a partial contact of the organs; producing a palatal, a continuant, and a nasal.

Filial. F is a consonant, and the antecedent of the base of the first syllable, representing its own proper sound, f; (*enunciate,*) which is an aspirate, obstructed at the lips by a partial contact of the organs; producing a labial and a continuant.

I, the base of the first syllable, is a vowel, representing its own short sound, i; (*enunciate,*) which is a short, simple vocal.

L is a consonant, and the consequent of the base of the first syllable; representing its own proper sound, l; (*enunciate,*) which is a subvocal, obstructed at the hard palate by a partial contact of the organs; producing a palatal, a continuant, and a liquid.

I is a consonant, and the antecedent of the base of the second syllable, representing the sound of y, y; (*enunciate,*) which is a vocal and a coalescent, modified at the teeth.

A, the base of the second syllable, is a vowel, representing its own short sound, a; (*enunciate,*) which is a short, simple vocal.

L is a consonant, and the consequent of the base of the second syllable, representing its own proper sound, l; (*enunciate,*) which is a subvocal, obstructed at the hard palate, by a partial contact of the organs; producing a palatal, a continuant, and a liquid.

DRILL IN FULL ORTHOGRAPHIC PARSING.

Impossibility is a simple, derivative polysyllable, accented on the fourth and second syllables. Possible, the base of the word, is modified by the prefix im, signifying not, and the suffix ity, signifying the state or condition. The word signifies, "that which can not be."

It is spelled, orthographically, i, m, p, o, s, s, i, b, i, l, i, t, y, and phonetically, i, m, p, o, s, i, b, i, l, i, t, i.

I is a vowel, the base of the first syllable, representing its own short sound, i; (*enunciate,*) which is a short, simple vocal.

M is a consonant and the consequent of the base of the first syllable, representing its own sound, m; (*enunciate,*) which is a subvocal, obstructed at the lips by a partial contact of the organs producing a labial, a continuant and a nasal.

P is a consonant, and the antecedent of the base of the second syllable, representing its own sound, p; (*enunciate,*) which is an aspirate, obstructed at the lips by a perfect contact of the organs producing a labial and an abrupt.

O, the base of the second syllable, is a vowel, representing its own short sound, o; (*enunciate,*) which is a short, simple vocal.

S is a consonant, and the consequent of the base of the second syllable, representing its own proper sound, s; (*enunciate,*) which is an aspirate, obstructed at the gums, by a partial contact of the organs; producing a dental and a continuant.

I, the base of the third syllable, is a vowel, representing its own short sound, i; (*enunciate,*) which is a short, simple vocal

B is a consonant, and the antecedent of the base of the fourth syllable, representing its own proper sound, b; (*enunciate,*) which is a subvocal, obstructed at the lips by a perfect contact of the organs; producing a labial and an abrupt.

I, the base of the fourth syllable, is a vowel, representing its own short sound, i; (*enunciate,*) which is a short, simple vocal.

L is a consonant, and the subsequent of the base of the fourth syllable, representing its own proper sound, l: (*enunciate,*) which is a subvocal, obstructed at the hard palate by a partial contact of the organs; producing a palatal, a continuant and a liquid.

I, the base of the fifth syllable, is a vowel, representing its own short sound, i; (*enunciate,*) which is a short, simple vocal, modified at the teeth.

T is a consonant and the antecedent of the base of the sixth syllable; representing its own proper sound, t; (*enunciate,*) which is an aspirate, obstructed at the teeth or gums, by a perfect contact of the organs; producing a dental and an abrupt.

Y, the base of the sixth syllable, is a vowel, representing the short sound of i, i; (*enunciate,*) which is a short, simple vocal modified at the teeth.

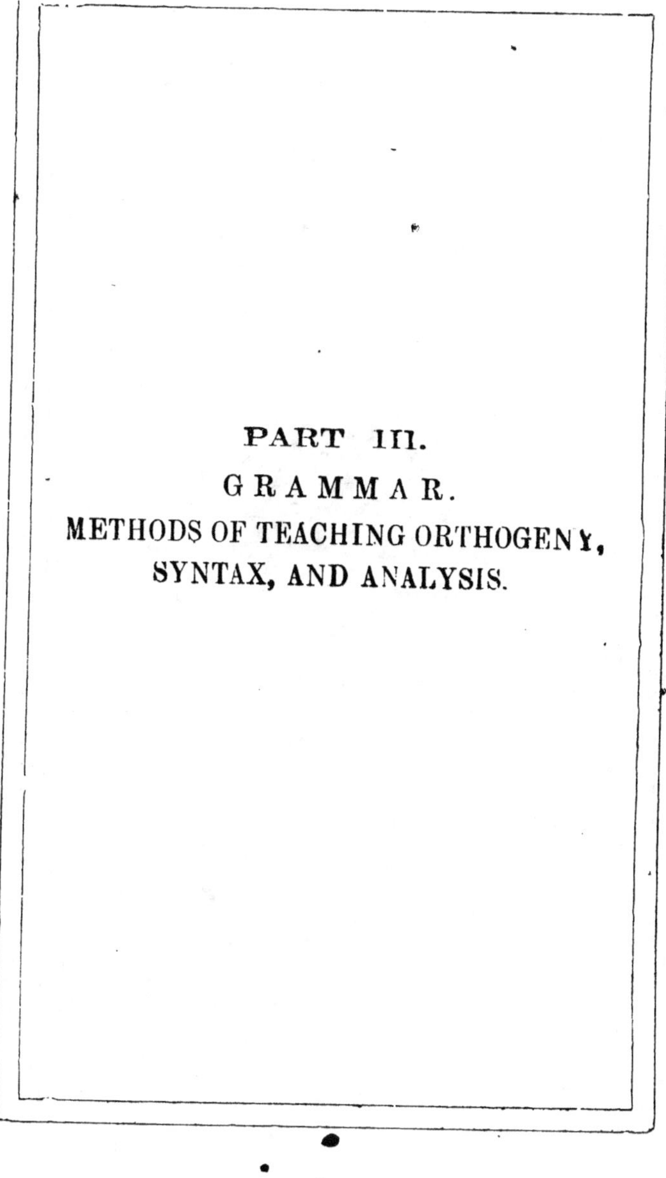

PART III.

GRAMMAR.

METHODS OF TEACHING ORTHOGENY, SYNTAX, AND ANALYSIS.

INTRODUCTION.

PROPER AGE FOR COMMENCING THE STUDY OF GRAMMAR.

There is no subject of school study about which there is a greater disparity of opinion prevailing among teachers than that of the age at which children may commence the study of Grammar.

Some teachers would have children commence Grammar as the first *study* in books after they have learned to read well, or even before; others of our best educators would defer it till the faculties of the mind are *all* measurably developed; a third class would not have Grammar studied at all, as a distinct science. I conceive that, by an adaptation of which the subject is susceptible, children may commence Grammar as soon as they can read fluently and intelligibly. Geography may be introduced before children can read fluently, as a means of securing *study in reading lessons*, and of training the hand and eye in drawing maps. I should, therefore, introduce Geography at this point, in this volume, were it not for breaking in upon a systematic arrangement of the branches.

Object lessons in common things, and Natural History; also experiments in Chemistry and Natu-

ral Philosophy, may well precede the study of Grammar also.

ORAL INSTRUCTION BEFORE THE BOOK.

No lesson should be required of a young pupil in the text-book, till he has had a preliminary drill; and the teacher is satisfied that he comprehends the subject so far as his lesson in the text-book extends.

Should the teacher fail in making the class, or any member of a class, understand any particular part of the subject, by the preliminary drill, it would be worse than in vain to require such a class, or individual, to memorize it from the text-book. Such a pupil or class must lay aside that subject for awhile, and take up some other more simple; or, lay aside the study of Grammar till the mind is more matured.

THE METHODS OF PRELIMINARY DRILL.

The main object of the following pages, given to PRIMARY TEACHING, is to illustrate and exemplify the method of preliminary drill, preparatory to lessons to be memorized from the text-book.

A similar course has been pursued with numerous classes in the Model Department of the Normal School, and Grammar has never failed to be a treat for the children.

THE ORDER OF LESSONS.

The order pursued in the following pages, in taking up the different subjects for lessons, is that of simplicity; commencing with the most simple and obvious of subjects, viz: the noun, and proceeding with its modifications and classes, as the child can bear them, and so advancing to other parts of speech and their modifications and classes, till the whole ground shall have been passed over in its *plainest* form. All exceptions, idioms, and irregularities, save such as are obviously violations of rules, are studiously avoided in this method of primary teaching, as tending to confuse the mind by too great a degree of complexity and obscurity.

METHOD OF INTRODUCING RULES.

No rule should be introduced till the necessity for it is understood by the class. There is, then, no difficulty in then memorizing it even in the oral drill. Children will thus obtain the great fundamental principles of construction, of syntax, while they are learning to distinguish the parts of speech, their classes and modifications.

WRITING EXERCISES.

There are many advantages in the plan of written exercises proposed in parsing; some of which are: 1st. It secures study in the preparation of a *parsing lesson*, which otherwise might be evaded under various pretexts. 2d. It affords a means of teaching spelling, as explained in article 52, page 85. 3d. Rapid improvement in penmanship can be secured by close attention to this matter on the part of the teacher. 4th. It paves the way to composition, by the scholars' taking a part of the difficulties, before entering upon them in combination. 5th. It effects the more equal advancement of a class, by securing more equal amounts of application outside of the recitation.

Remark.—The ordinary writing book may be used for this exercise, and the time otherwise given to writing from copies.

GENERAL PLAN OF CONDUCTING RECITATIONS.

The method of conducting a recitation in Grammar, as explained in the subsequent pages, illustrates the *general method* of conducting recitations in all branches. It assumes, that the class is an organized assembly, with the teacher for Chairman. No scholar has a right to the floor (using parliamentary language) till he is recognized by the teacher. The raising of the hand signifies, that he wishes to obtain the floor, but does not give him a right to it without the assent of the Chairman. The teacher should be particularly watchful on this point; otherwise scholars conceive, that whenever they raise the hand they may speak. Thus the object of raising the hand is defeated, and *disorder* is the result,

MUTUAL CRITICISM OF SCHOLARS.

Scholars are required, in the recitations, to criticise each other. Without special care, on the part of the teacher, he will deprive the scholars of this privilege by doing too much of it himself. Scholars will learn vastly more by criticising, than by being criticised. "It is more blessed to give than receive."

They should also be encouraged to criticise each other out of school hours—of course, in a kindly manner.

METHOD OF USING PART III.

For Primary classes in Grammar, it is not supposed that the teacher consulting this work will be governed mechanically by my divisions of the general subject into LESSONS, or that he will follow implicitly my arrangement of the parts of speech, and their classes and modifications, in his STEPS. With the exception of the adjective and the particles, which for want of room are not provided for, I conceive the arrangement adopted the best, though other teachers may prefer to follow the arrangement of their text-books.

The main object in view in the preparation of these primary lessons will be to exhibit, as clearly as possible, the combination of oral instruction with memoriter lessons from text-books; and it is believed that if a teacher will consult these successive LESSONS and STEPS in his own preparation for the successive recitations and exercises, he will obtain some hints which may serve as guide boards or beacon lights in his course.

The methods of using the Outlines and Definitions, etc., under the head of Advanced Teaching, will appear sufficiently in connection with them.

METHOD OF TEACHING GRAMMAR TO PRIMARY CLASSES.

1

PRELIMINARY REMARKS AND EXPLANATIONS,

The class should be able to read fluently and intelligently. They should be provided with books, grammars of some kind, and all of the same kind. It is not necessary nor desirable that they should have *primary* grammars. The larger and fuller grammar has to be purchased, after the primary has been used one session.

Most Normal Schools, throughout the country, now make use of either Brown's or Clark's Grammars as text books. My references will be made chiefly to Clark's Grammar, revised edition.

2.

LESSON I.

First Step—Nouns. Let the teacher define a Noun in the simplest possible manner, *i. e.*, as a name, and illustrate the definition by examples, thus:

Teacher. A noun is a name. Every noun is a name, and every name is a noun. Your names are nouns, and my name is a noun. Can you think of any other nouns?

The scholars raise their hands.

Teacher says to one—"John, you may mention some noun."

John mentions some name, as "house," "stone," "boy."

Teacher. Why is house a noun, John?

John. Because it is a name.

So the teacher should proceed with every member of the class, until all can not only give nouns, but can define them correctly.

3.

SECOND STEP—NOUNS—IMMATERIAL OBJECTS. As scholars will in the first place select the names of material substances, the teacher will secondly bring to their notice the names of immaterial substances and abstract qualities, thus:

Teacher. Is mind a noun? As many as think it is may raise the hand.

Several do not raise their hands, perhaps; among whom is Samuel.

Teacher. Samuel, why is n't mind a noun?

Samuel. I never saw a mind.

Teacher. But then you have a mind, I suppose, or are you all body and clothes? There are many things which you cannot see, which still must have names, as we have to talk about them. Did you, any of you, ever see the wind? or did you ever see a love or a friendship? Yet you do n't doubt that you possess and enjoy these things. Each one of the class may give such a noun.

The teacher will then call on the pupils individually by name, when such nouns as sound, health, goodness, breath, life, death, weight, lightness, smell, etc., may be brought out by the class; possibly some adjective, as new, or soft, or sweet, by Jane.

Teacher. Jane, why is sweet a noun? Did you ever see a sweet?

Jane. No, sir; but I have tasted of a sweet apple.

Teacher. True, you have tasted of an apple, and the apple was sweet. But what sort of a thing is the sweet without the apple? Now, how many of the class can tell me the name of that quality of the apple which makes it taste sweet?

Hands are raised.

Teacher. Sarah.

Sarah. Sugar.

Teacher. Sugar is a substance, not a quality.

James. Juice.

Teacher. Juice is also a substance, not a quality. If I were speaking of the quality which makes the apple sweet, I should not call it the sweet of the apple. What would I call it?

All hands come up, and eyes glisten.

Teacher. Mary.

Mary. Sweetness.

Teacher. Yes, that is the name of the quality. Can you give me any other quality of apples? Each scholar may think of some quality of an apple and give it, when called on. James, what quality do you think of?

James. Hardness.

Teacher. Susan.

Susan. Softness.

The teacher should pursue this course, till the class are familiar with the names of qualities taken abstractly.

4.

THIRD STEP. DRILL IN THE GRAMMAR. Direct the scholars to turn to page 148 of Clark's Grammar, Sentence I.

Teacher. You may tell me all the nouns you see in the second line: "A large ship traversing the ocean by the force of the wind."

James. Ship—ocean—wind.

Teacher. Why are these words nouns?

James. Because they are names.

Teacher. Are there no other names in that line?

James, perhaps, hesitates.

Teacher. Class. [Several hands rise.]

Remark. It will be noticed that when the teacher uses the word "Class," that no pupil speaks; but all who are able to respond raise their hands. The teacher then calls on some one to give the answer.

Teacher. Mary, you may give me the other nouns in that line.

Mary. Large, and force.

Teacher. Why is force a noun, Mary?

Mary. It is the name of something.

Teacher. Very well. Why is large a noun?

Mary. It is a name.

Teacher. Name of what? Did you ever see a large?

Mary. I never saw a force either.

Teacher. What property of the wind drives the ship? Is it not the power of the wind? What other name is there for power? Class. [Hands rise.] Susan.

Susan. Force.

Teacher. Is not force then the name of that which drives the ship? Could the wind drive the ship, if it had no force? Let us now see about large. Is large the name of anything, Mary?

Mary. Yes, sir; a large house is a name.

Teacher. House is a name of that in which people live; but what sort of a thing is a large? How many think large is the name of anything, now?

In a similar way, each member of the class may be called on to give the nouns in a line. The teacher will select such lines from Clark's Grammar, or any other, as may be best adapted to the particular scholar with whom he is dealing. Children will most easily and certainly select the names of material objects.

The lesson assigned for the scholar to learn from the book, is, in this case, nothing more than the definition of a noun. And the teacher will be careful in these primary exercises to require the class to learn nothing from the book which he has not made plain, and pleasant, in the preliminary drill.

5.

LESSON II.

First Step—Recitation of Lesson assigned.

Teacher. How many can define a noun?

Hands rise; and the teacher calls upon those who were the dullest in the previous exercise, to give the definition. Having thus satisfied himself as to the amount of study bestowed, he proceeds to another preliminary drill, on the modifications of nouns, taking them in the order of their simplicity, taking those modifications first, always, which are the most obvious to the child.

6.

Second Step—Number. *Teacher.* I will tell you something more about nouns. They are singular or plural. If a noun means one of that thing which it is the name of, it is singular; if it means more than one it is plural. For instance, horse is a singular noun, because it means a single horse; but horses is a plural noun, because it means more than one horse.

Teacher. The class, all together. Is bird singular or plural?

The class answer in concert without raising hands when the words "all together" are used.

Teacher. Is birds singular or plural?

Class. Plural.

Teacher. How is it with boy?

Class. Singular.

Teacher. Give me the plural of boy.

Class. Boys.

Teacher. Is girls singular or plural?

Class. Plural.

Teacher. Give me the singular of girls.

Class. Girl.

Teacher. Very well; now the plural of fox.

Class. Foxes.

Teacher. Box. *Class.* Boxes. *Teacher.* Ox *Class.* Oxes—oh no, oxen.

Teacher. Very well; try again. Mouse. *Class.* Mice. *Teacher.* Louse. *Class.* Lice. *Teacher.* House. *Class.* Hice—no, no, houses.

Teacher. You are right now. Again; Moose.

Class. Mooses. *Teacher.* Papoose.

Class. Papooses. *Teacher.* Goose. *Class.* Gooses; ha, ha, geese.

7.

Third Step—Gender. *Teacher.* Now, children, I wish to tell you about gender. The name of a male is a noun of the masculine gender. The name of a female is a noun of the feminine gender. For instance; boy is a noun of the masculine gender, girl is a noun of feminine gender. Floor is a noun of the neuter gender.

Teacher. What gender is man? All together.

Class. Masculine.

Teacher. How many can tell me why man is masculine? [Hands rise.]

Teacher. Samuel. *Samuel.* It is the name of a man. *Teacher.* Jane. *Jane.* It is the name of a female.

Teacher. What gender is lady? [Hands rise.]

Teacher. Mary. *Mary.* Feminine.

Teacher. What gender is desk? [No hands rise.] What gender did I tell you those nouns were which were neither masculine nor feminine? [Hands rise.] *Teacher.* Sarah. *Sarah.* Neuter.

Teacher. Very well. What gender is desk, then? [All hands up.]

Teacher. All together. *Class.* Neuter.

8.

Fourth Step—Parsing. The class are now prepared to commence the process of parsing. The teacher will lead the way by giving an example thus.

Teacher. You may all look at the first noun in the first line of Sentence I, 148, of Clark's Grammar, and I will parse it for you.

Science is a noun, singular number, neuter gender. Do you think you can parse a word now?—[Some hands rise.]

Teacher. Jane, you may parse mind, in the same line.

Jane. Mind is a noun.

Teacher. What number?

Jane. Singular. *Teacher.* What gender?

Jane. Neuter. *Teacher.* Now, you may parse it again. *Jane.* Mind is a noun, singular number, neuter gender.

Teacher. Very well. You may all parse it in concert.

Class. Mind is a noun, singular number, neuter gender.

Teacher. Very well. Sarah, you may now parse ship.

Sarah. Ship is a noun, neuter gender, singu lar number.

Teacher. You may all parse ship.

Class. Ship is a noun, (*in confusion*) singular number, neuter gender, neuter gender, singular number.

Teacher. You may give the number before the gender. Take the noun, John, in the line: "I, John, saw these things." James, you may parse it.

James. John is a noun.

Teacher. Why? *James.* It is a name.

Teacher. Go on. *James.* Singular number.

Teacher. Why? *James.* It means only one.

Teacher. What gender? *James.* Masculine.

Teacher. Very well. You may all parse John.

Class. John is a noun, singular number, masculine gender.

9.

Fifth Step—Person. *Teacher.* I will now tell you something else about nouns. If a noun is the name of the speaker or writer, it is in the first person. If it is the name of a person spoken to, it is in the second person; and if it is the name of a person or thing spoken of, it is in the third person. For instance: John, in the sentence we have just had, is in the first person, because John was the name of the writer. If I should say, "George, shut that door," George would be in the second person, because it would be the name of the person spoken to. But door would be in the third person, because it is spoken of.

What person is Daniel, in the expression used by the King: "O, Daniel! servant of the living God?" All together.

Class. Second person. *Teacher.* Why? *Class.* Daniel is spoken to.

Teacher. Now, we will parse a few words. I will parse John for you first. John is a noun, third person, singular number, masculine gender.

You may follow the same order in parsing that I did in giving person, number and gender.

Teacher. Eliza, you may parse Esther in the second sentence, in Lesson II.

Eliza parses as directed, in this manner: Esther is a noun, third person, singular number, feminine gender.

Teacher. You may all parse it in concert.

The *Class* parse in concert. They can be kept together by the teacher's beating with his hand, or pointer.

It will be noticed, that no definitions are called for, while parsing, as is practiced by most teachers and recommended in most grammars, since the days of Kirkham. However, if the scholar is wrong, or hesitates, showing doubt or ignorance of any point, the teacher at once calls for the definition necessary to set the scholar right. If the scholar parsing cannot give the required definition, the teacher says, "Class:" when all who can give it raise their hands; and the teacher calls on the scholar most unlikely to give it. If he fails, then on another, and so on till the definition is correctly given.

10.

SIXTH STEP — CLASSES OF NOUNS. *Teacher* Nouns are divided into two classes, for the purpose of showing us where to use capital letters.

General names, or such as apply to many persons or things, are called common nouns; for the reason that they belong in common to many objects. The noun man is common; it belongs in common to many persons. James Buchanan is called a proper noun; it belongs, properly, or peculiarly, to one person. I will give you several common nouns, and you may give proper names that belong to the same class of things. For instance: under the common noun, girl, we find the proper nouns, Susan, Mary, Eliza, etc.

What proper noun comes under the common noun boy?

Class raise their hands.

Teacher. William. *William*. Samuel.

This course may be pursued with each of the scholars, until they are all able to distinguish the classes of nouns.

Then the teacher calls on them to parse; giving the class of the noun first in order after the noun, then the modifications as before.

The exercise is closed by assigning to the class, for a lesson to be learned from the book, the definitions of the two classes of nouns, as well as the definitions of person, number, and gender. These definitions are pointed out in the grammar by the teacher; and some one of the duller scholars is asked to show, in his own book, what the lesson is, in order that the teacher may be sure that the class understand what they are to learn for the next recitation.

11.

LESSON III.

First Step. The recitation of the lesson assigned, and the grading of the scholars according to their merits, in the teacher's register.

12.

Second Step—Case. Verb. *Teacher.* Nouns have one more property, or modification; that of case. In order that you may understand this property, I shall introduce you to another kind of word; or, as the grammarians call it, another part of speech. A verb is a word that denotes action, or being, or state of being.

When I say, "The bird flies," the word flies denotes the action of the bird, or tells what the bird does; hence, it is a verb. In the sentence, "Mary reads;" reads is a verb for a similar reason. In the sentence, "The stone lies on the ground," the word lies does not express action, but simply state of being.

Now, you may give me the verbs in these sentences; all together: "The horse runs."

Class. (In concert.) Runs. *Teacher.* Why?

Class. It tells what the horse does. *Teacher.* Does it denote action or being? *Class.* Action.

Teacher. "The boy chops wood." In this sentence, what is the verb, John?

John. Chops. *Teacher.* Why? *John.* It denotes action. *Teacher.* Very well.

13.

THE THIRD STEP—DRILL IN VERBS. *Teacher.* You may now open your grammars to the 65th page and find some of the verbs in Sentence I.

James, in the first sentence, what is the verb, and why?

James. Feels, because it denotes action.

Teacher. Sarah, in the next sentence?

Sarah. Rose; it denotes action.

This course may be pursued till the class have all been reached, and can give the verbs in these simple sentences, and the reason for such words being verbs. It will be noticed, that *appear* and *seems* are verbs, because they denote being, or state of being.

14.

FOURTH STEP—SUBJECT AND OBJECT. *Teacher.* If I say, "The boy drives a team;" what is the subject of the remark, what is the principal thing talked about? Class raise their hands.

Teacher. Susan. *Susan.* Boy.

Teacher. Right. The subject of a sentence is that word in a sentence about which the verb asserts something. Now, the verb drives asserts an action of the subject, boy; and the noun, boy, is in the condition of a subject. Grammars call this condition the "nominative case." They might better call it the "subjective case," or condition. But, since nearly all grammars agree in this matter, we will call it so too.

Teacher. Let us take the same sentences again. What object does the boy drive?

Class raise hands.

Teacher. John. *John.* Team. *Teacher.* Yes. Then team is in the condition of an object, and we will say, that it is in the objective condition or case.

We can now parse these nouns, boy, and team, in full.

I will parse boy for you, but will first write the form by which I parse it, on the board. [The teacher writes.] *Species? Class? Person? Number? Gender? Case? Construction? Rule?* Now, I will parse it by this form; then, you may all parse it by the same form, in concert. The *teacher* using the pointer, as he proceeds, parses thus: Boy is a noun, common, third, singular, masculine, nominative, because it is subject of the verb, drives He then calls on the class to parse the same word, guiding them by pointing at the successive questions in the form, on the board. The same course is pursued with team, the teacher giving, as its "construction," "being the object of the verb drives."

The teacher assigns for the next lesson, those definitions which he has brought out and exemplified in this exercise. This lesson is to be studied and prepared for the next exercise. The definitions to be assigned, are these, viz: of the noun, common noun, proper noun; gender, masculine, feminine; person, first person, second person, third person; number, singular number, plural number case, nominative case, objective case.

15.

LESSON IV.

First Step—Recitation. The manner of conducting this recitation is this:

The scholars being seated, on the recitation bench, the teacher calls one most likely to fail, by name. He or she *rises.* The scholar rises for several reasons. 1st. He feels more responsibility in the recitation, when thus made more prominently the object of observation. 2d. The rest of the class can hear what he says more plainly. 3d. Other scholars, who are sitting, cannot so easily prompt him without being heard by the teacher. The teacher then proposes one word for definition, not the first, necessarily; perhaps the most difficult. If the scholar fails in this, the teacher proposes it to the class, for the purpose of keeping their attention, by saying, "Class." All who are able to answer, raise their hands; and the teacher calls upon those least likely to do so, to give the definition or answer the question. This course is pursued till every member of the class is reached and his merit or demerit ascertained and recorded in the class register.

16.

Second Step—Parsing. The teacher directs the class to turn to page 65 of Calrk's Grammar, or to any similar collection of sentences, in any other grammar. He writes out the *form for parsing a noun* on the board, as given before, in section 14, page 117. Then some one of the more apt scholars is called on to parse Science in the sentence, "Science enlarges and strengthens the mind," by the form—standing while he parses; the rest of the class signifying any error by raising their hands; when the teacher calls on some one, so signifying, to correct the error, or the supposed error. A scholar having parsed a word, is excused, and the class parse in concert; the teacher keeping time for them by pointing in succession to the several questions in the *form*.

I will parse the words Science and Mind, in the manner they should be parsed in this exercise. *Science* is a noun, common, third, singular, neuter, nominative, being the subject of strengthens and enlarges, according to the Rule, A noun or pronoun which is the subject of a finite verb, must be in the nominative case. Mind is a noun, common, third, singular, neuter, objective, being the object of the verbs strengthens and enlarges, according to the Rule, The object of a transitive verb must be in the objective case.

The teacher will be careful to give only such nouns to parse, as are subjects or objects of verbs; introducing or requiring nothing in the parsing exercise, which has not been fully understood by previous explanation and drill. If the book does not furnish a sufficient number of appropriate examples, sentences may be written on the blackboard.

In parsing, the words person, number, gender, and case, are omitted; because they are given in the form on the blackboard, and because they are just as plainly signified, when omitted, as when expressed. No definitions are required, we repeat, when parsing, unless the pupil, in his parsing, makes an error or hesitates; when he is corrected or prompted by the teacher's calling for the appropriate definition; the forgetting or neglecting of which was the cause of the pupil's error or hesitancy.

The hour, or half hour, for the recitation, is thus occupied in parsing, by individuals, and by the class in concert, leaving only time enough to assign another lesson.

17.

THIRD STEP—ASSIGNING A LESSON IN WRITING. The next lesson is the parsing of the words in writing, which have been parsed orally in the class. *Teacher.* Scholars, you will hand me, at the next recitation, a written parsing lesson. You may write, on paper, with ink, very neatly, and with correct spelling, the parsings of the same words which have been parsed in this recitation. Now, you will be careful to have paper, ink, and pens, all ready at the regular hour in which you study this lesson, and I will help you a little then, if necessary. I would like to have you fold your papers neatly, as merchants and lawyers fold their papers for filing, and write your name across one end, on the outside. The teacher will then show the manner of folding by taking a half-sheet and folding it before the class. He will write his name, on the folded paper, as he wishes the scholars to write theirs

18.

LESSON V.

FIRST STEP—CRITICISING WRITTEN EXERCISES The written exercises are collected by one of the scholars; and the teacher reads one of them aloud for the class to criticise. They are directed to watch for errors and to raise their hands if they notice any. Should any hands rise, the teacher calls on some one who raises his hands to mention the error and correct it. If he should fail, then the teacher calls on others, till the error is corrected. The pupil who made the error is required to give the definition or rule which he neglected or violated in making the error. The same course is pursued till this paper and the others are disposed of. The teacher will be careful to bestow any praise, that is deserved, for neatness in the execution of the mechanical part of the exercise, and he will grade the pupils in his register according to their accuracy in parsing and spelling; and according to the neatness evinced in writing and folding, and superscribing their own names on the papers.

Time should be reserved for another drill in oral parsing, even though all the written exercises are not criticised before the class. They may be criticised by the teacher out of school hours, and the errors corrected with a lead pencil or red ink, on the paper, so that the scholar will understand them, and the paper returned to him at the next recitation.

19.

Second Step—Drill in Oral Parsing. This drill may consist of parsings of the same class of words as before, provided the class are found quite deficient in their written exercises; and the same course may be pursued through several lessons until the majority of the class are able to parse the words assigned, according to their stage of advancement, correctly.

20.

LESSON VI.

First Step—Criticising Written Parsings.

Second Step—Possessive Case. The possessive case may be introduced, and the declension of nouns; and, after being explained, the definition of the possessive case and other cases, also, the declensions of nouns may be assigned for study, in connection with some nouns to be parsed in writing, which have not been parsed orally, and which are in the constructions already explained, viz: the subject of a verb, the object of a verb, the possessive case, denoting possession, origin, design, etc. (See Clark's Grammar, pages 83 and 84.)

21.

LESSON VII.

First Step—Recitation of definitions of cases, and the declensions of nouns.

Second Step—The Examination of the paper of one of the scholars, while the other scholars, having their papers in their hands, give their agreement or disagreement with the paper read.

THIRD STEP—INTRODUCTION OF THE PRONOUN.—*Teacher.* If I should say: "Jane studies with all Jane's might?" how could you better express that idea? [Hands rise.]

Teacher. Susan. *Susan.* "Jane studies with all her might," would sound better to me.

Teacher. Right. What word do you use instead of Jane's? *Class.* [Hands rise.]

Teacher. Mary. *Mary.* Her. *Teacher.* Then her is a pronoun, because a pronoun is a word used instead of a noun. Now, you may all open to page 209, and see if you can tell me which are the pronouns. How many of you see a pronoun in the sentence: "The evil which he feared has come upon him." [Hands rise.] *Teacher.* Henry. *Henry.* Which. *Teacher.* What does which stand in place of? *Henry.* Evils. *Teacher.* Right. Samuel, what pronoun in the same sentence? *Samuel.* He. *Teacher.* Why is he a pronoun? *Samuel.* Because it stands in the place of John. *Teacher.* Right. Do any of you see another pronoun in the same sentence? [Hands rise.] *Teacher.* Ellen. *Ellen.* Him. *Teacher.* What does him stand in place of? Ellen. *Ellen.* It stands in the place of he. *Teacher.* Right.

The same course may be pursued till the majority of the class can distinguish pronouns. The next lesson assigned for study, will include the definition of the pronoun, and a new parsing lesson of nouns; the teacher being careful to assign no nouns in different constructions from those he has already explained.

22.

LESSON VIII.

First Step—Recitation of the definition of pronouns.

Second Step—Classes and Cases of Pronouns.

Teacher. There are three classes of pronouns. I will endeavor to describe them, so that you can tell them apart. Let me have your attention very closely.

A personal pronoun is one that always stands for the same grammatical person.

A relative pronoun is one that may stand for any grammatical person, and connects clauses.

An interrogative pronoun is one that is used for asking a question.

The pronoun he always stands for the third person or some person spoken of. The pronoun I always stands for the speaker or for the first person. Thou, always stands for the second person. He, I and thou, are, therefore, personal pronouns. The pronoun who may stand for any one of the three persons; for the first person, second person, or third person. In the expression, "I, who teach," what person does who stand for? Class. [Hands rise.] *Teacher.* Susan. *Susan.* First person. *Teacher.* In the expressions, "You, who study;" "Our Father which art in heaven," what person do who and which stand for? [Hands rise.] John. *John.* The third person. *Teacher.* What does who stand for, John? *John.* It stands for you.

Teacher. Right. What does you stand for, when I say, "You, who study?" Does it stand for the person spoken of, or the person spoken to? *John.* It stands for the person spoken to. *Teacher.* Then who stands for the person spoken to, for it stands for the same that you does. In the expression, "Thou who runnest," what person does who stand for? [Hands rise.] *Teacher.* Jane. *Jane.* Second person. *Teacher.* Very well. Then you see that who does not always stand for the same grammatical person, as the pronoun I does.

In the question, "Who comes there?" who stands for the answer of the question, and for that reason is a pronoun. It is also used for asking that question, and is for that reason an interrogative pronoun.

How many can tell the pronouns in the line, "I, who was present, know the particulars." [Hands rise.] *Teacher.* Julia. *Julia.* I and who are pronouns. *Teacher.* Yes. Now I will write those definitions that I gave you, of the different kinds of pronouns on the board, and you may copy them on to your papers and recite them at your next recitation. You may also learn the declensions of the personal pronouns, on page 89. I do not wish you to learn the definitions of the different classes of pronouns in the grammar; they will only perplex you.

23.

LESSON IX.

First Step — Recitation of the Definitions given on the blackboard and copied the day previous; also of the Declensions of personal pronouns.

Second Step—Form of Parsing Pronouns.—This may be written on blackboard thus: *Species? Class? (Sub-class?) Agreement? Person? Number? Gender? Rule? Case?* Construction? Rule?*

Teacher. I will now parse a pronoun for you by the form. In the sentence, "When the Saxons subdued the Britons, they introduced their own language," they is a pronoun, personal, and agrees with Saxons in the third, plural, masculine, according to the rule, A pronoun must agree with its antecedent, or the noun or pronoun which it represents, in person, number, and gender. They is in the nominative case, being the subject of the verb introduced, according to the rule; A noun or pronoun, which is the subject of a finite verb, must be in the nominative case.

Now, you may parse the same word in concert, as I point to the form

The class then parse this word in concert. Their, in the same sentence, is parsed by some one of the pupils, following the form, and the teacher asking for definitions when the pupil errs or hesitates. Then the class parse the same word in concert, following the form as the teacher points to the several questions in it.

This exercise is co itinued with other pronouns, on the same page, till the time expires; when the teacher assigns the same pronouns for a parsing esson in writing, for the next recitation.

24.

LESSON X.

First Step—Criticism of one of the written exercises, with the comparison of the other exercise by the scholars. The teacher then collects the papers, for criticism out of school hours.

Second Step—Relative Pronouns. *Teacher.* I wish you to attend now more particularly to the relative pronouns. How many can give me the definition of a relative pronoun? [Hands rise.] *Teacher.* Sarah. *Sarah* repeats the definition. If she fails or errs, some other pupil is called on for it. Then the class is called on to repeat it, in concert, several times, till all can give it correctly. *Teacher.* A relative pronoun is one used to introduce a sentence, which qualifies its own antecedent. Turn to page 91, and see who can tell me what sentences, who connects? [No hands rise.] *Teacher.* I will tell you; "The youth was applauded," is one sentence, and "Who was speaking," is another, since they both have verbs in them, as every sentence must have a verb in it. Now, try the next sentence.—What is said about he? Samuel. *Samuel.* "Man whom you described." *Teacher.* No. "We saw man," is one sentence; what is the other? —*Samuel.* "Whom you described." *Teacher.* And what connects the two sentences? *Samuel.* Whom, I guess. *Teacher.* You guess right. Then what kind of a pronoun is whom? Class. [Hands rise.] *Teacher.* James. *James.* Relative. *Teacher.* Why? *James.* It connects those sentences. *Teacher.* Very well. Who can tell me the relative pronoun in the next sentence? [No hands rise.] *Teacher.* "Mount the horse," is one sentence; what other sentence is there included in it? [Hands rise.] *Teacher.* Susan. *Susan.* "Which I have chosen." *Teacher.* Right, and what stands for horse and connects the clauses? [Hands rise.] *Teacher.* Mary. *Mary.* Which. *Teacher.* Very well. Now, Mary, you may parse *which* by the form.

Mary parses *which;* any corrections, signified by the class, or otherwise necessary, are made by the teacher, by calling on Mary for the appropriate definitions. The class then parse it in concert, till they all are able to harmonize.

The parsing lesson now assigned for writing, is these same relative pronouns, which have been parsed by the class orally.

25.

LESSON XI.

SECOND STEP—THE VERB—TENSES. *Teacher.* We will resume the study of the verb. How many can give me the definition of the verb. [Hands rise.] *Teacher.* Sarah. *Sarah.* A verb is a word used to express the act, being, or state of a person or thing.

Teacher. Right. The class may give the definition in concert.

The class repeat the definition until all can give it correctly.

The course to be pursued with the verb is similar to that pursued with the noun, viz: taking the most obvious feature first, and others in order, as they become more complex. The distinction of tense appears to me the simplest and easiest modification, in connection with the verb.

Teacher. There are three kinds of time: present, past and future. All actions are performed in present time, or past time, or future time. Each kind of time has two tenses; the first and second. The first tense of each kind is called the present, past, future. The second of each kind is called the prior present, prior past, and prior future. I will give you the form of these tenses with the verb learn: *Present*, I learn; *Past*, I learned; *Future*, I shall or will learn. The class may give the forms in concert as I call for them. *Teacher.* Present. *Class.* I learn. *Teacher.* Past. *Class.* I learned. *Teacher.* Future. *Class.* I shall or will learn. *Teacher.* I would like to have you give the same tenses of some other verbs. Take study, and go through with it in the same way.

The class may all follow the teacher in inflecting the present tense, with the persons and numbers, giving them the proper pronouns.

Teacher. You will be able to get the forms of the tenses more easily by means of these signs: *now*, being the sign or test of the present; *yesterday*, the sign or test of the past; and, *shall or will*, the signs of the future.

You will not find the signs, *now* and *yesterday*, often in connection with verbs, in books; but you can always apply them to their respective tenses and make sense. They are applied in this way: *Present*, I learn now; *Past*, I learned yesterday; *Future*, I shall or will learn.

Now, you may give, in concert, the verb write in these three tenses, with the signs. I will beat time and you may give them. *Class. Present.* I write now; *Past* I wrote yesterday; *Future,* I shall or will write. *Teacher.* Pretty well. You may give them again.

The drill is continued with tenses in a variety of verbs, until all are able to give the tenses correctly. If any scholar is slow and careless in the concert exercise, he is called on to give the tenses separately, till his attention is secured.

26.

SECOND STEP—PRIOR TENSES. *Teacher.* The prior tenses have these signs. The prior present, *have, hadst,* or *has;* prior past, *had* or *hadst;* prior future, *shall* or *will have;* I will apply them to the verb learn. *Prior present,* I have learned; *Prior past,* I had learned; *Prior future,* I shall or will learn. Now, you may give them as I call for them.

Teacher. Prior present. *Class.* I have learned. *Teacher.* Prior past. *Class.* I had learned. *Teacher.* Prior future. *Class.* I shall or will have learned.

Teacher. Prior future. *Class.* I shall or will have learned.

Teacher. Very well. Now take the verb write and give the names of the prior tenses and their forms as I beat time with the pointer.

It may be well in any more difficult concert exercise, in which many of the class hang behind or fail of getting the exercise, to require the class to give each form twice. The laggards will then be able to catch the forms.

Teacher. You may now give all the six tenses, with their signs, as I call for them, and you may all give each form twice. All together. Present. *Class.* I learn now, I learn now. *Teacher.* Prior present. *Class.* I have learned, I have learned. *Teacher.* Past. *Class.* I learned yesterday, I learned yesterday. *Teacher.* Prior past. *Class.* I had learned, I had learned. *Teacher.* Future. *Class.* I shall or will learn, I shall or will learn. *Teacher.* Prior future. *Class.* I shall or will have learned, I shall or will have learned.

Teacher. You may now copy these signs from the board as I write them, and they will be your lesson for the next recitation. [The form of writing them will be found in Sec. 58.] The teacher writes on the board: "Signs of the tenses." Indicative mood. *Present*, (now.) *Prior present*, have, hast, or has. *Past*, (yesterday.) *Prior past*, had or hadst. *Future*, shall or will. *Prior future*, shall or will have.

You may learn the names of the tenses, and their signs, for your next lesson, so that you can all write them on the black board, at the next recitation, without looking on your papers. You may also learn the definitions of these tenses as given on pages 115–116 of Clark's Grammar.

27.

LESSON XII.

First Step—Recitation of definitions of tenses; and writing out the tenses, and their signs on the board or on slates.

Second Step—Moods. *Teacher.* There are several different manners of expressing actions or states of being. These different manners grammarians call moods. The indicative mood, that which you have been learning thus far, simply indicates a fact or asks a question, as, He learned, Did you study? The potential mood expresses power, possibility, liberty or necessity, and always uses these auxiliary or helping verbs, may, can, or must; and might, could, would or should. I will give you the four tenses in this mood; then you may see if you can give them in concert: *Present.* I may, can, or must learn; *Prior present,* I may, can, or must have learned; *Past,* I might, could, would, or should learn; *Prior past,* I might, could, would, or should have learned. Now, you may see if you can give the present tense, with its different persons and numbers. Give each twice, all together. First person. *Class.* I may, can or must learn, I may, can, or must learn. *Teacher.* Second person. *Class.* Thou mayest, canst, or must learn, Thou, etc. *Teacher.* Third person, etc. This drill may be continued in this form, till the class are all familiar with the variations of these signs, as applied to the different persons and numbers. Then the other tenses of the potential may be taken up in the same manner.

Teacher. I have told you the signs of the four tenses in the potential mood. I will repeat these signs, once more; and you will notice that they are taken in pairs; that the perfect tenses differ from the others by taking, after them, the word have.

The teacher repeats these tenses; then calls on the class, thus:

Teacher. You may give me these tenses of the potential mood, in concert, each twice. Present. *Class.* I may, can or must learn, etc. *Teacher.* Prior Present. *Class.* I may, can or must have learned, etc. *Teacher.* Past. *Class.* I might, could, would, or should learn, etc. *Teacher.* Prior Past. *Class.* I might, could, would, or should have learned, etc. The concert exercise must be continued till *all* the class can join in promptly and correctly. In case any pupil fails, he should be taken, separately, and drilled, till he overcomes the difficulty.

28.

THIRD STEP—PARSING VERBS. *Teacher.* You may now turn to page 91. I will take a verb and parse it for you, as far as you will be able to understand me. In the third sentence, ***have been***, is a verb, in the indicative mood, prior present tense, first person, singular number, to agree with its subject, I, according to rule, on page 195. A finite verb must agree with its subject, or nominative, in person and number.

I will now write the partial form, on the board, for parsing the verb, by which I parsed this verb, thus: *Species? Mood? Tense? Person? Number? Construction? Rule?*

You may now parse the same verb, by this form, and give each particular called for, by the form, twice, as I point.

The class now follow the form, as directed, and

parse the verb, have been; then other verbs: the teacher calling on individuals to select the successive verbs as they occur, and to parse them. Then, after a verb has been parsed *correctly*, by an individual; or, after he has been corrected by the class and teacher, in the manner before described, the class, in each instance, are called on to parse the same verb, in concert; giving the *entire* parsing, twice only, repeating each particular once, in each parsing.

29.

Fourth Step. The teacher prescribes for the next lesson, the definitions of the words; verb, mood, indicative mood, potential mood, tense, present tense, prior present tense, past tense, prior past tense, future tense, prior future tense; also, for a parsing lesson, in writing, the same verbs as have already been parsed, orally, in this exercise.

30.

LESSON XIII.

First Step—Recitation of lesson prescribed, and examination of the written exercises, and the hearty approval of every point in every scholar that admits of it; especially, the neatness in folding papers, and superscribing their names; neatness in the arrangement of the writing on the page; freedom from blots and blurs, etc.

31.

Second Step—Imperative Mood. *Teacher.*—There are three other moods beside the indicative and potential. You will know them by these pe culiarities, which I shall give you. The imperative mood is used for commanding, entreating, exhorting and permitting. It has no subject expressed. Take, for example: "George, shut the door." Shut, is a verb in the imperative mood, because it is used for commanding, etc. The teacher should give examples of all the different particulars embraced in the definition of the imperative mood, and then proceed to parse a verb in this mood by the form already given. The class should also parse, individually, and in concert, other examples, in preparation for writing.

32.

THIRD STEP—INFINITIVE MOOD. A similar course may be pursued with the infinitive mood, and embracing the signs of two tenses; to, being the sign of the present tense; to have, the sign of the prior present tense.

FOURTH STEP. A lesson should be prescribed, embracing the definitions pertaining to the verb, as far as the class have advanced; also, a parsing lesson, to be prepared, in writing, embracing verbs in the imperative and infinitive moods.

33.

LESSON XIV.

FIRST STEP—RECITATION, and EXAMINATION of written exercises.

SECOND STEP—VOICE. *Teacher*, I wish now to explain the most difficult thing to understand, that you will find in the whole subject of Grammar. It is VOICE.

Voice shows the relation of action expressed by the verb, to its subject. If the verb shows that the subject acts, it is in the active voice. If the verb shows that the subject is acted upon, it is said to be in the passive voice; because, passive means receiving or suffering an action or influence. For example: "George runs." In this sentence, the verb shows that the subject, George, acts; also, in the sentences, "The boy drives the horse;" "The stove warms the room;" the verbs show that the subjects act. But, in this sentence, "The horse is driven by the boy," the subject is acted upon, or receives the action, or is passive to it. The verb is said to be in the passive voice, because the subject is acted upon, or is passive to the action.

Now, you may look at some verbs in the Grammar, and tell me, if you can, whether they are in the active or passive voice.

Turn to page 118, and take the verbs as they occur in Sentence 37, and tell me whether they are active or passive, and why?

John, you may select the last verb, and tell me which voice it is in. *John.* Have been happier. *Teacher.* Susan. *Susan.* I don't think happier is a verb. Have been, is a verb. *Teacher.* Right, Susan. John, can you tell me what voice have been is in? *John.* I don't know. [Hands rise.] *Teacher.* How many think have been is in the active voice? [Several hands rise.] *Teacher.* How many think have been is in the passive voice? [Several other pupils raise their hands.] *Teacher.* How many don't know anything about it? [All raise their hands, with a smile.] *Teacher.* I see you don't understand it. I told you that voice was a difficult matter to get hold of. The truth is, that verb has no voice, according to my definition, as it does not denote action. What was my definition of the active voice? [Hands rise.] *Teacher.* Mary. *Mary.* The active voice shows that the subject acts. *Teacher.* Very well. How many can give me the definition of the passive voice? [Hands rise.] *Teacher.* Sarah. *Sarah.* The passive voice shows that the subject of the verb is acted upon. *Teacher.* Very well. Have been, or the verb to be, and other verbs which do not denote action, are said to be in the active or passive voice, according to their form. If such verbs have the form of verbs, whose subjects act, we will say they are in the active voice; or, if they have the form of verbs whose subjects are acted upon, we will say, they are in the passive voice.

Now, William, take another verb, and give its voice. *William.* Hast been taught, is a verb in the passive voice. *Teacher.* Why? *William.* Because the subject is acted upon. *Teacher.* Right. Samuel, another verb. *Samuel.* Had not found, is neither active nor passive, as I see. It don't denote action, but that there wasn't any action. He did n't find them. *Teacher.* Not, is no part of the verb. You may omit not. Now, tell me what voice had found is in, Samuel. *Samuel.* The active voice. *Teacher.* Why? *Samuel.* Because it shows, that the subject acted, if you leave out not. *Teacher.* Very well, Samuel.

So the class are all called on, individually, to give the voice of one or more verbs.

THIRD STEP—PARSING by the form.

FOURTH STEP—PRESCRIBING A LESSON.

This should include a review of definitions, for the verb and its modifications, also definitions written out on the blackboard, for voice, active voice, and passive voice. These definitions should be copied by the scholars on to their slates, or on to paper, so that they may have no excuse for not learning them. These definitions are not all found in any Grammar.

34.

LESSON XV.

FIRST STEP—RECITATION.

SECOND STEP—CLASSES.

It will hardly be necessary to go through with the method of drill for the classification of verbs. The classification which we adopt does not agree with Brown's; consequently, if that Grammar is used, definitions must be written out on the board. Such definitions may be found in this volume, Part III, Section 60.

35.

THIRD STEP—PARSING.

The complete form for parsing verbs may now be given; and the class will need drilling on this form, in connection with the form for pronouns and nouns, for many days—perhaps weeks—in connection with written lessons.

36.

GENERAL DIRECTIONS.

The remaining Parts of Speech.

The Adjective, Participle, Adverb, Preposition, Conjunction, and Exclamation, may be made subjects of lessons, occasionally, to give variety to the drills in parsing verbs, pronouns, and nouns.

The adjective would have been introduced more properly, immediately after the nouns, in this course of lessons; but, from its greater simplicity, it was thought preferable to give all the space to the more complex forms and facts involved in the noun, pronoun and verb.

37.

THE RULES OF SYNTAX.

The most important of these rules will be learned in connection with the drills already given, without assigning special lessons for learning them. Such lessons should, however, be given, sooner or later, and the scholars should be required to give them *by number*, as they are called for, promiscuously, by the teacher. The advantage of this is, that they can afterwards refer to them by number; thus saving much time and labor in the parsing lessons, both oral and written. The more difficult rules for construction, as, for example, that for the predicate nominative, should have special drills, and entire lessons devoted to them; otherwise, they never will be well understood.

38.

It is an excellent plan to give parsing lessons in the examples of false syntax, furnished for correction in the grammar used, confining the attention of the class chiefly to the words which violate the rules; requiring, that a pupil, before parsing the word assigned him, correct it, and give the reason for his correction; then that he parse it in full.

39.

HORIZONTAL PARSING.

Much more progress may be made, in a given time, after a class shall have become tolerably familiar with all the parts of speech, by pursuing the horizontal method of parsing.

THE FIRST STEP, in this method, is to call on the class for the PARTS OF SPEECH, only, as they occur in any given passage. THE SECOND STEP is to give the CLASS only to which each word belongs; for example, (see Clark's Grammar, pages 104, 119, and 154). Let the scholars, in succession, as they sit, give the classes of the words, as they occur, thus: A, indefinite; man, common; of, not classified; a, indefinite; lively, common or qualifying; imagination, common; has, irregular, transitive, etc.

THIRD STEP—The CASES only, of nouns and pronouns.

FOURTH STEP—The CONSTRUCTIONS only, of the nouns and pronouns.

FIFTH STEP—The RULES only, which apply to the cases of nouns, pronouns and verbs.

SIXTH STEP—The CONSTRUCTION and RULES of all the words, as they occur, in succession.

Much time may be saved, by adopting any one of these steps, which the class may seem most to need. Thus, those points on which the class are well posted, may be laid aside, for the time, and their attention directed, exclusively, to those in which they are found most defective.

40.

GENERAL CAUTIONS.

This entire plan demands the exercise of the closest watchfulness, on the part of the teacher, that no material points are omitted; that nothing, which has once been passed over, should be so long neglected, in the drills, as to be forgotten.

The FORMS OF PARSING, for all the parts of speech, should be well memorized, and so frequent practice should be given, in the use of them *all,* that no one can be forgotten.

Care should be taken, that only ONE CONSTRUCTION be given to each word, except to double relatives, which, from supplying two cases, are in two constructions. Nouns and pronouns, in APPOSITION, are too frequently parsed as if also in the same construction as the word with which they are in apposition. The fact of their being in apposition, is sufficient to determine their case, and any other construction would be superfluous. The PREDICATE NOMINATIVE, is not unfrequently parsed by teachers who enjoy some reputation, as being in the objective case, and governed by an intransitive or passive verb. The scholar should be drilled long, and thoroughly, on this point, till he accustoms himself to ascertain that an intransitive or passive verb is used; and, that the noun after it, means the same thing as the noun before it.

In the distinction of PERSONAL AND RELATIVE pronouns, there is generally more obscurity and error than in any other part of Grammar. It arises, in part, from their inappropriate names; but chiefly, from the erroneous or obscure definitions used for them.

A personal pronoun is too frequently defined as one which relates to persons, and a relative pronoun as one which relates to an antecedent. Both of these definitions are abominable in themselves, and lamentable in their results.

In all the parsing exercises, constant care should be exercised in SELECTING SUCH SENTENCES AND WORDS, for drill, as will best exemplify the principles presented. From a want of such care, arise confusion, embarrassment, disgust and discouragement.

Again; scholars should neither be required, nor permitted, to parse a word any farther than the class have been taken along together, and a FORM has been given.

NOTE.—The various models found in CLARK'S GRAMMAR, pp. 104, 105, and 154, may be profitably consulted by the teacher.

METHOD OF TEACHING ADVANCED CLASSES.

41.

PRELIMINARY REMARKS.

When, by the method described in the foregoing pages, or by any other, a class can distinguish all the parts of speech, and parse them in the more obvious constructions, a review of the entire subject should be commenced, with the use of OUTLINES.

Some teachers decry outlines altogether, and confine themselves and their scholars to the order and substance of the text-book, or what is worse, to no order or substance, except to such as appears in gas and vanishes in forgetfulness.

My experience is, that classes making use of outlines as guides to investigation, are much more independent, thorough and critical, in their study; and, that they obtain more correct, liberal and comprehensive views from such investigation, than without outlines. Outlines, used properly, will never limit investigation; but every well-trained pupil understands, that any facts, or principles, or items not provided for in the outlines, must be incorporated into it by himself; and he thus enjoys the satisfaction of an original discoverer.

Not only so, but it is an excellent plan to require a class, having used outlines enough to appreciate the logic of their arrangement, to make out outlines, each pupil for himself, and to present them, on paper, to the teacher, for examination. Then the teacher may select some one or more of these, for presentation to the class. The pupil will copy his own work on to the board.

42.

METHODS OF USING OUTLINES.

First Method. Instead of assigning a given number of pages, in the text-book, for scholars to study, for recitation, an outline of a subject may be copied on to the blackboard, by one of the pupils, from a manuscript prepared by the teacher. The class will all copy the outline on to slates or loose paper. It is then expected, that at the next recitation every pupil will be prepared to give the whole of the outline on the board, entirely from memory; also, any definitions, explanations, and applications, that the outline or the subject may call for. The teacher does not, ordinarily, call on one individual to write out the whole outline, but distributes it in such portions, as may be convenient, to different pupils. These portions, so assigned, they may write, immediately, on the board; and describe them, when they are again called on, by the teacher. After having assigned the different topics of the outline, to the class, (and each of the topics, if the class is large, may be given to several different scholars,) the teacher may occupy any time, before scholars who have had topics assigned them are ready to report, in examining others who have had no topics assigned them, orally, by questions; or, by proposing topics for them to discuss, without having written any portion of the outline on the board. Such a course would be necessary, with a large class and a small blackboard.

Teachers using outlines, should not lay aside the ordinary methods of assigning lessons, and of recitations, entirely. They may adopt this method of reporting, occasionally, in advance lessons; always in review lessons; or, as the nature of the subject, and the aptitude and discipline of the pupils may require.

43.

Second Method. An outline may be assigned to only one pupil, for him to use in investigating and mastering a subject. He will be expected to give his report, on that subject, at the next recitation, either without the written outline before him, in any form, or with the outline written on the blackboard, *from memory*, in presence of the class. In the latter case the pupil, in giving his report, takes his place, at the board, with the pointer, and directs the attention of the class to the several topics, sub topics, and distinct items, as he amplifies them with definitions, explanations, exemplifications, illustrations and applications. These may be drawn from books, or from the pupil's own experience and observation.

It is perceived, that the scholar thus obtains the power, almost unconsciously, of speaking systematically, and, at length, on any subject that he may have properly and thoroughly investigated. To such pupils as are the best disciplined, *advance subjects* may be assigned, without outlines. It is then expected that they will prepare their own outlines, and present them, as their own, on the blackboard, at the time of giving their report.

A definite time should be appointed, for giving the report; also, a definite amount of time, in which to give it; as five minutes, ten minutes, or fifteen minutes, according to the age of the pupil, the time occupied by the whole recitation, and the demands of the subject assigned for investigation.

The most interesting public examinations that I have ever attended, have been conducted on this plan. Special subjects were assigned to individual pupils, on which to report or deliver lectures before the public audience. The audience, of course, are informed of the plan adopted, in the preparation for the examination; and, that it is not designed so much to exhibit the scholars' knowledge of the branches generally, as to test their mental power in grasping a subject, and in communicating their views under embarrassing circumstances.

The audience should be urged to criticise the pupil, during the delivery of his lecture. Other pupils also, especially members of the same class, should consider themselves free to criticise, to correct misstatements, or to fill up omissions.

44.

METHOD OF CRITICISING REPORTS.

The scholars should do most of the criticising. They will learn much more by criticising than by being criticised.

But system should be secured in these criticisms; or nothing definite, or satisfactory, will be accomplished.

The order to be followed may be this: at the conclusion of a report, before the pupil reporting has taken his seat, the teacher may call on the class for criticisms, on—1st, Pronunciation; 2d, Spelling; 3d, Arrangement of the Outline, including, also, omissions or repetitions; 4th, Definitions; 5th, Promiscuous matters.

Lastly, the teacher makes any additional criticisms, remarks, or explanations required. The pupil having a special subject assigned him, is, of course, excused from preparing the lesson assigned to the class.

By giving the subjects, in order, to different pupils, on successive days, reviews will be accomplished in a manner more interesting and impressive than in that generally pursued. The subjects having been passed over once in review, as far as the class have advanced, the same order may be pursued by other pupils, as by those who first had them for special study and reporting.

45.

Ordinary Method of conducting a recitation with an advanced Grammar Class.

The teacher has a register for this class as for all others. He calls the names of the pupils, as he finds them in his register; sometimes in the direct order, sometimes in the inverse order; sometimes in the direct order, omitting alternate names; then in the inverse order. By this method of calling on the members of a class, he secures uncertainty, on the part of a pupil, as to when he may be called on; and, certainty, on his own part, that no pupil is neglected in the recitation. He grades each pupil as he recites; which grading shows who has been called on.

A scholar's name being called, he rises, and the subject of a section is proposed for him to discuss. If he should fail to reach all the matter of the section, the teacher will reach his knowledge or ignorance of those points, by questions.

In the case of parsing, or correction of false syntax, the pupil, when called on, rises and parses the word, or corrects the sentence, without interruption from the class; but when he concludes, the teacher calls on the class for criticism, by pronouncing the word "Class." Other pupils, who have criticisms to offer, raise their hands, and are called on, by name, separately, to give them. The teacher will call on those first, who are generally the least inclined to offer criticisms. He will also call on any pupil, for criticisms or corrections, who is seen to have remitted his attention or interest in the recitation. Such criticisms are given, by the pupil, sitting. No pupil, when standing, resumes his seat, without permission from the teacher. It is well, in case a pupil fails in a topic or question proposed to him, to pass it to the next pupil, and if he fails, to call on the class. That being disposed of, a second topic or question is proposed to the scholar first having failed; and so on, till the teacher is satisfied, as to his grade, for the recitation.

46.

OUTLINES.

Remark. The following outlines are accompanied only by the definitions of such words as, I conceive, are inadequately, or incorrectly defined, in most Grammars. It is not supposed, that this number of *The Normal* is to be used as a text-book. But, it is hoped that both teachers and scholars will find it serviceable as a reference book, in their daily preparation for recitations.

47.

GENERAL OUTLINE OF GRAMMAR.

Remark. This outline was introduced, in Part II, page 49, and the definitions and explanations given, in connection with it, for the purpose of keeping the chain of Outlines unbroken from the General Outlines of Knowledge, in Part I, to those of Orthoepy and Orthography, in Part II.

OUTLINE OF ORTHOGENY.

ORTHOGENY,	Noun, extended on page 150. Verb, " " 157. Pronoun, " " 162. Adjective, Participle, Adverb, Conjunction Interjection or Exclamation.

48.

DEFINITIONS, EXPLANATIONS, AND REMARKS.

ORTHOGENY. For definition, see Part II, page 45, section 9. For definitions of the parts of speech, see any text-book in general use.

49.

OUTLINE OF THE NOUN.

- **Noun,**
  - Terms: **Phrase, Sentence, Clause,** Apostrophe, **Parse.**
  - Classes,
    - Common,—Sub-Classes,
      - Collective and individual.
      - Verbal and non-verbal,
      - Abstract and concrete,
      - Diminutive and non-diminutive.
    - Proper,
  - Modifications,
    - Number,
      - Classes,
        - Singular,
        - Plural.
      - Methods of forming the Plural,
        - Regular,
        - Irregular,
        - Foreign,
          - Latin,
          - Greek,
          - French.
    - Gender,
      - Classes,
        - Masculine, Feminine.
        - Common, Neuter.
      - Formation of Feminine,
        - By another word,
        - By change of termination,
        - By prefix.
    - Person,
      - Classes,
        - 1st,
        - 2d,
        - 3d.
    - Case, —Outline extended on next page.
  - **Form of Parsing,** Species, Class, (Sub-class,) Person, **Number, Gender,** Case, Construction, Rule.

OUTLINE OF THE NOUN—Continued.

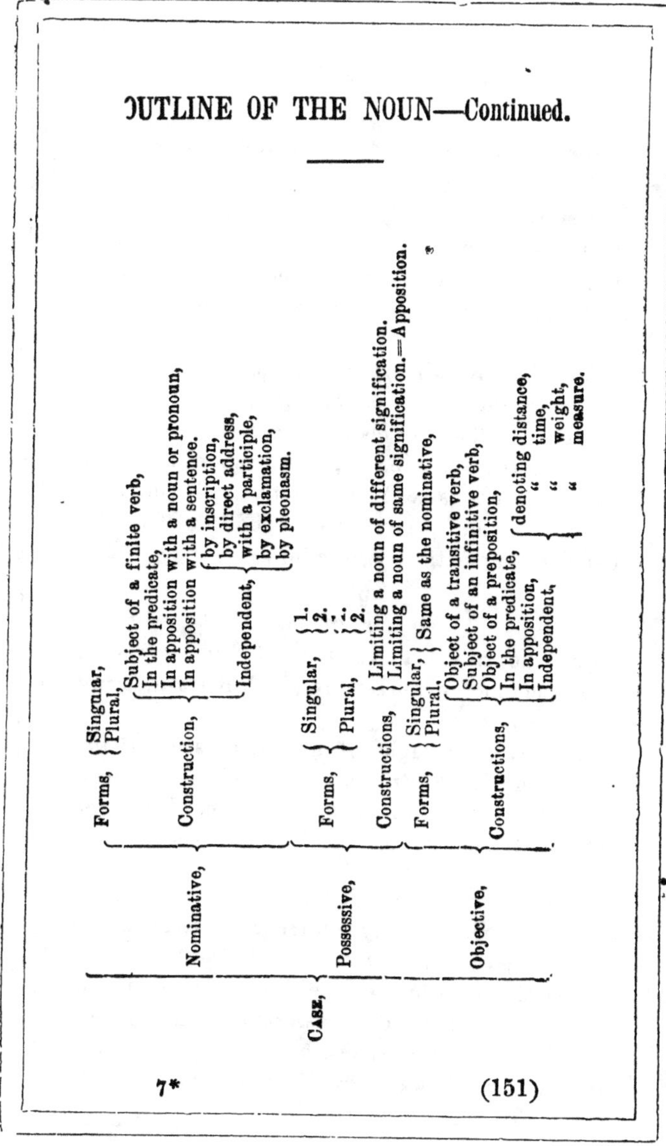

- **Case,**
  - Nominative,
    - Forms, { Singular, Plural,
    - Construction,
      - Subject of a finite verb,
      - In the predicate,
      - In apposition with a noun or pronoun,
      - In apposition with a sentence.
      - Independent,
        - by inscription,
        - by direct address,
        - with a participle,
        - by exclamation,
        - by pleonasm.
  - Possessive,
    - Forms,
      - Singular, { 1. 2.
      - Plural, { 1. 2.
    - Constructions,
      - Limiting a noun of different signification.
      - Limiting a noun of same signification.—Apposition.
  - Objective,
    - Forms, { Singular, Plural, } Same as the nominative,
    - Constructions,
      - Object of a transitive verb,
      - Subject of an infinitive verb,
      - Object of a preposition,
      - In the predicate,
      - In apposition,
      - Independent,
        - denoting distance,
        - " time,
        - " weight,
        - " measure.

50.

DEFINITIONS, EXPLANATIONS AND REMARKS.

NOUN—A name.

Remark. *Terms* include all those technical words necessary to an understanding of the sub ject, and not elsewhere introduced into the outline They should all be defined, by the pupil, in giving a report.

CLASSES. Results of an arrangement of similar things, according to some definite plan

Remark. The sub-classes of common nouns are only noticed in parsing, when the noun falls into one of the sub-classes in the first vertical column.

MODIFICATION. Any form or condition of words, used for grammatical distinction.

51.

CONSTRUCTIONS.

CONSTRUCTION. The method of framing a word into a sentence or phrase, by which it acquires any given modification.

Remark. Examples of nouns, in some of the more difficult constructions of the several cases, will be given, in which I differ somewhat from both Clark and Brown.

52.

NOMINATIVE IN THE PREDICATE.

Explanation. Every sentence is divided into two parts; the Subject and Predicate. The subject is that of which something is assérted: the predicate is that which is asserted of the subject, and always includes the verb of the sentence. The noun which follows an intransitive or passive verb and denotes the same thing as its subject, is said to be a predicate noun, and is always in the same case as the subject. The subject of a finite verb (*i. e.*, a verb not in the infinitive mood,) is in the nominative case; consequently a noun in the predicate, with a finite verb, must be in the nominative case.

Example First. "Gold is a *metal.*"

Metal is a noun, common, third, singular, neuter, nominative, being in the predicate with the intransitive verb, is, and denoting the same thing as the subject, gold.

Remark. Words, in this construction, are too frequently parsed in the objective case, and are said to be governed by the intransitive verb, which can have no government.

Example Second. "He was named John."

John is a noun, proper, third, singular, masculine, nominative, being in the predicate with the passive verb, was named, and denoting the same thing as he, the subject of the verb:

53.

APPOSITION WITH A SENTENCE.

Example. "He asked me to visit him in the country; a *privilege* of which I gladly availed myself."

Privilege is a noun, common, third, singular, neuter, nominative, in apposition with the sentence, "He asked me to visit him in the country."

54.

NOMINATIVE CASE INDEPENDENT.

These constructions are exemplified and explained, in Clark's English Grammar, pages **85** and **231.**

55.

SUBJECT OF THE INFINITIVE.

Remark. Strangely enough, this construction is overlooked by Brown, and many other excellent grammarians.

Explanation. In the abridgement of a subordinate sentence, used as the object of a transitive verb, the finite verb of the sentence is changed into the infinitive, and its subject into the objective case, provided it differs from the subject of the principal sentence.

Example. "Susan desires, that Samuel may go away." This sentence, abridged, takes this form: Susan desires Samuel to go away.

Brown, and many other grammarians, would parse Samuel as the object of desire. This is plainly not the sense. Susan does not desire Samuel, but desires the action, implied in the subordinate sentence. Then the subordinate sentence is the object of the verb, desire, and not Samuel. The usage of all languages puts the subject of the infinitive, in this construction, in the objective form. We see this, more plainly, in English, by the use of the pronoun, in a similar sentence. Unabridged, "John understood that he said," etc.; abridged, "John understood him to say" etc.

Rule, for subject of the infinitive.

The subject of the infinitive is commonly in the objective case.—Sometimes in the nominative. See Clark's Grammar, page 189.

56.

OBJECTIVE IN THE PREDICATE.

Explanation. By Clark, intransitive and passive verbs take the same case after them as before them, when both words refer to the same thing.

In the last construction, the subject of the infinitive is put in the objective. If, then, this infinitive is an intransitive or passive verb, and has a noun in the predicate, denoting the same thing as its subject, it will be in the same case, viz: the objective.

Example First. "I thought him to be a *scholar.*" Scholar is in the objective, in the predicate; or, as we say more briefly, is a predicate objective.

Example Second. "Zachariah wished him to be called *John.*"

John is parsed thus: John is a noun, proper, third, singular, masculine, objective in the predicate, with the passive verb, to be called: according to Rule 21, Brown; him, being the objective subject before it.

OBJECTIVE CASE INDEPENDENT.

Nouns expressing distance, time, weight, and measure, are often put in the objective case, without a governing word.

Explanation. In such examples as the following, "He walked a mile," "She studied an hour,'

"It weighed a pound," etc., there is no preposition, which, being supplied, will make good sense or euphony. Usage does not warrant us in supplying any preposition, to govern these objectives; hence, we say, they are in the objective independent.

57.

DRILL ON THE PRECEDING CONSTRUCTIONS.

The teacher will do well to assign for a lesson to an advanced class, perhaps for several lessons, the several constructions of nouns; requiring each scholar to bring in sentences, written on paper, exemplifying each construction, with the exemplifying word underscored. These sentences should not be copied from any Grammar.

The time of the recitation may be taken up by each scholar's parsing a word, in one of his own sentences, he having first written the sentence on the blackboard. The order of proceeding should be this: the teacher calls on one pupil to write a sentence exemplifying the predicate nominative, and so on till each scholar has been called on, and till each construction has been thus exemplified, one or more times, on the blackboard.

Then each scholar may be called on, the second time, to parse the word, in his own sentence, in the required construction.

If one pupil should fail, in giving a correct example, for any required construction, another should be called on to give it.

58.

OUTLINE OF THE VERB.

VERB,

- **Terms:** Subject, Object, Preterit, Finite,
- Classes,
  - As to Form, — Regular, Irregular, Defective, Redundant.
  - As to Use, — Transitive, Intransitive.
- Modifications —
  - Form, — Ordinary, Emphatic, Progressive.
  - Voice, — Active, Passive.
  - Mood, — Ind., Sub., Poten., Imp., Inf., Part.
  - Tense, — Present, Prior Present, Past, Prior Past. Future, Prior Future.
  - Person, — 1st, 2nd, 3rd.
  - Number, — Singular, Plural.
- Principal Parts,
  - Names, — Present Indicative, Past Indicative, Present Participle, Past Participle.
  - Tests, — (now,) (yesterday,) (-ing,) (having.)
- Signs,
  - Indicative.
    - Pres., (now,) Past, (yesterday.)
    - Future, shall or will.
    - Prior Present, have, hast, or had.
    - Prior Past, had, or hadst.
    - Prior Future, shall have or will have.
  - Potential.
    - Present, may, can, or must.
    - Past, might, could, would, or should.
    - Prior Present, may, can, or must have.
    - Prior Past, might, could would, or should have.
  - Subjunctive, — If, though, unless, except, etc.
  - Imperative, —Its uses are its Signs.
  - Infinitive — Present, To; Prior Present, To have.

OUTLINE OF THE VERB—CONCLUDED.

Form of Parsing,	Species, Classes, (Principal Parts,) (Form,) Voice, Mood, Tense, Person, Number, Construction, Rule.
Form of Parsing Participles,	Species, Classes, { Time, Voice, } Derivation, Construction, Rule.

59.

DEFINITIONS, EXPLANATIONS AND REMARKS.

Remark. The greater part of the definitions required in giving a report on the outline of the verb, can be obtained from all grammars. I shall only give such definitions as, I conceive, are generally given erroneously.

VERB. A word used to assert action, being, or state of being.

Explanation. The word *assert* is used here, with the meanings of affirm, deny, ask a question, command, exhort, intreat, permit, suppose, grant, or state a condition.

REGULAR VERB. One that makes its preterit or past tense, and past participle, by adding *ed* to the present, according to Definition 120, Clark's Grammar.

TRANSITIVE VERB. One that requires an object to complete its meaning.

Remark 1. A common definition of a transitive verb is: "One that has an object *after it.*" This last expression, "after it," is constantly misleading the pupil; for, in the case of relative and interrogative pronouns, the object is always before the verb. In the passive voice, also, the object being used as the subject, is, necessarily, before the verb.

Remark 2. Some contend, that passive verbs are intransitive. By the faulty definition, given above, they are right. In truth, however, they are entirely wrong, or all our dictionaries are wrong. For the dictionaries give all verbs, which admit of the passive voice, as transitive. But, should the objector say, that dictionaries do not give passive verbs at all; then I answer, that I conceive they do, just as much as they give infinitive verbs, or finite verbs, or any other kinds, which take their names from their modifications.

Remark 3. Every transitive verb admits of a passive voice; and no intransitive verb can be passive, when used intransitively; for the reason, that the passive verb always uses its object for its subject, and intransitive verbs have no objects.

VOICE. That modification of the verb, which distinguishes the relation of the verb to its subject.

ACTIVE VOICE. That form which verbs assume, whose subjects act.

Explanation. By this definition, all intransitive verbs are in the active voice, for they have the *form* of transitive verbs in the active voice.

PASSIVE VOICE. That form which a verb assumes, to denote that its subject is acted upon.

60.

TESTS AND SIGNS.

Explanation. The use of tests and signs, in aiding pupils to form the principal parts and subordinate parts of verbs, is given on pages 128–133.

Remark. In the FORM OF PARSING, *principal parts*, and *form*, are inclosed in parentheses, to show that they are not given, in parsing all verbs.

The *principal parts* only, of irregular verbs, are noticed in parsing; and the *form* only, when it is emphatic or progressive.

61.

CONSTRUCTION OF VERBS AND PARTICIPLES.

Remark. The *construction* of finite verbs, is generally simple; but the construction of infinitives and participles demands close attention.

In addition to Clark's Rules, or rather in the place of his tenth, I would use this

RULE. *Infinitives and participles have the construction of nouns, adjectives, or adverbs.*

In parsing infinitives and participles, the pupils should give their construction in this manner: "With the construction of a noun, being the subject of," etc.

62.

EXAMPLES OF PARSING INFINITIVES.

To show this more plainly, I will give several examples.

"To steal is base."

To steal, is a verb, irregular, transitive; steal, stole, stealing, stolen, active, infinitive, present, with the construction of a noun, being the subject of the verb, is.

"He desired to go."

To go, is a verb, irregular, intransitive, go, went, going, gone, active, infinitive, present, with the construction of a noun, being the object of the verb, desired.

"He was unwilling to be called a shirk."

To be called, is a verb, regular, transitive, passive, infinitive, present, with the construction of an adverb, limiting the adjective, unwilling.

"This is the time to study."

To study, is a verb, regular, transitive, active, infinitive, present, with the construction of an adjective, relating to the noun, time.

63.

EXAMPLES OF PARSING PARTICIPLES.

"I saw the sun *rising*."

Rising is a participle, imperfect, active, from rise, rose, rising, risen, with the construction of an adjective. relating to the noun, sun.

"By being rejected, his fortune was made."

Being rejected, is a participle, imperfect, passive, from reject, etc., with the construction of a noun, being the object of the preposition, by.

64.

OUTLINE OF THE PRONOUN.

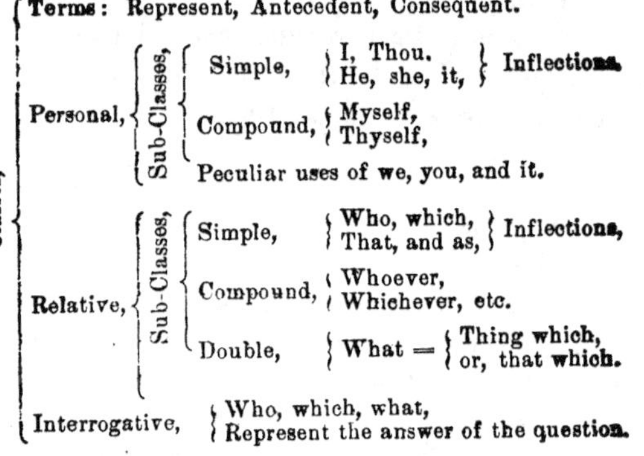

Modifications—the same as nouns.

Form of Parsing,
- Species, Class, (sub-class,)
- Agreement, { Person, Number, Gender, Rule.
- Case,
- Construction, Rule.

65.

DEFINITIONS, EXPLANATIONS AND REMARKS.

Represent. To stand in the place of, with similar properties.

Antecedent. A word going before a pronoun, and represented by it.

Consequent. A word coming after a pronoun, and represented by it.

Remark. An interrogative pronoun always represents a consequent found in the answer of the question.

PERSONAL PRONOUN. One that is always used for the same grammatical person.

Remark 1. Brown's definition, "A personal pronoun, is a pronoun that shows, by its form, what person it is," appears to me only to apply to the pronoun I; the letter I, being used for the number one. But I see nothing in the *form* of the other personal pronouns to indicate their person, whether first, second, or third.

Remark 2. The common definition given for a personal pronoun, by the great majority of scholars and teachers, viz: "One that stands for persons," should be hooted out of every schoolroom.

RELATIVE PRONOUN. One that is not always used for the same grammatical person; and connects clauses.

Remark 1. Clark's definition for a relative pronoun, is a good one, but I have framed mine as antithetic to that for the personal pronoun.

Remark 2. The common definition for a relative pronoun, viz: "One that relates to an antecedent," is worse, if possible, than that for a personal pronoun. If any other teacher finds it necessary to use as much labor, as I do, in smoking out these vermin, from their lurking places, he has my most heartfelt sympathy and commiseration.

INTERROGATIVE PRONOUN. One that is used for asking questions.

66.

EXAMPLES IN PARSING SIMPLE PRONOUNS.

"I, who was present, know the particulars."

I is a pronoun, personal, representing the name of the speaker, and agreeing with it in the first, singular, common, according to Rule 4, Clark. It is in the nominative, being the subject of know, according to Rule 1, Clark.

Who is a pronoun, relative, representing its antecedent, I, and agreeing with it in the first, singular, common, according to Rule 4. It is in the nominative, being the subject of was, according to Rule 1.

"He pursues just such studies as he likes."

As is a pronoun, relative, representing its antecedent, studies, and agreeing with it, in the third, plural, neuter, according to Rule 4. It is in the objective, being the object of, the verb, likes, and governed by it, according to Rule 3.

"What will become of us without religion."

What is a pronoun, interrogative, representing the answer of the question, in person, number and gender unknown; according to Rule 4. It is in the nominative, being the subject of, will become, according to Rule 1.

67.

EXAMPLES IN PARSING DOUBLE RELATIVES

"Shall I hide from Abraham *what* I do?"

What is a pronoun, relative, double, equivalent to *thing which*. *Thing*, the antecedent part, is a noun, common, third, singular, neuter, objective, being the object of hide, and governed by it, according to Rule 3. *Which*, the relative part, is a pronoun, relative, representing its antecedent, thing; and agreeing with it in the third, singular, neuter, according to Rule 4. It is in the objective, being the object of do, and governed by, it, according to Rule 3.

"Let the lad become *what* you wish him to be."

What is a pronoun, relative, double, equivalent to, *thing which*. *Thing*, the antecedent part, is a noun, common, third, singular, neuter, indefinite, in the predicate, after the intransitive verb, become, according to Rule 6; lad, being the subject objective, before the same verb. *Which*, the relative part, is a pronoun, relative, representing thing, and agreeing with it, in the third, singular, neuter according to Rule 4. It is in the objective in the predicate, with the intransitive verb, to be; according to Rule 6; him, being the subject objective before the same verb.

68.

OUTLINE OF BROWN'S RULES OF SYNTAX.

Agreement	Nouns with nouns; Rules III, XXI. Pronouns with nouns; Rules V, VI, VII, VIII. Verbs with subjects; Rules IX, X, XI, XII. Verbs with verbs; Rule XIII.
Relation.	Adjectives to nouns and pronouns; Rules I, IV. Participles to nouns and pronouns; Rule XIV. Adverbs to verbs, etc.; Rule XV. Conjunctions to words and sentences; Rule XVI. Prepositions to words; Rule XVII. Interjections, no relation; Rule XVIII.
Government.	Subject of finite verb; Rule II. Subject of infinitive verb; no rule given. Object of verbs; Rule XX. Object of prepositions; Rule XXII. Possessive case; Rule XIX. Infinitives; Rules XXIII, XXIV. Participles; Rule XIV. Case absolute; Rule XXV.

69.

REMARKS AND EXPLANATIONS.

Remark 1. This outline differs from Brown's arrangement but in a few particulars, viz: 1st. Agreement and relation are separated. 2d. Rule 2. which he includes in agreement, I place in government, as I conceive a verb governs or controls the case of its subject, just as much as the case of its object. 3d. Rule 21 is placed under the head of agreement, for the reason that it is a plain case of agreement.

Remark 2. The subject of the infinitive is provided for, in Part III, section 55.

Remark 3. This outline should be assigned for a lesson to the whole class, for review as directed in Part III, Section 42; and to individuals, for reporting, as explained in Section 43.

The teacher will require each pupil reporting to give a sentence, containing a word, exemplifying the construction to which each rule relates.

70.

OUTLINE OF ANALYSIS.

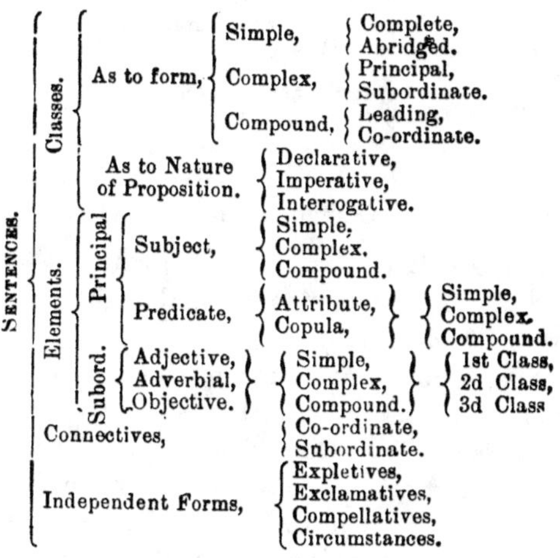

Form of Analysis.

1. Classify the sentence, { as to form, as to proposition.
2. Give complex subject.
3. Give simple subject.
4. Describe modifiers of subject, in order, by giving structure, nature, and class.
5. Give base of the modifier, and describe its modifiers, in order, as before.
6. Give complex predicate.
7. Give simple predicate.
8. Give attribute and copula.
9. Give modifiers, and desrcibe them, as before.

Remark. Elements of the third class are first described as elements, then as sentences according to this form.

8

OUTLINE OF ANALYSIS—CONCLUDED.

Abridgment.
- Abridged Sentences.
  - As to Nature, { Substantive, Adjective, Adverbial.
  - As to Construction, { Participial, Absolute, Infinitive, Participial Noun.
- Method of Abridgment, Remove the Connective, etc. See Section 82.
- Order of Analysis, { 1st, in the abridged form, 2d, in the expanded form.

71.

DEFINITIONS, EXPLANATIONS AND REMARKS.

ANALYSIS; see Part II. page 46, section 9.

SENTENCE. An enunciation of a thought, including a verb and its subject.

SIMPLE SENTENCE. One that contains but one proposition, or one assertion and its subject.

COMPLETE SENTENCE. One whose verb is finite.

ABRIDGED SENTENCE. One whose verb is in the infinitive or participial mood.

COMPOUND SENTENCE. One that contains two or more simple or complex sentences, of equal rank.

LEADING SENTENCE. The first simple or complex sentence, comprised in a compound sentence.

COÖRDINATE SENTENCE. Any other sentence than the first, and of equal rank with it, in a compound sentence.

COMPLEX SENTENCE. One that contains a complete subordinate sentence as a constituent part.

PRINCIPAL SENTENCE. The entire complex sentence, including all its subordinate sentences.

SUBORDINATE SENTENCE. One that is used to modify some word or phrase in another sentence

72.

ELEMENT. Any part of a sentence; including words, phrases and subordinate sentences.

PRINCIPAL ELEMENTS. Those without which a sentence cannot exist. They are the subject and predicate.

SUBJECT. That of which something is asserted. See Part III, Section 59, Verb.

PREDICATE. The assertion made of the subject.

ATTRIBUTE. That property, quality, characteristic, name or circumstance, asserted of the subject.

COPULA. That which joins the attribute to the subject and makes the assertion.

Remark. The verb, to be, with its various modifications, is commonly used as the copula; and any other verb can be resolved into the verb, be, and the peculiar attribute which it expresses.

SUBORDINATE ELEMENTS. All elements, other than the principal elements. They are adjective, adverbial, and substantive.

ADJECTIVE ELEMENT. One that modifies a noun.

ADVERBIAL ELEMENT. One that modifies any thing else than a noun.

Explanation. The word noun, in these last two definitions, is understood to include any word, phrase or sentence, which assumes the functions of a noun.

OBJECTIVE ELEMENT. One which is used as the object of a transitive verb or participle.

73.

Simple Element. One without its modifiers.

Complex Element. A simple element, with its modifiers. The simple element is also called the base of a complex element.

Compound Element. One comprising two or more simple or complex elements of equal rank, connected by coördinate conjunctions, expressed or understood.

Element of First Class. One whose base is a single word.

Element of Second Class. One whose base consists of a preposition and its object, including infinitives.

Element of Third Class. One whose base is a subordinate sentence.

74.

Connective. Any word that joins words, phrases or sentences.

Coördinate Connective. One that joins sentences or elements of equal rank.

Subordinate Connective. One that joins elements of unequal rank.

75.

Independent Forms. Those which have no grammatical construction in a sentence.

Expletives. Those introductory words that are superfluous in the construction of a sentence.

Examples. 1st. "*It* is plain he can do it." 2d. "*John*, he is a fine fellow.' 3d. "*There* is a reason for that." *It*, *John*, and *there*, in these sentences, form no part of the construction, and are hence called expletives.

COMPELLATIVES. Names of persons addressed.

CIRCUMSTANCES. Phrases containing the case absolute, with a participle. See Clark's Grammar, page 232, Note III.

EXCLAMATIVES. Words, expressing emotions, including interjections, and case absolute by exclamation. See Clark's Grammar, page 278.

76.

EXAMPLES OF ORAL ANALYSIS BY THE FORM.

SIMPLE SENTENCES.

1. *I repent*, is a simple declarative sentence, of which I is the simple subject unmodified; and repent, the simple predicate, unmodified.

2. *Both parties disgraced themselves*, is a simple declarative sentence, of which *both parties* is the complex subject; of which *parties* is the simple subject, modified by *both*, a simple adjective element of the first class. *Disgraced themselves*, is the complex predicate, of which *disgraced* is the simple predicate, modified by *themselves*, a simple objective element of the first class.

3. *Spirits less vigorous would have shrunk from such dangers*, is a simple declarative sentence, of which, *spirits less vigorous*, is the complex subject, of which *spirits* is the simple, subject modified by *less vigorous*, a complex adjective element of the first class, of which *vigorous*, the base, is modified by *less*, a simple adverbial element of the first class.

Would have shrunk from such dangers, is the complex predicate, of which *would have shrunk*, is the simple predicate, modified by, *from such dangers*, a complex adverbial element of the second class, of which *dangers*, the noun of the base, is modified by *such*, a simple adjective element of the first class.

4. *Did his natural intrepidity forsake him at the approach of death?* is a simple interrogative sentence, of which, *his natural intrepidity* is the complex subject, of which *intrepidity* is the simple subject, modified by *his* and *natural*, two simple adjective elements of the first class. *Did forsake him, at the approach of death*, is the complex predicate, of which *did forsake* is the simple predicate, modified by *him*, a simple objective element of the first class; also by, *at the approach of death*, a complex adverbial element of the second class, of which *approach*, the noun of the base, is modified by *the*, a simple adjective element of the first class; also by, *of death*, a simple adjective element of the second class.

77.

COMPLEX SENTENCES.

5. The *chief misfortunes that befall us in life can be traced to vices and follies which we have committed*, is a complex declarative sentence, of which, *the chief misfortunes that befall us in life*, is the complex subject, of which, *misfortunes* is the simple subject modified by *the* and *chief*, two simple adjective elements of the first class; also, by *that befall us in life*, a simple adjective element of the third class. It is also a simple declarative subordinate sentence, of which, *that* is the connective and simple subject, unmodified. *Befall us in life*, is the complex predicate, of which *befall* is the simple predicate, modified by *us*, a simple objective element of the first class; also, by *in life*, a simple adverbial element of the second class. *Can be traced*, and all that follows, is the complex predicate, of which, *can be traced* is the simple predicate, modified by *to vices*, and and all that follows it; a compound adverbial element of the second class, of which *vices or follies*, the nouns of the base, are modified by *which we have committed*, a simple adjective element of the third class. It is also a simple declarative subordinate sentence, of which *we* is the simple subject unmodified. *Have committed which*, is the complex predicate, of which, *have committed* is the simple predicate, modified by *which*, a simple objective element of the first class; also, the connective of the subordinate sentence.

6. *That he is dishonest is manifest*, is a complex declarative sentence, of which, *that he is dishonest* is the simple subject, an element of the third class; also, a simple declarative subordinate sentence, of which *that* is an expletive, and *he* the simple subject, unmodified; *is dishonest*, is the simple predicate, unmodified, *dishonest* being the attribute, and *is*, the copula.

7. *My desire is that you may improve*, is a complex declarative sentence, of which, *my desire* is the complex subject; of which, *desire* is the simple subject, modified by *my*, a simple adjective element of the first class.

Is that you may improve, is the simple predicate, of which, *is* is the copula, and, *that you may improve*, is the attribute; also, a simple declarative subordinate sentence, of which *that* is the connective subordinate, and *you*, the simple subject, unmodified. *May improve*, is the simple predicate, unmodified.

78.

COMPOUND SENTENCES.

8. *I expect that she will come, but I intend to return*, is a compound declarative sentence, of which, *I expect that she will come*, is the leading logical declarative sentence, of which, *I* is the simple subject, unmodified, and, *expect that she will come*, is the complex predicate, of which, *expect* is the simple predicate, modified by *that she will come*, a simple objective element of the third class: also a simple declarative subordinate sentence of which *she* is the simple subject, unmodified, and, *will come*,

the simple predicate, unmodified. *But I intend to return*, is the coördinate simple declarative sentence, of which *but* is the coördinate connective, and, *I* the simple subject, unmodified; and, *intend to return*, is the modified predicate, of which, *intend* is the simple predicate, modified by, *to return*, a simple adverbial element of the second class.

79.

WRITTEN ANALYSIS.

Remark 1. Much time can be gained, in recitations, by adopting the following plan of exhibiting the analysis of sentences on the blackboard.

Remark 2. Many scholars can be engaged, at once, on as many different sentences assigned them, provided there is sufficient blackboard. If not, those who cannot be accommodated at the board, can write their sentence in the analyzed form, on their slates, or on paper, which the teacher can examine, in order, as he passes around the class.

Remark 3. After having given a written analysis, of a sentence, on the board, the pupil should analyze it orally, and receive the criticism of the class and teacher.

I have found the discipline of analysis much more vigorous and satisfactory, when the written and oral methods are combined, than when either is used alone.

Remark 4. Besides, there is so much *beauty* in the logical arrangement of a sentence, as presented to the mind, through the eye, that it would well repay the labor, even if it took more time; but it does not. A class will accomplish more, in extent and thoroughness, in the same length of time, by first analyzing their sentences, on the board.

Remark 5. I shall present the written analysis of the sentences, as analyzed orally, on page 171, *et seq*.

80.

EXAMPLES OF WRITTEN ANALYSIS.

SIMPLE SENTENCES.

1 { I
repent.

2 { Parties | Both
disgraced | themselves.

3 { Spirits | vigorous | less
would have shrunk | from dangers | such.

4 { intrepidity { his
natural
did forsake { him
at approach { the
of death.

COMPLEX SENTENCES.

5 { misfortunes { The
chief
{ that
befall { us
in life,
can be traced { to vices
(and)
[to] follies } { we
have committed | which

6 { { (That)
he
is dishonest
is manifest.

7 { desire | my
is { (that)
you
may improve.

COMPOUND SENTENCE.

8 { I
expect { (that
she
will come (but) { I
intend | to return

81.

EXPLANATIONS.

1. Sentences and elements of the same rank, stand in the same vertical column. Hence, in the analysis of a sentence, the principal elements stand

in the first column; subordinate elements of the first degree stand in the second, and so on.

2. To prevent a subordinate sentence from appearing like two elements, it is preceded by a brace.

3. Words supplied, to make out a construction, are enclosed in brackets.

4. Words not forming a part of the construction, although expressed in the sentence, are enclosed in a parenthesis. Such words are conjunctions, and independent forms.

5. Words having a double use, have a line drawn under them. Such words are relative pronouns, since they are used as connectives and pronouns; also, conjunctive adverbs, since they are used both as connectives and modifiers.

6. Double relatives must be separated into their two parts, in written anaylsis; since the antecedent part belongs in the principal sentence, and the relative part, in the subordinate.

82.

ABRIDGMENT.

DEFINITIONS, EXPLANATIONS AND REMARKS.

Abridgment. That part of analysis which treats of contracting sentences, by rejecting connectives, suppressing subjects of verbs, and changing the verbs from the finite moods to infinitives and participles.

Abridged Sentence. One whose verb is an infinitive or participle.

Substantive Abridged Sentence. One that is used as the subject or object of a verb.

Adjective Abridged Sentence. One that is used to modify a noun, pronoun, or substantive clause

Participial Abridged Sentence. One whose leading word of construction is a participle.

Infinitive Abridged Sentence. One whose leading word of construction is an infinitive.

Absolute Abridged Sentence. One whose leading word of construction is the nominative case absolute.

Method of Abridgment. Remove the connective, change the finite verb to an infinitive or participle, and suppress the subject, provided it is the same as that of the verb in the principal sentence.

ORDER OF ANALYSIS.

1st. Analyze in the abridged form. 2d. Expand the sentence by supplying the connective and subject, and changing the mood of the verb to a finite mood. 3d. Analyze in the complete form.

Remark. In written analysis, these two forms of the subordinate sentence, may be connected by a curving sign of equality.

Note.—Teachers, who use Clark's Grammar, will find the various sentences classified and exhibited with great precision by the use of his System of Diagrams.

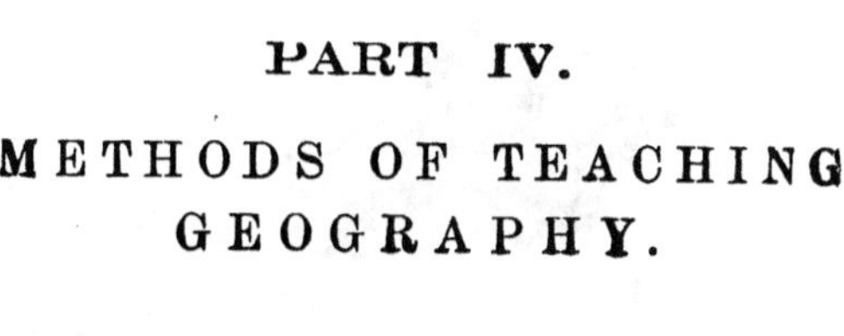

PART IV.

METHODS OF TEACHING GEOGRAPHY.

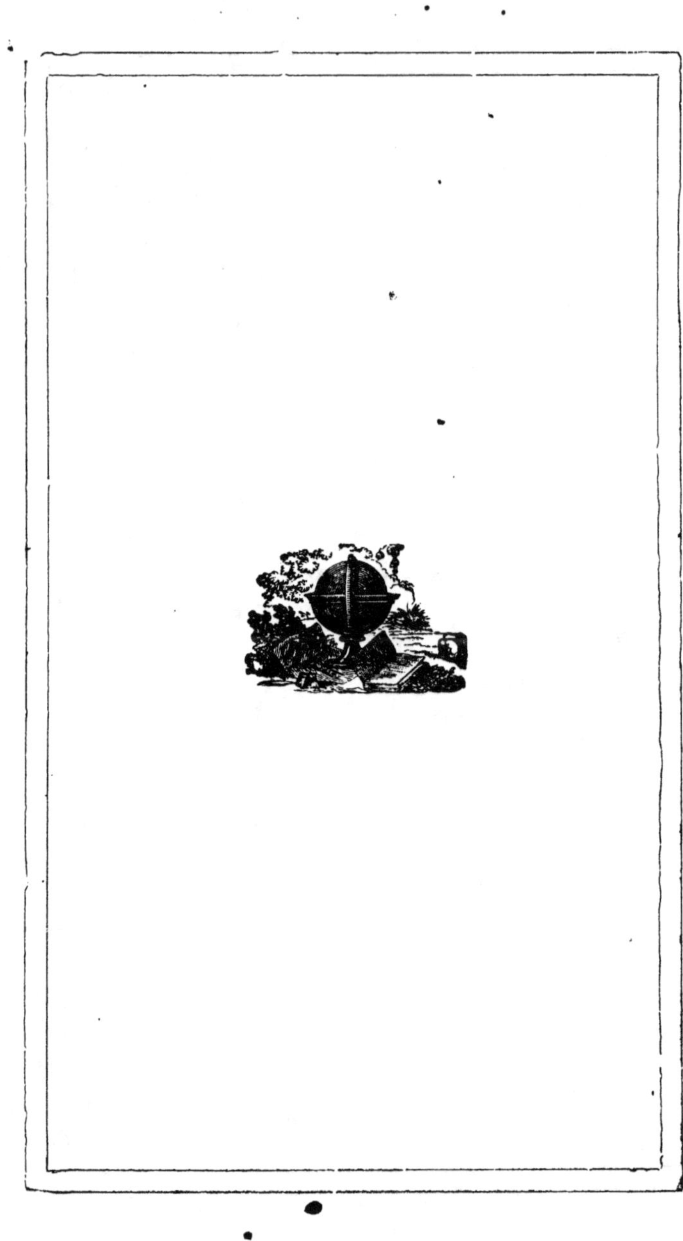

INTRODUCTION.

PROPER AGE FOR COMMENCING THE STUDY OF GEOGRAPHY.

As soon as the child is able to read well enough to obtain ideas from what he reads, in as difficult a class of sentences as those found in the primary Geography, proposed to be used, it is desirable that he have the advantages of the variety which the Geography will give to his reading lessons. It would be folly, of course, to set such a child to studying a book designed for higher classes.

It is a great mistake to keep a child confined to one book, whether Speller, Reader, or Geography; or to keep him confined to books entirely; a slate and pencil are indispensable concomitants of books, from the first.

ORAL INSTRUCTION BEFORE THE BOOK.

I may repeat here, what I said in reference to Grammar. No lesson should be required of a young pupil, in the text-book, till he has had a preliminary drill, and the teacher is satisfied that he can comprehend the subject, so far as the lesson in the text-book extends.

NECESSITY OF APPARATUS IN TEACHING GEOGRAPHY.

Some teachers suppose, that apparatus is only necessary in High Schools and Colleges; others, that it does not belong to them to purchase it; and multitudes of others do not know what it is, and would not know what to do with it, if it were placed in their hands. This is obvious, from the manner in which the apparatus, furnished by the State of Ohio, has been abused, neglected and destroyed, in the large majority of schools, where it has been placed. "It is of no account," says one. "I don't know what to do with it," says another. "Take away your fly-traps," says a third. "Them things will do for play things; I don't know what other use to make on 'em," says the fourth; and so on through every variety of ignorance and stupidity.

Of the twenty thousand dollars' worth of apparatus supplied to the schools by the State of Ohio, if at this time all that remains in our country schools were put up at auction, to be bid for by the teachers who have used the apparatus, I doubt whether one hundred dollars would be offered for it. Such is the lamentable ignorance prevalent among teachers in this direction, that Normal Institutes should be established in every county, to be in session long enough to instruct every teacher, at least, in the use of the blackboard and globe, and then no certificate should be granted to any one who could not show a good degree of facility in applying the illustrations.

I say, then, that a globe is indispensable to the correct teaching of primary classes in Geography. I know of a child who had learned Parley's little Geography, "by heart," at school and could repeat it from one end to the other, who, when she saw a small globe, in her father's hand, as he brought it home, addressed him thus: "Pa, what is that round thing in your hand?" The father replied; "It is a globe, Fannie." "A globe? What is that?" "Why it shows what shape the world is." "Why, Pa, is the world round like that?" "Hav'nt you repeated a hundred times, the world is round and like a ball flies swinging in the air?" "Oh, yes, Pa, but I never knew it before."

If that girl's teacher had had a globe, she would not, probably, have known what use to make of it. A globe of the most convenient size only costs a dollar. If the teacher has n't a dollar to buy a globe, and cannot borrow it, he ought to make one, or make use of an orange or an apple; or, if he cannot spare those, for such a purpose, he might use a piece of chalk, a potato, or his fist.

OBJECTS TO BE AIMED AT IN TEACHING PRIMARY GEOGRAPHY

1st. Learning to Study. Study is necessary to any desirable progress in learning to read; for if the scholar only reads while he is engaged in his class, he can only be familiarizing his eye with the forms of words some fifteen or twenty minutes, at most, during the day; while the scholar who *studies*, may be engaged in the same operation several hours each day. The progress of the latter will be more than proportionally rapid and satisfactory.

2d. Learning to DRAW. The use of the hand and eye, in drawing, is conceded, by all intelligent Educators, to be an important aim in the education of every person. The drawing of Maps, on the slate, blackboard or paper, is an easy and excellent introduction to the art.

Map Drawing also imprints the local geography on the mind, more correctly and permanently than any other method; it also affords the necessary variety to school exercises, to make them healthful and pleasant.

3d. Learning to READ. The consideration of this object has been forestalled in discussing the others. I will, however, add, that since Geography may be made more interesting than any *reading lesson*, it will more thoroughly arouse the pupil to voluntary effort in the preparation of his lessons, which, of course, will secure more rapid advancement in intelligent and intelligible reading.

4th. Learning GEOGRAPHY.

This is a worthy object, but less in importance, in my estimation, than any other mentioned, at the age at which a scholar should commence the study.

METHODS OF PRELIMINARY DRILL.

Many of the following pages will be given to the various plans to be adopted in preliminary drills, involving the use of the globe, of the blackboard, of the neighborhood and township; and of anv travel that the scholars may have enjoyed, for illustration; also, of maps both small and large.

METHODS OF CONDUCTING RECITATIONS.

The methods of conducting recitations have been so fully explained and exemplified, in the preceding branches, that comparatively little attention will be given to them in Part IV.

METHOD OF USING PART IV.

The teacher will consult it, in his daily preparation for his classes.

TEXT-BOOKS USED.

Monteith & McNally's series of Geographies are highly recommended as the best now before the public; and I shall refer to them continually, in the following pages, for the material of illustration and exemplification in the methods described

OBJECT LESSONS.

In connection with the lessons in Geography, it is well for a teacher to make use of various *objects*, not only for illustration, such as globe and maps, but of common things, such as corn, wheat, apples, woods of various kinds, etc.; also to bring before the class, the productions of foreign countries, or to induce the scholars to do so. Such *objects* serve by suitable conversation, to arouse thought, to train children to observe, and to connect *book lessons*, with EXISTING THINGS

METHOD OF TEACHING GEOGRAPHY TO PRIMARY CLASSES.

1.

PRELIMINARY REMARKS AND EXPLANATIONS.

Remark 1. The class should be able to read the simple style of the Primary Geography used, *intelligently;* not necessarily, fluently. They should all be provided with some Primary Geography, and all with the same kind.

Remark 2. The teacher should be provided with a five-inch globe, at least. Such a globe, mounted on a stand, can be purchased for one dollar. It would be well for the teacher to provide himself also with maps of the town, township, county and state, in which his school is situated.

Remark 3. It is understood that Geography is the first branch of science, to which the pupil is introduced; that it comes in connection with a Second or Third Reader, but does not displace it.

2.

LESSON I.

FIRST STEP—HOW TO SECURE BOOKS. The teacher having called a reading class to the recitation seat, ascertains how many have Geographies, and how many have the right kind. He finds the children wide awake with the idea of taking up a new study, in a new book. It is only necessary for him to say, that those who can obtain the book used by the class, can study Geography, and that it will be impossible for others to join the class. He will then inquire how many there are who think they cannot get the book. If any, he should visit the parents, or write a note and send it by the hand of the pupil, who will use all a child's eloquence, in connection with the note, to obtain the desired book. The child will not fail, unless the parent is absolutely too poor or too drunken to purchase it; in which case, the teacher should supply the book himself, or apply to the Directors, or other benevolent individuals, to do it. No child will be permitted to remain behind his class, from poverty, by the TRUE TEACHER.

3.

SECOND STEP—EXCITING AN INTEREST. *Teacher.* You have new Geographies, some of you; by to-morrow, I hope you will all have them. You see it is full of pictures and maps; and reading that tells you about the pictures and explains the maps. Geography is a very interesting study. Why, see; here is the picture of the Natural Bridge, which is ten times as high as this house, and is one solid rock. A boy once climbled to the top of it, by cutting steps, with his jack-knife, into the rock. When he got up so high that he could n't jump down, he tried to go down by his steps, and could n't do it, without falling; then all that he could do, was to try to cut his way to the top of the bridge, several hundred feet. Do you suppose he ever reached the top? He did, and all the people, for miles, had collected on the bridge to see him. Then, here is a picture of Bunker Hill Monument, where the British soldiers were mowed down by the bullets of American farmers and mechanics, when the British wanted to make slaves of them. Here also, are beautiful pictures of a great many fine buildings and large cities. By studying Geography, you will find out all about them. Is not Geography an interesting study?

4.

Third Step—Explanation of Maps. *Teacher.* Now, I want to show you about these maps, that are painted so prettily. See, here is the map of the Western Hemisphere. How many can tell me what a map is for? [Hands rise.] Well, John, what do you think a map is for? *John.* (*Hesitatingly.*) Maps show how the countries look. [Several hands spring up.] *Teacher.* Isaac. *Isaac.* I don't think the countries look that way, all red and yellow. *Teacher.* No; the country is generally green in the summer. Maps are not designed to show the color of countries, but their shape on the surface of the earth. Here, I'll draw a map of our school yard for you, on the blackboard. [Teacher draws.] See, here is where the front fence runs; here are the side fences. Now, where shall I put the school-house? Here? Where the wood-house? Here? And, here the pump stands; and here the outhouse, and here the walk to the gate, etc., etc. In the same way I could draw a map of the town, and could show you, on the map, where each one of you lives. How many would like to learn to draw maps? [All hands come up.] Well; I will show you to-morrow.

5.

FOURTH STEP—THE GLOBE. Here is a Globe. It is designed to show the shape of the Earth, in which we life. You see it has maps on it. Now, I can show you where the country is, in this globe, on which you live. See, here is North America, and here are the Great Lakes, and just about there, [sticking a pin,] is where you are now. This globe is five inches in diameter, or through it; and fifteen inches, or a little more than a foot, in circumference, or around it. How large do you suppose this great ball is, on which we stand? (*Stamping.*) Why, it is eight thousand miles through it, and twenty-five thousand miles around it, and it takes a whole year to travel round it. Perhaps, some one of you knows some person that has sailed round the world.

6.

FIFTH STEP—ASSIGNING A LESSON. *Teacher.* You may now open your books, those of you that have books, to this picture of the Earth, and we will see if we can read Lesson I. I will read the fine print, and you may read the coarse print.

All look on, now, and see if I read right. [Teacher reads.] "What is the planet, on which we live, called?" John you may read the coarse print. [*John reads.*] "It is called the Earth." *Teacher.* Very well. You see that the coarse print answers the question in fine print. I will read the next question. [Reads.] "What is the shape of the Earth?" Mary, you may read the answer. *Mary reads.* "It is very nearly round." *Teacher.* Now Samuel, you may read the next question. *Samuel reads.* "Do we live on the outside or inside of the Earth?" *Teacher.* Susan, you may read the answer. *Susan reads.* "On the outside." *Teacher.* Very well. Now you all see how to read this. I wish you to read over the questions and answers, so many times to yourselves, when you go to your seats, that you can give me the answers without looking on the book, when you come to me, to recite to-morrow. How many of you think that you will be able to answer all the questions in Lesson I, by to-morrow morning? [All hands rise.] Very well. You may take your books home to-night, if you have a mind to, and study your lesson at home; I shall not be surprised if you get two lessons, but I shall only hear you recite one. You may go to your seats now, in order.

7.

LESSON II.

First Step—Have all Books? *Teacher.*—How many have books today? [Books rise.] If any have not yet got the books, the teacher decides in his own mind, how they may be provided, and informs the scholars deficient, how it can be done.

8.

Second Step—Recitation. The teacher having enrolled the names of the pupils in his register, calls from the register the name of one pupil; say,

Amanda. [Amanda rises.] *Teacher.* [With Globe in his hand.] "What is the planet, on which we live, called?" *Amanda.* "It is called the Earth." *Teacher.* Very well. Amanda is excused. James, [James rises.] "What is the shape of the Earth?" *James.* "It is round." [Hands rise.] *Teacher.* Sarah. *Sarah.* "It is very nearly round." *Teacher.* Right, Sarah. James is excused.

Remark. Scholars, when offering criticisms or corrections, do it sitting; but never without permission from the teacher.

Teacher. I will ask you all a question not in the book. Is the earth round, like a plate, or like the stove pipe, or like this ball? How many can tell? [Hands rise.] Maria. *Maria.* It is round like a ball. *Teacher.* Then it is a ball, is n't it? How deep must a hole be, to go through this globe, right through the center. [No hands rise.]—*Teacher.* Five inches. But how deep would a well have to be to go down through the Earth, right through the center? [No hands rise.] How far through did I say the Earth was, yesterday? [Some hands rise.] Henry. *Henry.* Eight hundred miles. *Teacher.* Eight thousand miles; and how long would it take to go through such a well or tunnel, if you could go in a railroad car, with the speed of thirty miles an hour? Well, it would take more than twenty days, traveling twelve hours a day. That would be a long journey, in a tunnel, would n't it?

Thus the lesson is pursued, by proposing the

questions, in the book, till all the scholars have been reached, one or more times. If any scholar fail on one question, he is tried on another; and then on another, till the teacher satisfies himself as to the amount of study the scholar has bestowed on his lesson. He is then graded, accordingly, in the register.

9.

Third Step—Drawing on Slates. *Teacher.* I wish you to draw this map of the Western Hemisphere, on your slates, for a part of your next lesson; and bring your slates when you come to recite. I will draw it for you, on the blackboard. The teacher first draws the circle by taking a string as a radius, holding one end, in one hand stationary, on the board; the other end, with a piece of chalk, in the other hand, he carries around on the board, forming the circle. He then draws the continent, with the general divisions, prints the names, and makes a dot, in a small figure, representing his own State, in the map. The children are thus encouraged to do what they see done, and perhaps will even try to excel the master, in drawing a map. He requires them only to draw the outline for the first lesson.

10.

Fourth Step—Dismissing the Class. The next lesson being assigned, and the grades of the class being read aloud for their encouragement or incitement, they are dismissed from the recitation seat, in order, by calling their numbers, as written in the class register.

11.

LESSON III.

First Step. The teacher examines the slates, points out the excellences and errors of each drawing; gives his attention to the evenness of the curve; the shape and position of the countries; the size and regularity of the letters in the printing. He finds several of the class who could not make a circle, and so failed of doing anything. Instead of scolding them, or making any discouraging comparisons, he takes a slate and makes a circle; then tells all the scholars to make one. He then proceeds to draw the map, on the slate, requesting them all to follow him on their own slates as he draws, holding his slate before the class.

Thus by encouragement, by aid judiciously given, map-drawing is fairly commenced, and will not be laid aside, till the study of Geography is abandoned.

It will be well to include the consideration of map-drawing, in the grading.

Second Step—Recitation.

Third Step—Assigning the next Lesson, including the drawing of the same map, with the gulfs and lakes, in addition to the outline of the continent.

12.

LESSON IV.

First Step--Examination of Drawings.

Second Step—Recitation. This recitation should be conducted, with the globe in the hand of the teacher; and the scholars should be called upon to decide which is land and which is water, on the globe; also which is the Western and which is the Eastern Hemisphere, and the Northern and the Southern Hemisphere, on the globe.

In fact, the globe should be constantly in use, in every recitation, to give correct ideas of the relative size of countries; their true direction from each other, which never can be obtained from maps.

Third Step—Assigning next Lesson, including another drawing lesson. It may be the same map, with the lakes, seas, islands, and all the details as far as given.

13.

LESSON V.

First Step—Examination of Maps.

Second Step—Recitation.

Third Step—Points of Compass. The teacher should be careful, that the scholars get clear and correct ideas of direction, not only on the map, but on the Earth itself. He should begin with the school-room, and have the class understand definitely the four cardinal points of the compass, in the school-room. The pupils should obtain them from the rising and setting sun. He should also use the globe, in this connection, and show how these directions lie on the globe.

Having explained the eight most important points of compass, in connection with the globe, the teacher proceeds, somewhat thus, in questioning the class.

Teacher. (*Holding the globe in his hand.*)—Which way is North America, from South America, on this globe? You may all answer together. How many of you can point towards South America, on the Earth? As many as can, may do it.

Which way is Europe from North America, on the globe? Now, if you were about to start for Europe, which way would you travel?

Which way is Asia from North America?

The scholars give various answers. One says East; another, West; another, it is on the other side, etc.

Teacher. You may point now, if you can, towards Asia.

The class have the same difficulty in pointing as in telling the direction.

Teacher. If a fly were walking on this globe, which way would it go from North America to reach Asia. All together.

Class. East, West, (*in confusion.*)

Teacher. Would it not reach Asia, if it should walk, continuously, in any direction? East, West, North or South?

Then, which way would you go on the Earth's surface, to reach Asia?

But, you may now point directly towards Asia, without reference to traveling.

Most of the scholars point downwards.

Teacher. Some of you are right; Asia is on the other side of the Earth, but not directly opposite to us.

If a hole were dug down through the Earth, where would it come out?

Class. In Asia. In the ocean.

Teacher. Some of you are right and some wrong. A hole would not come out in Asia, if dug directly down ; it would have to be inclined somewhat towards the north. Do you think a person, in going through such a hole or tunnel, would come out head foremost or feet foremost in Asia? Such a hole will never be made, but the people, in Asia, stand with their heads pointing nearly in the same direction that our feet do.

Thus, no pains should be spared to connect the *words of the book* with the IDEAS OF EXISTING THINGS.

The great and crying evil of teaching, is, that *book* knowledge is kept isolated from REAL knowledge; and the evil, generally, begins with the first lessons of the child, and ends with the last lessons of the collegiate graduate.

14.

LESSON VI.

CONCLUSION OF PRIMARY TEACHING. I shall conclude these explanations of Primary Teaching, by a few general remarks.

Remark 1. The most common phenomena, as the rising and setting of the sun, should be explained to a primary class, from time to time, in order to give interest and variety to the study.

Remark 2. The globe should be kept constantly in hand, that no erroneous impressions may be derived from maps, with regard to the true position of places.

Remark 3. The same map should be assigned to the class, for drawing lessons, several days in succession. They should only be required to draw the outline, on the first day. Then, in successive days, they should make new drawings, embracing all the work of the previous days, and should add, in order, first the larger bodies of water, and islands, if any; secondly, rivers and mountains; thirdly, boundaries of political divisions; and, lastly, localities of cities and towns. The printing of names should keep pace with the other work.

Remark 4. The drawings may be made on paper, after a sufficient practice on slates. Drawing, of course, will not be confined to maps; though every map in the book should be so learned, that the scholars can go to the blackboard and draw it, without looking on the book, at all, while drawing it.

Remark 5. The teacher should instruct the class to look out the pronunciation of the geographical names in the vocabulary, at the end of the book.

Remark 6. Frequent reviews should be taken; sometimes, by the maps; sometimes, by outlines, prepared by the teacher; sometimes, by asking promiscuous questions on the matter passed over in one week. Scholars should have opportunity to prepare themselves for reviews, as well as for advanced lessons. A wide awake teacher will excite more interest in the review lesson than in the advance lessons

METHOD OF TEACHING INTERMEDIATE CLASSES.

15.

PRELIMINARY REMARKS AND EXPLANATIONS.

Remark 1. The class should be able to read the style of the Intermediate Geography, intelligently and fluently. They should be able to write a legible hand, with facility; and should be trained in the use of the dictionary, in ascertaining the pronunciation, spelling and meaning of words. They should, of course, all be provided with dictionaries, either Webster's Academic, or Worcester's Comprehensive.

Remark 2. The teacher should be provided with a five-inch globe, and a set of Outline Maps. Instead of Outline Maps, the teacher *can* make use of any maps whatever, of large size, situated so far from the class, that the names cannot be recognized. The beautiful Maps in McNally's Geography are well adapted to this use. The pupil can draw a series of outline maps of a larger size, making use of McNally's maps for his guide (omitting all the small cities and towns), and introducing the course of rivers and all boundary lines—and when finished, tack them to the wall, or blackboard, for class exercises.

16.

Remark 3. It is supposed, that those who study Intermediate Geography, are also studying Arithmetic, Reading and Spelling.

Remark 4. In graded schools, a half hour should be devoted to this recitation. In ungraded district schools, not less than fifteen minutes are required to arouse any degree of interest that will be profitable in the least.

Remark 5. Some teachers require their pupils to purchase "Topic Books," at an expense nearly half as great as that of the Geography. I think all the advantages of Topic Books can be secured without them, and more. Instead of the pupil's using a Topic Book, when he is learning his lesson, and reciting, he will do better to write on paper, or on his slate, the topics of his lesson, when he is studying; and use them in the recitation, in the manner described below. All speculations in books, and, especially, in those which are not indispensable, are likely to raise complaints from parents, and to impair a teacher's influence. Should a teacher introduce any books whatever, he will find it a matter of economy to furnish them to his scholars at cost.

17.

LESSON I.

FIRST STEP—TOPIC LISTS. *Teacher.* My young friends, we commence, to-day, in a new Geography. You will pursue a very different course, in this work, from what you did in studying the Primary Geography. I was accustomed to ask you the questions, in that book, and you to answer them, in the very words of the book. I shall not ask the questions, in this book, but wish you to prepare TOPIC LISTS, when you study your lessons, and to recite your lessons from them. I will write the first one for you, on the board. [He writes.] *Geography? Earth? Earth's Surface? Land? Water? Natural Divisions? Artificial Divisions? Political Divisions? Mathematical Divisions? Physical Geography? Includes what? Political Geography? Includes what? Mathematical Geography? Includes what? Divisions of Geography?* I will let this Topic List remain on the board, and you may copy it, on to loose paper, or into your writing books, in a very neat style, and study your lesson by it. Some of the topics you will find discussed or explained, in the coarse print, in the answers of the book; and some of them, in the fine print, in the questions.

18.

SECOND STEP—EXPLANATION OF THE METHOD OF RECITING. *Teacher.* Children, when you come to recite, I shall ask you no questions. But, I wish each one to bring his Topic List, and to recite from that. I shall give each of you an equal amount of time, to recite in; and we will see who can go over the most ground, and in the most correct manner.

19.

THIRD STEP—CONCERT EXERCISE ON MAP AND GLOBE. *Teacher.* We will now take a short exercise on an Outline Map.

The teacher places a Map of the World, in a conspicuous position, and calls on the class to go over with him, in a concert exercise, the principal bodies of land and water; also, the Hemispheres, Eastern and Western, Northern and Southern. In the concert exercise, the class give each name twice, as they proceed; that, at the second pronunciation of the word, all may join in.

When it shall be found that all can harmonize, in the concert exercise, as the teacher only points to the different localities, a scholar may be called on to give the localities, pointing for himself. Then the class may go over the same concert exercise, while a pupil points.

Then the globe may be used, instead of the map, for the same concert exercises; the teacher holding it in his hand. Thus the time allotted may be occupied. The teacher, having designated the extent of the lesson again, dismisses the class, in order.

20.

LESSON II.

First Step—Division of Time. The teacher *needs* at least a half hour for this recitation. If his school is well classified, he can allow this amount of time; possibly more. According to the number of scholars in the class, and the time of the recitation, he should assign, not less than one, nor more than two minutes, for each scholar to recite in. There is a great advantage in giving a definite time to each scholar. It excites the scholar to a more thorough preparation; to a more rapid utterance; to greater activity of thought; to a greater accuracy of expression; all this from the fact, that he is graded on what he accomplishes, in the time assigned him, and on the manner in which he accomplishes it.

21.

Second Step—The Recitation by Topics. The teacher, having the names of his class enrolled, calls on a pupil, from his register, to commence the recitation. He commences with the Topic List, and goes as far, and as well as he is able, till his time expires; when the class are called on for criticism. All scholars, having criticisms to offer, raise their hands. The teacher gives permission to some one, who is least inclined to offer criticism, to do so. Then, on others, till all errors, of the pupil reciting, shall have been reached. The pupil, having recited, is then graded. The teacher calls on another scholar to go on with the recitation, commencing with the topics where the first scholar left off; and so on, with other pupils, over and over the Topic List till all of the scholars are called on; or until the time is spent. The grading shows, which scholars are called on. If any are omitted, they should, of course, be first, in order, at the next recitation.

22.

Third Step—Concert Exercise, on Map and Globe. If time should remain, after the recitation from the topics assigned, it may always be employed to good advantage, in concert exercise, as before described. Indeed, it will be well to reserve a part of the time, after a few of the first recitations by top ics, for this purpose, even though all the scholars are not called on to recite, at each recitation.

Remark. Scholars will be inclined to mention every topic, before amplifying it. This is awkward. They should proceed with the subject matter, without mentioning the topics, unless especially requested to do so.

In this way, they soon become able to pursue a continued and systematic course of thought, orally; improving, from day to day, in rapidity of utterance, precision of language, and clearness of expression.

23.

Fourth Step—Assigning a Lesson. The teacher will do well, for a few of the first lessons, to write down the topics, on the board, which the class can copy, after they take their seats, provided they sit in the recitation room; if not, the teacher should write the topics, on the board, before the recitation commences; that the scholars may copy them, during the recitation. The topics, thus used from day to day, should, each of them, be written neatly, in a blank book, procured for the purpose.

Scholars will thus form, for themselves, a *Topic Book*, which will be used also in reviews. In doing it, particular attention should be given to spelling, capital letters, neatness of arrangement, and economy in the use of paper. The teacher should have regular times for examining the Topic Books. If other books cannot be obtained by the pupil, a part of the writing book may be set apart for this purpose; though a few sheets of paper, folded twice, and properly covered and stitched, make a more convenient book.

24.

LESSON III.

First Step—Recitation by Topics.

Second Step—Explanation of Terms, in Mathematical Geography. The globe should be used, for this purpose. The diurnal and annual revolutions can be shown as going on, simultaneously, by suspending the globe by a string, from the hand; or better, from a nail driven into the ceiling.

25.

LESSON IV.

First Step—Recitation by Topics.

Second Step—Explanation of Points of Compass. The points of compass should be explained by the rising and setting sun, by the use of the globe; also, by practice on the surface of the Earth itself, by requiring scholars to point in the direction of various countries, as ascertained from the globe.

26.

LESSON V.

First Step—Recitation by Topics.

Second Step—Explanation of Terms, used in next lesson, by the use of the globe.

Third Step—Concert Exercise on the globe, of mathematical points, (poles,) lines, and divisions. The teacher conducts this, by holding the globe in his hand, and pointing with his pencil to the several localities of such points, lines, and divisions, while the class proceed, in concert, to name them. The class may also add, in the concert exercise, the lengths of diameter and circumference in miles

27.

LESSON VI.

FIRST STEP—RECITATION BY TOPICS

SECOND STEP—EXPLANATION OF ZONES, by the globe.

Remark. Zones can hardly be well explained, or understood, from the map alone; the same is true of meridians and parallels of latitude.

Teacher. I wish to show you about the Zones; why they are marked, as you find them on the map, here. You notice, that this globe is supported by an inclined wire, representing its axis. It is inclined 23½ degrees to the plane of this table. So the Earth is inclined 23½ degrees to an extended plane, passing through its own centre as it goes on in its orbit, and the center of the sun. If the Earth's axis stood upright, there would be neither zones nor seasons—no summer nor winter here, nor anywhere else, on the Earth.

I will now suppose my hat to be the Sun, as it stands here on the table. This globe represents the Earth, in its orbit or path, as it passes around the Sun. I will place the axis so that it shall incline towards the north, and place the globe in the eastern part of its orbit. [The teacher takes a position east of the table, with the globe in his hand, inclined towards the north.] Now, you will see, that the Sun, my hat there, would shine equally, on both poles; but as the Earth passes on towards the northern part of its orbit, keeping its axis always inclined towards the north, the Sun does not shine on both the north and the south pole. When it arrives at the northern part of its orbit, the axis inclines directly away from the Sun, and since the Sun shines only on half the globe at once, it cannot reach the north pole with its rays of light and heat, but they fall short of it, 23½ degrees; just as much as the axis is inclined.* They also pass over beyond the south pole, 23½ degrees. By varying the inclination, you can see this more plainly. If the axis lies down flat, the Sun shines on the southern hemisphere only, and its rays do not strike north of the equator; that is, they do not come within 90 degrees of the north pole, because the axis is now inclined away from the Sun, 90 degrees. Again; if the axis stands upright, you can see that the Sun's rays would reach the north pole; that is, since there is no inclination, the rays do not fall short of either pole or go over either pole. You will then perceive, that just as much as the Earth's axis is inclined, just so much will the sun fail of reaching one pole, while it shines just as much over the other. You will notice, too, that this pin, [the teacher should insert the pin in the direction of a radius of the globe,] inserted into the globe, at the southern tropic, 23½ degrees from the equator, will have the Sun directly over its head, when the Earth is at the northern part of its orbit.

I will now carry the globe around to the western part of its orbit, and will stick another pin into the globe, at the equator. You now see, that the Sun is overhead, at the equator, but as the Earth passes on towards the south, the pin will be inclined away from the Sun. The Earth is now at the southern point of its orbit, and I will stick a pin in at the northern tropic; and you see that its head points directly towards the Sun. Now, these two pins inserted at the tropics are at the greatest distance north and south, where the Sun can be over the heads of the people, on the Earth. If the Earth's axis were more, or less, inclined, this would not be so.

All that part of the Earth's surface, then, between the tropics, has the Sun directly overhead, sometime during the year, and hence, is the hottest part of the Earth, and is called the torrid, or burning zone. Those parts around the poles, within a circle, 23½ degrees from the poles, since the rays of the Sun do not reach them, at all, during some part of the year, are very cold, and are called frigid or frozen zones; while these larger belts, between the torrid and frigid zones, are called temperate zones.

Third Step—Assigning the Lesson.

28.

LESSON VII.

First Step—Recitation by Topics.

Second Step—Questions on the explanation of the Zones, as given yesterday.

Teacher. Class, how much is the Earth's axis inclined? How many can tell? All who can, may raise their hands. [Hands rise.] *Teacher.* Jane. *Jane.* Twenty-three and a half degrees. *Teacher.* How many think Jane is right? [Nearly all hands rise.] How many think she is wrong? [No hands rise.] Well, Isaac, don't you know any thing about it? *Isaac.* No, sir; I forgot. *Teacher.* I hope you will try to remember, now. *Isaac.* I don't know what degrees mean. *Teacher.* *That* was explained some time ago; but I will show you again. [He draws a circle, on the board, and divides it circumference into four parts.] Each one of these parts is divided into 90 parts, which are called degrees; so any circle, here on the globe, or off from it, is divided into four times 90 degrees, or 360 degrees. Now, how many of the class can tell me what a degree is? [Hands rise.] *Teacher.* John. *John.* A degree is a 360th part of a circle. *Teacher.* Very well. Isaac, can you tell me now, what degrees are? *Isaac.* Yes, sir; degrees are 360th parts of a circle. *Teacher.* And, how many of these degrees is the Earth inclined? *Isaac.*—Twenty three and a half. *Teacher.* [Turning the globe so that its axis is horizontal.] Can any of you tell me how much the Earth's axis is inclined now? [No hands rise.] *Teacher.* I will show you. [Taking the globe from the stand.] Now the axis is not inclined at all, as it stands upright. Now it is inclined 23½ degrees; now 45 degrees. Now it is turned down, one quarter of the way around, or 90 degrees. If it is turned entirely round, it makes the circuit of 360 degrees, thus. *Teacher.* How many can tell me how wide the torrid zones are? [All hands rise.] *Teacher.* Sarah. *Sarah.* Twenty-three and a half degrees. *Teacher.* How many agree with Sarah? [Some hands rise.] Look at the globe, and see if the torrid zones do not extend 23½ degrees north, and 23½ degrees south of the equator.

Thus, the teacher will reach the scholars' mistaken notions, and chase them away, one after another; and he will find it necessary, to repeat the process, all along, or he inculcates more error than truth, even though he understands his subjects well, and explains them with clearness and accuracy.

THIRD STEP—ASSIGNING A LESSON FOR REVIEW, BY TOPICS. This review should extend over all the ground thus far passed over.

29.

LESSON VIII.

FIRST STEP—RECITATION OF REVIEW LESSON.

SECOND STEP—ASSIGNING AN ADVANCE LESSON in divisions of land and water.

Teacher. I have written out the topic lists, by which you can study and recite your next lesson.

TOPIC LIST FOR NATURAL DIVISIONS OF LAND.

— Land —	Continent,	How situated? How surrounded?	Volcano,	Crater? Materials [thrown out?
	Island,	How situated? How surrounded?	Hill,	
	Peninsula,	How situated? How surrounded?	Valley,	
	Isthmus,	Connects what? Lies between what?	Desert,	
	Cape,	Projects from what? Projects into what?	Shore, or	
	Mountain,	Where situated? Extending in what [direction?	Coast?	

Teacher. In studying your lesson, by the topic list, you will learn the definitions of all the natural divisions, as continents, islands, etc.; then you may look out three such divisions, on your map, and describe them as the topic list requires.

For instance, when you come to *Isthmus*, you

will learn the definition as you find it in the book. Then you will find an isthmus on the map of the world, or any other map, and describe it, by telling what two bodies of land it connects, and what two bodies of water it lies between. Then find two more, and prepare yourselves to describe them, in the same way; and so of all the natural divisions of land.

You may also, each one, prepare yourselves to draw, on the board, without any map before you, some continent, island, peninsula and cape; so that the rest of the class can tell what division you have drawn. You will practice in drawing these on your slate.

30.

LESSON IX.

First Step. The teacher will assign some kind of natural division of land, to each pupil, for drawing on the board. If the board is not large enough, some of the pupils may use slates.

Second Step. While the class are thus engaged in drawing, the teacher will call on individuals, in succession, from his register, to recite their lesson from the topic list, the scholar having the topic list in hand, but using it as little as possible.

Third Step. When all have thus recited, returning to their drawings, as they are excused, from the topic list, each drawing may be examined thus:

Taking, for instance, the drawing of some one, who was required to draw an Island, the teacher says: How many can tell what island? As many as can, may raise the hand. [Hands rise.] *Teach-*

er. Mary. *Mary.* Madagascar. *Teacher.* How many agree with Mary? [Hands rise.] How many disagree? [Hands rise.] Susan, what do you think it is? *Susan.* I do n't know ; I don't think it is Madagascar. It runs East and West; Madagascar runs North and South. *Teacher.* Well, Henry, you drew this : what did you design it for? *Henry.* Cuba. *Teacher.* It is quite similar to Cuba, both in direction and shape. In this way, each drawing may be examined and criticised.

31.

FIRST STEP—WRITING TOPIC LIST.

TOPIC LIST FOR NATURAL DIVISIONS OF WATER.

- **Ocean,** how surrounded.
  - north?
  - east?
  - south?
  - west?
- **Sea,**
  - projects from what?
  - projects,
    - into what?
    - or between what?
- **Gulf or Bay,**
  - projects from what?
  - projects into what?
  - or, between what?
- **Strait,**
  - lies between what?
  - connects what?
- **Sound,**
  - projects from what?
  - projects,
    - into what?
    - or between what?
- **Channel,**
  - lies between what?
  - connects what?
- **Lake,**
  - situated where?
  - class,
    - fresh,
    - salt.
  - streams,
    - inlets,
    - outlets.
- **River,**
  - rises where?
  - flows in what direction?
  - empties where?
- **Frith, or Estuary.**
- **Brook, Creek, Rivulet, Rill.**

You will pursue the same course, in preparing this lesson, with these topics, as with those of yesterday; also, in drawing.

32.

LESSON X.

FIRST STEP—ASSIGNING DIVISIONS OF WATER FOR DRAWING.

SECOND STEP—RECITATION.

THIRD STEP—ASSIGNING A LESSON. You will next take a lesson on the Map of North America. I wish you to practice, in drawing North America, so that you can draw the boundaries of all the countries in it, and locate the capitals. You need not draw the bodies of water any farther than they form boundaries.

You may also prepare yourselves to give the boundaries of the countries, from the outline map, either before you have drawn them, or after you have drawn them; also, to give the name of the capital of each country.

33.

LESSON XI.

FIRST STEP—DRAWING THE MAP OF NORTH AMERICA, either on the board or on slates.

SECOND STEP—RECITATION. While the class are generally engaged in drawing, individuals are called on, successively, to give the boundaries of North America, and each of the countries; also, the capital of each.

THIRD STEP—ASSIGNING A LESSON. *Teacher.* For your next lesson, you may practice, in drawing the outline of North America, and the principal islands, peninsulas, capes, and mountains; also prepare yourselves to describe them by the topic lists, I gave you, a few days since. How many have the topic lists? [Hands rise.] John, you have the topic lists; you may write, on the board, the topic list for natural divisions of land. Susan, you may write the topic list, for natural divisions of water, on the board. Now, those who have lost them, can copy them, and then, I hope, they will copy them into their Topic Books.

GENERAL DIRECTIONS

FOR THE STUDY OF COUNTRIES, EMPIRES, KINGDOMS, AND STATES.

Remark. I do not deem it advisable to confine scholars, for any lesson, *exclusively* to map studies, as is proposed in Monteith & McNally's Geography. I would make map-studies a part of every lesson, in connection with every country, empire, kingdom, or state.

34.

Direction I.—Map-Drawing. The practice of map-drawing, should be kept up, without intermission. Besides drawing on slates, and on blackboard, pupils should be required, in order, one or more every day, to bring in a finished map, drawn on paper, not always, necessarily, of the country assigned for study of the class. These may be drawn, mathematically, and proportionally, larger or smaller than the map in the atlas or book, by drawing the marginal lines first, in proportion to the marginal lines of the printed map, taking them one-half, two-thirds, or twice as large, or in any other proportion. Then the scholar will use dividers, and divide the marginal lines into as many equal parts as those of the printed map; then draw the lines of latitude and longitude. If these lines are curved, he can bend a piece of whalebone or hickory, prepared for the purpose, by extending a string from end to end, to keep it bent in the proper curve. By loosening or tightening the string, the curve can be varied to meet the demands of any line, on any map. The lines having thus been drawn and numbered, with the degree of latitude or longitude, the paper is ready for commencing the map.

By the use of these squares, thus formed by the lines of latitude and longitude, noticing the position of each point, and direction of each line, as to which square it is in, and which part of the square, and the proportional distance, in each corresponding square, a map can be drawn with correctness and beauty. The lines of latitude and longitude should be drawn in ink; the boundaries, rivers, etc., should first be drawn with a pencil, afterwards with ink.

35.

Direction II.—Preparation and Use of Topics. Scholars should, in the main, prepare their own topics, as they have only to copy them from the bold faced type, as **Boundaries, Situation**, etc. Such natural divisions of land and water may be added, as occur in the country assigned for a lesson. These may be proposed, or written on the blackboard, when the lesson is assigned, at first, by the teacher. Soon, however, the scholar will be able to bring in these topics, without any direction from the teacher. I think the writing of such topic lists, a valuable exercise for the pupil, and that he ought not to be deprived of it by using printed topics. The method of recitation, by topics, has already been fully described, and I will merely add, that scholars should be encouraged to recite, without looking at the topic list, and without any prompting or questioning from the teacher.

As has before been stated, a definite length of time should be assigned, for each pupil to use in reciting; and the more he can accomplish, in this time, and the better he can do it, the higher should his grade be, on the class register, for each recitation.

Strict attention should be given to penmanship, in preparing topics and copying them into the Topic Book, for review lessons. Much care should be bestowed, on precision and propriety of language, in the recitations. Such attention and care, are generally the most effectual when given in the form of encouragement, rather than in the form of fault-finding.

36.

Direction III.—Review Lessons. Review lessons should be assigned frequently. I prefer to give them, in connection with the divisions of the subject-matter, rather than to assign them periodically, as many teachers do. In completing the

study of the States, on any map, for instance, I would propose a review of those States ; so, in completing the study of the Grand Divisions, I would have the whole reviewed, even if it should take several lessons to accomplish it.

37.

DIRECTION IV. — PRONUNCIATION. Scholars should be required to consult the pronouncing vocabulary, before they come to the recitation. If there should be none, in the Geography used, they should have access to some dictionary that contains one ; or, if this is not practicable, the teacher, at least, should have such a dictionary, or gazetteer, on his table: and no geographical name should be permitted to pass, without a definite and certain knowledge of its pronunciation. The teacher will do well, in case any doubt arises, to require some scholar to look out the word, during the time of recitation.

METHOD OF TEACHING ADVANCED CLASSES.

38.

INTRODUCTORY LESSON.

In commencing a term of school, it is desirable for the teacher to define the position that Geography holds in Science, in relation to other branches. This can be done by referring to Part I. The teacher should make an introductory exercise, as the scholars are not prepared for recitation, by presenting so much of the GENERAL OUTLINE as is necessary for the purpose. It may be given thus:

- Knowledge,
  - Literature,
  - Sciences,
    - Geotics.
      - Geography,
        - Mathematical,
        - Physical,
        - Phenomenal,
        - Descriptive.
      - Geology,
      - Mineralogy,
      - Chemistry,
      - Botany,
      - Zoology.
    - Mathematics,
    - Therapeutics,
    - Physics.
  - Arts.

Having written so much of the General Outline, he should present the definition of every term used, beginning with Knowledge. These definitions are found in Part I. But the teacher should not confine himself to bare definitions; he should occupy the whole time, allotted to this recitation, in such illustrations and exemplifications of these definitions, as will make them intelligible and interesting to his pupils. He will thus have delivered a systematic introductory lecture, and will have given his pupils an earnest of his ability to manage the class in a novel and interesting manner.

The scholars should be requested to copy the outline so presented, in order that they may be able to report on it from time to time, and that each may have an entire course of outlines, embracing the whole subject of Geography. The teacher will also assign a lesson for the next exercise; state, if possible, at what time the class may expect to be called on for a recitation. As it is supposed that the class are already familiar with Geography, to a considerable extent, it is not desirable, perhaps, to follow the course of any text-book that may be used in the class, but to follow the course marked out in the Outline of Geography, as presented below. The teacher will give as much of it, for successive lessons, as his class can well manage. It will be seen, however, that a variety of text-books, in an advanced class, is no bar to its progress, but decidedly a means of greater interest and improvement. There is no objection, however, to all the class having a book of the same kind; but all the class should be in possession of one or more besides the common text-book. They should all have access to Physical Geography, which may be found in the new edition of McNally's Geography; also to some good system of Histories, as Willard's School Histories.

Before proceeding further with the method of teaching advanced classes, it will be necessary to present the Outline of Geography.

39.

I. Mathematical Geography.

- **1. Position.**
  - Distance from,
    - Sun, 95 million miles,
    - Moon, 240 thousand miles,
    - Other planets, variable,
    - Nearest fixed star, 40 trillion miles.
  - Inclination of axis —23° 28 min.
  - Direction of axis
    - towards North Star.
    - parallel with itself.
  - Form of Orbit
    - Ellipse,
      - major axis,
      - minor axis,
      - eccentricity.
- **2. Form.**
  - Proofs that the Earth is globular.
    1. Circumnavigation.
    2. Appearance of ship at sea,
    3. Shadow on the Moon,
    4. Appearance of Polar Star,
    5. Appearance of Clouds in Horizon,
    6. Suspended weights,
    7. Force of Gravity,
    8. Analogy.
    9. Actual Measurement.
  - Proofs that the Earth is an oblate spheroid,
    1. Varying vibration of pendulum,
    2. Centrifugal Force,
    3. Analogy,
    4. Measurement of degrees of latitude.
- **3. Magnitude.**
  - Diameter,
    - Equatorial, 7924 miles,
    - Polar, 7898 "
    - Mean, 7912 "
    - (difference 26 miles.)
  - Circumference, 25,000 miles.
  - Area, 197,000,000 square miles.
- **4. Motions and Velocities.**
  - Diurnal,
    - Velocity at Equator 1000 miles per hour.
    - Proofs,
      - Table turns under pendulum,
      - Falling body strikes east of vertical line,
      - Necessary assumption in all astronomical calculations.
  - Annual,
    - Velocity, 68,000 miles per hour in orbit.
    - Proofs,
      - Aberration of light,
      - Change of Seasons,
      - Necessary assumption in all astronomical calculations.
  - In common with solar system.
    - Velocity per hour 3,500 miles.
    - Proof,
      - Approaching and receding of fixed stars in opposite parts of the heavens.

MATHEMATICAL GEOGRAPHY—*Concluded.*

5. Points, Lines, Divisions,
- 1. Axis,
- 2. Poles,
- 3. Diameter,
- 4. Circumference,
- 5. Equator,
- 6. Tropics,
- 7. Polar Circles,
- 8. Parallels of Latitude,
- 9. Meridians of Longitude,
- 10. Zones,
- 11. Hemispheres,
- 12. Horizon, { sensible, rational,
- 13. Colures.

6. Means of Representing,
- 1. Globe,
- 2. Tellurian,
- 3. Armillary sphere,
- 4. Orrery,
- 5. Maps,
- 6. Charts.

40.

II. PHYSICAL GEOGRAPHY.

1. Structure and Materials.

Geology, Mineralogy, Chemistry.
- Igneous Rocks, Metamorphic Rocks, } Inorganic,
- Aqueous Rocks—Organic,
  - Primary,
  - Secondary,
  - Tertiary,
  - Quaternary.

2. Temperature.

Temperature,
- At the surface variable,
- Depth of invariable temperature,
- Increase of temperature downwards.

3. Land.

Extent, Proportion, Distribution, Analogies of Continents.

Divisions,
- 1. Continent, 2. Island, 3. Peninsula,
- 4. Isthmus, 5. Cape, 6. Promontory,
- 7. Shore or Coast, 8. Banks, 9. Shoals.

Physical Geography—*Continued.*

Surface.

- Mountain,
  - 1. Ranges,
  - 2. Systems,
  - 3. Groups,
  - 4. Peaks.
    - Directions,
    - Distribution,
    - Analogies,
    - Slope,
    - Counter-Slope.
  - 5. Volcanoes,
    - Active,
    - Intermittent,
    - Extinct.
- Hill,
- Plain,
- Valley,
  - High,
    - Table Land,
    - Plateau,
  - Fertile,
    - Prairie,
    - Selva,
    - Pampa,
    - Steppe,
  - Barren,
    - Sandy,
    - Salt,
    - Alkaline.
      - Causes and Uses.

4. Water.

Classes.

- Fresh,
  - Soft,
  - Hard,
- Salt,
  - Ocean,
  - Lake,
- Mineral,
  - Acidulous,
  - Chalybeate,
  - Sulphurous,
  - Saline,
    - Localities,
    - Composition,
    - Weight,
    - Points of
      - ebullition,
      - congelation.

Divisions.

- Oceans and Seas.
  - Characteristics,
    - color, saltness, temperature, depth, quantity, level, extent, taste, motions.
- Lake,
  - Fresh,
  - Salt,
    1. with Inlets and Outlets,
    2. with Inlets and no Outlets,
    3. with Outlets and no Inlets,
    4. with neither Inlets nor Outlets,
    5. Subterranean,
    6. Periodical.

PHYSICAL GEOGRAPHY—*Continued.*

Divisions.

- Gulf,
- Bay,
- Strait,
- Channel,
- Sound,
- River,
  - 1. Extent,
    - Source,
      - in Mountains,
      - in Lakes,
      - in Springs.
    - Mouth,
  - 2. Velocity of
    - stagnant,
    - gentle,
    - rapid,
    - Rapids,
    - Cataracts,
    - Cascades,
  - 3. Magnitude,
    - length,
    - breadth,
    - depth,
  - 4. Drainage,
    - extent,
    - Water-Shed,
    - Basins or Bottoms,
      - 1st,
      - 2nd.
  - 5. Delta,
    - Fluvial,
    - Lacustrine,
    - Maritime.
  - 6. Direction,
  - 7. Locality,
    - Ordinary,
    - Subterranean,
    - On elevations of their own forming.
  - 8. Uses,
    - Navigable,
      - for what vessels,
      - to what extent.
- Estuary,
- Canal,
- Well,

5. Atmosphere.

- Composition,
  - essential,
  - accidental.
- Color,
- Height, | how determined.
- Temperature, | Limits on surface, in
  - Torrid Zone,
  - Temperate Zone,
  - Frigid Zone.
- Weight,
  - at surface,
  - at height of three miles,
  - ratio of diminution upward.
- Fluidity.
- Elasticity.
- Moisture,
  - Limits of ratio to the atmosphere.
  - Dew, Fogs, Clouds, Rain, Hail, Snow, Frost.

PHYSICAL GEOGRAPHY—*Continued.*

- **Climate,**
  - Classes,
    - Continental or excessive,
    - Insular,
  - Circumstances modifying,
    - Latitude,
    - Height above the Sea,
    - Proximity to bodies of water,
    - Slope of country,
    - Position and direction of Mountain Chains,
    - Nature of soil,
    - Degree of cultivation.
    - Prevalent winds,
    - Annual quantity of rain.
  - Isothermal Zones.
    - Torrid,
    - Hot,
    - Warm,
    - Temperate,
    - Cold,
    - Frigid,
      - Boundaries,
      - How determined.
      - Productions.
  - Salubrity,
    - Causes modifying,
      - Temperature
      - Soil,
      - Moisture,
      - Cultivation.
- **Uses,**
  - Natural,
  - Artificial.

6. Productions.

- Minerals.
  - Non-Metallic.
    - Non-combustible,
      - Air,
      - Water,
      - Building materials,
      - Statuary "
      - Ornamental "
      - Drug, "
      - Chemical "
    - Combustible,
      - Coal,
        - Anthracite,
        - Bituminous,
        - Cannel,
      - Naphtha, Petroleum,
        - Liquids,
      - Sulphur,
      - Amber.
        - Distribution,
        - Abundance,
        - Locality,
        - Uses.

Physical Geography—*Continued.*

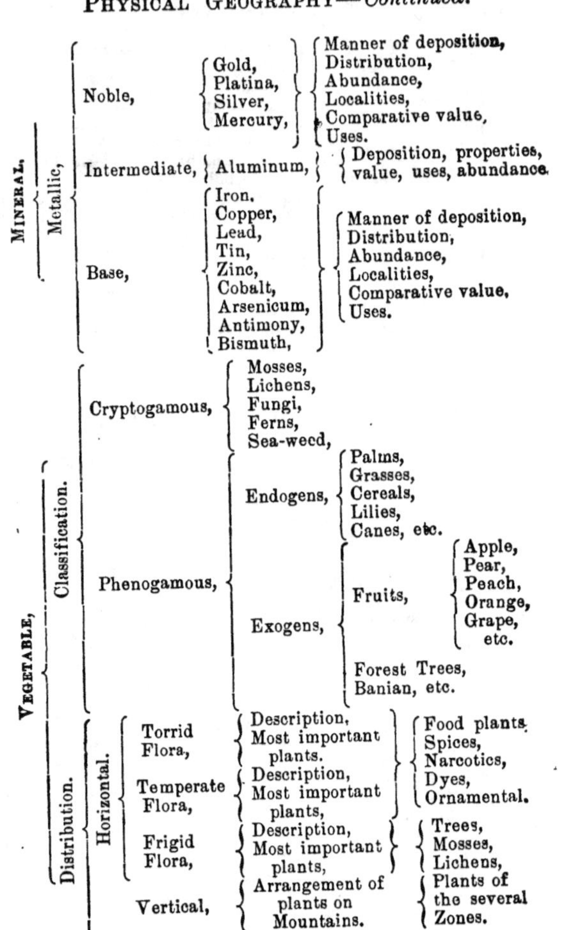

PHYSICAL GEOGRAPHY—*Concluded.*

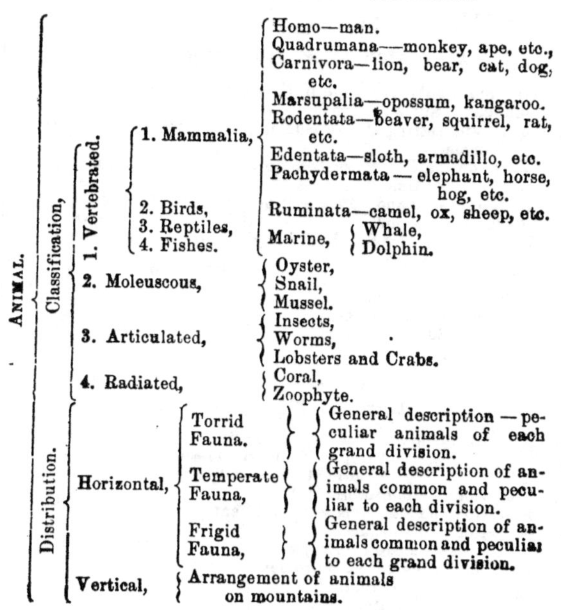

- **ANIMAL.**
  - Classification,
    - 1. Vertebrated.
      - 1. Mammalia,
        - Homo—man.
        - Quadrumana—monkey, ape, etc.,
        - Carnivora—lion, bear, cat, dog, etc.
        - Marsupalia—opossum, kangaroo.
        - Rodentata—beaver, squirrel, rat, etc.
        - Edentata—sloth, armadillo, etc.
        - Pachydermata—elephant, horse, hog, etc.
        - Ruminata—camel, ox, sheep, etc.
        - Marine, Whale, Dolphin.
      - 2. Birds,
      - 3. Reptiles,
      - 4. Fishes.
    - 2. Moleuscous,
      - Oyster,
      - Snail,
      - Mussel.
    - 3. Articulated,
      - Insects,
      - Worms,
      - Lobsters and Crabs.
    - 4. Radiated,
      - Coral,
      - Zoophyte.
  - Distribution.
    - Horizontal,
      - Torrid Fauna. General description—peculiar animals of each grand division.
      - Temperate Fauna, General description of animals common and peculiar to each division.
      - Frigid Fauna, General description of animals common and peculiar to each grand division.
    - Vertical, Arrangement of animals on mountains.

10*

41.

III. Phenomenal Geography.

1. Astronomical Phenomena.

1. Day and night—variation in length of day and night.
2. Change of Sun's declination.
3. Rising and setting of the Sun north of east and west, in Summer.
4. Where on the Earth's surface do the days begin?
5. Difference of time.
6. No absolute up and down, east or west.
7. Change of Seasons.
8. Appearance of the Sun in the frigid zones.
9. Eclipses,
   - Solar,
   - Lunar.
10. Changes of the Moon.
11. Precession of Equinoxes.
12. Meteors,
    - Shooting Stars,
    - Falling Stars.

2. Terrestrial Phenomena.

1. Formation and structure of the Earth.
2. Internal heat,
   - Depth of invariable temperature.
   - Ratio of increase downwards.
3. Elevation of Mountains.
4. Elevation and subsidence of Continents.
5. Elevation and subsidence of Islands.
6. Volcanoes—Causes of Eruptions.
7. Earthquakes—Causes, Movements and Effects.
8. Springs,
   - Perpetual,
   - Intermittent,
   - Periodical,
   - Artesian Wells,
   - Salt Springs,
   - Hot Springs,
   - Fire Springs.

   (all:) explanation, uses.
9. Rivers,
   - Origin,
   - Formation of channels,
   - Formation of bottoms,
   - Formation of oxbows, bayous, and islands,
   - Formation of deltas,
   - Elevation of bed above surrounding country,
   - Running up hill.
10. Caves,
    - Mountain,
    - Subterranean,

    (both:) Causes, Stalactites, Stalagmites, Gases, Rivers, Lakes.

PHENOMENAL GEOGRAPHY—*Continued.*

11. Natural Bridges,
    - cause,
    - most remarkable.
12. Causeways,
    - cause,
    - columns,
        - shape,
        - size.

3. Oceanic Phenomena.

1. Saltness, Causes, Limits of per centage.
2. Temperature, in Torrid, Temperate, and Frigid Zones; in currents.
3. Depth, Deepest Sounding, Method of Sounding.
4. Density, at surface, at depth of a mile.
5. Level,
    - Variation, Apparent Variation,
        - elevation of land,
        - depression of land.
6. **Motions,**
    - Waves.
        - Cause,
        - Height—"Billows mountain high"?
        - Force,
        - Direction,
        - Rate of travel,
        - The Bore,
        - Uses.
    - Tides.
        - Causes,
        - Tide opposite the Moon,
        - Direction and rate of travel,
        - Later daily recurrence,
        - Tides in rivers—many at the same time,
        - Spring and neap tides,
        - What six concurring circumstances will give the highest tide?
        - Extraordinary local tides—causes.
        - Uses.
    - Currents.
        - Constant.
            - Antarctic drift,
            - Pacific equatorial,
            - Indian "
            - Atlantic "
            - South Atlantic,
            - Brazil,
            - South connecting,
            - Cape,
            - Gulf Stream,
                - N. branch,
                - S. "
            - Arctic,
                - E. branch,
                - W. "
            - Japan,
            - Grassy Sea,
            - (all the above:) causes, extent, direction, force, temperature, color, effects.
            - Counter, Under,
                - means of determining,
                - effects,

Phenomenal Geography—*Continued.*

6. Periodical Currents,
   - of Red Sea,
   - of Persian Gulf,
   - of India Ocean,
   - of China Sea,
     - causes,
     - effects.

7. Coral,
   - Coral animalculæ,
     - No. of genera and species,
     - description,
     - habits.
   - Classes,
     - Reef,
     - Branch,
     - Brain.
     - Organ pipe, etc.
   - Formations
     - Atolse,
       - habitable part,
       - lagoon,
     - Reefs,
       - encircling,
       - barrier,
       - fringing,
         - causes,
         - shape,
         - localities,
         - uses,
         - dangers.
   - Chalk beds,
     - how formed,
     - how forming.

4. Atmospheric Phenomena.

1. **Weight,** cause, methods of determining, rate of diminution upwards, effects, force.
2. **Pressure,**
   - cause,
   - illustrations,
   - effects,
     - preserves liquidity of water,
     - prevents vacuums,
     - raises water in pump and siphon,
     - raises mercury in barometer,
     - combination with water to maintain life of fish.
3. **Resistance,**
   - cause,
   - illustrations,
   - effects,
     - flying of birds,
     - difference of descent,
     - retarding velocity of railroad cars.
4. **Temperature**—cause of variation, rate of diminution upward.
5. **Boiling** point of water—variation upward and downward.

Phenomenal Geography—*Continued.*

- **6. Wind.**
  - auses,
    - Heat,
    - Electricity,
    - Revolution of the Earth,
      - operations of each
  - Velocity and force of,
    - Gentle, Brisk, High, Violent, Hurricane.
  - Direction,
    - means of determining,
    - upper and lower currents.
  - Classes.
    - Constant or Trade,
      - explanation,
      - zones of calms,
        - equatorial,
        - tropical,
          - northerr
          - southern.
      - Limits,
        - North and South,
        - East and West.
      - Uses.
    - Periodical,
      - Land and Sea breezes,
        - localities,
        - explanations,
        - periods.
      - Monsoons, Etesians, Northers,
        - localities,
        - explanations,
        - extent,
        - periods.
    - Variable,
      - localities,
      - explanations,
      - Local,
        - Simoom,
        - Rhamsin,
        - Harmattan,
        - Sirocco,
        - Pamperos,
        - Bora.
    - Whirlwinds, Hurricanes, Tornadoes, Typhoons,
      - localities,
      - explanation,
      - chief periods.
    - Water Spouts,
      - locality,
      - explanation,
      - attending phenomena.
  - Navigation,
    - Former ignorance in relation to.
    - Late improvements.
    - Gen'l principles,
      - from Europe to America,
      - " U. S. to Europe,
      - " N. Y. to Francisco,
      - " U. S. to China.

Phenomenal Geography—*Continued.*

- 7. Moisture.
  - Evaporation,
    - proofs,
    - extent,
    - average annual from sq. rod,
      - Temperate Zone,
      - Torrid Zone.
  - Dew,
    - explanation,
    - Dew point,
      - depending on what?
      - how determined?
    - Dew at midday—"pitcher sweats,"
    - circumstances favoring,
    - circumstances preventing,
      - explanation,
    - Frozen—frost,
    - uses?
  - Mists, or Fogs,
    - explanation,
    - condition of moisture,
    - localities of dense fogs,
    - periods of fogs.
  - Clouds,
    - explanation—how differ,
    - height,
    - Classes,
      - Cirrus,
      - Cumulus,
      - Stratus,
      - Nimbus,
        - description of each.
    - uses,
  - Rain,
    - explanation,
    - distribution,
      - General principles,
        - from equator to poles,
        - from sea to interior,
        - on east and west shores
        - in Tropics,
        - in Temperate Zone,
        - in Frigid Zone.
    - Regions,
      - Rainless,
      - Periodical rains,
      - Frequent rains,
        - where.
  - Snow,
    - explanation,
    - snow crystals,
    - extent superficially,
    - Snow line,
      - in Torrid Zone,
      - in Temperate Zone,
      - in Frigid Zone.
  - Glaciers,
    - explanation,
    - character and appearance of ice,
    - localities,
    - extent,
    - motions,
    - effects.

PHENOMENAL GEOGRAPHY—*Concluded*.

7. Moisture.
   - Avalanches,
     - explanations,
     - localities,
     - effects.
   - Icebergs,
     - explanation,
     - dimensions,
     - proportion above water,
     - localities,
     - extent,
     - effects,
       - cool southern climate,
       - distribute rocks over bottom of [sea,
       - boulders on present continents,
   - Hail,
     - explanation,
     - dimensions,
     - localities,
     - effects.

IV.—ELECTRICAL PHENOMENA.

1. Thunder and Lightning.
   - Explanation,
   - Classes,
     - Zigzag,
     - Sheet,
     - Globular,
     - Heat.
   - Protection,
     - Rods,
       - inventor,
       - extent of protection,
       - best materials,
       - best arrangement.
     - Localities to be avoided
   - Localities,—when most abundant.
2. Mariner's Light.
   - explanation,
   - localities.
3. Aurora Borealis.
   - explanation,
   - appearance,
   - localities.

V.—OPTICAL PHENOMENA.

1. Rainbow.
   - explanation of
     - primary,
     - secondary.
   - classes,
     - solar,
     - lunar.
   - limits,
     - in time,
     - in place.
2. Halos Corona.
   - explanation,
   - indication.
3. Mock Sun, Mock Moons.
   - explanation,
   - localities.
4. Mirage.
   - explanation,
   - localities,
   - effects.
5. Inverting images in air.
   - explanation,
   - localities,
6. Ignis fatuus.
   - explanation,
   - localities,
   - effects.

VI.—Political Geography.

Government.

1. **Patriarchal.**
   - Political divisions,
   - Chief officer, Subord'te officers,
     - term of service,
     - how appointed,
     - extent of power.
2. **Absolute Monarchy.**
   - Political Divisions, — Empire, Kingdom.
   - Chief Officer, Subord. Officers,
     - time of service,
     - how appointed,
     - extent of power.
   - Branches of Government,
     - how established,
     - extent of jurisdiction,
     - officers, how app'ted.
3. **Limited Monarchy.**
   - Political Divisions, — Empire, Kingdom.
   - Chief Officer,
     - how appointed,
     - extent of power.
   - Coordinate branches of Government,
     - how established,
     - extent of jurisdiction,
     - officers, how app'ted.
4. **Aristocracy.**
   - Political divisions,
   - Chief Officer,
     - how appointed,
     - extent of power,
   - Coordinate branches of Government,
     - how established,
     - extent of jurisdiction,
     - officers, how app'ted.
5. **Republic.**
   - Political divisions, — State, Duchy.
   - Chief Officer, Subord. Officers,
     - time of service,
     - how appointed,
     - extent of power.
   - Coordinate branches of Government,
     - how established,
     - extent of jurisdiction,
     - officers, how app'ted.

Races.

1. Caucasian,
2. Mongolian,
3. Malay,
4. American,
5. African.

- Color,—skin, hair, eyes,
- Features,
  - eyes, nose, cheekbones, forehead,
  - mouth, lips, chin, hair.
- Nations included,
- Number estimated,
- Distinguishing characteristics,
- Government,
- Languages,
- Civilization,
- Religion.

POLITICAL GEOGRAPHY.—*Continued.*

State of Society.

1. Classes, as to manner of living.
   - Roving Tribes,
   - Nomadic Tribes,
   - Fixed Nations,
     - mode of subsistence,
     - mode of habitation,
2. Classes, as to social condition.
   - Enlightened,
   - Civilized,
   - Half Civilized,
   - Savage,
     - Attainments in Arts and Sciences,
     - Systems of Education,
     - Political power,
     - Religion,
     - Humane institutions.

Religion.

1. Christians.
   1. Roman Catholic,
   2. Greek Church,
   3. Protestant,
   4. Nestorians,
      - Founders,
      - Ecclesiastical system,
      - Officers,
        - how appointed,
        - extent of power,
      - Books of authority,
      - Worship,
        - objects,
        - modes,
      - Sects,
      - Number,
      - Embraced in what nations.
2. Jews.
   - Founders,
   - Ecclesiastical System,
   - Officers,
     - how appointed,
     - extent of power.
   - Books of authority,
   - Worship,
     - objects,
     - modes.
   - Sects,
   - Number,
   - Scattered through what nations?
3. Mahometans.
   - Founder,
   - Ecclesiastical System,
   - Officers,
     - how appointed,
     - extent of power.
   - Books of authority,
   - Worship,
     - objects,
     - modes,
   - Sects,
   - Number,
   - Embraced by what nations?
4. Pagans.
   - Books of authority,
   - Worship,
     - objects,
     - modes,
   - Sects,
   - Number,
   - Embraced by what nations?

POLITICAL GEOGRAPHY—*Continued.*

Artificial Productions.

- **Agricultural.**
  - Food,
    - Animal,
      - Beef,
      - Mutton,
      - Pork,
        - Butter,
        - Lard,
        - Tallow, etc.
    - Vegetable,
      - Cereals—Wheat, Corn, Oats, Barley, [Rye, etc.
      - Fruits—Apple, Peach, Pear, etc.
      - Roots—Potatoe, Beet, Turnip, etc.
  - Clothing,
    - Animal—Wool, Hair, Silk, Skins, etc.
    - Vegetable—Linen, Cotton, etc.
  - Animals for Labor,
    - Horse, Mule, Ox, Camel,
    - Reindeer, Dog, etc.
  - Fuel,
    - Animal—Tallow, Lard.
    - Vegetable—Wood, Charcoal.
  - Miscellaneous,
    - Cordage—Hemp, etc.
    - Medicines—Castor Bean, Oil of Pepper- [mint, etc
    - Dyes—Madder, Indigo, etc.
- **Manufactured.**
  - Raw,
    - Ores and precious stones
    - Clay and Sand,
    - Stone,
    - Timber,
    - Ivory,
    - Horn, etc.
  - Wrought,
    - Metals,
    - Hewed Stone,
    - Lumber,
    - Brick,
    - Yarn and Cloth,
    - Leather, etc.
  - Finished,
    - Machinery,
    - Cutlery,
    - Crockery,
    - Houses,
    - Furniture,
    - Clothing,
    - Shoes,
    - Hats,
    - Clocks,
    - Ornaments,
      - Diamond
      - Agate,
      - Opal, etc.
- **Miscellaneous**
  - Food—Fish, Game, etc.
  - Fuel,
    - Coal—Bituminous, Anthracite,
    - Oil.
  - Condiments,
    - Coffee, Tea, Sugar,
    - Spices, Salt.
  - Drugs,
    - Mineral—Calomel, etc.
    - Vegetable—Strychnine, etc.
  - Perfumes,
  - Paints,
  - Dyes,
  - Poisons—Corrosive Sublimate, Arsenic, etc.

POLITICAL GEOGRAPHY—*Continued.*

Employments.

Agriculture.
- Farmer, Gardener, Fruit Grower, etc.
- Grazier, Shepherd, Drover, Butcher, etc.
- Teamster, Chopper, Sawyer, etc.

Fishery. Whaleman, Codfisher, Oysterman, etc.

Manufactures.
- Miner, Quarryman, Lumberman, Trapper,
- Mechanics.

Commerce.
- Merchants,
  - Importers,
  - Jobbers,
  - Retailers.
- Transporters,
  - Sailors,
  - Boatmen,
  - Railroadmen,
  - Stage owners and drivers,
  - Teamsters and Draymen,
  - Stevedores.

Artists.
- Architects,
- Designers,
- Musicians,
- Painters,
- Sculptors,
- Engravers,
- Daguerreans.

Professions.
- Teachers.
- Ministers,
- Physicians,
- Lawyers.

History.

Ancient Countries. / Modern Countries.
- Dynasties, Kings, Wars, dates.
- Extent of Conquests,
  - over what countries,
  - under what kings and generals,
- Decline and Fall,
  - under what king,
  - by what nation and king subdued.
- Change of Governments,
  - by whom effected,
  - causes of decay,
  - effects on civilization and religion.
- Battles,
  - date,
  - locality,
  - number of men engaged on each side,
  - generals,
  - causes,
  - number slain on each side,
  - consequences.
- Extent of Conquests,
  - over what countries,
  - under what kings and generals.

Political Geography—*Concluded.*

Education.

1. Diffusion and extent of Knowledge,
   - among the common people,
   - among higher classes.
2. Libraries,
   - Public,
   - Private,
     - by whom established,
     - number of volumes,
     - conditions of use.
3. Instruction.
   - Public, or Free,
     - Universities,
     - Normal Schools,
     - High Schools,
     - Common Schools,
       - classified
       - unclassified,
     - Number of Teachers
     - Number of Pupils,
   - Private or Pay.
     - Universities,
     - Normal Schools,
     - High Schools,
     - Grammar Schools,
       - endowed,
         - Chairs,
         - amounts.
       - charges,
       - Number of Teachers,
       - Number of Pupils.

Literature, Sciences, and Arts.

Literature,
- what form the most generally cultivated?
- what form the most highly cultivated?
  - Historical?
  - Periodical?
  - Poetical?
  - Metaphorical?
- most noted works,
  - names?
  - authors?

Sciences,
- what the most generally understood?
- what the most highly cultivated?
- most noted discoveries?
  - character?
  - discoveries?
  - consequences?

Arts,
- what the most generally cultivated?
- what the most highly cultivated?
- most noted inventions?
- most noted works?
  - character?
  - inventors?
  - consequences?

Miscellaneous.

Natural Curiosities, Artificial Curiosities, Places and objects of Interest, Distinguished Persons, Manners and Customs, Languages, Traveling Facilities, etc., etc.

43.

DESCRIPTIVE GEOGRAPHY.

1. Boundaries,
2. Latitude and Longitude,
3. Surface,
4. Mountains,
5. Volcanoes,
6. Plains,
7. Islands,
8. Peninsula,
9. Capes,
10. Isthmus,
11. Bodies of Water,
12. Rivers,
13. Noted Springs,
14. Climate,
15. Isothermal Line,
16. Soil,
17. Natural Currents,
18. Natural Productions,
19. Square Miles,
20. Population,
21. Race,
22. State of Society,
23. Capital,
24. Chief Towns,
25. Employments,
26. Facilities for Traveling,
27. Agricultural Productions,
28. Manufactured Productions.
29. Miscellaneous Productions, { Slaves, Emigrants, Fish, Tar, etc.
30. Religion,
31. Education,
32. Morality,
33. Manners and Customs,
34. Languages,
35. History.
36. Literature, Arts and Sciences.

44.

SUCCEEDING LESSONS.

The class will pursue this course of Outlines, in successive lessons, with frequent reviews, till it shall have been mastered.

Then they will commence Descriptive Geography, taking one or two Political divisions for a lesson, using the Topic List on page 235, in the preparation and recitation of their lessons.

The Teacher of an ungraded or country school, can make a division of the class, according to the ability of the scholars, by assigning the whole Topic List, as a guide for the lesson of the most advanced scholars, and only such topics as are found in the text-book used, to scholars less advanced. These two divisions may recite as one class.

The general plan of managing the recitation of an advanced class, is the same as for a secondary class, the difference being in the greater range of topics examined, and in the greater amount of time allowed each scholar for a recitation.

USE OF APPARATUS.

45.

The remaining pages of Part IV. will be given to the description and use of the Globe and Tellurian, and their use in the explanation of Astronomical Phenomena. The matter was originally written by me, several years since, for a text-book, to accompany Holbrook's School Apparatus. Most of it was transferred to the Teacher's Guide to Illustration, a work prepared by F. C. Brownell, for a similar purpose, and published in Hartford, Ct., 1857. That is a valuable work, and should be in the hands of every teacher.

TERRESTRIAL GLOBE.

46.

A Globe should invariably precede the use of maps, to avoid the erroneous impression, with children, that the earth is flat; and the Hemisphere Globe may be used in connection with the Hemisphere Map.

For several reasons, a five-inch globe is preferable, in a common school, to one of any other size. While it shows the spherical form as well as any other, and is large enough to give a distinct view of the principal divisions of land and water to all the members of any ordinary class in Geography, it is not so large but that it can be held in the hand conveniently for familiar illustration; nor is it so large but that it can be made of solid, firm material, without too much increase of weight, which secures it against destruction in case of a fall.

Again, anything that is desirable to be taught by the use of a globe to an ordinary Geography class, can be taught better with a small globe, elevated on a simple pedestal, or suspended by a cord, than by a large globe, costing ten or twenty times as much, surrounded and encumbered by a frame work, horizon and meridian, as such globes usually are.

The fact, that where both a large and a small globe are in possession of teachers, the former is *showed* to visitors, and the latter *used* to instruct scholars, is a sufficient indication of the comparative utility of the two.

But an *outline* globe is preferable, in primary in

struction, to one so much crowded with names as to render the forms of seas and continents obscure and incorrect. The details of particular countries are studied better on maps than on globes. If the minutiæ of Geography should be studied on globes, then ought globes to be large enough to embrace the details of countries and towns, which, of course, is impossible within any ordinary limits of expense.

47.

APPLICATIONS.

I.—THE SHAPE OF THE EARTH.

That the earth is spherical, appears from the following proofs and illustrations:

Proof 1*st.* The earth has been traveled around.

Illustration. As a fly crawling around the globe, in any continuous direction, comes back to the starting point, so travelers have passed around the earth, in nearly all directions, and returned to their homes.

Proof 2*d.* The shadow of the earth on the moon is always circular.

Illustration. The globe always casts a circular shadow, whereas no other body, in all positions, will do so. Try a cylinder, a cone, oblate and prolate spheroids, and then the globe.

Proof 3*d.* The upper part of an approaching object is seen first, as a ship at sea.

Illustration. Insert a pin into the globe, and turn the globe. The outer extremity is first seen, when approaching, and disappears last when receding.

Proof 4*th*. A horizontal line diverges from any horizontal plane surface. The divergence is eight inches for the first mile, thirty-two for two miles, six feet for three miles, and so on.

Illustration. Apply a straight edge to the globe, and it is seen to coincide with it but a short distance.

Proof 5*th*. Vertical lines, at any considerable distance from each other, are not parallel, but diverge toward different parts of the heavens.

Illustration. Insert two or more pins, perpendicularly to the surface of the globe, at some distance from each other, and they are seen to diverge outward and to converge toward the center, *i. e.*, are not parallel to each other, as they would be, if inserted perpendicularly into a plane surface.

Proof 6*th*. The North Star rises as we travel north, and declines as we go south, till we reach the equator, when it disappears.

Illustration. The globe being on a stand, let the north pole be directed toward any small object, as a nail in the ceiling. If that nail represent the north star, and a short pin a traveler, and the pin be moved from the pole toward the equator and across it, then will it appear that the globe will intercept the line of vision from the traveler to the star soon after crossing the equator.

Proof 7*th*. Analogy.

Remark. As all other bodies in the heavens are spherical, except Comets and Saturn's rings, it is reasonable to conclude, that the earth is likewise a sphere.

Proof 8th. Were the earth ever a fluid, (and there is sufficient evidence to show this to be a fact,) the force of gravity would have compelled it to take the form of a sphere.

48.

THE EARTH A SPHEROID.

That the earth is not a perfect sphere, but a spheroid, having the polar diameter shorter than the equatorial, appears from the following proofs:

Proof 1st. A pendulum vibrates more rapidly as it is carried from the equator toward either pole.

Remark. The frequency of the vibrations of a pendulum depends upon the force of gravity, and gravity varies as the squares of the distances from the center of the earth vary inversely. Since, then, a pendulum vibrates more rapidly near the pole than near the equator, it is inferred that the surface at the pole is nearer the earth's center than at the equator.

Proof 2nd. A degree of latitude, on the earth's surface, as indicated by the stars, is longer near the poles than near the equator, showing that the surface is there flattened.

Remark. By accurate measurement of degrees in the torrid and frigid zones, the polar diameter is found to be twenty-six miles shorter than the equatorial diameter, or as 301 to 302.

Proof 3d. Were the earth ever in a fluid state, the centrifugal force, arising from its revolution on its axis, would compel it to assume the form of an oblate spheroid.

49.

II. MATHEMATICAL LINES AND DIVISIONS.

1. *Diameter.* Any straight line extending through the center of the earth from surface to surface.

2. *Circumference.* Any circle on the earth's surface which has the same diameter as the earth.

3. *Axis.* That diameter about which the earth revolves. (*Poles.* The extremities of the axis.)

4. *Great Circle.* Any circle which divides the earth's surface into two equal parts.

5. *Small Circle.* Any circle which divides the earth's surface into two unequal parts.

6. *Equator.* The *great circle,* equally distant from the poles.

7. *Tropics.* Two *small circles,* 23½ degrees from the equator.

8. *Polar Circles.* Two *small circles,* 23½ degrees from the poles.

9. *Meridians.* *Great circles* passing through the poles and the equator.

10. *Parallels of Latitude.* *Small circles* parallel to the equator, either north or south of it.

11. *Zone.* A belt or girdle surrounding the earth.

Torrid Zone. That portion of the earth's surface between the tropics.

Temperate Zones. The two belts between the tropics and polar circles.

Frigid Zones. Those portions of the earth's surface included by the two polar circles.

Hemispheres Any two equal divisions of the

earth; as, northern and southern, eastern and western.

REMARK. All mathematical lines and divisions are imaginary.

Illustration. By the use of the globe, on which the imaginary circles are drawn, the other lines and divisions can be clearly pointed out and explained.

50.

III. MOTIONS OF THE EARTH.

The two most important motions of the earth, are the Diurnal Motion, or that around its axis; and the Annual Motion, or that in its orbit around the sun.

Illustration, 1. With the Globe on the stand, make it revolve on the inclination wire or axis. This will represent the diurnal motion. If at the same time, the globe is carried around any object representing the sun, it will illustrate the annual motion.

Illustration, 2. The better method of combining these motions is to suspend the Globe by a cord attached to a nail in the ceiling. By this means, the elliptical form of the orbit may be shown, as the two motions combined.

51.

IV. THE RELATIVE POSITION OF PLACES.

The true relative position of places is not shown on maps, except in comparatively small areas; and the globe should be in the hand of the teacher of Geography at every recitation, in order that the scholars may obtain the true direction and approximate distance of every County, State, or Town, from their place of residence and from each other.

Remark. It will be seen by the globe that any place, as San Francisco, may be said to be in three directions from any other place, as London. San Francisco can be reached by traveling in a continuous line on the earth's surface, either S. W. or N. E., or by electricity, in a straight line through the earth. Asia is both east and west of America, likewise on the opposite side of the earth.

From the relative position of places on the earth's surface, the inhabitants receive different relative appellations.

Antipodes, are those living diametrically opposite. They have opposite seasons, and opposite days and nights.

Antœci are those living under the same meridian, but on opposite parallels of latitude. They have opposite seasons, but the same days and nights, though the days of one are always equal to the nights of the other, disregarding atmospheric refraction of light.

Periœci are those living on the same parallel of latitude, but under opposite meridians. They have the same seasons, but opposite days and nights; *i. e.*, when it is noon with one, it is midnight with the other.

52.

V. NO ABSOLUTE UP AND DOWN.

Remark. *Up* and *down* are merely relative terms, used in connection with direction to or from the earth's center. With respect to the stars or space at large, that direction which we call *up* at midday is *down* at midnight. And at any time, that direction which is *up* to any person on one side of the earth, is *down* to any person on the other side.

Illustration, 1. Insert a pin into the globe and turn the globe on its axis. It will be seen that the direction which would be called *up* by a person similarly situated on the earth is constantly changing.

Illustration, 2. Insert two pins at antipodes, as in America and Asia. It will be seen that the heads point in opposite directions, *i. e.*, the direction which is *up* to one is *down* to the other.

53.

VI. PHENOMENA.

SUCCESSION OF DAY AND NIGHT.

Day and night are caused by the revolution of the earth on its axis, bringing any place between the two polar circles once in the light of the sun at each revolution.

Illustration, 1. In a darkened room, having in it only one lighted candle, it will be seen that one-half the surface of the globe is illuminated and the other half is in shade. Insert a pin at your place of residence, and turn the globe on its axis. It will come round alternately into light and shade, or into day and night.

Illustration, 2. By daylight, a window or any other object may be taken for the sun, and the imagination can picture the illumined hemisphere on the side toward the sun; or the large ball of a lunarian can be used in connection with the globe.

THE CHANGE OF SEASONS.

The change of seasons is produced by the inclination of the earth's axis to the plane of its orbit, as shown by the inclination of the axis of the globe.

Illustration. The change of the seasons may be shown by carrying the globe, with the axis continually directed toward the north, about any object assumed as a sun.

54.

TRADE WINDS.

The trade winds are caused by the revolution of the earth on its axis from west to east, in connection with the current of air flowing toward the equatorial region, to supply those portions of space from which the air rises by the action of the sun's heat.

Illustration. (With the globe in hand.) It is supposed that the Sun is shining directly on the equator. Those parts of the earth's surface about the equator, being much heated, rarefy the air in contact with them. The air thus rarefied rises; other air from the north and south, within and beyond the tropics, flows in to supply the place of the air so elevated. But as the atmosphere partakes of the motion of that part of the earth's surface with which it is in contact, and as the surface at the tropics and beyond them does not move as rapidly from west to east as at the equator, since those circles are smaller than the equator, it is plain that if air, with the eastward motion of the tropics, say 900 miles an hour, were instantaneously transported to the equator, where the eastward motion of the earth's surface is 1000 miles an hour, the air so transported would have a relative backward or westward motion of 100 miles an hour. But as it is not transported instantaneously, but flows with a moderate velocity, its westward motion, though considerable, is not so great. It must be remembered, that the motion toward the equator is combined with the backward or westward motion, giving the trade winds a southwesterly direction north of the sun, and a northwesterly direction south of the sun. Where the two currents would meet, which is always a few degrees behind the sun, in its course from one tropic to the other, the equatorial zone of calms is found.

55.

VII. ABSOLUTE AND RELATIVE TIME.

It is considered 12 o'clock, M., at any place on the earth's surface when the sun is on the meridian of that place.

But as the sun has an apparent motion from east to west of 15 degrees an hour, or 360 degrees in 24 hours, evidently it cannot be 12 o'clock at the same time, at any two places not on the same meridian.

Then at any place, as Boston, lying on a meridian east of any other place, as New Orleans, it must be 12 o'clock, or noon, before it is noon at the latter place, because the sun will reach the meridian of Boston sooner, in its westward course, than it will the meridian of New Orleans.

Hence, if it is noon at Boston, it will be forenoon at New Orleans, and if it is noon at New Orleans it will be afternoon at Boston. While then absolute time is the same in all places, relative time is later at places lying east of us, and earlier at places lying west of us.

Illustration. Insert a pin at Boston, another at New Orleans, assuming any object on a horizontal line with the globe for a sun. Turn the globe on its axis, from west to east, it is seen that the pin at Boston comes under the assumed sun before the pin at New Orleans.

56.

VIII. MEASUREMENT OF DISTANCES.

Take a narrow tape, and make it the same length of the equator on the globe. Divide by folding into 5 equal parts. Mark with pencil or pen these divisons. In the same manner subdivide these divisions into 5 other equal parts. Call each 1000 miles. Again divide these as many times as convenient.

A scale is now made by which distances, from place to place, may be ascertained, the comparative length of different routes or voyages known, etc. These, as fast as ascertained, should be committed to memory, or written down for future reference. This is found to be an amusing and instructive exercise, valuable in family or school, to keep children out of mischief, and to imprint on their minds some of the most important geograpical knowledge.

57.

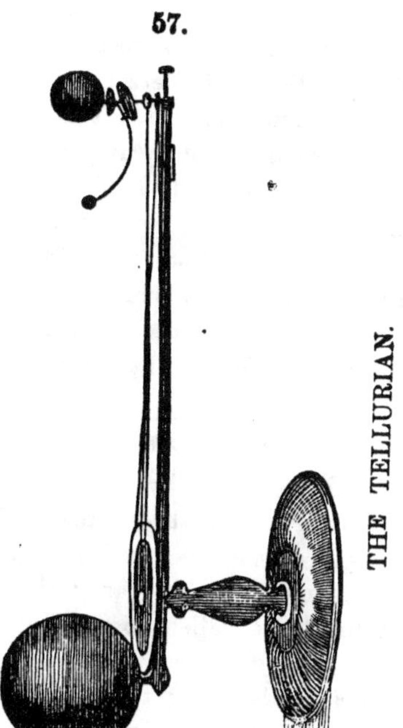

THE TELLURIAN.

This instrument is designed to illustrate all the phenomena resulting from the relations of the Sun, Moon and Earth, to each other. The most important of these phenomena are the succession of day and night; the change of seasons; the change of the Sun's declination; the different lengths of day and night; the rising of the Sun north of east in summer; the changes of the Moon; solar and lunar eclipses; spring and neap tides; the later daily recurrence of the tides; the length of days on the Moon; the appearance of the Earth to observers on the Moon; the harvest Moon; the difference of a synodical and sidereal revolution of the moon; the precession of the equinoxes and the difference of a solar and sidereal year. All these phenomena may be explained by the Tellurian, with a simplicity that brings them within the comprehension of a child. Before passing to an explanation of the manner in which they may be illustrated, I shall describe the construction of the instrument, and give directions for its adjustment.

58.

CONSTRUCTION.

The Tellurian, as seen by the cut, consists of the stand; the arm; the three fixed pulleys; the handle; the three movable pulleys; the inclination wire; the moon's orbit plane; the extension screw, and the three balls representing the Sun, Earth, and Moon. Of these three balls, the globe is three inches in diameter; the small ball, seven-eights of an inch, giving nearly the true proportionate size of the moon; and the large ball, five inches, the true proportionate size of which would be nearly twenty-eight feet. The proportionate distance of the moon from the earth would be seven and a half feet; while the earth should be placed at the distance of two thousand nine hundred and sixty-nine feet from the sun. It is perceived, that an instrument, giving the true proportionate sizes and distances, could not well be constructed: and were it constructed, would require either a telescope or microscope to examine it.

Notwithstanding the proportions are not preserved in the Tellurian, the causes of the various phenomena appear much more clearly than if they were.

Of the three fixed pulleys, only the upper and larger one is seen in the figure. There are three corresponding movable pulleys on the end of the arm, each moving independently of the other. The upper pair of pulleys, one movable and one fixed, being connected with a cord passing around both, serve to give motion to the moon around the earth. The middle pair, connected by a cord in a similar manner, give a slow motion to the moon's orbit plane. The lower pair being both of the same size and connected by a cord, preserve the parallelism of the inclination wire or axis of the earth.

The extension screw is for the purpose of tightening the cords when they become slack by use.

59.

ADJUSTMENT.

In setting up the instrument, screw the upright standard, to which the arm and fixed pulleys are attached, into the circular base; place the movable pulley, with the orbit plane, on the wire at the end of the arm; arrange the cords around the respective pairs of pulleys, crossing the cord which goes around the upper pair, (this is the longest cord of the three;) place the globe on the inclination wire and the sun or large ball on the wire in the handle; then turn the stand so that the dividing line, between Aries and Pisces, on the horizontal circle on the large fixed pulley, shall be on the east side of the center; again, by applying the thumb and finger to the lower and movable pulley, turn the inclination wire and globe on it, so that the north pole of the globe shall be directed toward the north star. The instrument is now adjusted.

If by means of the handle the arm is turned around, it will be observed, that the sun and earth revolve around a common centre of gravity; that the sun revolves on its axis by coming in contact with the large pulley; that the moon revolves around the earth thirteen times while the earth goes around the sun once; that the parallelism of the earth's axis is maintained, always pointing toward the north. The revolution of the earth, on its axis, is effected by striking the globe lightly with the finger. The motion of all the balls should be from west to east, in the southern part of their orbits.

60.

DAY AND NIGHT.

The succession of day and night is best represented by placing a short lighted candle on the center of the large fixed pulley, in a darkened room. Half of the globe will then be seen to be in light and half in shade. Insert a small pin at your place of residence on the globe, as nearly as may be, and turn the globe on its axis with the finger, from west to east on the south side. It will be noticed, that the place, thus designated, is alternately in light and shade, or in day and night. And, if the pin is supposed to be an observer, it will see the sun coming into view, or rising over countries or seas at the east, and passing around over its meridian, disappearing or setting behind countries and seas lying in the west.

61.

VARIATION IN LENGTH OF DAY AND NIGHT.

If the arm of the Tellurian, adjusted as already explained, be turned so as to bring the globe directly west of the yellow ball or sun,* both poles will be illuminated by the light of the candle, as if proceeding from the Sun, and all parts of the globe, excepting the poles, will come successively and equally into light and shade, when it is made to revolve equally on its axis. At this point, then, in the earth's orbit, as well as at the opposite point, the days and nights will be equal all over its surface. Hence, the east and west points of the Earth's orbit are called by astronomers equinoctial points or equinoxes, from *æquus*, equal, and *nox*, *noctis*, night.

But as the earth passes on in its orbit from the western equinox toward the south, since the axis continues directed toward the north, the light will gradually extend over the north pole and recede from the south pole. The northern hemisphere will thus become more than half illuminated, and the southern proportionally less. Now, it will be perceived that any place north of the equator will remain longer and longer in light at each diurnal revolution as the earth advances, until it arrives at the southern point of its orbit. Here the light

* When the words *Sun*, *Earth*, and *Moon*, begin with capitals, they refer to the bodies, in the heavens; but when they begin with small letters, they refer to the balls which represent them on the Tellurian

will extend over the north pole twenty-three and a half degrees, and fall as far short of the south pole, giving the longest possible day to the northern hemisphere, and the shortest possible night.

Notice, too, that all places north of the Arctic Circle will make more than one entire revolution in light, and thus have a day of more than twenty-four hours in length.

Again, turn the arm and carry the globe through the northern part of its orbit, it will readily appear why the inhabitants of the northern hemisphere have nights longer than days in that part of the Earth's orbit.

That both poles must have days and nights of six months each, is also apparent.

62.

THE CHANGE OF SEASONS.

The inclination of the Earth's axis, together with its parallelism, influences more or less all terrestrial phenomena. The attentive pupil must have already seen, that the variation in the length of day and night is the result of this cause. If so, he is prepared to understand in what manner the change of seasons is brought about by the same means.

Let the arm of the Tellurian be directed toward the south, then the earth's axis will be inclined toward the sun, and a line extending from the earth's center to the sun's center, will pass through the tropic of Cancer. Hence, an observer on that tropic would, at noon, see the Sun directly overhead when the Sun and Earth are in this position with regard to each other, and all the inhabitants of the northern temperate and frigid zones would see the Sun at its greatest altitude. This must be midsummer, or as it is termed by astronomers, the summer solstice. Observe that the longest day occurs at this time in the northern hemisphere, and that the Sun is more nearly vertical when on the meridian at all places north of the tropic of Cancer than at any other time of the year; *i. e.*, the Sun shines a larger portion of the twenty-four hours on this part of the Earth's surface, and emits a larger amount of rays on any given space than at any other time.

Now, move the arm around toward the east; as the inclination of the axis continues toward the north, it becomes less and less inclined toward the sun as the earth moves on to the eastern part of its orbit. Being at the eastern point, it is neither inclined to nor from the sun, but the extremities or poles are equally illuminated. As before shown, this is one of the equinoxes, and as it succeeds summer, it must be the autumnal equinox. The sun is now vertical at the equator; in other words, "is crossing the line."

Again, turn the arm toward the north; observe that the north pole is carried into darkness, while the south pole is brought more and more into light. If the earth has reached the north point of its orbit, the axis is inclined away from the sun, and the southern hemisphere is more directly under its influence. The sun will now be vertical at the tropic of Capricorn, and shine a longer portion of the twenty-four hours on the southern hemisphere, and with greater intensity, while the days are shorter, and the rays more oblique on the northern hemisphere than at any other time of the year. Here, then, must be the winter solstice to the inhabitants of the northern hemisphere.

Carry the arm around toward the west, at the same time make the globe revolve on its axis; observe that the days become longer and longer in the northern hemisphere, while the earth is prosecuting this part of its annual journey. The globe having arrived at the west point of its orbit, occupies the same relative position with regard to the candle as the Earth with regard to the Sun, at the vernal equinox. The sun is now visible at both poles, and is again crossing the line.

Thus having followed the round of the seasons, we cannot but admire the simplicity of the mechanism which produces such varied and beautiful results. Were the axis perpendicular to the plane of the orbit, there could be no change of seasons, but unvarying arid heat would prevail in the equatorial regions; while perpetual frosts would reign over a much larger portion of the Earth's surface than under the existing arrangement.

The tropics, so called, because at these lines the Sun turns back toward the equator, depend for their locality upon the axial inclination, being necessarily as many degrees from the equator as the axis is inclined from the perpendicular. Were the axis to lie down on the plane of the orbit, the tropics would be in the poles, and the polar circles at the equator.

63.

RISING AND SETTING OF THE SUN NORTH OF THE EAST AND WEST POINTS OF THE HEAVENS.

Since the Sun never comes further north than the tropic of Cancer, how is it, that morning and evening, even in our latitude, it casts its rays on the north side of our dwellings and other objects during the summer months?

In order to understand this the more readily, let us consider the appearance of the Sun at the poles. About the 20th of March it begins to make its appearance, gradually rising into view as it makes the entire circuit of the horizon every twenty-four hours. Higher and higher it rises, passing around the heavens, almost entirely parallel with the horizon, until, at midday, corresponding to our midsummer, it reaches the altitude of twenty-three and a half degrees, and from that time winds downward, and in three months is lost again behind the continent of ice.

At any place within the Arctic Circle, except at the north pole, once in the year at least, the sun will be seen directly in the north, as can be shown by the globe of the Tellurian. Below the Arctic Circle and near it, the sun will be seen just dipping below the horizon, a few degrees west of the meridian, and soon emerging as many degrees east of it. The farther south the observer is situated, the longer will the sun continue below the horizon, and the nearer will it rise and set in the east and west points of the heavens; in other words, the further north he is situated, the nearer will it rise and set to the north point of the horizon.

64.

SIDEREAL AND SOLAR DAY.

While the Earth is revolving on its axis, it is likewise revolving around the Sun; hence, an entire diurnal revolution which brings any locality under the same star, will not bring it into the same relation to the Sun.

Let the arm of the Tellurian be directed toward the north; insert a pin at any point on the equator of the globe; let the pin be directed toward the sun, (yellow ball,) which will be exactly south. Now turn the globe once on its axis, at the same time moving the arm forward a short distance toward the west. When the pin is brought around again toward the south, it is not directed toward the sun as before, but must make a part of another revolution to come round in the direction of the sun. The first is the sidereal; the second, the solar revolution or day. There will, of course, be one more sidereal revolution than solar in a year, however few or many there may be of either, unless the revolutions are in opposite directions, when there will be one less.

65.

REVOLUTIONS OF THE MOON.

The Moon has at least three revolutions: the first on its axis, the second around the Earth, the third around the Sun.

The Tellurian represents the Moon as presenting always the same side to the Earth. This is true to nature, and it gives the moon one revolution around the earth, as, obviously, all sides of the moon will be brought successively under the eye of an observer situated beyond the moon's orbit. The fact of one side being presented always to the Earth, has been attributed to the greater specific gravity of that side, making it hang down toward the Earth.*

66.

CHANGES OF THE MOON.

The changes of the Moon are the result of its opacity and its revolution about the Earth. We have new and full Moon once in twenty-nine and a half days, from the fact that its revolution around the Earth once in twenty-eight days, in connection with the common motion of these bodies around the Sun, bring them all into the same relation with regard to each other in that period. This period is called a *lunation* or *lunar month.*

Placing a strong light on the Tellurian, as before, turn the arm so as to bring the moon between the sun and earth. Evidently the dark side of the moon is now toward the earth, and this is the position of the three bodies at *new moon.* Thus situated, the sun and moon are said to be in *conjunction.*

Turn the arm again, and bring the moon around on the side of the earth opposite the sun.

---

*NOTE.—The difference of a sidereal and a synodical revolution can be shown in a manner similar to that of illustrating the difference of a sidereal and solar day.

The illuminated side of the Moon is now presented to the Earth. This is *full moon*, and the Sun and Moon, in this position, are said to be in *opposition*. As the Moon's orbit is not on the same plane with the Earth's orbit, the Moon is sometimes above and sometimes below the plane of the Earth's orbit or *ecliptic* at new and full. Hence we do not always see exactly the same hemisphere at full moon, or the crescent pointing in the same direction at new moon. The horns of the crescent will, however, always point away from the Sun, whether above or below; or, as we say, the Moon *runs high* or *runs low;* all of which can be clearly shown by the Tellurian.

The intermediate phases, as the quadrants and octants, are also seen by the Tellurian, but perhaps more clearly by the use of the Lunarian.

67.

ECLIPSES.

An eclipse is nothing more than an obscuration of the Sun or Moon by the interception of the Sun's rays.

An eclipse of the Sun, or a *solar eclipse*, is shown by turning the Tellurian arm until the moon casts a shadow on the earth's surface. An eye, situated at the place of the shadow, could not, of course, see the luminous part of the candle. So, on the earth's surface, wherever the shadow of the Moon falls, the Sun can not be seen, as it is in an eclipse. A solar eclipse commonly happens at new moon, and can be *total* when the Moon's center is in, or very near, the ecliptic, or when the Moon is at one of its *nodes*. Since, as shown by the Tellurian, the Moon is sometimes above and sometimes below the ecliptic, at this period, it is obvious that an eclipse can not happen at every new moon.

A *partial* eclipse will occur wherever a part of the Sun's disk is obscured by the intervention of the Moon.

A lunar eclipse is shown by turning the Tellurian arm until the moon comes into the shadow of the earth, either partially or entirely; giving a partial or total eclipse. Neither of these can happen at every full moon, in consequence of the obliquity of the moon's orbit to the ecliptic. The construction of the instrument is such that the moon's orbit plane will come into the same relation to the earth's plane once in eighteen revolutions of the earth around the sun. This arrangement corresponds to the Chaldaic period in nature, which gives the recurrence of nearly the same order of eclipses once in eighteen years and ten days. By means of this period, the ancients were enabled to foretell eclipses, but with no great degree of precision.

68.

TIDES.

Tides are the result of the unequal attraction of the Moon on the water on the Earth's surface, and on the inflexible mass of the Earth itself. They are influenced likewise by the Sun, and by the form and position of coasts and harbors.

Since the water under the Moon is 4,000 miles nearer to it than the centre of the Earth, it will be attracted by as much greater force than the Earth as the square of 240,000 is greater than the square of 236,000. Hence the water is heaped up under the Moon, and this elevated mass of water will pass around the Earth as far as continents will permit, once in twenty-four hours, or as often as the Earth revolves under the Moon. This will account for a tide once a day. But there are two tides daily. How is this?

Since the Earth's centre is 4,000 miles nearer to the Moon than the water on the Earth's surface opposite the Moon, the Earth is drawn away from this water on its surface opposite the Moon. And as the water under the Moon is drawn away from the Earth, so the Earth is as much drawn away from the water on the side opposite the Moon Hence, there will be a tide opposite the Moon as well as under it, and the two tides will be equal, or nearly so. This will give any place within the reach of tide-water two tides in a day.

69.

LATER DAILY RECURRENCE OF TIDES.

Tides happen about fifty minutes later every day, in consequence of the motion of the Moon in its orbit around the Earth.

This may be shown by giving motion to the Tellurian arm and the globe on its axis at the same time. Observe that any place on the earth must make more than an entire revolution to come around the second time under the moon, whereas if the moon were stationary, then a complete revolution would bring the same meridian again under it.

70.

SPRING AND NEAP TIDES.

It is found by observation, that the influence of the Sun on the tides is about one-fourth as great as that of the Moon.

By the Tellurian, it is shown, that when the Sun and Moon are either in opposition or in conjunction, their influences combine to produce a tide equal to the sum of the tides they would produce separately. This is called a spring tide, and will happen either at new or full moon.

Again, it is shown, that when the Moon is at its quadratures, the tide will be equal to the difference of the Sun's and Moon's tides separately. This is called the neap tide.

The highest tide possible, at any given place, will happen under the concurrence of the following circumstances, viz: The Earth in its perihelion, the Moon in its perigee, at one of its syzygies, and in the zenith or nadir.

71.

PRECESSION OF THE EQUINOXES.

The precession of the Equinoxes is the recurrence of the Equinoxes or any other period of the year before the Earth has made an entire revolution around the Sun.

It it is found that a year is twenty minutes and

seventeen seconds less than the time required for an entire revolution. This is occasioned by a change, not on the inclination of the Earth's axis, but on the direction of that inclination. To show this clearly, take hold of the lower movable pulley with the thumb and finger, and turn that pulley half the way round. In so doing, you will cause the axis of the Earth to point south instead of north, but with the same inclination still. In nature, it requires 12,934 years to make the change, and 25,868 years to bring the axis back again into its present position. Now, if you start the arm from the east, where the globe will be in the position of the autumnal equinox, and while you turn the arm, you at the same time turn the axis so that it shall incline easterly, you have only to carry the arm around to the south to bring the globe into the position of the autumnal equinox again; *i. e.*, a quarter of a revolution of the axis produces a precession of the equinox—equal to a quarter of the Earth's orbit. The precession, then, we see, is equal to the part of a revolution that the axis makes. It really makes a change of 50″.1 in a year, and the precession is the same, and it requires twenty minutes and seventeen seconds for the earth to pass that part of its orbit. Hence, as before stated, the year is so much less than the time required for an entire revolution.

PART V.

METHODS OF TEACHING MENTAL, PRACTICAL, AND THEORETICAL ARITHMETIC.

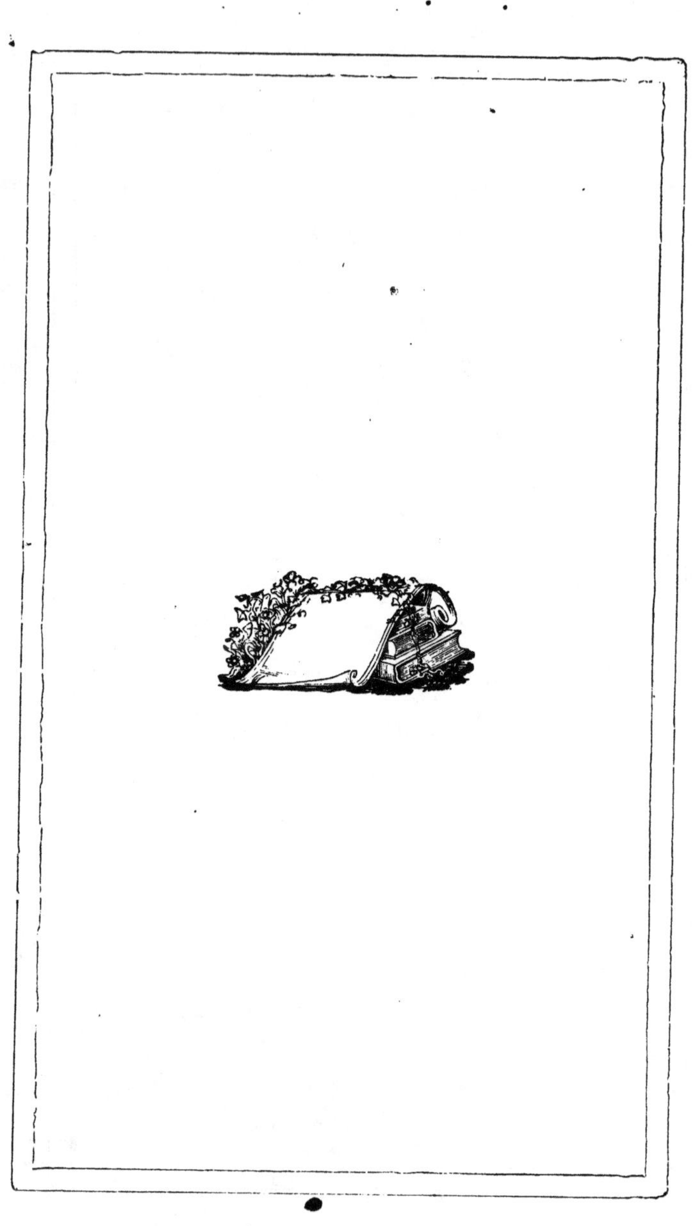

INTRODUCTION.

MENTAL ARITHMETIC.

THE OBJECTS aimed at by the true teacher for his class in Mental Arithmetic, are—

1st. *Distinct mental conceptions.* Some teachers make use of numeral frames, and a variety of other expedients, to aid their pupils in *realizing* the powers of numbers. I am of the opinion that such aids may be relied on too far; so far as to retard the operation of the mind in forming its own conceptions. The large majority of pupils will advance more rapidly and self-relyingly, without any visible representations whatever, and should they be needed, marks on the blackboard answer every purpose.

2d. *Clear views of cause and effect.* From the very first exercise in Arithmetic, the relation of cause and effect is ever before the mind; equally as much in answering the question, One and one are how many? as in the most complex problems, requiring a long continued course of analysis and synthesis for solution. In fact, every operation is but an application, in some form, of the law of cause and effect. Hence Arithmetic, and especially Mental Arithmetic, affords a fine field for the cultivation of the reasoning faculties. There is no better, if properly managed.

3d. *Certainty in the courses of reasoning.* This should be aimed at just as much, in the simpler steps, in the first lessons, as in the higher walks of more advanced stages. For if entire certainty is not secured in the preliminary steps, what else may be expected of the more advanced exercises than conjecture, doubt and uncertainty in the processes and results?

4th. *Precision in language.* This implies not only a clear distinction of abstract and concrete quantities, and the use of the necessary language to make such distinction without tautology, if possible; but it does not admit of any forms of false or doubtful syntax in the enunciation or solution of questions.

5th. *A thorough understanding of Fractions.*— There is no aspect in which a Mental Arithmetic class can appear to so good advantage before an examining committee, as in the ready and successful management of fractional numbers. A knowledge of powers and multiples is indispensable to free use of fractional quantities.

6th. *Rapidity in the solution of questions.* Certainty should be aimed at from the very first, but as the class advances emulation should be brought into play in exciting the minds of the *whole* class to rapid combinations and evolutions. Most astonishing results may be attained, even with sluggish minds, in this direction.

7th. *Artifices for abridging labor.* These should never be introduced till the scholar is well drilled in the full and logical forms of procedure, but then they may be used with great interest and effect.

8th. *Cultivation of Memory.* To this end no book should be used by the class, during recitation; and at every lesson more or less impromptu and "random questions" should be given. Examples of these will appear in the following pages.

WRITTEN ARITHMETIC.

THE OBJECTS to be aimed at in Written Arithmetic, are—

1st. *Correctness in operation.* Written Arithmetic looks more particularly to operations in dollars and cents, in the counting room, workshop, or market; and the teacher who should tolerate any want of accuracy in the operations of the pupil would be false to his interests.

2d. *Rapidity in operation.* When it is known, that by practice, two or three long columns of figures can be added with as much rapidity as one is, ordinarily, it is seen that there is abundant room for improvement, not only in scholars but in most teachers. Multiplication and division are equally susceptible of condensed operations, yielding remote results in "less than no time" to the expert calculator

3d. *Artifices for abridging labor.* Every possibility of cancellation should be familiar, every contraction in the fundamental rules, every use of aliquot parts, and factors, should be so frequently and so long dwelt upon by a class, that the "shortest method" will always afterward present itself, in business life, as if by intuition.

4th. *Ready and reliable means of proof.* As there are no "answers" to real business transactions, except such as the business man obtains for himself, it seems to me altogether preferable to accustom scholars in practical arithmetic, to prove their work from the first. Of course the "best methods" should be sought by the teacher, and practiced by the pupil, till he has little occasion for "the answer in the book." Books without answers are desirable for this end; but the teacher should be the more watchful and exacting in the matter of proofs, if the text book is furnished with answers.

THEORETICAL ARITHMETIC.

THE OBJECTS to be aimed at in Theoretical Arithmetic, are—

1st. *A thorough understanding of all the peculiar and common properties of numbers as high as twelve.* The demonstration and use of these properties are equally useful and interesting.

2d. *Development of reasoning faculties.* Geometry is frequently resorted to for this purpose and for no other. Theoretical Arithmetic is no less effectual, if pursued with as much rigor as the subject demands. The definitions and axioms should be as clearly stated, and the propositions as well connected, and as logically proved as those of Geometry; while for the great majority of pupils there is immeasurably a greater demand for the use of the principles of Arithmetic than for those of Geometry.

3d. *Cultivation of the power of accurate expression of thought.* There is no department of science where we find so much looseness in definitions and rules, as in Arithmetic, notwithstanding the multitude of text books on this subject, and the higher claims of each successive author, in this particular. This very looseness in authors affords the critical teacher a fine field, if not for display of his own acumen; yet for arousing the energies of his pupils to excel their text book.

4th. *A knowledge of the curiosities of the science.*

5th. *An acquaintance with the works of various authors.* It will be found a very desirable practice, in pursuing a course of Theoretical Arithmetic, to consult the various authors who have written on the subject. A more liberal and symmetrical view of the science is thus obtained than from any one author. Respect for authors is thus diminished, while the love for the truth is enhanced.

METHOD OF TEACHING MENTAL ARITHMETIC TO PRIMARY CLASSES.

LESSON I.

1.

First Step—How to secure Books. A course similar to that described on page 184, Sec. 2, may be pursued.

Second Step—Counting. *Teacher.*—Children, how many of you can count a hundred? [A majority raise their hands.] As many as can count ten may raise the hand. [Nearly all hands rise.] Now we will see. I will make some marks on the blackboard and you may all count them as I make them.

The teacher makes the marks, (circles,) on the board, and the children count in concert. He soon learns the ability of the class in counting; and drills those unable to count ten in counting marks, buttons, fingers, desks, windows, panes of glass, etc., till they can tell the number of objects as high as ten. They may then be required to make as many marks on the board as the teacher designates.

2.

THIRD STEP—PRELIMINARY DRILL ON LESSON I. Ray's Mental Arithmetic.

Teacher.—Children, you may now open your books to Lesson I., on page 8, as many as have books. Those who have no books may look over others' books to-day, but all who remain in the class must have books to-morrow. We can have no looking over after to-day.

Have you all found it? Charles, you may read the first question, beginning "James had an apple."

Charles reads the question.

Teacher.—How many can answer it? As many as can may raise the hand. [All hands rise.] Sarah, you may answer it. *Sarah.*—Two. *Teacher.* Susan, you may read the next question. *Susan* reads. *Teacher.*—How many can answer this question? The teacher will be careful to call on those pupils who are the most backward or inattentive.

In a similar manner, this lesson, or so much of it as the class can bear, is passed over in preparation for studying it.

Teacher.—Now I wish you to study this lesson which you have been reading, so that you can answer all the questions without the book, when you come again to recite. I will read the questions and you may answer them without looking on the book at all. How many will study this lesson and learn it well? [All hands rise.]

The class is now dismissed in order, and notes written to parents for the necessary books.

LESSON II.

3.

First Step—Recitation. The teacher reads the question to the whole class, and calls on one pupil by name for an answer. He will be careful not to omit any, but he should not pursue the order in which they sit. He may follow the order of his register for this class, forwards or backwards, taking all the names as they stand, or taking them alternately, backwards or forwards: or he may depart from this order, when he sees any scholar inattentive, by giving him a question.

Making Figures. As each scholar answers his question, he may go to the blackboard, and make the figures corresponding to the numbers used in the question and answer, and perform the operation by adding the figures as in Written Arithmetic. Of course, the mental operation comes first and the answer by this means. With a primary class it is much better thus to combine Written with Mental Arithmetic as they proceed.

Second Step—Preliminary Drill for next lesson.

Remark. The class will pursue the course described in Lesson II, for many days, until they acquire a knowledge of counting, of the use of figures, and the power of making them correctly on the slate or blackboard, till they can perform the operation of addition and subtraction by either the mental or written process; but when multiplication is reached the regular steps of a solution should be taught, which are as follows:—

4.

ADVANCED LESSON.

Recitation. Teacher reads a question for the whole class: "At 7 cents apiece what will 3 melons cost?" After waiting till most of the class have raised their hands as each has obtained the result, he speaks the word "class." Then all who have obtained the result raise their hands together. He calls on one pupil by name to give the result; then on all who agree with this result to raise their hands; then on all who have another result, to raise their hands; then on some individual, from his register, in order, by name, to give a solution of the question, which is done in the manner described in the following section.

5.

SOLUTIONS.

First Step—Scholar rises and repeats the Question. If he fails, the teacher says, "Class, who can give him the question?" Hands rise. The teacher then calls on some one to repeat the question. He repeats it without rising. First scholar, still standing, also repeats it.

Second Step—Scholar gives the Analysis, or explains the method of solving the question. If he fails, pursue the same course to correct him as in the first step.

Third Step—Scholar performs the Operations, and obtains the result.

Fourth Step—Scholar gives the Conclusion, as nearly as possible in the language of the question.

Remark. After the teacher has drilled the class in solutions, in multiplication, they may return to addition for a few solutions.

6.

FIRST EXAMPLE.—ADDITION.

Teacher reads, James had five cents, and he found seven more; how many had he then? When it is seen by hands rising that nearly all the class have obtained the result, he says "Class." Then all who have solved the question raise their hands together.

Teacher.—Henry, what is the result?

Henry.—Twelve.

Teacher.—How many agree? [Hands rise.] How many have a different result? [Hands rise.] Mary. *Mary.*—Twelve cents. *Teacher.*—Very well. Sarah, you may give the solution.

Sarah, rising, repeats (not reads) the question.

FIRST STEP. James had five cents, and he found seven more, how many had he then?

SECOND STEP. He had as many as the sum of five cents and seven cents.

THIRD STEP. Five cents plus seven cents are twelve cents.

FOURTH STEP. Therefore, if James had five cents, and found seven more, he then had twelve cents.

7.

SECOND EXAMPLE.—SUBTRACTION.

The teacher having read the question—

Maria, rising, gives the solution thus:

First Step. A boy having eight marbles, lost five of them, how many had he left?

Second Step. He had as many as the difference between five marbles and eight marbles.

Third Step. Eight minus five are three.

Fourth Step. Therefore, if James, having eight marbles, lost five of them, he had three marbles left.

8.

THIRD EXAMPLE—ADDITION AND SUBTRACTION.

Peter, rising, repeats the question.

First Step. A lady bought a comb for twenty five cents, some pins for ten cents, and some tape for six cents; she gave the shopkeeper seventy-five cents; how much change ought she to receive?

Second Step. She ought to receive as many as the difference between seventy-five cents and the sum of twenty-five cents, and ten cents, and six cents.

Third Step. Twenty-five plus ten, plus six, are forty one. Seventy-five minus forty-one are thirty-four.

Fourth Step. Therefore if a lady bought a comb for twenty-five cents, some pins for ten cents, and some tape for six cents, and gave the shopkeeper seventy-five cents, she ought to receive forty-one cents in change.

9.

FOURTH EXAMPLE—MULTIPLICATION.

Samuel, rising, gives the solution thus:

First Step. At four dollars a pair, what will five pairs of boots cost?

SECOND STEP. If one pair cost four dollars, five pairs will cost five times four dollars,

THIRD STEP. Which are twenty dollars.

FOURTH STEP. Therefore, at four dollars a pair, five pairs of boots cost twenty dollars.

10.

FIFTH EXAMPLE.—DIVISION.

Susan, rising, gives the solution thus:

FIRST STEP. If a man laid out one hundred dollars for cows, and paid twenty dollars for each cow he bought, how many cows did he buy?

SECOND STEP. If one cow cost twenty dollars, he bought as many cows for one hundred dollars as twenty is contained times in one hundred,

THIRD STEP. Which are five times.

FOURTH STEP. Therefore, if a man laid out one hundred dollars for cows, and paid twenty dollars for each cow that he bought he bought five cows.

11.

SIXTH EXAMPLE.—DIVISION.

William, rising, gives the solution thus:

FIRST STEP. If you should buy six oranges for twenty-four cents, how much would you pay for each orange?

SECOND STEP. To pay one cent for each orange would require six cents; then you would pay as many cents for each orange as six cents is contained times in twenty-four cents,

THIRD STEP. Which are four times.

FOURTH STEP. Therefore, if you should buy six oranges for twenty-four cents, you would pay four cents for each orange.

Remark. In examples of this kind the pupil is inclined to take it for granted that one kind of concrete quantity is contained in another kind of concrete quantity. Hence his analysis is likely to be thus: "Since you buy six oranges for twenty-four cents, each orange will cost as many cents as six is contained times in twenty-four."

Six what is contained times in twenty-four what? should be asked by the critical teacher.

For further examples and solutions I refer the teacher to Ray's Mental Arithmetic.

12.

VARIATIONS IN THE MANAGEMENT OF CLASSES.

1st. If a class is large, it will be better for each pupil, as his name is called from the register, to take but one step in a solution. Thus more of the class will be reached in a given time, and more general attention secured with less difficulty.

2d. It may be well occasionally to combine the second and third steps in one, i. e., let the pupil give the PROCESS and result of each operation proposed in the METHOD of solution; thus,

Henry, rising, gives the solution.

FIRST STEP. If three tuns of hay cost twenty-one dollars, what will five tuns cost?

SECOND AND THIRD STEPS. If three tuns of hay cost twenty-one dollars, one tun will cost one-third of twenty-one dollars, which is seven dollars; and if one tun cost seven dollars, five tuns will cost five times seven dollars, which are thirty-five dollars.

FOURTH STEP. Therefore, if three tuns of hay

cost twenty-one dollars, five tuns will cost thirty-five dollars.

13.

RANDOM EXERCISES.

A random exercise is such as is engaged in by the class without previous study, the teacher leading. These should be commenced with small integral numbers; and the teacher should proceed slowly in his lead, at first bringing in only addition and subtraction. As a class improves under the exercise, the operations of multiplication and division may be introduced; also, involution and evolution; also, fractional quantities.

I will give a few examples.

14.

Example 1st. *Teacher.* Class, take seven, add five, add eight, add five, subtract nine, subtract eight. How many have the result?

The pupils, as many as have followed the teacher and have obtained the final result, are expected to raise their hands.

Teacher.—James. *James.*—Twelve. *Teacher.* How many agree? [No hands rise.] How many have a different result. [Hand rises.] Sarah. *Sarah.*—Eight. *Teacher.*—How many agree with Sarah? [Hands rise.] Very well. How many can give the operations aloud? [Hands rise.] Susan. *Susan.* Take seven, add five, which gives twelve; add eight, which gives twenty; add five, which gives twenty-five; subtract nine, which gives sixteen; subtract eight, which gives eight, the final result. *Teacher.*—Very well, Susan.

15.

Example 2d. *Teacher.*—Class, take fourteen, divide by seven, multiply by twelve, multiply by two, add two, divide by twenty-five; how many have the result?

The same course is pursued in bringing out all the scholars, in ascertaining how many have followed the question, and how many have not, as before.

16.

Example 3d. *Teacher.*—Class, take nine, square it, subtract seventeen, take square root, double it, take the square root, take the square root; how many have the result?

17.

Example 4th. Take one hundred, multiply by nine-tenths, multiply by eight-ninths, multiply by seven-eighths, multiply by six-sevenths, multiply by five-sixths, multiply by four-fifths; how many have the result?

18.

Example 5th. Take eight, divide by four-fifths, divide by five-sixths, divide by six-sevenths, divide by seven-eighths. How many have the result?

19.

Example 6th. A monkey started up a mast sixty feet high; he ran up twenty feet, down eight feet, up fifteen feet, up seventeen feet, up six feet, jumped up five feet, and where was he?

20.

The variations of random exercises are, of course, endless. They serve for variety, and if properly managed will arouse any desirable amount of enthusiasm in a class. They should not, however, be relied on, to any great extent, as a means of suitable training, in Mental Arithmetic.

I will give one more example, involving a few contractions, which may be reached by the class in the appropriate successive drills on each contraction.

21.

EXAMPLE IN CONTRACTIONS.

Take eighteen, multiply by five, multiply by twenty-five, multiply by ten, take the square root, add ten, multiply by twelve and a half, divide by thirty-three and a third, multiply by ten, divide by sixteen and two-thirds, and what is the result?

Explanation. $18\times5=18\times\frac{10}{2}=90$, $90\times25=90\times\frac{100}{4}=2250$. $160\times12\frac{1}{2}=160\times\frac{100}{8}=2000$, $2000\div33\frac{1}{3}=2000\times\frac{3}{100}=60$, $60\times10=600$. $600\div16\frac{2}{3}=600\times\frac{6}{100}=$ **36.**

METHODS OF TEACHING WRITTEN ARITHMETIC.

PRELIMINARY REMARKS.

22.

Remark 1*st*. Written Arithmetic should be commenced with Mental Arithmetic. Scholars in Mental Arithmetic should be provided with slates, and they should be permitted to work out the examples, *while studying them*, on the slate. They should also be required to work them on the slate or blackboard *after* having solved them mentally.

23.

Remark 2*d*. In the management of a large class in Written Arithmetic, the principal difficulty to be overcome is that of reaching *all* the schol ars at *every* recitation. Unless this is done scholars are liable to remit their efforts, especially on such days as they may think the chances are against their being called on to recite.

This difficulty must be met, if possible, and every scholar must know that he will be held responsible at every recitation, for a thorough preparation of all the lesson. If in the division of time among the several classes it shall be found impossible to give time enough to Arithmetic, to reach every scholar, in each recitation, it will be better to have the recitation every other day, and the Grammar recitation every alternate day. Thus double the amount of time could be had for each recitation in these two leading subjects, by having them occur only half as often. By proper management in the use of blackboards and slates, every scholar in the largest class may be reached.

24.

Remark 3*d*. The blackboard should be sufficiently capacious, if possible, to accommodate all the class at once. To this end all the space on the walls of the room not taken up by windows and doors, to the height of six or seven feet, should be occupied by blackboard. It is sufficient to paint a hard firm wall that is laid on brick. If laid on lath, it should first be covered with the thickest, firmest wall paper that can be had, and then painted black. If, then, there is not room enough to accommodate all the scholars at the same time, those who cannot find room on the board for working examples, can work them on their slates as they sit on the recitation seats; and the teacher can pass around and look over the work of each scholar as often as a new example has been assigned and wrought.

25.

Remark 4*th*. In the earlier steps, especially, it is better to give the same example to all the class, to work simultaneously. But in review lessons, and in a more advanced class, it is better to assign different examples to each pupil, unless some examples more difficult than others should be assigned to several different pupils, or to all of them.

26.

Remark 5th. Some teachers think it necessary that scholars should understand the reasons of every rule, before they are permitted to use it in working out examples. This is plausible, but will be found to work badly. It is better, generally, for scholars to learn the practical working of a rule first, and thus have their curiosity excited to *inquire* why they have to do so and so, as the rule directs, to obtain the result; rather than to force the reasons upon them before they have any desire to know them. With a few of the quicker scholars, the latter plan will work well enough; but with the majority of most classes the former course is decidedly preferable. There is no trouble in feeding a hungry child, but the same food only disgusts him when he has no appetite. First excite the desire to know; then administer to the mind's cravings.

27.

Remark 6th. It hardly seems desirable to me to require scholars to give arithmetical rules precisely in the language of the book. I prefer that they should *describe the processes* in their own language; a rule in Arithmetic being "a description of a process for obtaining a required result." It is more necessary, perhaps, to require the rules verbatim from beginners.

28.

Remark 7th. Books without answers are preferable, for the reason that a strong temptation is removed to copy the answers from the book without solving the questions; for the reason also that scholars are more self-relying, and are made, by this means, better practical reckoners and accountants. If answers are not desirable in Mental Arithmetic, why in Written?

29.

Remark 8th. I would, if possible, avoid any text book in Arithmetic or Algebra which has a printed key in market. Keys are paralyzers, nuisances, and the teacher should be particularly watchful that keys are not resorted to by pupils in any of his classes.

30.

Remark 9th. The skilful teacher will always prepare his class for any difficulty which may meet them in the advance lesson. He may explain the difficulty orally; he may solve an example, not in the book, which shall meet the difficulty; he may give the class a preliminary drill on a rule, or on a series of more difficult examples under any rule, or in miscellaneous examples under a number of rules. Such preparation, judiciously given, more than anything else, is calculated to keep up the ambition of *all* a class, by removing all excuses for laziness and discouragement.

31.

Remark 10th. Small scholars should be required to bring their examples, wrought on slates or on paper, to the recitation, which the teacher will examine, as the FIRST STEP in every recitation. This will not prevent their working them again during the recitation.

32.

Remark 11th. The manner of conducting different recitations in Written Arithmetic are so similar that I shall give but two Lessons—as examples.

33.

PRIMARY LESSON.

FIRST STEP—THE TEACHER EXAMINES THE SLATE or paper of each pupil, to determine how much of the lesson assigned has been prepared, and how well the work has been executed. He points out the errors as he proceeds, giving as much encouragement in every case as possible, and as little censure.

SECOND STEP—RECITATION OF RULES OR TABLES assigned for the lesson.

THIRD STEP—WORKING THE EXAMPLES on the slates or blackboard. As in few schools there is blackboard enough to accommodate all the scholars, they will be called up in sections to the board without books, and will follow the orders of the teacher.

34.

Order 1st.—Prepare the board. This is done by erasing any former work, and dividing the board by vertical lines into equal spaces for each scholar. Each scholar draws a line at his right.

Order 2d.—Write the example. The teacher then dictates the example and all write it, both those at the board, on the board; and those on the recitation seat, on their slates.

Order 3d.—Perform the example. The teacher now has opportunity to note the readiness and correctness of each pupil in his work as he proceeds, whether at the board, or on the seat; or the failure or errors of any, or their inclination to copy from others' work.

Order 4th. James, you may explain your work. James proceeds to explain the example as he has solved it; and the teacher, at any error, either in the work or in the explanation, looks for the raising of hands by other members of the class, and if no pupil notices the error, he calls attention to it by the question, Why do you thus? or by any other that the case may require. When James has concluded his explanation, the class is called on for criticisms. After these are settled, the teacher may inquire, "How many understand James' explanation?" Hands rise. "How many do not understand the example?" If hands rise he may call on James again to explain the example, or on some other pupil, or he may explain it himself.

Order 5th.—Be seated.

35.

The teacher then calls up another section, and proceeds in a similar manner with them in the working of another example; and so on till the time has expired, or so far expired that he can only have time for the fourth step.

FOURTH STEP—PRELIMINARY EXPLANATION AND DRILL for the next lesson.

36.

ADVANCED LESSON.

Remark. The same course may be pursued with an advanced class as that described for a primary class, or the following method may be used.

FIRST STEP. *Teacher.*—Any who have reports to give may prepare their work on the board.

Scholars, then, to whom any classification, demonstration, or explanation was assigned at any previous recitation, for this recitation, take their places at the board and make any necessary preparation, as writing out the classification or work necessary for a demonstration.

SECOND STEP—RECITATION OF RULES OR TABLES by the rest of the class.

THIRD STEP—SCHOLARS AT THE BOARD GIVE THE DEMONSTRATION; and the same order of criticism from the class and from the teacher, as was described in the Primary Lesson, is pursued.

37.

FOURTH STEP—WORKING THE EXAMPLES. The course to be pursued is the same as described in the Primary Lesson, except that it will be found necessary to give each pupil a different example. These may be assigned by number to each pupil, he having the book in hand from which to take his data.

FIFTH STEP—THE EXPLANATION OF EXAMPLES. It is supposed that the teacher, in a preliminary drill has himself explained the working of the rule; and demonstrated the principles on which its different points are based. In this stage of the recitation, one pupil is called for the demonstration of one principle in connection with his example; and another for the demonstration of the same principle or another in connection with the explanation of his example. All under the same course of criticism, from other scholars and teacher, as has been before described.

SIXTH STEP—PRELIMINARY EXPLANATION AND DRILL **for next recitation.**

THEORETICAL ARITHMETIC.

38.

Remark. Instead of presenting the method of teaching Theoretical Arithmetic, I shall give a condensed view of the subject itself; leaving it for the teacher to apply the METHODS before described for Grammar and Geography.

I.—ARITHMETIC.

- **History,**
  - Ancient,
    - Euclid, B. C. 300, Greek Notation.
    - Archimedes, B. C. 250, Greek Notation.
    - Diophantes, A. D. 250, " "
  - Modern,
    - Lucca de Borga, A. D. 1484, Arabic Notation.
    - Nicholas Pike, A. D. 1776, " "
    - Daniel Adams, A. D. 1801, " "
    - Warren Colburn, A. D. 1825, Mental Arith'c.
- **Terms,**
  - Definition, Solution, Rule, Demonstration, { direct. / indirect.
  - Proposition { Problem, Corollary, Scholium, Lemma. / Theorem.
  - Hypotheses, Axiom, Discussion.
  - Unit, Quantity, { Magnitude. / Multitude.
  - Numbers
    - { Integral, / Fractional, } { Abstract, / Concrete, } { Even, / Odd, } { Simple, / Comp'nd.
    - { Cardinal, / Ordinal, } { Prime, / Composite, } { Rational. / Surd. }
- **Classes,**
  - As to uses:—Abstract, Applied.
  - As to characters:—Particular, General.
  - As to operation:—Mental, Written, Theoretical.
- **Divisions,**
  - Preliminaries { Notation, / Numeration.
  - Fundamental Operations,
    - Addition, / Multiplication, } Increase.
    - Subtraction, / Division, } Diminution.
  - Applications,
    - 1 Comp. Numbers, 2 Com. Fractions, 3 Decimals, 4 Ratio and Proportion, 5 Percentage, 6 Partnership, 7 Allegation, 8 Exchange, 9 Partnership, 10 Involution, 11 Evolution, 12 Mensuration, 13 Analysis.

39.

DEFINITIONS, EXPLANATIONS AND REMARKS.

ARITHMETIC. The Science of Numbers

HISTORY. Notice of the most prominent writers, and of the progress of the Science of Arithmetic.

ANCIENT HISTORY. That which applies to time previous to A. D. 1400.

MODERN HISTORY. That which applies to time subsequent to A. D., 1400.

EUCLID was the first writer on Mathematics whose works have come down to us. He wrote on Geometry and Optics, as well as on Arithmetic. He established a school for Mathematics at Alexandria in Egypt, which Ptolemy Lagus, the Egyptian Monarch, attended. When the pupil inquired of Euclid, if there was no easier method of learning Mathematics, Euclid replied, "There is no royal road to Geometry."

Although he was the first writer on Mathematics, he was indebted to Thales and Pythagoras, celebrated teachers, for much contained in his works.

ARCHIMEDES flourished in Syracuse. He made many discoveries in Mathematics, and inventions in Mechanics. One of the former was the ratio of the cylinder to the inscribed sphere; one of the latter was an arrangement of mirrors by which he set the Roman fleet on fire. He also discovered the means of obtaining the specific gravity of bodies. Several fragments of his writings are extant, but nothing on Arithmetic.

Diophantus flourished at Alexandria. The time at which he wrote is not definitely known. But his works remain, both on Arithmetic and Algebra. He was the first writer on Algebra.

Lucca de Borga is worthy of note, as being the first European writer who made use of the Arabic Notation.

40.

Definition. Such a description of an object as includes everything of the kind, and excludes everything else.

Solution. A process by which a required result is obtained.

Rule. A description of a general process for obtaining a required result.

Demonstration. A course of reasoning by which the propriety of a Rule is made obvious; also a course of reasoning by which a proposed truth is established.

Direct Demonstration. One that commences with known truths; and by a course of reasoning establishes the proposed truth.

Indirect Demonstration. One which assumes the proposed truth to be false, and then proves that an absurdity will result from the assumption. This is also called a Reductio ad absurdum.

Proposition. That which requires a solution, or a demonstration.

Problem. A question proposed for solution.

Theorem. A truth requiring a demonstration to establish it.

Corollary. A truth deduced from a preceding proposition.

Scholium. A remark on a preceding proposition, showing its application, restriction, or extension.

Lemma. A subsidiary proposition.

Hypothesis. A supposition made either in the statement or demonstration of a proposition.

Axiom. A self-evident truth.

Discussion. A course of investigation by which the properties, relations, and applications of any number, proposition, or rule, are demonstrated.

41.

Quantity. That which can be increased, diminished, or measured.

Magnitude. Undivided Quantity; also that form of quantity which answers the question, How much?

Multitude. Quantity made up of distinct parts; also that form of quantity which answers the question, How many?

Unit. A single thing, either a whole or a part.

Number. One, or more, or less; also an expression for Quantity.

Integral Number. An expression for one or more whole or entire units.

Fractional Number. An expression for one part of a unit, or more than one equal parts of a unit.

Abstract Number. A number taken without reference to substance, time, space, or their properties.

CONCRETE NUMBER. A number applied to substance, time, space, or their properties.

EVEN NUMBER. One which can be divided by two without a fractional quotient.

ODD NUMBER. One which cannot be divided by two without a fractional quotient.

SIMPLE NUMBER. One in which the units expressed, are all of the same value.

COMPOUND NUMBER. One in which the units expressed are of different values.

CARDINAL NUMBER. One used to denote multitude, or how many.

ORDINAL NUMBER. One used to denote the order or rank of an object.

PRIME NUMBER. An integral number which can be divided by no other integral number than itself and unity without a fractional quotient.

Remark. There is no term in Mathematics which has had so many bungling, worthless definitions, as this.

Ray's definition: "A prime number is one that can only be exactly divided by itself and unity." Since every number can be exactly divided by every other, with either an integral or fractional quotient, there is no prime number according to this definition.

Again, in Ray's Higher Arithmetic, we find this: "A prime number is one that can be exactly divided by no other whole number but itself and unity." Since every whole number will exactly divide every other number whether fractional or integral, there can be no prime number according to this definition; moreover, the grammatical sequence of *but* to *other*, is, to say the least, inharmonious.

Again, Thompson's definition is still worse: "A prime number is one which cannot be produced by multiplying any two or more numbers together, or which cannot be exactly divided by any whole number except a unit and itself." Since every number can be produced by multiplying itself by unity, or some integral number by some fractional number, there is no prime number according to Thompson.

Loomis' definition involves the same absurdity.

Leach & Swan's definition is passable.

Davies' definition is the best, most simple and concise

Rational Number. One whose exact root can be expressed by figures.

Surd Number. One whose exact root cannot be expressed by figures.

42.

Classes. Results of arrangement according to a given plan.

Abstract Arithmetic. That form of Arithmetic which makes use of abstract numbers.

Applied Arithmetic. That form of Arithmetic which makes use of concrete numbers.

Remark. Book-keeping and Mensuration may be mentioned as examples of Applied Arithmetic.

Particular Arithmetic. That form of Arithmetic which makes use of figures to express particular values.

General Arithmetic. That form of Arithmetic which makes use of letters to express general values. It is also called Algebra.

Mental Arithmetic. That form of Arithmetic in which the operations are carried on entirely in the mind, without the use of visible characters.

Written Arithmetic. That form of Arithmetic in which the operations are carried on by the aid of visible characters.

Theoretical Arithmetic. That form of Arithmetic which investigates principles, and demonstrates rules; also, that gives a clear, connected, and systematized arrangement of all the principles and rules involved in the subject.

43.

Preliminaries. Preparatory processes.

FUNDAMENTAL OPERATIONS. Processes on which all others are based; or those without which no others can be performed.

APPLICATIONS. All other processes than the preliminary and fundamental.

44.

II.—NOTATION.

- Signs,
  - of Operation
    - Increase $+$, $\times$, ab $(\ )^n$
    - Diminution $-$ $\div$ $\frac{a}{b}$, a)b(, $\sqrt[n]{\ }$
  - of Relation $=$, :, ::, $>$, $<$.
  - of Deduction $\therefore$,
  - of Aggregation $\overline{\quad}$, ( ), [ ], { }.
- Characters,
  - Roman or Literal,
    - History,
    - Forms, I, V, X, L, C, D, M, —.
    - Origin of each.
    - Ratios of increase, { 2, 5 }
    - Laws of arrangement, { 1, 2, 3 }
  - Arabic or Figural,
    - History,
    - Forms, 1, 2, 3, 4, 5, 6, 7, 8, 9, 0.
    - Classes,
      - Significant, or digits.
      - Zero, cypher, or naught.
      - Separatrix.
    - Origin of each,
    - Radix,
    - Fundamental Law.
    - Value,
      - Simple,
      - Local.

45.

DEFINITIONS, EXPLANATIONS AND REMARKS.

NOTATION. Any visible method of indicating operations or relations; also of expressing quantity.

SIGN. A mark or combination of marks to indicate an operation or relation, deduction or aggregation.

OPERATION. Process involved in a solution.

INCREASE. Augmentation. The act or result of making larger.

DIMINUTION. Decrease. The act or result of making less.

RELATION. Bearing.

46.

The sign + signifies *add to;* and is read, *plus.* It has its origin in the fact that two lines thus placed seem to be the simplest manner of expressing the act of addition.

The sign × signifies *multiply by*, and is read *into.* It has its origin in tallying, or keeping accounts of several successive additions of the same quantity, which consists in crossing obliquely other marks. This is an abridged or simplified form of tallying.

The sign of contiguity, as represented in ab, is used only in letters, or in Algebra.

The sign $()^n$, or the exponent, signifies that the quantity immediately before it, or the quantity contained in the parenthesis to which it is attached, is to be multiplied by itself a number of times, one less, than there are units in the sign.

The sign — signifies *subtract from*, and is read *minus.* It seems to have originated in the sign +; one of the marks having been taken away, suggesting the idea of subtraction; and the mark left, a difference.

The sign ÷ signifies *divide by;* and is read, *divided by.* Its origin is plainly, that of dividing or separating one line into two parts, by the use of another.

The sign $\frac{a}{b}$ signifies *divide by*, or the result of having divided one quantity by another, and is read *over*, as a over b; or in this example, $\frac{17}{13}$, seventeen over thirteen.

The sign a)b(signifies that the quantity at the right of the first curved line is to be divided by the quantity at the left. In Algebra the divisor is placed at the right of the line curving to right.

The sign $\sqrt{}$, or the radical sign, signifies that the square root of the quantity to which it is prefixed, is to be taken. If a figure is placed before the sign, then such a root is to be taken as is indicated by the figure, which is called the index.

47.

The sign = signifies *equality*, and is read, *is equal to.* Its origin is found in the fact that it is the simplest method of expressing to the eye the idea of equality.

The signs $> <$ signify inequality, and are read *is greater than*, and *is less than;* the greater quantity being placed at the opening, and the less at the apex of the angle.

The sign of ratio : is an abridged form of the sign of division. In the French form of writing the ratio, however, the divisor is placed before the sign, and the dividend after it. It is read, *as*, *as*, in the first couplet and *to* in the second.

The sign of proportion : : is an abridged form of the sign of equality; the extremities only of the line being used. It is read *so is*.

The sign of deduction .·. seems to have its origin in the fact that there are three terms in a syllogism; the two first being true the third must follow. It is read *therefore.*

48.

The signs of aggregation are the bar ‾‾, which signifies that the numbers over which it is placed are to be taken together as one number; also, the parenthesis, ( ); the brackets, [ ]; and the braces, { }, which signify that the quantities enclosed by them respectively are to be taken together, as one quantity.

Remark. The use of technicalities not hitherto defined in this work, for the explanation of the signs, is not strictly philosophical; but as this classification is only used in reviews, and as the signs are an inseparable part of Notation, the demands of the case seem to warrant this departure from rigid philosophical usage, in the arrangement.

49.

Characters. Any written or visible forms used to express numbers.

Verbal Characters, or Verbal Notation. Visible words used to express numbers.

Roman Notation. That notation which makes use of seven Capital Letters, to express numbers.

Arabic Notation. That which makes use of ten figures to express numbers; also a separatrix.

50.

History of the Roman Notation. Notwithstanding the Roman alphabet seems to be but a modification of the Greek alphabet, the Romans adopted an entirely different notation for numbers.

While the Greek notation makes use of the letters in their original order and number to express numbers, the Roman notation, in part, seems to have been in use before the Roman people adopted the Greek letters or formed an alphabet at all, as their origin will show. The several capital letters, which more nearly corresponded to the original marks of the notation, were subsequently adopted.

Origin of the Roman Characters. In counting, or in keeping an account, it is obvious that one or more vertical lines is as simple a method as could be adopted for the first few units. The letter I was afterwards used as most nearly resembling such a vertical line.

When the number equal to the fingers and thumbs on both hands had been reached, it was natural and easy to cross the vertical lines signifying ten. In transferring this method of tallying, or of keeping accounts, it was after a while discovered that a simple cross would answer as well as all the marks of the original tally. Hence a cross was adopted for ten, and afterwards an X for the cross.

Either half of the cross was used for five, but the letter V, corresponding to the upper half, was finally adopted.

The initial of Centum, which signifies one hundred, was adopted, after the introduction of the alphabet, to save the trouble of writing ten crosses or X's.

Either half of the letter C in its angular form [

was used to represent fifty; but since the letter L corresponds to the lower half it was finally adopted.

The initial of Mille, which signifies one thousand, was also used to represent one thousand. Following the law of taking halves, a half of this letter was taken for five hundred. It was finally supplanted by the letter D, the letter which seemed most nearly to correspond to it.

Ratio of Increase. From the origin of these characters it is seen that they increase in the alternating ratio of five and two.

Laws of Arrangement. 1st. A letter, not of greater value, being placed after another gives the sum of the values represented by the letters separately.

2d. A letter of less value being placed before another, gives the difference of the values represented by the two letters standing separately.

3d. A horizontal line drawn over any letter or letters increases their value one thousand times.

51.

History of the Arabic Notation. The Arabic figures were introduced into Europe during the tenth century, by the Crusaders. From the Arabic these figures have been traced to the sacred books of the Brahmins in India. The Brahmins claim that they are a gift of the god Brahma. They are probably the invention of some ingenious priest of that heathen deity.

Origin of the Figures. In keeping accounts, one mark would naturally represent one. Two horizontal marks with a connecting line would stand for two, thus: Z. Three horizontal marks with connecting lines would stand for three, thus: 3; and four marks, either arranged in the form of a square or triangle, would stand for four, thus: □, 4. Five marks in this form 5 was the original figure five of this notation. Six marks, thus: 6, the original figure six. The figure eight was made by placing two squares near each other, thus: 8; and seven, by omitting one of these marks, thus: 7; nine by adding one more mark to the figure eight, thus: 9. The zero was originally a circle, and seems to have been suggested from counting *around* the fingers and thumbs, as held in a circular position. Hence once around was denoted by the figure 1, and 0. Twice around by 2 and 0, and so on.

From this last arrangement seems to have been suggested the law of the notation, in which its superior utility consists. For, by placing any other figure in the place of the zero to make the numbers between ten and twenty, we have the law established.

Separatrix. A mark used in the Arabic notation to separate units from tenths, in other words, integers from decimal fractions.

Remark. The separatrix is always written, or supposed to be written, at the right of the unit's place. Though not called a figure, it is still the most important character in the notation.

Radix of the Arabic Notation. The number expressing the number of times the value of any figure is increased or diminished as it is removed one place to the left or right, to or from the separatrix. It is ten.

Fundamental Law of the Arabic Notation. Every significant figure has its value multiplied by ten every time it is removed to the left, towards or away from the separatrix; and divided by ten every time it is removed one place to the right, towards or away from the separatrix.

52.

Remark 1st. Figures at the right of the separatrix express, obviously, by the law of the notation, fractional quantities; as tenths, hundredths, etc. Such figures are called decimal figures, and the quantities expressed by them are called decimals, or decimal fractions.

Remark 2d. The removal of figures is often accomplished relatively by changing the place of the separatrix. This can also be done in whole numbers, by annexing cyphers or other figures; and in the fractional figures by interposing cyphers or other figures between the separatrix and the given figures.

Simple value of a Figure. Its worth when standing in the first place at the left of the separatrix.

Local Value of a Figure. Its simple value multiplied or divided by such a power of ten as is indicated by the order of the place that the figure occupies at the left or right of the place of unity.

53.

III.—NUMERATION.

Orders.—Units, Tens, Hundreds, Thousands, etc.
Periods.—Units, Thousands, Millions, Billions, etc.

Methods,
- National,
  - French.
  - English.
- Practical,
  - Preparatory.
  - Final.
- Derived,
  - by Tens.
  - by Hundreds, etc.

54.

DEFINITIONS, EXPLANATIONS AND REMARKS.

NUMERATION. Any method of expressing the values of figures in words.

ORDERS. Places occupied by the several figures being counted towards the left and right from the separatrix.

UNITS. The first order, at the left of the separatrix; also, the first order of integral numbers or integers.

TENS. The second order of integers.

HUNDREDS. The third order of integers.

TENTHS. The first order at the right of the separatrix; also the first order of decimal fractions.

HUNDREDTHS. The second order of decimal fractions.

PERIODS. Groups of orders, named and used to facilitate numeration.

FRENCH METHOD. That method of numeration in which three orders constitute a period.

ENGLISH METHOD. That in which six orders constitute a period.

Remark. The names of the orders in both methods are the same as far as the ninth, or hundreds of millions; after which they take different names, the tenth being called in the French method, billions, and in the English method, thousands of millions.

55.

Names of the Periods.—1st, Units. 2d, Thousands. 3d, Millions. 4th, Billions. 5th, Trillions. 6th, Quadrillions. 7th, Quintillions. 8th, Sextillions. 9th, Septillions. 10th. Octillions. 11th, Nonillions. 12th, Decillions. 13th, Undecillions. 14th, Duodecillions. 15th, Tridecillions. 16th, Quadrodecillions. 17th, Quindecillions. 18th, Sexdecillions. 19th, Septodecillions. 20th, Octodecillions. 21st, Nonodecillions. 22d, Vingintillions. 23d, Unvingintillions. 24th, Duo-vingintillions, etc. 32d, Trigintillions. 42d, Quadrogintillions. 52d, Quingintillions. 62d, Sexagintillions. 72d, Septuagintillions. 82d, Octogintillions. 92d, Ninogintillions. 102d, Centillions. 103d, Uncentillions. 104th, Duocentillions, etc. 202d, Duocentillions, etc. 1002d, Millillions, etc.

Derived Methods of Reading Numbers. These are readings with the assumption of some other order than units as the base.

Example.—304.06 may be read as tens, thus: thirty tens, and four hundred and six thousandths of a ten. The same number may be read as tenths, thus: three thousand and forty tenths, and six tenths of a tenth.

56.

TOPIC LIST FOR DISCUSSION OF FUNDAMENTAL OPERATION.

1. Definition.
2. Terms, and definitions.
3. Signs—form, signification, reading.
4. Rules, Demonstrations.
5. Proofs, Demonstrations.
6. Comparison with other operations
7. Contractions, Demonstrations.
8. Use of negative quantities.

Remark. The four fundamental operations may each be discussed very thoroughly by following this TOPIC LIST as a guide in the investigation. I shall omit many of the most obvious considerations in my discussion, as these can be obtained from all Arithmetics. Pupils, however, should be required in these discussions to reach every point, whether obvious or obscure.

57.

DISCUSSION OF ADDITION.

5. PROOF 1st. Add the columns downwards.

PROOF 2d. REJECT THE NINES from each quantity, also from these excesses so obtained, also from the sum of the quantities; then, if the excess of the excesses of the several quantities is equal to the excess of the sum of the several quantities, the work is supposed to be right.

Demonstration. Since by the sixth Theorem—Ray's Algebras—the difference of the same powers of any two numbers is divisible without a fractional quotient, by the difference of the numbers, any power of ten, minus any power of one, is divisible by ten minus one. In other words, any power of ten is one greater than a multiple of nine. This may be expressed thus:

$(10)^n - (1)^n$ is divisible by $10-1$ without a fractional quotient, or $(10)^n-1$ is divisible by 9, without a fractional quotient.

But if a unit of any integral order gives one for a remainder, when divided by nine, then any figure in any order will give itself for a remainder when its local value is divided by nine. Hence the figures expressing any integral quantity will express so many remainders, when the quantity is separated into the parts expressed by the local values of the several figures used to express it, and each part is divided by nine. Now if the sum of these figures, or remainders, be divided by nine, the true remainder for the whole quantity will be obtained. Thus, 7896, separated into parts as described, gives

7000	and	7	remainder,
800	and	8	"
90	and	9	"
6	and	6	"

The true remainder from the given quantity is thus obtained by rejecting the nines from these figures, either as they stand in the vertical column or in the given quantity.

58.

One example will suffice to show the process of Rejecting Nines, and of proving addition by this process.

EXAMPLE FOR PROVING ADDITION BY REJECTING NINES.

Quantities,	7896	3	Excesses
	4567	4	
	3864	3	
Sum,	16327	1 final excess,	from the excesses from the sum.

Process. *First quantity.* 6+8=14, which gives 5 as an excess, 5+7=12, which gives 3 as an excess 3 is placed in the column of excesses. It will be noticed that no attention is paid to the figure 9

Second quantity. 7+6=13; 4, excess. It will be noticed that no attention is given to 4 and 5, as they are equal to nine.

Third quantity. 4+6=10; 1, excess. 1+8=9, hence 3 is the excess of the third quantity. Rejecting nine from these excesses, we have 1 for a final excess. Rejecting nine from the sum of the quantities, which is done by simply noticing that 7+2=9 and 3+6=9, 1 remains as the excess of the sum of the quantities. This being equal to the final excess of the quantities as before obtained, the work is supposed to be right.

The concluding link in the chain of demonstration is this: Since we have found the remainders of the several quantities, when divided by nine, to give a final remainder equal to the remainder from the sum of the several quantities, the sum is supposed to be correct.

Remark 1st. Any other figure would answer as well as 9 for this form of proof, save that 9 gives us its remainder more readily by this method of *rejection*, than other figures would their remainder, by the process of DIVISION.

Remark 2d. This property of nine, viz.: that it will *divide any number with the same remainder, as that which the sum of the figures, expressing the number gives, when divided by nine*, results obviously from its being one less than the radix of the notation. If the radix were eight, seven would have the same property.

59.

PROOF 3d. REJECT THE ELEVENS from difference of the sums of the alternate figures in the several quantities; also from the difference of the sums of the alternate figures in the sum of the several quantities; then if the excess of the excesses, from the several quantities, is equal to the excess of the sum of the quantities, the work is supposed to be right.

Demonstration. By theorem 8th, Ray's Algebras, the sum of the same odd powers of two quantities is divisible without a fractional quotient by the sum of the quantities. Hence $(10)^n+1^n$ is divisible by $10+1$, or 11, when n is an odd number. Then $10+1$, $1000+1$, $100,000+1$, etc., are divisible by 11; in other words, the odd powers of ten lack one of being divisible by 11, or give —1 for a remainder. If the figure 1 in all the odd places taken in its local values gives —1 for remainders, then any other figure will give itself with the minus sign for a remainder,—i. e., as 10, 1000, 100,000, or any other odd power of 10 gives —1 for remainders. 20, 2000, 200,000, etc., will give —2 for remainders, when divided by 11. Hence every figure in any odd place may be taken with the minus sign, for the remainder, when its own local value is divided by 11.

In a similar manner, by Theorem 7th, Ray's Algebras, it may be proved that each figure in the even places will give itself with the plus sign for a remainder, when its local value is divided by 11.

Now if the *sums* of these two series of remainders are equal to each other, they will cancel each other, and there will be no remainder when the quantity which the figures express is divided by 11; or if these sums are not equal, their difference gives the same remainder as the quantity which they express gives when divided by 11. If there should be an excess of the negative figures, the true remainder will be obtained by subtracting that excess from 11. Such being the case, we can add the two sums of alternate figures, and find the difference of the two sums, remembering that the series of figures in the odd places give minus remainders.

This process is much abridged, by subtracting the left hand figure of each quantity from the next, and the resulting remainder, from the next figure, and so on. The final remainder will always be the remainder with the proper signs.

60.

EXAMPLE FOR PROVING ADDITION BY THE REJECTION OF ELEVENS.

Quantities,	7896	—2	Excesses.
	58731	+2	
	206	+8	
	41	—3	
Sum,	66874	5 final excess,	from excesses / from the sum

Taking the first quantity: 8—7=1, 9—1=8, 6—8=—2 the excess.

Taking the second quantity. 8—5=3, 7—3=4, 3—4=—1, 1—(—1)=2.

Taking the third quantity: 0—2=—2, 6—(—2) =+8.

Taking the fourth quantity: 1—4=—3.

Then the sum of these excesses, arranged at the right of their respective quantities, is +5.

Taking the sum of the quantities: 6—6=0, 8—0=+8, 7—8=—1, 4—(—1)=+5.

61.

Demonstration of this method of finding the difference of the sums of alternate digits.

Let a, b, c, d=four figures expressing any quantity, including four orders.

Then b—a, c—(a—b) d—[c—(b—a)] will represent the several steps of the subtraction. The last quantity, being reduced, so that each letter shall have its essential sign, and then arranged, the result will be d—c+b—a, which corresponds to the demands of the case.

Again, take an odd number of letters representing the figures standing in the several orders, perform a similar operation, and the result will also correspond with that obtained by subtracting the sum of the figures in the even places from the sum of the figures in the odd places.

Scholium. It will be noticed that in those quantities expressed by an even number of figures, that the process of subtraction must commence at the left, or the excess obtained will be affected with the wrong sign.

62.

Comparison of addition with other fundamental operations.

1st. It is similar to multiplication; both being operations of increase.

2d. It is the opposite of subtraction.

3d. It is the indirect opposite of division.

63.

Contractions. 1st. The addition of two or more columns at once.

2d. Multiplication is but a contraction of addition, in the case in which the quantities to be added are alike.

64.

Use of Negative Quantities.

Remark 1*st.* The Teacher will do well to give his classes practice in the negative quantities under all the fundamental rules.

Remark 2*d.* My limits will not permit the discussion of the other fundamental operations; but the discussion becomes more interesting as the class proceeds, from one to the other, in order.

Remark 3*d.* The contractions in multiplication and division are worthy of close study; and demand thorough demonstration, each of them. Leach & Swan have given a better variety of such contractions than other authors.

65.

COMPOUND NUMBERS.

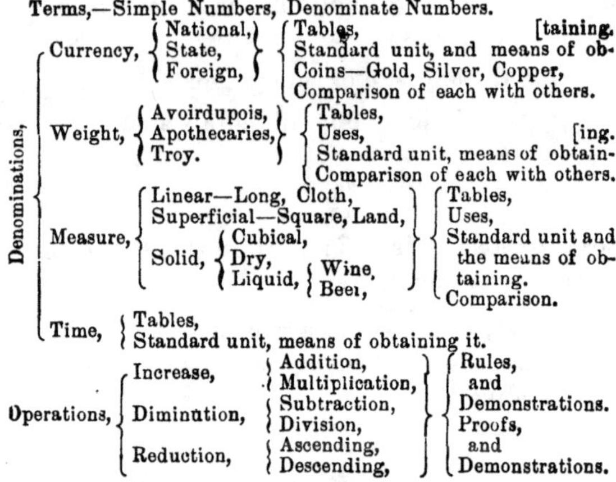

Remark. All the standard units are determined, directly or indirectly, from the length of the day or the time of a revolution of the Earth on its axis, as ascertained by astronomical observation. A pendulum, beating seconds, has a certain length. A linear foot is now determined by the pendulum. Dry and liquid measures are determined by the number of solid feet or inches. A cubic foot of pure water weighs 1000 ounces, and the standard pound is thus determined.

Hence it is seen that any variation in the length of the day will cause a variation in all the denominations, of every kind.

66.

COMMON FRACTIONS.

PRELIMINARIES.

- **Numbers,**
  - Terms—Unit, Integer, Factor, Reciprocal, Root.
  - Classes,
    - Prime, { Absolute, Relative.
    - Composite, { Multiple, Power.
  - Properties,
    - 1, 2, 3, 4, 5, 6, 7, 8, 9, 10, 11, 12.
    - Demonstration of the properties of each number. *Remark.*—Properties, of 9 and 11, depend on their relation to the radix, 10.
- **Factoring,**
  - Rules, { by inspection, by division.
  - Scholium.—Use the primes no further than the square root of the number to be resolved. Demonstration.
- Greatest Common Divisor.
  - Rules for integers, { by primes, by division. Demonstration.
  - Rule for Fractions, { Divide the G. C. D. of numerators by the L. C. M. of denominators. Demonstration.
- Least Common Multiple,
  - Rules for Integers, { by primes, { 1st. 2d. by division, Demonstration.
  - Rule for Fractions, { Divide the L. C. M. of numerators by the G. C. D. of denominators. Demonstration.

ESSENTIALS.

Terms,—Numerator, Denominator.

Classes, { as to value—Proper, Improper, and Mixed Numbers. as to form—Simple, Compound, Complex.

Value, { Equal to, Greater than, Less than } Unity.

Comparison of Fraction with Division, { Numerator=Dividend, Denominator=Divisor, Value=Quotient.

Propositions, 1, 2, 3, 4, 5, 6. Demonstrations.

OPERATIONS.

- Reduction of Fractions of Simple Numbers,
  - Integers or mixed numbers to fractions,
  - Fractions to integers or mixed numbers,
  - Fractions to lower or higher terms,
  - Compound Fractions to Simple,
  - Complex Fractions to Simple,
  - Fractions to equivalent fractions, with C. D.
  - Fractions to eq. Frac. with L. C. D.

- Increase and Diminution,
  - Addition,—Subtraction.
  - Multiplication and Division,
    - Integers by fractions,
    - Fractions by integers,
    - Fractions by fractions,
    - Mixed No. by Mixed No.
- Reduction of Fractions of Compound Numbers.
  - Fract. of one denomination to frac. of another,
  - Integers of different denominations to fraction of higher denominations,
  - Fractions of higher denomination to integers of lower denomination,
  - Quantity of several denominations to fraction of another quantity.

67.

DEFINITIONS, EXPLANATIONS AND REMARKS.

A Common Fraction. A Fraction whose numerator and denominator are both expressed

Preliminaries. Preparatory steps.

Terms. Words not otherwise introduced in the classification.

Unit. One, either integral or fractional.

Integer. A whole number, or a number con sisting only of entire units.

Factor of a Number. A divisor which gives an integral quotient.

Remark. Factors are more generally considered integers, unless otherwise designated.

Reciprocal of a Number. The result of dividing unity by that number. This result is said to be the reciprocal of the given number.

Remark. The reciprocal of a number may be obtained by changing it to the fractional form, if it be a mixed or integral number, and then inverting the fraction.

Root of a Number. Any factor, whether fractional or integral, which being multiplied by itself shall produce a given number. *Explanation.* Such a factor of a number is called, if multiplied into itself once, its square root; twice, its cube root; thrice, its fourth root; and so on.

Classes. Results of arrangement according to some given plan.

Prime Number. Any integer which can only be divided by itself and unity without a fractional quotient.

Absolute Prime. The same as a prime.

Relative Primes. Integers which have no common integral factor, save unity.

Composite Number. Any integer resulting from the product of other integers than itself and unity.

Multiple of a Number. Any product, which results from taking a given number, either fractional or integral, an integral number of times. Such product is called a multiple of the given number.

Power of a Number. The result of taking a number a given number of times as a factor.

Explanation. A number taken once as a factor, is the number itself, and is the first power. A number taken twice as a factor, is multiplied, or is to be multiplied into itself once, and is the second power. A number taken three times as a factor is the third power, and so on. The nought power of every number is unity, or the result of dividing a number by itself.

Remark. Pupils should be well drilled in primes and their powers before commencing the study of the Least Common Multiple. It is a good plan for the teacher to call for the primes, in concert, from the class, and to notice which of the class can go the farthest in giving them. It is well for the class to give each prime twice in the concert exercise, that the slower pupils may learn them. The powers of the smaller primes should be learned by a similar method. No pupil should be permitted to do anything with Least Common Multiples till he thoroughly understands the nature of primes and powers.

68.

PROPERTIES OF NUMBERS.

1 is the nought power of every number.

1 is any power of itself.

1 is any root of itself.

1, used as a multiplier, does not increase the multiplicand.

1, used as a divisor, does not diminish the dividend.

2 is a factor of any integral number whose unit figure is divisible by 2, without a fractional quotient.

Demonstration. Every integral number expressed by more than one figure is made up of tens and units. The tens are divisible by 2; if the unit figure is also divisible by two without a fractional quotient, then the whole number is divisible by 2.

3 will divide any number without a fractional quotient, the sum of whose figures it will divide in the same manner.

Explanation. The figures of any number are the figures used in writing the number.

Remark. This property of three depends on its being a factor of 9.

Remark. The properties of the other numbers are discussed in most Arithmetics, and my limits forbid my pursuing them further.

The properties of nine and eleven, however, are discussed in section 58, page 310.

FACTORING. The process of separating numbers into their prime factors.

Remark. Long and numerous drills must be given in factoring before commencing the study of the Greatest Common Divisor, and Least Common Multiple. The teacher will commence such drills by giving small numbers, and requiring the class to separate them by the mental process, and to give what power of each prime factor is contained in each given number.

69.

DEMONSTRATION OF SCHOLIUM. Since every divisor smaller than the square root of a number, must give a quotient larger than the square root, and every divisor larger than the square root must give a quotient smaller; if every prime number smaller than the square root proves not to be a factor, no prime number larger can be, for the reason, as before stated, that it must give as a quotient one of the primes less than the root, which is impossible; as they have already been tried, and found not to be factors.

70.

Demonstration of Rule by division for finding the Greatest Common Divisor.

The G. C. D. of two numbers must be the same as that of the smaller number and the remainder after the smaller number has been taken out of the larger number as many times as possible.

Illustration. Take the two lines A——B C——|——|E——D, apply the shorter to the longer; it is evident that after the shorter shall have been applied to the longer as many times as possible, that the greatest common divisor or measure of the two lines A B, and C D, must also divide or measure the difference E D, after it has exactly measured the line C E, which is but the line A B, repeated on the line C D.

Since then the G. C. D. of the remainder after division of the larger number by the smaller, is the same as that of the two given numbers, if this remainder is not itself the G. C. D., it may be taken out of the smaller as many times as possible, and then the G. C. D. of what remains after this second division will be the G. C. D. of the less of the given numbers and the remainder, and if so, then of the two given numbers. This process of dividing the last divisor by the last remainder must evidently be continued till there is no remainder, then the last remainder, which is also the last divisor, is the G. C. D. of the two given numbers.

71.

RULES FOR OBTAINING L. C. M. BY PRIMES.

1st. Multiply together the highest powers of each of the prime factors contained in any of the given quantities.

Demonstration. The L. C. M. is the product of the highest powers of each of the prime factors, found in any of the given quantities; for it must contain as many of each kind of prime factor as any number contains, or it would be impossible to divide by that number. No more factors of any one kind can be taken out the L. C. M. than it contains; but if any given number should contain more of such factors than the L. C. M., in attempting to divide the L. C. M. by such a number it would be attempting to take out more of one kind of prime factor than the L. C. M. contains, which would be impossible. Nor should the L. C. M. contain more of any one kind of prime factor than the largest number of such prime factor contained in any one of the given quantities, as such would obviously be superfluous.

2d. Take the largest of the given numbers, multiply it by such factors contained in the other numbers as are not provided for in the largest number, or by factors already taken from other numbers.

Example. 12, 18, 20, 24, 50.

By the first rule, 8 is the highest power of 2 contained in any of the given numbers, nine is the highest power of three, 25 the highest power of 5 and there are no other prime factors in the numbers, save 1, which does not affect the L. C. M Hence $8\times9\times25=1800$, =L. C. M., for it contains all the 2's in all the numbers, since it contains as many as there are in 24, which contains more than any other. So also 1800 contains all the 3's since it contains as many as 18, which has more than any other. So also of the 5's in 50. By the second rule I take 50, which contains one 2 and two 5's, but 24 contains three 2's as factors, hence two of them are not provided for in 50, but must be by multiplying 50 by 4. Again, the 3 in 24 is not yet provided for; this must also be multiplied into the former product of 50 and 4. All the factors of 20 are provided for, but 18 has two 3's, and as only one 3 has as yet been put into the L. C. M., another must be multiplied into it. Hence we now have for the L. C. M., $50\times4\times3\times3=1800$.

2nd Example. 20, 30, 40, 50, 60.

By the first rule we have $8\times3\times25=600$=L. C. M.

By the second rule we have $60\times5\times2=600$=L. C. M.

3d Example. 24, 34, 44, 54.

By the first rule we have $8\times27\times11\times17$=L. C. M.

By the second rule we have $54\times2\times11\times17\times2$ =L. C. M.

4th Example. 23, 33, 43, 53.

By the first rule we have $3\times11\times23\times43\times53$= L. C. M.

By the second rule we have $53\times43\times3\times11\times23$ $=$L. C. M.

72.

Demonstration of the rule for obtaining the L. C. M. by division.

Take the numbers 6, 8, 9, 12, 15, 18, 20, 24, 25; divide these by 2, and we shall obtain the quotients and undivided numbers, 3, 4, 9, 6, 15, 9, 10, 12, 25. Now this divisor 2 will answer for all the first powers of 2 contained in any of the given numbers; consequently those first powers of 2 are all rejected, and this divisor 2 is retained for them in the L. C. M.

Dividing again by 2 we shall obtain the quotients and undivided numbers, 3, 2, 9, 3, 15, 9, 5, 6, 25. This second divisor 2 will answer for all the second factors of 2 in any of the given numbers. It is therefore retained, as a factor of the L. C. M. Dividing again by 2 we obtain 3, 1, 9, 3, 15, 9, 5, 3, 25. This third divisor 2 answers for all the third factors of 2 contained in any given numbers. Hence it is obvious that dividing by the several prime factors as long as two or more of the given numbers can be divided without a fractional quotient, is merely for the purpose of rejecting superfluous factors, and retaining the necessary factors, for the L. C. M.

Remark. How much easier and shorter is the process of selecting the necessary factors according to Rules 1st or 2nd than to reject the unnecessary factors, according to the Rule, by division. According to Rule 1st the necessary factors are 8×9

$\times 25=1800$. According to Rule 2d they are $25\times 8\times 9=1800$. The L. C. M. is thus obtained at a glance, with scarcely any effort.

Remark. The skillful teacher will not permit his pupils to learn the Rule by division at all; or, if they have already learned it, he will drill them on the other rules till they will be glad to let it alone.

73.

ESSENTIALS.

TERMS OF A FRACTION. The numbers used to express it.

NUMERATOR. That term of a fraction which is written above the line, and expresses the number of parts taken, by the fraction.

DENOMINATOR. That term of a fraction which is written under the line, and shows the number of parts into which the unit of which the fraction expresses a part, is taken. It also names the parts taken.

74.

PROPOSITIONS.

1. Multiplying the numerator multiplies the fraction.
2. Multiplying the denominator divides the fraction.
3. Multiplying both terms by the same number, does not alter the value of the fraction.
4. Dividing the numerator divides the fraction.
5. Dividing the denominator multiplies the fraction.

6. Dividing both terms by the same number does not alter the value of the fraction.

DEMONSTRATIONS.

Prop. 1. Because it increases the number of parts while their size remains the same.

Prop. 2. Because it diminishes the size of the parts while their number remains the same; and it diminishes the parts, because the unit is thus divided into a greater number of parts, and of course each part becomes as many times less, as the divisor is times greater.

Prop. 3. Because it increases the number of parts, as many times as it diminishes their size.

Prop. 4. Because it diminishes the number of parts while their size remains the same.

Prop. 5. Because it increases the size of the parts while the number remains the same; and it increases the size of the parts because the unit is thus divided into a less number of parts; each part being as many times greater as the divisor is times less.

Prop. 6. Because it diminishes the number of the parts as many times as it increases their size.

75.

Reduction. Change of form without changing the value.

Remark. From want of room I shall only discuss a few of the operations of fractions; and those, to show the application of the propositione in their demonstrations.

REDUCTION OF FRACTIONS TO LOWER TERMS

Demonstration, Prop. 6.

REDUCTION OF FRACTIONS TO HIGHER TERMS.

Demonstration, Prop. 3.

REDUCTION OF COMPOUND FRACTIONS TO SIMPLE.

Demonstration. Take $\frac{3}{4}$ of $\frac{5}{6}$.

Since multiplication is taking one number as many times as there are units or parts of a unit in another, taking $\frac{3}{4}$ of $\frac{5}{6}$ is a case of multiplication; hence may be expressed thus: $\frac{3}{4}\times\frac{5}{6}$. Then 3 times $\frac{5}{6}$ (Prop. 1,) is $\frac{15}{6}$, but since the multiplier is $\frac{1}{4}$ of 3, this product is four times too large, and must be divided by 4. But (Prop. 2,) $\frac{15}{6}\div4=\frac{15}{24}$. By observing the two operations it is seen that the numerators have been multiplied together for a new numerator, and the denominators for a new denominator. Hence the ordinary rule is demonstrated.

76

Remark 1. Reduction of Complex Fractions to Simple is demonstrated in a similar manner, after having first shown that it is a case of division.

Remark 2d. In examining classes this may be considered a test question, "Why does dividing the denominator multiply the fraction?" Such an answer as this is often given, "Because it shows that the fraction is divided into a less number of parts;" or this, "Because it increases the parts:' or this, "Because the number of the parts is less, therefore they must be greater." All these answers are worthless, the latter, which is more frequently given, is absurd. This answer may be given, Because by dividing the denominator we divide the *unit* of which the fraction expresses a part, into a less number of parts: consequently, each one of the parts is of greater value.

Remark. The analytical method of demonstrating the operations of fractions should not be neglected. I will give one example of this method in division. Divide $\frac{3}{4}$ by $\frac{5}{6}$.

$1 \div 1 = 1$. $1 \div \frac{1}{6} = 6$. $\frac{1}{4} \div \frac{1}{6} = \frac{6}{4}$. $\frac{3}{4} \div \frac{1}{6} = \frac{3 \times 6}{4} = \frac{18}{4}$. $\frac{3}{4} \div \frac{5}{6} = \frac{18}{4} \div 5 = \frac{18}{4 \times 5} = \frac{18}{20}$. By noticing the last steps of this process it is seen that they correspond to the ordinary rule for the division of one fraction by another; viz: Invert the divisor and proceed as in multiplication.

77.

Remark 3d. The division of a mixed number by a mixed number without reducing them to improper fractions gives an excellent drill, and should not be omitted. Such an example as this for instance, $19\frac{8}{9})3994\frac{2}{5}($, involves a difficulty that few scholars will surmount without help; for, in performing the division it is found that the divisor is not contained twice in 39, and if it is assumed that it is contained once the second partial quotient is 10. The difficulty may be overcome in two ways; first assume that the divisor is contained twice in $39 + \frac{9}{10}$, which assumption holds, as the second nine is $\frac{9}{10}$ of a unit standing in the place of the first nine. Secondly, assume that it is contained once in 39, thus making the first quotient figure 1, then the second partial quotient will be 10; the first figure of which being added to the former figure makes the first figure of the quotient 2, as before. The second quotient figure will be 0.

It is not claimed that this method of dividing one mixed number by another, is of any practical value in business operations; only, that it gives a clearer view of the theory of the Arabic Notation; and that it affords the means for an excellent drill in a class of apt scholars.

Remark 4th. In reducing a fraction of a larger denomination to integers of lower denominations, a course is too often pursued which involves absurdity in the notation. For instance, if $\frac{3}{7}$ of a mile is to be reduced to integers, the work is generally performed thus, $\frac{3}{7}$m$\times 8 = \frac{24}{7}$fur.$= 3\frac{3}{7}$ fur.$\times 40 = \frac{120}{7}$ rods$= 17\frac{1}{7}$ rods$\times 16\frac{1}{2} = \frac{16\frac{1}{2}}{7}$ ft.$= 2\frac{2\frac{1}{2}}{7}$ ft.$\times 12 = \frac{30}{7}$ inches$= 4\frac{2}{7}$ inches.

This is plainly a string of absurdities; for 8 times $\frac{3}{7}$ of a mile is $\frac{24}{7}$ of a mile, and not $\frac{24}{7}$ of a furlong. Again, $3\frac{3}{7}$ fur.$\times 40$ is not equal to $\frac{120}{7}$ rods, but is equal to $120 + \frac{120}{7}$ furlongs.

A better method is this: $\frac{3}{7}$m$= \frac{24}{7}$ fur.$= 3\frac{3}{7}$ fur., $\frac{3}{7}$ fur.$= \frac{120}{7}$ rod$= 17\frac{1}{7}$ rods, $\frac{1}{7}$ rod$= \frac{16\frac{1}{2}}{7}$ ft.$= 2\frac{2\frac{1}{2}}{7}$ ft., $\frac{2\frac{1}{2}}{7}$ ft.$= \frac{30}{7}$ inch$= 4\frac{2}{7}$ inches; then $\frac{3}{7}$ mile$=3$ furlongs, 17 rods, 2 feet, $4\frac{2}{7}$ inches.

Remark 5th. Nearly every operation in fractions admits of several different methods; that of dividing one fraction by another admits of at least twenty different methods. It is an excellent plan to propose to a class to bring out all the different methods which they can discover or invent for each operation; also the demonstrations for the several methods.

78.

DECIMAL FRACTIONS.

Terms—Separatrix, Price, Cost, Quantity, Unity.

- Preliminaries,
  - Notation—Rule.
  - Numeration—Rule.
- Classed,
  - Terminal,
    - Origin,
    - No. of figures—method of determining.
  - Circulating,
    - Origin,
    - Notation, Rule,
    - Numeration, Rule,
    - Value: how determined,
    - Classes,
      - Pure, / Mixed, — Single, / Double, etc.
      - Repetends,
        - Imperfect,
        - Perfect, — 1st, 2d, 3d, 4th. — Properties,
- Operations,
  - Reduction of Fractions of Simple Nos.
    - Com. to Dec.
    - Dec. to Com.
    - Decimal to lower terms,
    - Decimal to higher terms.
  - Increase—Addition, Multiplication, / Diminution—Subtraction, Division, — Rules, / Demonstration,
  - Reduction of Fractions of Compound Numbers,
    - Decimal of higher denomination to integers of lower,
    - Integers of lower denomination to decimal of higher,
    - One quantity to decimal of another.

79.

DEFINITIONS, EXPLANATIONS, AND REMARKS.

Decimal Fraction. A Fraction whose denominator is not expressed; but is understood to be such a power of ten as is indicated by the number of figures at the right of the separatrix.

Criticism. In consulting Ray's Higher Arithmetic, I find this definition of a decimal fraction:

"A Decimal Fraction is one which derives its name from the Latin word *decem*, meaning ten; and is so called, because its denominator is always 1 with cyphers annexed; being either 10 or the product of several 10's."

This definition is worthless because it includes a large class of common fractions. Read Prof. Davies, in his University Arithmetic—"A decimal fraction is one in which the unit is divided according to the scale of tens."

Remark. The separatrix is the most important character used in decimals, and no pains should be spared to impress this on the minds of pupils.

Rule for Notation. 1st. Write the separatrix. 2d. Determine the place of the given denomination. 3d. Assume this place, so determined as the place of units, and write the given quantity, as if whole numbers.

Remark 1st. The difficulty in most rules for writing decimals is that the pupil is compelled to write them twice; once, to obtain the correct number and arrangement of figures, and again, to place them in proper relation to other decimals with which he may wish to combine them. By this rule he will write them where he wants them in the first instance.

Remark 2d. In large classes of *Teachers* I have seldom found more than two or three individuals (frequently none) who were able to write decimals correctly. Take examples of these kinds, for instance:

One hundred million ten-thousandths.

Fifteen million fifteen thousand and fifteen hundred ten-millionths.

Forty-five million forty-five thousand and forty-five hundred thousandths.

Forty-five million forty-five thousand and forty-five hundred-thousandths.

Remark 3d. Such common fractions as $\frac{3}{1000}$ and $\frac{4}{60000}$, having denominators of many more figures than the numerator are the proper examples to test a class in reducing common fractions to decimals. It is not an uncommon thing for a class to obtain almost as many different results as it contains pupils, in consequence of the misplacement of the separatrix. A thorough teacher will pay particular attention to this matter.

80.

Demonstration of the rule for multiplication of decimals.

Rule. Multiply as in entire numbers and point off as many figures from the right of the product as there are in both of the factors.

Demonstration. Assume that both factors are entire numbers, then since removing the separatrix towards the left divides either of the factors, as many times by ten, as there are figures thus placed at the right of the separatrix; and since the product must be as many times divided by ten as both the factors, it follows that the rule is correct.

81.

Demonstration of the rule for the division of decimals.

Rule. Divide as in whole numbers, and point off as many figures, at the right of the quotient, for decimals, as the decimal figures in the dividend exceed those in the divisor.

Demonstration. Assume first that both dividend and divisor are whole numbers, then of course the quotient is also a whole number: but since dividing the dividend divides the quotient, and dividing the divisor multiplies the quotient. and since re moving the separatrix towards the left divides either quantity as many times by ten as there are figures thus placed at the right of the separatrix, in each of the numbers, it follows then as many more times as the dividend has thus been divided than the divisor, so many times must the quotient be divided by ten; in other words, so many figures must be cut off from the right of the quotient as the dividend has been divided more times by ten than the divisor has been thus divided.

82.

RATIO.

Terms—Antecedent, Consequent, Couplet, Value of Ratio.

Signs— : $\frac{a}{b}$

Relations,
- of subtraction—how much greater?—Difference.
- of division—how many times greater?—Quotient.
- of involution.
- of evolution.

Classes,
- as to arrangement, — English, French.
- as to origin, — Direct, Inverse.
- as to combination, — Simple, Compound.
- as to value, — of equality, of greater inequality, of less inequality.

Comparison of English Ratio.
- with Division, — Antecedent=Dividend. Consequent=Divisor, Value=Quotient.
- with Fractions, — Antecedent=Numerator. Consequent=Denominator. Value=Value.

Comparison of French Ratio,
- with Division, — Antecedent=Divisor, Consequent=Dividend. Value=Quotient.
- with Fractions, — Antecedent=Denominator, Consequent=Numerator, Value=Value.

Scholium,—Ratio can only exist between quantities of the same kind.

Rule for finding value of Ratio.

Laws,	English Ratio,	1. Ant.—Cons.×Value of Ratio. 2. Cons.—Ant.÷Value of Ratio.
	French Ratio,	1. Ant.—Cons.÷Value of Ratio. 2. Cons.—Ant.×Value of Ratio.

Geometric Series, { Law, Value.

Propositions, 1, 2, 3, 4, 5, 6.

83.

DEFINITIONS, EXPLANATIONS, AND REMARKS.

Ratio. A combination of two or more terms in pairs, for the purpose of comparison by division.

Remark. The result of such division is often called ratio; more correctly, it is the value of the ratio.

Terms. The numbers between which the comparison is instituted.

Antecedent. The first or lefthand term of a pair comprised in a ratio.

Consequent. The second or righthand term of the pair comprised in a ratio.

Couplet. A pair of terms including an antecedent and consequent.

Value of Ratio. The quotient arising from dividing one term of a ratio by the other.

Relations. Bearings.

Relation as determined by subtraction, answers to the question, How much greater is one number than another? It is the same as the difference.

Relation as determined by division, answers the question, How many times is one number greater than another? It is the same as the quotient.

Relation as determined by involution or evolution answers the question, What power or root is one number of another? It is the same as the exponent or index of one number, when placed equal to another, as its power or root.

English Ratio. That in which the antecedent is to be divided by the consequent.

French Ratio. That in which the consequent is to be divided by the antecedent.

Remark. It is not to be supposed that all English mathematicians adopt what is called the English Ratio, or that all French mathematicians use what is called the French Ratio. Davies seems first to have introduced the inverted or French ratio into American books. He did not follow the French author whose work he translated in this particular. Most works on Natural Science retain the old or English form, and in their ratios suppose that the first term is to be divided by the second.

Several of the more recent Arithmetics have adopted the English Ratio, as Stoddard's, Dodd's, etc.

84.

Direct Ratio. That in which more requires more; or less requires less.

Inverse Ratio. That in which more requires less; or less requires more.

Remark. Many arithmeticians reject this distinction as useless. In my opinion, however, it affords a fine means of drill, in the discussion of problems in compound proportion.

Simple Ratio. That involving but one couplet.

Compound Ratio. That involving two or more simple ratios, combined with the sign of multiplication.

Ratio of Equality. That in which the terms are equal; or that in which the value is unity.

Ratio of Greater Inequality. That in which the value is greater than unity.

Ratio of Less Inequality. That in which the value is less than unity.

Remark. It will be noticed that a French Ratio of greater inequality may be identical with an English Ratio of less inequality.

Series. A succession of terms, each of which is derived from one or more preceding terms by some known law.

Geometric Series. One in which each term is derived from the preceding term by a constant multiplier or divisor. It is sometimes called Continued Proportion.

Remark. This constant multiplier or divisor is equivalent to the value of any single ratio, or couplet comprised in the series.

Propositions. The same as those for fractions, substituting the terms antecedent and consequent for numerator and denominator.

85.

PROPORTION.

Terms,—Proportional, Mean Proportional, Last Proportional, Third Proportional, Fourth Proportional, Homologous, Analogous, Extremes, Means.

Signs,— :, ÷, ::, =, ∴, { Signification, Reading.

- Classes,
  - as to origin, { Direct, Inverse.
  - as to combination, { Simple, Compound, Conjoined.
- Names of Single Terms,
  - First term=First Antecedent=First Extreme.
  - Second term=First Consequent=First Mean.
  - Third term=Second Antecedent=Sec'd Mean.
  - Fourth term=Sec'd Consequent=2d Extreme.
- Names of Pairs of Terms,
  - First and Second=First Couplet,
  - First and Third=Antecedents,
  - First and Fourth=Extremes,
  - Second and Third=Means,
  - Second and Fourth=Consequents,
  - Third and Fourth=Second Couplet.
- Laws,
  - Fundamental, Product of Extremes=Product of Means.
  - Derived,
    1. Product of Extremes÷one mean=other mean.
    2. Product of Means÷one extreme=other extreme.
- Rules for statement,
  - for Simple Proportion.
  - for Compound Proportion.
- Methods of Solution,
  1. by Fundamental Law,
  2. by Ratio,
  3. by Cancellation.

86.

DEFINITIONS, EXPLANATIONS, AND REMARKS.

PROPORTION. A combination of two equal ratios, with the sign of equality.

PROPORTIONAL. Any one of the terms of a proportion.

MEAN PROPORTIONAL. One of two equal means in a proportion.

THIRD PROPORTIONAL. The fourth term of a proportion in which the means are equal.

Remark. Such a proportion is often written with only three terms; thus: (4:8:16)=(4:8::8:16).

Homologous Terms. Those occupying the same place in two or more couplets. Two or more consequents are homologous terms; also two or more antecedents.

Analagous Terms. Such as are found in the same couplet.

Extremes. The first and last terms of a proportion.

Means. The second and third terms of a proportion.

Signs. Symbols indicating a relation, operation or sequence.

Sign of Ratio, (:). It is an abridged sign of division, and is read as in this *Example*, 4:6::8:12.

Reading.—As 4 is to 6, so is 8 to 12.

Sign of Equality, (::). It is an abridged form of the ordinary sign of equality, being the extremities of the lines. It is read as in the example above, "so is."

Sign of Sequence or Deduction, (∴). It is explained, section 47, page 299.

Direct Proportion. That which involves direct ratios.

Inverse Proportion. That which involves inverse ratios.

Simple Proportion. That which consists of simple ratios only.

Compound Proportion. That which contains one or more compound ratios.

Conjoined Proportion. That form of a compound proportion, in which each antecedent is equal in value to its consequent.

Remark Conjoined proportion is used in reducing coins of the two countries through the medium of other countries. It is often called the Chain Rule.

Demonstration of fundamental law:

1st. Take 6:8::12:16. Expressing each ratio fractionally $\frac{8}{6}=\frac{16}{12}$. Multiplying each fraction by 6, we have $8=\frac{16\times6}{12}$; for, multiplying equals by equals the products will be equal. Again, multiplying the last two equal quantities by 12, we have $8\times12=16\times6$, which gives the product of the means, 8 and 12, equals the product of the extremes, 6 and 16.

2d. Take 6:8::12:16. Since every consequent is equal to its antecedent multiplied by the value of their ratio: $8=6\times\frac{4}{3}$; and $16=12\times\frac{4}{3}$. Hence we perceive that the extremes 6 and 16 contain the same factors as the means 8 and 12. 6.12 and $\frac{4}{3}$ being the factors of the extremes; 6, $\frac{4}{3}$, and 12, being the factors of the means. Since the products of equal factors are equals, and the means and extremes contain equal factors, the products of the extremes and means must be equal.

Methods of Solution. *By Ratio.* Multiply the first term of the second couplet by the value of the ratio, obtained from the first couplet. *By cancellation.* Consider all antecedents, excepting the last, as denominators, all consequents and the last antecedent as numerators of a compound fraction. Then cancel as in the reduction of a compound fraction.

87.

PERCENTAGE.

Terms,—Percent, Rate percent.
Notation,—Rule, Consider hundredths as units, and write as in whole numbers.
Sign (%). This sign has been recently introduced; and is read percent.

Cases,
- 1st, To find any given percent of a number, Rule.
- 2d, To find what percent one No. is of another, Rule.
- 3d, To find a No. when any percent of it is known, Rule.
- 4th, To find a No. when any percent greater or less is given, Rule.

88.

GAIN AND LOSS.

Remark. 100 percent represents the No. on which any gain or loss accrues.

Cases, {1, 2, 3, 4} =the same general cases in percentage.

89.

COMMISSION.

Remark.—100 percent represents the No. on which commission is charged.

Terms, { Agent, Commission-Merchant, Factor, Correspondent, Principal, Rate of Commission.

Cases, {1, 2, 3, 4} =the same general cases in percentage.

BROKERAGE.

Terms,
- Consigner, Consignee, Bill of Exchange, Check, Draft, Bond,
- Rate of Brokerage, Proceeds or cost.

Cases, {1, 2, 3, 4} =the same general cases in percentage.

90.

STOCKS.

Terms,
- Joint Stock Company, Stock, Share, Certificate, Stockholders, Dividend, Rate of Dividend.
- Par Value, Face, Nominal Value, Real Value, Market Value, Rise and Fall.
- At par, Above par, Below par, At a premium, At a discount, Discount.
- Stock Broker, Stock Jobber, Investment, Commission, Rate of Commission,

Cases,=Cases in Percentage.

91.

INSURANCE.

Terms, { Policy, Premium, Underwriter, Out-Door, Rate of Insurance, Take a Risk, Cover.

Classes, {
- Fire,
- Marine,
- Life,
- Health,
- Stock, etc.

Cases,=Cases in Percentage.

TAXES.

Classes, {
- Direct, { Poll, Property,
- Indirect, { Customs or Duties, } { Ad valorem, Allowances, Specific, } { Tare, Draft, Leakage, Breakage.

Cases, { for specific duties, Rule, for ad valorem duties—Cases=Cases in percentage.

92.

INTEREST.

Quantities and Symbols, {
- Principal=P. Compound Interest=C. I.
- Interest=A. Compound Amount=C. A.
- Rate=R. Logarithm=Log.
- Time in { Years=T. Months=m. Days=d.
- Amount=A.=P+I.

Classes, {
- Simple,
- Compound,
- Annual,
- Mixed.

Legal Rates, {
- 8, Ga., Ala., Mi., Fl.
- 7, N. Y., S. Ca., Mi., Wis., Io.
- 5, La.
- 10, Texas.
- 6, In all other States and in U. S. Courts.

Remark. 100 percent represents the principal.

Rules, {
- General. $P\times T\times R=I$.
- Special, for 6 percent, { $\left(\frac{m}{100}+\frac{d}{3000}\right)\times\frac{P}{2}=I$. $\frac{P}{100}\times\frac{m}{2}=I$.

Cases in Simple Interest,

1 Given, { P. T. R. } Required, I. $P \times R \times T = I.$

2 Given, { P. I. T. } Required, R. Rule $\left\{ \frac{I}{P \times T \times ,01} = R. \right.$

3 Given, { P. I. R. } Required, T. Rule $\left\{ \frac{I}{P \times R} = T. \right.$

4 Given, { I. R. T. } Required, P. Rule $\left\{ \frac{I}{R \times T} = P. \right.$

5 Given, { A. R. T. } Required, P. Rule $\left\{ \frac{A}{\$1, + R \times T} = P. \right.$

6 Given, { A. R. T. } Required, I. Rule $A - \frac{A}{\$1, + R \times T.} = I.$

Cases in Compound Interest,

1 Given, { P. R. T. } Required C A. Rule $P \times (1+R)^T = C\ A.$

2 Given, { P. R. T. } Required C I. Rule $P \times (1+R)^T - P. = C\ I.$

3 Given, { C A. R. T. } Required P. Rule $\frac{C\ A.}{(1+R)^T} = P.$

4 Given, { C I. R. T. } Required P. Rule $\frac{C\ I}{(1+R)^T - 1} = P.$

5 Given, { C A. P. T. } Required R. Rule $\sqrt[T]{\frac{CA}{P}} - 1 = R.$

6 Given, { C A, P. R. } Required T. Rule $\frac{\text{Log. C A} - \text{Log. P.}}{\text{Log. } (1+R.)} = T.$

93

BANKING.

- Banks,
  - of Issue,
  - of Discount,
  - of Deposit.
- Officers,
  - Directors,
  - President,
  - Cashier,
  - Tellers.
- Notes,
  - Classes,
    - Negotiable,
    - Non negotiable,
    - Bank,
    - of hand.
  - Essentials,
    - Signature,
    - Date,
    - Promise to pay,
    - Value received.
  - Persons,
    - Maker,
    - Payee,
    - Holder,
    - Endorser.
  - Terms,
    - Face, Protest, Payable on Demand, Payable on Time, Payable on Sight, Proceeds, Avails, Cost, Time to Run, Day of Maturity, Nominally Due, Legally Due.
  - Partial Payments,
    - *Remark.*—Interest must not draw interest.
    - Rules,
      - United States,
      - Connecticut,
      - Vermont.
  - Discount,
    - Quantities,
      - Face of Note, A.
      - Avail or Cost, C.
      - Rate, R.
      - Time,
        - in Years—T.
        - in Months—m.
        - in Days—d.
      - Bank Discount—D.
    - Classes,
      - True Discount,—$I=P\times R\times T$.
      - Bank Discount,—$D=A\times R\times T$.
    - Cases of Bank Discount
      1. To find discount of a note. $A\times R\times T=D$.
      2. To find proceeds of a note. $A-A\times R\times T=C$.
      3. To find face of a note for given proceeds, $\frac{C}{1-R\times T}=A$.

94.

EXCHANGE.

- Classes,
  - Foreign,
  - Domestic,
  - Circular.
- Bills,
  - Sight=Checks,
  - Time.
- Endorsements,
  - Special,
  - in Blank.
- Acceptance.
- Rate,
  - in favor,
  - against.
- Standard—Amount of pure gold or silver in coin.
- Reduction of Currencies,
  - direct,
  - circular=chain rule.
- Foreign Coins,
  - English, French, German, Spanish, Russian,
    - Gold, Silver, Platinum, etc

95.

INVOLUTION.

- Power,
  - Degrees,
  - Exponent,
    - positive,
    - negative.
- Propositions,
  - Adding exponents multiplies the quantities.
  - Subtracting exponents divides the quantities.
  - Multiplying an exponent involves the quantity.
  - Dividing an exponent evolves the quantity.
- Properties,
  - of 1. Every power of 1 is 1.
  - of numbers less than 1. Powers, higher than the first, are less than the number.
  - of 0th power of numbers. Always=1.
- Rule,
  - Demonstration,
  - Applications.

96.

EVOLUTION.

- Root,
  - Degrees,
  - Sign,
  - Index,
  - Fractional Exponent.
- Propositions. The same as in Involution.
- Properties,
  - of 1. Every root of 1 is 1.
  - of number less than 1. Every root higher than the first is greater than the number.
  - of 0th root of numbers. Always=1.
- Rules,
  - for Square root, for Cube root, for any root,
    - Demonstration,
      - Geometrical,
      - Arithmetical,
      - Algebraic.
    - Applications.

97.

ARITHMETICAL PROGRESSION

Arithmetical Series, { Ascending, Descending.

Quantities and Symbols, { First term=a. Last term=l. Common difference=d. Number of terms=n. Sum of series=s.

Cases,

Case	Given	Required	Rule
1	a. n. d.	l.	$a+d(n-1)=l$.
2	n. l. d.	a.	$l-d(n-1)=a$.
3	a. n. l.	d.	$\frac{l-a}{n-1}=d$.
4	a. l. d.	n.	$\frac{l-a}{d}+1=n$.
5	a. l. n.	s.	$\frac{(a+l)n}{2}=S$.

98.

GEOMETRICAL PROGRESSION.

Geometrical Series, { Ascending, Descending.

Quantities and Symbols. { First term=a. Last term=l. Common Ratio=r. Number of terms=n. Sum of series=s.

Cases,

Case	Given	Required	Rule
1	a. r. n.	l.	$a \times r^{n-1}=l$.
2	l. r. n.	a.	$\frac{l}{r^{n-1}}=a$.
3	l. a. n.	r.	$\sqrt[n-1]{\frac{l}{a}}=r$.
4	l. a. r.	s.	$\frac{l \times r-a}{r-1}=S$.
5	a. r. n.	s.	$\frac{a \times r^n-1}{r-1}=S$.

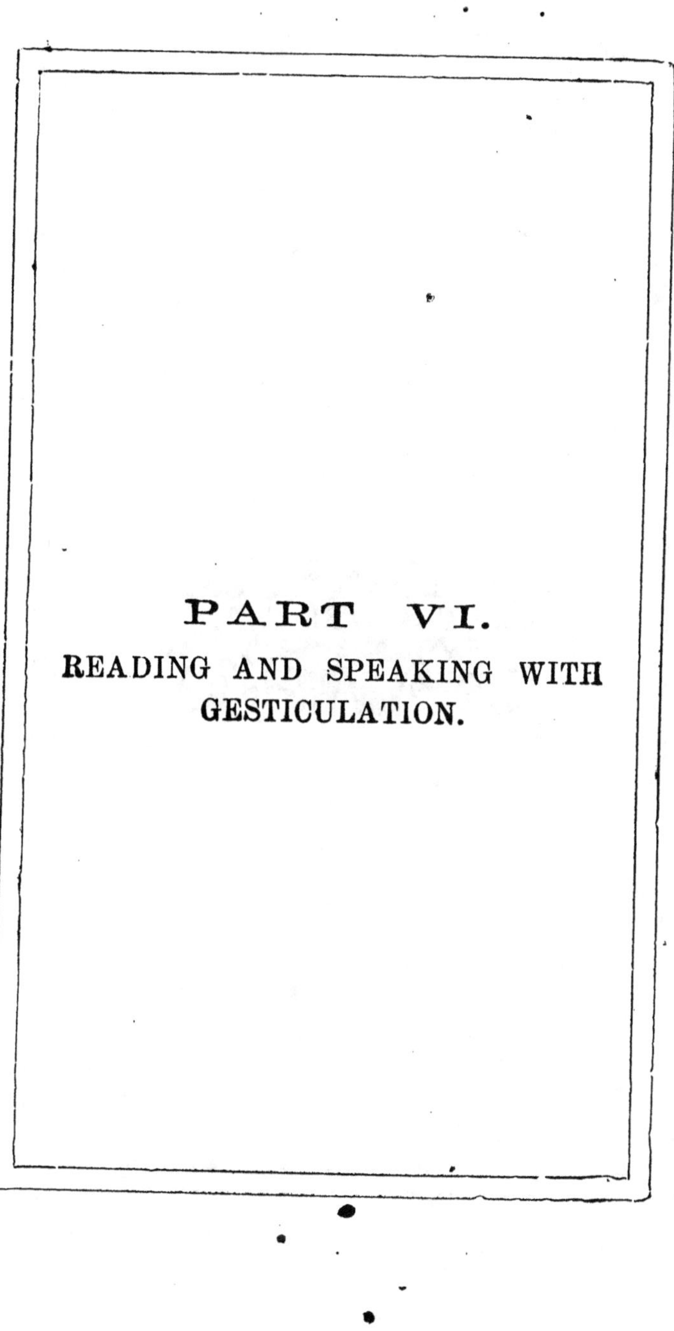

PART VI.

READING AND SPEAKING WITH GESTICULATION.

INTRODUCTION.

It is universally conceded, that no branch is so much neglected in our common schools as reading. Resulting from this abuse there is more, vastly more, disagreeable reading and speaking, even among professional men, whose habits, in this particular, are for the most part fixed in their primary instruction, than illogical thinking or false reasoning. Yet there is less being done by leading Educators, or by those guardians of our public schools, the School Examiners, either in the way of scrutiny or remonstrance, in this branch, than in any other of the common branches.

It becomes the true Teacher, and especially such an one as may have the *training* of Teachers, to give his best efforts to this subject. I shall endeavor to do so. Amid the avalanches of books for reading and declamation that overwhelm us, not one that I have examined presents a just and appropriate arrangement of the subject, and much less a systematic plan of teaching it, e. i., so simple as to be available in our common schools, and so thorough as to meet the demands of the subject.

If I succeed no better than my numerous predecessors, it will not be for want of attention to the subject, or of experience in teaching it, or of a determination to accomplish what is required.

The OBJECTS to be aimed at in the study of Elocution, and of course in teaching it, are

1st. THE ACQUISITION OF GENERAL KNOWLEDGE.

It may be said, that good vocal delivery is not necessary in this point of view. I answer, that he who can make others appreciate the sense and scope of an author, will surely be most likely, himself, to comprehend the author, and that in the effort to impress others with ideas read or declaimed, he himself receives the deepest impression.

2d. THE ACQUISITION OF A LOVE FOR READING.

It is a complaint on the part of many parents that their children have no love for their books. Though the difficulty lies chiefly with the parents themselves, in not supplying their children with books and papers suitable for their age, and advancement; yet the proper training of the voice, and with it the mind—for the former is impossible without the latter—is an efficient means for inciting children and youth to read for the pleasure it affords them. Show me a "good reader" and I will show you a person that has become so, not so much by class drill, or by self-training in vocal delivery, as by silent and intelligent reading incited by it.

3d. THE IMPROVEMENT OF THE MEMORY, JUDGMENT, AND TASTE.

Though these faculties of the mind are more

particularly cultivated by proper training in vocal delivery, every other faculty is reached and improved.

4th. Improvement of the Social Faculties.

Instead of that vacuity, frivolity, and tendency to gossip and flirtation, which too generally prevail in social gatherings, we might, as the result of proper vocal culture, have such occasions enlivened and enriched, or, at least, varied with readings, recitations, personations, or the telling of anecdotes, with such spontaneous criticism, remarks, additional readings, recitations, speeches, stories, and fun as they would provoke, all of which cultivated vocal delivery is calculated to improve and embellish.

4th. Improvement of the Health.

The person who learns to make correct use of the organs of speech, and with them of the entire system in finished vocal delivery, can hardly be affected with any serious disease of the chest or spine. At any rate, the exercise is better than all the poisons, under the various names of nostrums, cordials, tonics, expectorants, panaceas, and cod liver oils, that have ever been consumed. Whitefield could "drive off a fever by a good pulpit sweat." The bronchitis can never lay aside a person who cultivates a good vocal delivery. Such a person may, with reasonably correct habits otherwise, defy the consumption, and all its concomitant evils.

5th. A Graceful Carriage and Address.

Many parents send their children to dancing

schools, at a great hazard of their morals, to improve their manners. A *proper training* in elocution will accomplish the same object more directly, without any such risk.

6th. A PREPARATION FOR PUBLIC LIFE.

How many men of good abilities and superior culture otherwise, are comparatively inefficient and unsuccessful from improper training and use of their organs of speech. Audiences wearied, instruction unimparted, justice unattained, real virtue and true benevolence unsustained, are some of the lamentably notorious effects of the pernicious and repulsive habits of a large class of public men in their elocution.

7th. THE PREVENTION AND CORRECTION OF THE FOLLOWING LIST OF IMPROPRIETIES.

IMPROPRIETIES IN PERSON AND COUNTENANCE.

1. Improper Walk to the Rostrum; too much on the heel, too noisy, too stooping, too slow, too rapid. Improper attitude on floor or rostrum; too nearly equal on both feet, too long on one foot, too frequently changing the position, too much bent over, shoulders too much drawn forward, chest too much contracted, too much wriggling and twisting, rocking, or weaving the body.

2. Improper Bow; too much in the neck, too quick and snappish, too low, too familiar or disrespectful, too much to one side, too stiff and formal.

4. Improper Manner of Holding the Book or Manuscript; too much with both hands, too much before the face, too near the breast or abdomen,

too stiffly, so as not to admit of the ready turning of leaves or of gesticulation.

5. Improper Position of the Head; too much forward, too much backward, too much on one side, too much throwing the hair back, too much nodding, too much shaking, too immovable.

6. Improper Use of the Eyes; too much out of the window, too much at the pillars or walls, too much towards the floor, too much at one individual in the audience, too much at one part of the audience, too much closed, too wide open, with too little interest or confidence in the audience.

7. Improper Action of the Mouth; too much closed, lips too near together, teeth too nearly shut, too much spitting.

8. Improper Expression of Countenance; too "shame-faced," too stupid, too unvarying, too much lacking any expression, too little in accordance with the sentiment uttered.

9. Improper Use of Hands and Fingers; too stiff and straight, too much clinched, behind the back, in the pockets, in the arm-hole of the vest, too much on the hip, fingers playing with each other or with the dress, or with buttons, watch chain, or pencil or string, stroking the face or beard, running the fingers through the hair.

10. Improper Gesticulation; too unfrequent, too frequent, too feeble, too violent, too periodical, too much with one hand, too much with both hands, too low, too much bending the arm at the elbow, gesticulating when looking on the book or manuscript, no gesticulation, unsuited to the senti-

ment uttered, too soon or too late for the sentiment, too stiff, too angular, too much in straight lines out from the body, pointing to the ears, eyes, or other features, not being accompanied with the eyes.

11. Improper Recognition of Individuals in the Audience; with smiles not called for by the sentiment of the piece.

12. Improper Manner of leaving the Rostrum, too hasty, too noisy, too impudent, too sneaking.

IMPROPRIETIES OF BREATH AND VOICE.

1. Improper Times of taking Breath; in the midst of a syllable, in the midst of a word, where no pause is required, after a sentence rather than before.

2. Improper Method of taking Breath; too little at a time, with too much noise.

3. Improper Use of Breath in producing Sound; too wasteful through harsh or impure tones.

4. Improper Articulation; too hurried, too careless, too indistinct, too particular on unimportant words and unaccented syllables.

5. Improper Pronunciation; wrong sound of vowels, wrong sound of consonants, accent placed on wrong syllables.

6. Improper Pitch; too high, too low, too monotonous.

7. Improper Force; too feeble, too faltering, too feeble on unimportant words, too loud, too unvarying, too loud on unimportant words, diminu

tion of force from the beginning to the end of every sentence.

8. Improper Rate; too rapid, or too slow to suit the sentence or the piece.

9. Improper Inflection on any word, phrase or sentence.

10. Improper Emphasis; on the wrong word or words, too little, too much, of the wrong kind, emphatic pause too short, emphatic pause too long, no emphatic pause.

11. Improper Quality of Voice; too husky and impure in tone, too nasal, too guttural, too tremulous, too boisterous, too shrill, too much mumbling, too apathetic, too affected, too sniffling.

12. Improper Ending of Sentences; too abrupt, too drawling, with too much of a tone, too much alike.

13. Improper Transition; from one key to another, from one degree of rapidity to another, from one sentiment to another, from one paragraph to another, from one personation to another.

14. Improper Style of Delivery; unfitted to the sentiment, too grave, too comic, too stern, too trifling, too sad, too joyful, too earnest, too unfeeling, too sarcastic, too sneering, too contemptuous, too ridiculous, too much of a sing-song, too monotonous.

15. Improper Appearance; too bold, too timid, too pompous, too effeminate, too theatrical, too ministerial, too tame, too vehement, too conceited, with too much affectation, too simpering, too silly, too much embarrassed, too much frightened at

your friends, too much affected with the blind staggers.

16. Improper Personation; too slight portrayal of character, character overdone, character not correctly personated.

17. Improper conception of the subject matter

ELOCUTION.

1.

Elocution, { Departments. Management of the Person. Vocal Culture. Gesticulation.

2.

DEFINITION AND EXPLANATION.

Elocution. The art of expressing thought and feeling, by means of articulate and gesticulate language.

Explanation. By referring to the General Outline of Grammar, page 39, it will be seen, that Natural Language is divided into Articulate and Gesticulate; and that Artificial Language is divided into Articulate and Written; Elocution comprises both divisions of Natural Language; but the first only, of Artificial Language.

3.

DEPARTMENTS OF ELOCUTION.

- Departments,
  - Reading,
    - Silent,
    - Audible.
  - Speaking,
    - Declamation,
    - Oratory,
      - Premeditated,
      - Extempore.

4.

DEFINITIONS, EXPLANATIONS AND REMARKS.

Reading. The perusal or utterance of thought and feeling, as seen expressed in Written Language.

Silent Reading. The perusal of Written Language without utterance.

Audible Reading. The utterance of thought and feeling, as immediately obtained from Written Language.

Remark 1*st*. No work on Elocution with which I am conversant attempts a definition of Reading.

Remark 2*d*. Silent Reading does not strictly come under the definition of Elocution, yet from its inseparable connection with the subject, it seems necessary to introduce it.

Speaking. The utterance of thought and feeling, with the eyes free from Written Language.

Declamation. The speaking of another's composition.

Oratory. The speaking of one's own composition in an impressive manner.

Premeditated Oratory. That in which the composition has been previously studied.

Extempore Oratory. That in which the composition is accomplished simultaneously with the delivery.

5.

MANAGEMENT OF THE PERSON.

Management of the Person. {
- Manner of taking Position,
- Manner of Bowing,
- Position of the body, { Standing, Sitting.
- Position of Upper Extremities,
- Position of Lower Extremities,
- Changes in Position,
- Carriage of the Head,
- Management of Mouth, { Lips, Teeth.
- " Lungs,
- " Eyes,
- Expression of Countenance,
- General Appearance,
- Manner of leaving the Stage.

} { Directions, Errors, Methods of Drill.

6.

DIRECTIONS AND EXPLANATIONS.

MANNER OF TAKING POSITION. The pupil rises when his name is called, and passes with a firm and elastic tread, to one side of the stage, and ascending in a quiet and graceful manner, takes his position where he can best be seen by all the audience; and with just a moment's respectful view of the audience he bows, to the ladies first, if the sexes are separated, then to the gentlemen; or if the sexes are intermingled he bows to the whole audience.

7.

MANNER OF BOWING. In bowing, the whole frame should bend slightly, the neck somewhat more than other parts. The right hand may wave gracefully to the audience, especially to the ladies, or both hands may be thrown forward gracefully, greeting the whole audience.

Remark 1. No explanation or plate can give a correct idea of this greeting, any more than of gesticulation. It can only be learned from a living example.

Remark 2. It is not desirable that all the members of a class should give the same form of bow or of greeting, in commencing reading or speaking, but that a class should be trained in a variety of forms.

8.

Position of the Body. Whether standing or sitting, the body should be erect, the shoulders thrown back, and the chest made protuberant.

9.

Position of the Upper Extremities. The hands should hang as the force of gravity, only, will place them. No force should be applied to make them hang down or to project the fingers downward, or to draw them together. Hanging without thought in such a position they are ready when needed for gesticulation. The awkward and disrespectful positions of the hands, as in the pockets, or behind the back, should be carefully avoided. The fingers should not be permitted to work or play with each other, or with the buttons or clothes.

10.

Position of the Lower Extremities. The weight of the body should rest on one foot, rather than on both. The foot not sustaining the body should be thrown slightly forward or backward of the other, and should touch the floor with the ball rather than the heel.

11.

Change of Position. This may be accomplished by throwing the weight on the foot at rest, and by those movements which animated delivery requires. No change should be made *directly* forward, or directly sideways; but in an oblique direction. Changes must not be too frequent; nor so unfrequent as to tire the spectator.

12.

Carriage of the Head. The head should be sustained respectfully erect, not stiffly so. Much grace is exhibited by a handsome carriage of the head. In animated delivery it must partake of the spirit of the piece in its motions, but all bobbings, noddings, and shakings not called for by the sentiment of the piece, must be most scrupulously avoided.

13.

Management of the Mouth. The almost universal fault of keeping the mouth too much closed, the lips and teeth too near together, needs the particular and continued attention of the trainer and the trained. Drills on the vowel sounds with the mouth as widely opened as possible, consistently with clear enunciation of the several sounds, have a good effect towards curing this bad habit. The difference of the same vowel sounds with the teeth closed and the teeth well apart, may be dwelt on by teacher and scholar.

14.

Management of the Lungs. The great evil in the use of the lungs is that they are permitted to remain too nearly in a collapsed condition. Full and deep respiration should be *practised*, and the habit established of commencing the delivery of a sentence, with full rather than with exhausted lungs.

15.

Management of the Eyes. The eyes possess more expression, and magnetic power, than the entire man besides; and the person who cannot use them for impressing, convincing, or persuading his audience, can accomplish nothing in the way of oratory, sacred or secular. A vacant stare at the audience, or at one place in the midst of the audience or out of it, should be carefully avoided. The eyes should meet, intelligently and feelingly meet, those of distinct individuals, whose sympathy with the speaker cannot fail to arouse him to higher effort, and more complete success. The magic influence of the eye in rousing the indifferent, in suppressing opposition, in awakening sympathy, no speaker can afford to undervalue or neglect.

16.

Expression of the Countenance. The expression of the countenance depends so much on that of the eyes, that little need be said further about it; yet. if in addition to a want of a sympathy of the eye with the sentiment uttered, there shall be a stupid. impudent, or sneaking expression of the countenance, the exhibition becomes intolerably repugnant.

17.

General Appearance. The general appearance must be in keeping with the varying sentiment of the piece delivered. The entire system must participate in and exhibit the sentiment. It is this self-abandonment which distinguishes the effective speaker, this forgetfulness of self and the yielding of every faculty to the absorbing, overpowering current of thought and feeling, which constitutes the finished actor, or orator.

18.

Manner of Leaving the Stage. The stage or rostrum may be left without any demonstration, farther than a quiet, self-possessed retreat. But in case the audience have exhibited warm sympathy with the speaker, a low bow is a suitable acknowledgment; and in case applause is continued, a repetition of bows while the speaker retreats is desirable. In some cases a circular bow and a corresponding sweeping gesture with the hand is admissible.

19.

METHOD OF DRILLING A CLASS.

Remark 1. Awkwardness and bashfulness are only exhibitions of self-consciousness. These evils can never be directly overcome in the scholar; but they will vanish as he becomes interested in his teacher, and in the exercises.

Remark 2. All exercises should be commenced as concert exercises, the teacher first giving the example. By this means the teacher, perceiving who are the most successful, can excuse such by twos or threes, and thus reach, by degrees, those who need special attention.

Remark 3. These drills must be introduced with prudence into schools, where they are new, and not much time given to them; a few minutes previous to each reading exercise. Otherwise the idea will get out that "the teacher spends so much time in his new-fangled notions that the scholars do n't learn anything."

Remark 4. These drills may commence with the most advanced reading class, after they shall have had a training in the articulate sounds for a few weeks.

20.

TEACHER'S DIRECTIONS TO PUPILS.

Direction 1. The class will take their places on the floor at such distances that their hands will not interfere in gesticulation.

Remark 1. It is desirable that as many as possible stand where their feet can be seen by the teacher.

Direction 2. You may all take the *First Position* as I take it, body on left foot, right foot forward, head erect, hands down, not stiffly. *Second Position.* Body forward on the right foot, the left foot touching the floor with the toe only. First Position again. *Third Position.* Body on the right foot, the left in front. *Fourth Position.*

Body on the left foot, the right behind, resting on the toe. First Position again, hands on the hips, with fingers on the abdomen, thumbs back, elbows back, let them touch each other if possible, hands down.

Direction 3. Bow forward with head and body. Bow to the right. Bow to the left. Bow forward and accompany the bow with the appropriate gesture of both hands. Bow to the right, with the accompaniment of the right hand. Bow to the left with the accompaniment of the left hand. Bow to each other and take your seats.

Remark 1. In repeating this drill, as it may be necessary to repeat it several days in succession, the ingenious teacher will introduce new movements, and vary the order of the transitions from any one position to the others. He may also introduce a series of gesticulations as will be explained under the head of Gesticulation.

Remark 2. The management of the mouth, eyes, countenance, and general appearance, and leaving the stage, will come up in connection with the Individual Drills in Vocal Culture.

VOCAL CULTURE.

21

I.—PRONUNCIATION.

- **Breathing.**
  - Errors. See introduction page 352.
  - Objects to be attained.
  - Methods of drill.
- **Articulation.**
  - Sounds—see Part II. Chart No. 1. Page **52**
  - See Introduction Page.
  - Objects to be attained.
  - Methods of drill.
- **Accent.** (See Part II. Page 50. Section 16.)
  - Common.
    - Primary,
    - Secondary,
    - etc.
  - Discriminative.
    - Nouns from Verbs.
    - Adjectives from Nouns.
    - Adjectives from Verbs.
  - Emphatic.
  - Poetical.
- **Rules.**
  1. Follow the usage of the best Speakers.
  2. Consult the best Dictionaries.
  3. Avoid any peculiarity that attracts attention.

II.—MODULATION.

- **Pitch.**
  - Terms: Key. Monotone.
  - Classes—Medium, High, Very High, Low, Very Low.
  - Errors. See Introduction Page 352.
  - Objects to be attained.
  - Methods of Drill.
- **Force.**
  - Classes.
    - Sustained.
      - Medium, Strong, Very Strong.
      - Weak, Very Weak.
    - Varying.
      - Swell, Vanish, Wave.
      - Radical Expulsive Stress.
      - Radical Explosive Stress.
      - Vanishing Stress.
  - Errors. See Introduction Page 352.
  - Objects to be attained.
  - Methods of Drill.
- **Rate.**
  - Classes—Medium, Fast, Very Fast, Slow, Very Slow.
  - Errors. See Introduction Page 353.
  - Objects to be attained.
  - Methods of Drill.

Inflections.
- Classes.
  - Simple.
    - Rising.
      - Rising Slide.
      - Bend,
    - Falling.
      - Falling Slide.
      - Partial Close.
      - Perfect Close.
  - Compound.
    - Double Slide.
    - Upper Circumflex.
    - Lower Circumflex.
    - Emphatic Sweep.
      - Rise.
      - Fall.
- Errors. See Introduction Page 353.
- Objects to be attained.
- Methods of Drill.
- Rules 1—8.

Emphasis.
- Classes.
  - Common, Antithetic,
  - Cumulative, Deferred,
  - Conventional.
- Methods.
  - By Elevation or Depression of Pitch
  - By Increase or Diminution of Force.
  - By Increase or Diminution of Rate.
  - By Whisper.
  - By Emphatic Sweep.
  - By Rise or Fall of Emphatic Sweep.
  - By Upper Circumflex.
  - By Lower Circumflex.
  - By Emphatic Pause.
  - By Change of Tone.
  - By Gesticulation.
  - By Change of Countenance.
  - By Change of Position.
- Errors. See Introduction Page 353.
- Objects to be attained.
- Methods of Drill.

Tone.
- Classes.
  - Pure, Orotund, Guttural, Nasal Aspirate,
  - Smooth, Harsh, Shrill, Husky, Tremulous,
- Errors. See Introduction page 353.
- Objects to be attained.
- Methods of drill.

Transition.
- Classes.
  - Of Sense, in Parenthesis, "Aside," etc.
  - Of Paragraphs, Chapters, etc. [etc.
  - Of Personation, in Dialogue, Colloquy,
- Errors. No Change, Too Little Change, Too Much Change.
- Objects to be attained.
- Method of Drill.

III.—STYLE OF DELIVERY.

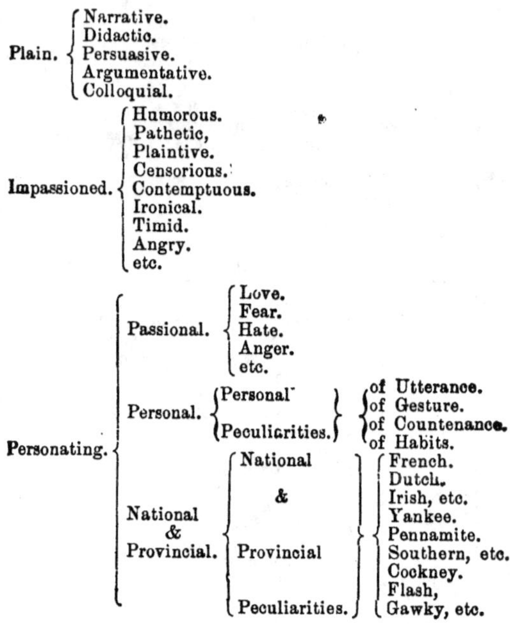

- Plain.
  - Narrative.
  - Didactic.
  - Persuasive.
  - Argumentative.
  - Colloquial.
- Impassioned.
  - Humorous.
  - Pathetic,
  - Plaintive.
  - Censorious.
  - Contemptuous.
  - Ironical.
  - Timid.
  - Angry.
  - etc.
- Personating.
  - Passional.
    - Love.
    - Fear.
    - Hate.
    - Anger.
    - etc.
  - Personal.
    - Personal Peculiarities.
      - of Utterance.
      - of Gesture.
      - of Countenance.
      - of Habits.
  - National & Provincial.
    - National & Provincial Peculiarities.
      - French.
      - Dutch.
      - Irish, etc.
      - Yankee.
      - Pennamite.
      - Southern, etc.
      - Cockney.
      - Flash,
      - Gawky, etc.

22

DEFINITIONS, EXPLANATIONS, REMARKS AND DRILLS.

VOCAL CULTURE. The training of the organs speech for the more effective expression of thought and feeling.

Remark. For definitions of PRONUNCIATION, ARTICULATION, ACCENT and its divisions, see Part II, pages 50 and 51, section 16. See also Drill in articulate sounds, pages 23 and 55, section 17.

23

DRILL IN BREATHING—TEACHER'S DIRECTIONS TO PUPILS.

Remark. The Class will stand during the exercises.

Direction 1. Throw the shoulders back, place the hands on the hips with the thumbs backward, carry the elbows as near back to each other as possible, without moving the hands from the hips.

Direction 2. Draw in breath noiselessly while I raise my hand. Exhale noiselessly while my hand falls. Extend the lungs to their utmost capacity, while you repeat the inhalation

Direction 3. You may exhale suddenly as I drop my hand, but without any sound whatever.

Remark. Deep breathing is a healthy exercise, calculated to enlarge the volume of the chest, and may take the place, to some extent, of out-door exercise. Proper vocal culture will require deep breathing in all the exercises.

Direction 4. Inhale as long as I raise my hand; as I bring it down slowly utter the sound of *a*, and we will see who can give it unbroken, the longest. We will try this again; again; again; very well.

Remark. This exercise serves to train the pupil to the economical use of breath, to the habit of taking breath before commencing the delivery of a sentence, rather than in the evil habit of taking breath where the sense requires no pause; and that of catching the breath in the midst of a syllable.

Remark. Its chief advantage is in training the voice to a full, clear and strong delivery on the lower tones, and the teacher should direct his special attention to this form of training, giving the vocal on a lower key, and requiring its utterance with greater force, as the class can bear it.

Direction 5. Inhale while I raise my hand, and in as low a tone as possible utter the sound *o*. Again, louder; again, louder.

Remark. Breath is spent much more rapidly in giving low tones than higher ones.

Remark to the Teacher. You will now excuse a few of those who exhibit the greatest capacity of chest and drown the voices of the rest.

Direction 6. (Calling the names of such) you may rest while I find the voices of the remainder of the class.

Remark. Thus, in turn, sets of two or three or more may be excused after each effort, until you discover who have the feeblest voices, or the least control of them, and who of course need the greatest amount of attention and encouragement, to drill themselves in this exercise in their rooms, or in any other suitable place. Perseverance will not only serve to increase the power of the voice, but will actually increase the growth of the chest one, two, three inches or more, in a few weeks.

Remark. No person who is faithful in this exercise, attending to it daily, and several times a day, need fear the consumption or bronchitis; nor need he be deterred by making himself hoarse for the first few days. Hoarseness will of necessity result from any sufficient self-training, but should not be carried too far.

24.

DRILL IN ARTICULATION AND ACCENT.

Each scholar in turn may be called on to take his place in one end or corner of the room, and be required to read any passage which he may select in this book or any other, in a whisper, till he can be heard distinctly all over the room. The teacher will take his place as far as possible from the scholar, and inform him of the articulate sounds in which he fails. The pupil of course selects passages from the book without mentioning the page, so that he shall be understood, if at all, entirely by the distinctness and force of his articulation in the whispering exercise. Every pupil in the class will be called, and those who find the most difficulty in making their reading intelligible, must be trained repeatedly, and sufficiently, to reach the end aimed at in the drill. Short passages may be assigned, which involve difficult combinations of subvocal and aspirate sounds. Collections of such may be found in almost any reading book.

25.

PITCH.

PITCH. That quality of the voice which depends on the tension of the vocal chords, and the extent of the opening of the articulatory organs.

HIGH PITCH. That which results from a more than ordinary tension of the vocal chords, and a less than ordinary opening of the articulatory organs.

Remark. For definition and enumeration of *Articulatory Organs*, see page 48, section 11.

LOW PITCH. That which results from a less than ordinary tension of the vocal chords, and more than ordinary opening of the articulatory organs.

KEY. The average pitch on which any given passage is delivered.

MONOTONE. The same pitch, either high, medium, or low, with no variation, other than required by accent and cadence.

Remark. The Monotone is often thought to be Unvarying Low Pitch.

26.

DRILL ON PITCH.

Exercise 1. The class may be called on to give the sound *o*, in a medium pitch, with the teacher, and several times, till he perceives that they have all the same pitch. Then, the same sound in a low pitch; then, in a very low pitch; then, in a high pitch; then, in a very high.

Remark. This exercise must be varied and continued, till all the class get not only the knowledge of pitch, but till every scholar, whether possessed of a musical ear or not, can give a sound in any pitch required.

Exercise 2. The teacher will select some short passage, and require the class to read in concert, first in the ordinary pitch; then a little lower; then lower still, and so on, until a point is reached, where but a few of the better male voices can read with a distinct articulation. Then, commencing again with the ordinary pitch, the reading of the passage may be repeated, and varied in the ascend ing scale, till as high a pitch as may be consistent with distinct articulation is reached.

Remark 1. In pursuing these drills, females must be trained by themselves occasionally, while the males rest, and the plan of exercising the more powerful voices by twos and threes practised, till the most feeble voices and the most timid girls are reached, and their difficulties met by special training.

Remark 2. This exercise must be varied and continued, till every scholar can read any passage assigned, in any pitch required, unaccompanied by the teacher or other scholars.

Remark 3. Particular attention must be paid to those scholars who have acquired the habit of reading or speaking on too high or too low a key for their voice. Every voice has its own key, on which it can sustain continued delivery with the greatest ease to itself, and with the greatest satisfaction to an audience.

Remark 4. By frequent daily repetition of these exercises, on single sounds, and on sentences, in a low pitch with ever increasing force, a depth and strength of voice can be acquired which may be used, when required, with great effect in delivering emphatic words or passages. The exercise is well calculated to give the greatest compass and flexibility to the voice, and to bring it perfectly under control in this particular.

Remark 5. Constant attention must be given to the QUALITY of the voice in all these drills. No husky, guttural or nasal tones should be tolerated;

but if necessary, special drilling should be given to every pupil who does not possess a clear, full, ringing voice; in other words, PURE TONE. One of the more common causes of impure tone is a want of sufficient opening of the teeth and lips. If that be the difficulty, illustrations of the difference of tone resulting from this cause must be given by the teacher, and the pupil must have no peace till the difficulty be removed.

27.

EXAMPLES FOR DRILL IN PITCH.

LOW PITCH.

Hold! Shame! Beware! It is impossible! Scorn to be slaves. May my tongue cleave to the roof of my mouth.

Bless the Lord, O my soul, and all that is within me bless his holy name.

HIGH PITCH.

O, fie. My stars. Good enough. *Victory* (they all shouted) VICTORY, (as loud as they could scream), VICTORY.

To arms! the Greek! they come, the Greek!! the Greek!!!

VARYING PITCH OR COMPASS.

Falling.

I know not what course others may take, but as for me, give me liberty or give me death!

Rising.

What! to attribute the sacred sanctions of God, and nature, to the massacres of the Indian scalping knife; to the cannibal savage, torturing, murdering, devouring, drinking the blood of his mangled victims!

28.

FORCE.

FORCE. That property of the voice which depends on the power with which air is driven over the vocal chords, by the action of the respiratory organs.

Remark. For the definition and enumeration of the *Respiratory Organs*, see page 48, section 11.

SUSTAINED FORCE. That which is continued through the delivery of a word, phrase, or sentence.

MEDIUM FORCE. That of ordinary delivery in the conversational or didactic style.

STRONG FORCE. That of *loud* tones.

VERY STRONG FORCE. That of *vociferous* tones.

WEAK FORCE. That of *soft* tones.

VERY WEAK FORCE. That of *subdued* or almost *suppressed* tones.

29.

DRILL ON FORCE.

Remark 1. More difficulty is found in this matter of force, than in all others connected with reading and speaking. Many pupils, by previous bad habits, or by timidity, or by affectation, have no apparent power to make themselves heard beyond a few feet. Hence teachers, fellow pupils, and visitors, are perpetually annoyed by such shams. The first exercise must be directed to the remedy of this evil, and if necessary, the last.

Exercise 1. Let the class rise, take proper position, and give in concert the sound of *e*, in the medium pitch and with medium force; again, as the

the teacher says "louder," with increased force; and so on at the word "louder," with still increasing force, till vociferous tones are reached, at least by some of the class. Care must be taken that the medium pitch be preserved.

Let those having the strongest voices sit down (calling them by name). Go through with the same drill with the remainder of the class, excusing two or three at a time of those who are most distinctly heard till the feeblest voices are reached. Train these by themselves repeatedly, in a similar manner, giving the sounds of different letters, of different syllables and words. When some degree of force is developed on single words, short sentences may be read, by those timid, affected creatures till they can be heard in a remote corner of the room. After training several together, till this be accomplished, each such pupil may be taken separately and drilled till whatever force of voice or of character possessed shall be brought out and increased. The teacher may then pass into another room and shut the door, and require such pupils separately to read short sentences so that he can hear them; then longer ones.

This exercise must be resumed every day, for many days, perhaps for weeks, till the difficulty be entirely removed.

Exercise 2. Let the class give the sound of a vowel on a low pitch, and increase the force as before; again, on a very low pitch. Such pupils as succeed the best may be excused; while those whose voices are feeble must be trained in proportion to their need, especially to acquire force in low pitch.

Exercise 3. Reading in the monotone in very low pitch, with all possible force, serves to give great strength and compass to the voice. This exercise may be varied by concert reading on the monotone, in high pitch, and very high pitch, with increasing force; and by alternating from reading in monotone in high pitch, to reading in monotone in low pitch; from very high pitch, to very low, with different degrees of force as the teacher may direct, from medium to loud, very loud, vociferous; again from medium to soft, subdued, suppressed and whisper.

Remark 1. Too much attention cannot be bestowed in every drill on PURE TONE.

Remark 2. It is frequently necessary to drill the female voices separately, while the male voices rest.

31.

VARYING FORCE. That which is increased or diminished, or both increased and diminished on the same syllable.

SWELL. The increase of force on one syllable.

VANISH. The diminution of force on one syllable.

STRESS. Force applied to one part of a syllable more than to another.

RADICAL STRESS. That applied at the commencement of a syllable.

VANISHING STRESS. That applied at the end of a syllable. It is seldom used.

EXPULSIVE RADICAL STRESS. The powerful utterance of a syllable at its commencement, diminishing somewhat to the end.

EXPLOSIVE RADICAL STRESS. The violent bursting forth of sound at the commencement of a syllable, diminishing somewhat to the end.

Remark 1. The superiority of accomplished speakers consists much in the appropiate use of VARYING FORCE; a matter which is almost entirely overlooked in the majority of books on elocution.

Remark 2. Unremitting attention must be given in the following exercises to PURE TONE. No slender, aspirated, husky, nasal, or guttural sounds should be tolerated unless required by the nature of the piece delivered. Nothing short of a ringing tone, as clear and as sweet as a bell, should satisfy the trainer or trained.

32.

EXAMPLES FOR DRILL IN SUSTAINED FORCE.

Remark. Any of the following examples may be used for *Exercises* 1 or 3 in sustained force.

LOUD.

Look aloft. Watch, Watch.
To arms, to arms, the foe, they come, they come
Roll! on thou deep and dark-blue ocean, Roll!

SOFT.

Speak gently, she sleeps now.
Come then; expressive silence, muse His praise.

Ah! few shall part where many meet,
The snow shall be their winding sheet;
And every turf beneath their feet
Shall be a soldier's sepulchre.

WHISPER.

Hark! what is that noise? What can it be? Let us go and find mother!

Hush! hark! a deep sound strikes like a rising knell.

33.

EXAMPLES FOR DRILL IN VARYING FORCE.

O! Ah! Hold. Woe. Shoulder arms. Forward march. Rear column, halt.

Rouse, ye Romans! Rouse, ye slaves!

Strike! till the last armed foe expires,
Strike, for your altars and your fires,
Strike for the green graves of your sires,
God—and your native land.

Oh heaven! she cried. Can you not save him! Oh! save my husband.

34.

LAUGHING EXERCISE.

Remark. Exercise in concert laughing occasionally, is desirable, not only as a drill in varying force, but for its enlivening effects on a class.

Let the exercise commence on Ha! ha! ha! ha and make a real laugh of it; none of your dry, hollow, sham laughs—like this, Ha! ha! ha! but a real, genuine, hearty, old-fashioned laugh all around—Ha! ha! ha! ha! The exercise may be stopped by a sudden elevation of the hand as a signal.

EXAMPLE FOR THE LAUGHING EXERCISE.

What a funny old fellow that is! ha, ha, ha, ha. Did you ever see the like before? ha! ha! ha! ha! Just look at his nose once! if it is n't enough to make a horse laugh, ha! ha! ha! Oh my eyes! what a nose, ha! ha! ha! ha!

35.

RATE.

RATE. Rapidity of utterance, in the delivery of a sentence, or discourse.

Remark 1. The proper rate of delivery in every passage will depend on the nature of the thought and feeling expressed, yet it should not be so slow as to become a continuous drawl, nor so fast in any instance as to prevent distinct articulation.

Remark 2. "Reading too fast," is a common fault and much attention is demanded to correct it. In drilling a scholar, to correct too rapid reading, he will generally read slower by making pauses between all the words. This should not be tolerated, but he should be taught to prolong the vocals and sub-vocals, and to articulate the aspirates more distinctly.

Remark 3. Concert exercises will aid much in correcting too rapid reading, the teacher controlling the rate with his voice in each example at first. But they must not be relied on entirely.

36.

EXAMPLES FOR DRILL IN RATE.

Remark. Any sentence whatever may be taken as material for drill in correcting too rapid reading; this, for instance, or the following sentences:

SLOW AND DISTINCT.

God, who at sundry times and in divers manners; spake in times past unto the fathers by the prophets, hath in these last days spoken unto us by His dear Son.

O! Jerusalem! Jerusalem! thou that killest the prophets and stonest them that are sent unto thee.

how often would I have gathered thy children together, even as a hen gathereth her chickens under her wings, and ye would not!

RAPID AND DISTINCT.

How far wilt thou, O! Cataline, abuse our patience? How long shall thy madness outbrave our justice? To what extremities art thou resolved to push thy unbridled insolence of guilt?

37.

INFLECTIONS.

INFLECTION. The continuous elevation or depression of the pitch in the delivery of a syllable, word, phrase or sentence.

Explanation. By *continuous* elevation and depression is here understood that upward or downward sliding from one point to another, in the musical scale by which the voice is heard at every intermediate point.

SIMPLE INFLECTION. That which is entirely rising or entirely falling.

RISING INFLECTION. That in which the voice by a *gradual* tightening of the vocal chords and closing of the articulatory organs, glides from a lower to a higher pitch.

FALLING INFLECTION. That in which the voice by a *gradual* relaxing of the vocal chords and opening of the articulatory organs, glides from a higher to a lower pitch.

RISING SLIDE. The rising inflection continued through any single word standing independently, through several words, or through an entire sentence.

Explanation. The rising slide may be applied to such single words, as interjections, names of persons addressed, and equivalents for whole sentences; otherwise to several words in succession.

Bend. The rising inflection applied to a single word standing at the end of a phrase, clause or sentence, to denote incomplete sense.

38.

METHOD OF DRILL IN RISING INFLECTIONS.

Let the teacher select definite questions from this book, or any other, and read them with the rising slide; then with the bend, or rising inflection on the last word only, for the purpose of showing the correct manner of delivering them; also, for the purpose of showing the incorrect notation of such reading books as place the mark for the rising inflection on the last word only of a definite question.

Remark. If any mark is used, it ought to be placed at the beginning, rather than at the end of a question.

The teacher having illustrated the nature of the rising slide, and the manner of using it, with his own voice, will call on the class to read short questions in concert with himself; individuals in the class, to read the same, and other questions. In long questions, it will be well for the class all to take the pitch of the first word. This pitch should be much lower than the ordinary key, in order that the voice may have opportunity to rise through the whole question, without running so high, as to break.

Remark. In reading *very* long sentences, consisting of several clauses, or members, the voice will necessarily fall back at the commencement of every new clause to a pitch but a little higher than at the commencement of the preceding clause or member of the question. The pitch will become more and more elevated in every succeeding clause, till it culminates at the close of the last word of the entire sentence.

39.

EXAMPLES FOR DRILL IN RISING INFLECTIONS.

RISING SLIDE.

Do you deny that? Is that the man whom you expected? Did you arrive in town yesterday? Should we not all, both teachers, and scholars, be scrupulously careful to comply with the school regulations which we have adopted?

What? Might Rome then have been taken if these men who were at our gates had not wanted courage for the attempt? Rome taken, whilst I was consul?

Has Great Britain any enemy in this quarter of the world to call for all this accumulation of navies and armies? No sir, she has none.

Shall we acquire the means of effectual resistance, by lying supinely on our backs, and hugging the delusive phantom of hope, until our enemies shall have bound us hand and foot?

Do we never meet with charity which melts at suffering; with the honesty which disdains and is probably superior to falsehood; with the active beneficence which gives to others its time and its labor; with the modesty which shrinks from notice and gives all its sweetness to retirement; with the gentleness which breathes peace to all, and throws a beautiful lustre over the walks of domestic life?

Was it not enough that sorrow robed the happy home in mourning; was it not enough that disappointment preyed on its loveliest prospects; was it not enough that its little inmates cried in vain for bread, and heard no answer, but the poor father's sigh, and drank no sustenance, but the wretched mother's tears; was this a time for passion, conscienceless, licentious passion, with its eye of lust, its heart of stone, its hand of rapine, to rush into the mournful sanctuary of misfortune, casting crime into the cup of woe, and rob the parents of their only wealth, their child, and rob the child of her only charm, her innocence?

Do we intend to violate that most solemn obligation ever entered into by men, that plighting before God of our sacred honor to Washington, when, putting him forth to incur the dangers of war as well as the political hazards of the times, we promised to adhere to him in every extremity, with our fortunes and our lives?

Remark. Other examples may be selected from almost any reading book in use in the school; though these few afford sufficient material and variety for drilling a class on this inflection, viz: the Rising Slide.

40.

BEND.

As in Adam all die, so in Christ shall all be made alive.

Where the carcass is, there will the eagles be gathered together.

Remark. Other examples for drill in the use of the Bend may be taken from any part of this bock, or any other.

41.

Falling Slide. The falling inflection continued through any single word standing independently, through several words, or through an entire sentence.

Explanation. The falling slide may be applied to such single words as interjections, names of persons addressed, and equivalents for whole sentences; otherwise to several words in succession.

Partial Close. The falling inflection applied to a single word, commencing at a point above the key, and descending to it or slightly below it.

Perfect Close. The falling inflection applied at the end of a sentence, commencing with the key and descending far below it.

42.

METHOD OF DRILL IN THE FALLING INFLECTIONS.

Let the teacher select indefinite questions from this book or any other, and read them with the falling slide; and then with the perfect close, or falling inflection on the last word, only, for the purpose of showing the correct manner of delivering them, also for the purpose of showing the incorrect notation of such reading books as place the mark for the falling inflection on the last word, only, of an indefinite question.

The teacher having illustrated the nature of the falling slide, and the manner of using it, with his own voice, will call on the class to read short indefinite questions in concert with himself; then in concert, without his accompaniment; then on individuals in the class to read the same or other questions till they obtain the perfect control of the voice in this species of delivery.

Remark. It is a good plan to require the reading of an indefinite question occasionally with the rising slide, then again with the falling, till the difference is clearly discriminated, and till every voice in the class can give either, on any sentence that may be proposed.

A similar course may be pursued with the closes, as with the falling slide, contrasting them with the bend, and requiring the class, and individuals who most need the drill, to give the bend when the sense demands the partial close, and vice versa.

Remark. In the following exercises, selected more particularly for drill in falling inflections; rising inflections, particularly the bend, will necessarily occur, and suitable attention must be bestowed on their appropriate delivery.

43.

EXAMPLES FOR DRILL IN THE FALLING INFLECTION.

FALLING SLIDE.

Who is here so base that he would be a bondman?

Where is the man whose moral courage is equal to the test of rising and pleading this cause against this host of the licentious and profane?

How different would have been our lot this day had the revolution failed of success!

What can carry less the appearance of a design to fight than a man entangled with a cloak, shut up in a chariot, and almost fettered by a wife?

Who could guess,
If ever more should meet those mutual eyes,
Since upon a night, so sweet, such awful morn
should rise?

Remark. In very long indefinite questions consisting of several members, the voice takes a high pitch at the commencement of the first member and falls continuously to its end; then commencing the second member in a pitch not quite so high as at first, it falls to its end, and so on through the successive members; each member commencing and ending a little lower than the preceding member.

What place would be drearer than the future mansions of Christ to one who should want sympathy with their inhabitants; who could not understand their language; who would feel himself an alien there; who would be taught by those holy joys, of which he could not partake and for which he would have no relish, his own loneliness and desolation?

Why beholdest thou the mote that is in thy brother's eye, but considerest not the beam that is in thine own eye; or how wilt thou say to thy brother: Let me pull out the mote of thine eye, and behold a beam is in thine own eye?

To whom do we owe it, that the pure and powerful light of the gospel is now shed abroad over these countries, and rapidly gaining on the darkness of the western world; that the importance of religion to the temporal welfare, and to the permanence of wise institutions, is here beginning to be felt in its just measure; that the influence is not here as in almost every other section of Christendom, wrested to purposes of worldly ambition; that the holy Bible is not sealed from the eyes of those for whom it was intended; and that the best charities and noblest powers of the soul are not degraded by the terrors of a dark and artful superstition.

44.

PARTIAL AND PERFECT CLOSES.

Remark. The partial close is used to denote sense completed, but connected grammatically with that which follows; the perfect close is used to denote sense completed, but without grammatical connection with anything following. The closes are also both used, when given intensely, for emphasis, even when the sense is not complete, as will be shown under the head of Emphasis.

The history of the world is full of testimony to prove how much depends upon industry; not an eminent orator has lived but is an example of it.

With trembling hands, and faltering steps, he departed from his mansion of sorrow; his eyes were dazzled with the splendor of the light; and the face of nature presented to his view a perfect paradise. The jail in which he had been imprisoned stood at some distance from Pekin, and to that city he directed his course, impatient to enjoy the caresses of his wife, his children, and his friends.

Be perfect, be of good comfort; be of one mind, live in peace.

45.

SERIES.

Remark 1. In a succession of particulars, most reading books give directions to place the rising inflection on the last member of a commencing series, and on the last but one of a concluding series. Though no speaker, while earnestly engaged in delivering his own thoughts, ever conformed to these directions, it may be well, for the sake of the drill, to require a class to comply with these methods of delivery.

COMMENCING SERIES.

The poor, the sick, the aged and the wounded, were left to perish.

To advise the ignorant, to relieve the needy, and to comfort the afflicted, are duties that fall in our way almost every day af our lives.

CONCLUDING SERIES.

I protest against this measure as cruel, oppressive, tyrannical, and vindictive.

God was manifest in the flesh, justified in the spirit, seen of angels, preached unto the Gentiles, believed on in the world, and received up into glory.

Remark 2. In a long series, the bend may be used, to avoid monotony, occasionally, but no definite rule can be given in this matter. The judgment and taste of no two readers would agree; nor would any *good* reader be likely to deliver such a passage twice, precisely alike, in respect to the inflections. Take the following examples, for instance, on which the teacher and scholars can exercise their voices and their taste :

Neither blindness, nor gout, nor age, nor penury, nor domestic afflictions, nor political disappointments, nor abuse, nor proscription, nor neglect, had power to disturb him.

We do not pray, to instruct or advise God; not to tell Him news, or inform Him of our wants; nor do we pray, by dint of argument, to persuade God, and bring Him to our bent; nor that by fair speech we may cajole Him; or move His affection toward us by pathetic orations; not for any such purpose are we obliged to pray; but because it becometh and behooveth us to do so; because it is a proper means of bettering, ennobling, and perfecting our souls; because it breedeth most holy affections, pure satisfactions, and worthy resolutions; because it fitteth us for the enjoyment of happiness; and leadeth us thither; for such ends is devotion prescribed.

46.

METHOD OF DRILL IN ALL THE SIMPLE INFLECTIONS COMBINED.

Let the teacher select some piece in the reading book used, of rather simple grammatical constructions, and let the members of the class, each read one sentence, and describe his method of reading it, in respect to inflections. The remainder of the class will then be called on for criticisms; first, in the inflections given; secondly on the manner of describing them; thirdly, on the words miscalled; fourthly, on the words mispronounced, stating definitely what sound was given, and what sound the correct pronunciation requires. This course must be pursued several successive days, perhaps for weeks; at least, until every scholar shall become entirely familiar with the different inflections, and the technical names applied to them. No teacher should be satisfied, with calling the bend, the rising inflection; or with calling the partial close, the falling inflection, since there are other inflections of both kinds.

47

COMPOUND INFLECTIONS.

COMPOUND INFLECTION. A combination of both the rising and falling inflections on the same word, phrase, clause, or sentence.

DOUBLE SLIDE. The rising slide, or slides, on one member of an antithetic or conditional expression; and the falling on the other.

UPPER DOUBLE SLIDE. That in which the rising slide, or slides, precede the falling.

LOWER DOUBLE SLIDE. That in which the falling slide, or slides, precede the rising.

Note 1. The more emphatic member generally takes the falling slide.

Note 2. If the antithesis is between an affirmation or negation, the negation generally takes the rising slide.

Note 3. It will be noticed that the rising slide terminates with a bend, when used in connection with the falling, to form the double slide.

48.

EXAMPLES FOR DRILL ON THE DOUBLE SLIDES.

Art thou he that should come, or do we look for another?

Has God forsaken the works of his own hands, or does he always graciously preserve, and keep, and guide them?

As it was then, so it is now.

As in Adam all die, so in Christ are all made alive.

It is sown in corruption, it is raised in incorruption.

My son, if thou wilt receive my words, and hide my commandments with thee; so that thou incline thine ear unto wisdom, and apply thine heart unto understanding; yea, if thou criest after knowledge, and liftest up thy voice after understanding; if thou seekest her as silver, and searchest for her, as for hid treasure; then shalt thou understand the fear of the Lord, and find the knowledge of God.

You were paid to fight against Alexander, not to rail at him.

He declares Mr. Smith to be an honorable and trustworthy man, and not a hypocrite or knave, as you seem willing to insinuate.

49.

Circumflex. A combination of the rising and falling inflections on one syllable or word.

Upper Circumflex. That in which the rising inflection is heard first.

Lower Circumflex. That in which the falling inflection is heard first.

Remark 1. In the upper circumflex the rising inflection is often heard slightly, after the falling, as well as before it.

Remark 2. Mandeville calls the upper circumflex the wave; and the lower, the circumflex. McGuffey calls the upper circumflex, the falling circumflex, and the lower, the rising.

Remark 3. Though the circumflexes may be

placed in these two classes, their modifications and varieties are endless; no two being given precisely alike.

50.

EXAMPLES FOR DRILL ON THE CIRCUMFLEXES.

You *will* bring your grammar to-*morrow*?
You will bring *your* grammar to-*morrow*?
You will bring your *grammar* to-*morrow*?
You will bring your grammar *to-morrow*?

Ship *ahoy!* Ship *ahoy?*

If we have no regard for our *own* character, we ought to have some regard for the characters of *others*.

Were there *ten* cleansed, but where are the *nine*?

Should not children obey their parents in *all* things?

What will content you? Talent? No! Enterprise? No! Courage? No! Reputation? No! Virtue? No! The man whom you would select, should possess not one, but all of these.

Remark. The words *No* in this last example may be read with the lower circumflex, except the last, which should receive the upper circumflex, and perfect close, with considerable measure of force.

Where *grows?* Where grows it *not?*

What! Might Rome have been taken? Rome taken when I was consul?

Banished from Rome! Tried and convicted traitor!

Prince Henry. What's the matter?
Falstaff. What's the *matter?* Here be four of us have taken a thousand pounds this morning.

And this fellow calls himself a painter? A *Painter?* He is not fit to daub the sign of a country ale-house.

And this man is called a Statesman? A *Statesman!* Why, he never invented a decent humbug.

Remark. The last six examples are taken from McGuffey's Fifth Reader, where the words in italics are marked with the rising inflection. The class may read them with the rising inflection; also, with the upper circumflex and lower circumflex, and may then be called on to decide on the most appropriate delivery. If the upper circumflex be given to the words *Painter* and *Statesman*, ridicule is thrown on the idea given in the preceding sentences. If the same words be read with the lower circumflex, contempt is expressed for the persons spoken of.

A man who is in the daily use of ardent spirits, if he does not abuse his wife and children, will eventually ruin his health and character.

A lady who suffers herself to use tobacco, if she does not ruin her health and character, makes herself utterly repulsive and disgusting.

The boy who plays truant occasionally, if he does not thereby lose all interest in his studies, will become an unreliable and worthless citizen.

Remark. By the proper or improper use of the circumflexes in these last three examples, two entirely different sets of ideas will be given in reading them; hence, they are very good examples for the discrimination of the circumflexes.

51.

EMPHATIC SWEEP. The combination of the slides and circumflexes for the purpose of emphasis.

EXAMPLES FOR DRILL ON THE EMPHATIC SWEEP.

A cry of joyful *surprise* resounded through the court-room. The prisoner charged with *murder* was declared innocent.

If I would not consent to be *searched*, it was because I was a stranger to every one present; and because I had on my person a medal exactly *similar* to the one supposed to be stolen.

Remark. The above examples give the combination of the rising slide, upper circumflex, and falling slide, in the same order as here mentioned.

The poor girl paid him *thankfully*, when she learned that her bill was only *fifty cents.*

Remark. In this example, the first emphatic sweep consists of the rising slide and the upper circumflex, on the word *thankfully;* the second emphatic sweep consists of the rising slide, slightly developed, and the lower circumflex on *fifty cents.*

The man asked the Doctor whether he *killed* his wife. "No," said the Doctor. "Did you cure her?" "No." "Then you have no legal *demand*, according to our *contract*," said the man.

Remark. Let the pupil describe each of the emphatic sweeps in the preceding passage—i. e., tell what each one is made up of, which slides and which circumflex; also, in the following passage:

"It amazes me that ministers don't write better sermons; I am sick of the dull prosy affairs," said a woman in the presence of Dr. Nesbit.

"But it is no easy matter, my good woman, to write good sermons," suggested the Doctor.

"Yes," rejoined the lady, "*but you are so long about it;* I could write one in half the time, if I only had the text."

"O, if a text is all you want," said Dr. Nesbit, "I will furnish that; take this one from Solomon: 'It is better to dwell in a corner of a house top, than in a wide house with a brawling woman.'"

"Do you mean me, sir?" inquired the woman quickly.

"O, my good woman," was the response, "you will never make a sermonizer; you are too quick in making your application."

Remark. From these examples it will be seen that the emphatic sweep is the most complex form of inflection; and that it is made up of every possible combination of the slides and circumflexes; also, that the emphasis concentrates itself in the circumflex, the slides being introductory, or concluding in their character.

52.

RULES FOR INFLECTIONS.

Remark 1. The classification of sentences is given on page 168, section 71.

Remark 2. Interrogative sentences are divided for purposes of delivery, into Definite, Indefinite, Indirect, and Double.

DEFINITE INTERROGATIVE SENTENCE. One which may be answered by yes or no.

INDEFINITE INTERROGATIVE SENTENCE. One that requires some other answer than yes or no.

INDIRECT INTERROGATIVE SENTENCE. One which has the grammatical form of a declarative sentence.

DOUBLE INTERROGATIVE SENTENCE. One in which the disjunctive *or* occurs.

Remark 3. Scarcely a rule can be given for the inflections which is not liable to be modified or violated by emphasis or impassioned delivery. Some of the cases in which such modifications or violations most frequently occur will be given as exceptions.

Remark 4 It may be said: "If no rule is reliable, why give any rules?" I give them as indicative of the most common usage; but more, for the advantage of the drill which the examples under them afford.

53.

RULE I.

Simple and complex declarative sentences, are delivered with the bend, at the intermediate pauses; with the emphatic sweep, culminating on the emphatic words; and with the perfect close at the end.

Remark. The substitute for this rule, as given by authors who pay no attention to sentential structure, is substantially this: "Incomplete sense requires the rising inflection; and complete sense, the falling inflection."

54.

EXAMPLES FOR DRILL.

Simple Declaratives.

In thy sight, O Lord, shall no man be justified.

Many persons mistake the love, for the practice of virtue.

Complex Declaratives.

Lysimachus, the teacher of Alexander, being an austere man, and a near relation of Olympias, inured his pupil to hardy habits, which invigorated his constitution.

There are but few who know how to be idle and innocent.

As fame is but breath, as riches are transitory, and as life itself is uncertain, it becomes us to seek a better portion.

Ye who listen with credulity to the whispers of fancy, and pursue with eagerness the phantoms of hope; who expect that age will perform the promises of youth, and that the deficiencies of the present day will be supplied by the morrow, attend to the history of Rasselas, prince of Abyssinia.

55.

Exception 1. Earnest and sad delivery often require the partial close at the intermediate pauses.

56.

EXAMPLES FOR DRILL.

Earnest Delivery.

From thy throne in the sky, thou lookest; and hurlest the bolt of death.

To smile upon those we should censure, Lorenzo, and to countenance such as are guilty of bad actions, is bringing guilt on ourselves.

Ah! me, the laureled wreath that murder rears,
Blood-nursed and watered with a widow's tears,
Seems not so foul, so tainted, and so dread,
As waves the nightshade round the sceptic's head.

57.

Sad Delivery.

The path of sorrow, and that path alone,
Leads to the land where sorrow is unknown.

Touch not those ancient elms that bend their shade
O'er the patriots' graves, for 'neath their boughs
There is a solemn darkness even at noon
Suited to such as visit at the shrine

Of serious liberty. No factious voice
Called them unto the field of generous fame,
But the pure consecrated love of home.

58.

Exception 2. Negative sentences and clauses are generally delivered with the rising slide and with the lower circumflex on the emphatic word; hence they terminate with the bend, instead of the perfect close.

EXAMPLES FOR DRILL.

Friends, it was not our *purpose* to injure you.

It was not an *eclipse* that caused the darkness at the crucifixion of our Lord; for the sun and moon were not relatively in a position to produce an eclipse.

Now it is hardly to be supposed that he could have acquitted himself very well, as ill as he was last Saturday evening.

59.

Exception 3. The members of a series may be delivered partly or entirely with the partial close, instead of the bend, at the intermediate pause, or pauses, of the sentence of which they form a part.

Remark. Most writers on Elocution give definite rules for the delivery of series, dividing them into commencing and concluding series; but for the reason assigned on page 386, section 45, I consider such rules pernicious. Good taste, for the guidance of which no definite rule can be given in this case, must determine the proper and *peculiar* delivery of every series that may occur.

EXAMPLES FOR DRILL.

Love, joy, peace, long suffering, gentleness, goodness, faith, meekness, temperance, are the fruits of the spirit.

The science of Elocution is noble, elegant, pleasing, refining, useful, intricate, philosophical and wonderful; nevertheless some of the rules given by Elocutionists are trifling, erroneous and pernicious.

The fruits of the spirit are love, joy, peace, long suffering, gentleness, goodness, faith, meekness, temperance; against these there is no law.

For I am persuaded that neither life, nor death, nor angels, nor principalities, nor powers, nor things present, nor things to come, nor hight, nor depth, nor any other creature, shall be able to separate us from the love of God, which is in Christ Jesus, our Lord.

60.

RULE II.

Compound declarative sentences are delivered with the partial close at the termination of the leading, and of all the co-ordinate sentences except the last, which takes the perfect close.

EXAMPLES FOR DRILL.

Beauty is but a vain, a fleeting good;
A shining gloss, that fadeth suddenly;
A flower, that dies almost in the bud;
A brittle glass, that breaketh presently:
A fleeting good, a glass, a gloss, a flower,
Lost, faded, broken, dead within the hour.

And beside this, giving all diligence, add to your faith, virtue; and to your virtue, knowledge; and to your knowledge, temperance; and to your temperance, patience; and to your patience, godliness; and to godliness, brotherly kindness; and to brotherly kindness, charity.

I am crucified with Christ; nevertheless I live; yet not I, but Christ liveth in me; and the life which I now live in the flesh, I live in the faith of the Son of God, who loved me and gave himself for me.

Contrasted faults through all his manners reign;
Though poor, luxurious; though submissive, vain;
Though grave, yet trifling; zealous, yet untrue;
And e'en in penance, planning sins anew.

61.

Exception. If antithesis is expressed, one member will require the rising and the other the falling slide.

EXAMPLES FOR DRILL.

I could honor thy courage, but I detest thy crimes.

They slight my mean birth; I despise their mean characters.

You were paid to fight against Alexander; not to rail at him.

Let us retract when we can; not when we must.

It was by industry, perseverance and integrity that he obtained his political eminence; not by partizan tricks, chicanery and fraud, as most men of the dominant party obtain and retain their position and influence now.

62.

RULE III.

Definite Interrogative Sentences are delivered with the rising slide, commencing below the key and ascending above it.

Note 1. If the sentence is long, consisting of several members, it should be commenced with the pitch far below the key, and ascending through the first member it may conclude with the bend; the second member should commence with the pitch slightly higher than the first, and ascending through this member, it terminates with a bend somewhat higher than in the first member; and so on through all the successive members to the end of the entire sentence.

Note 2. Emphasis is generally given in definite questions by the lower circumflex.

63.

EXAMPLES FOR DRILL.

Did you say he walked to town yesterday?

Remark. Let successive scholars give the preceding sentence with the emphasis on each of the successive words, beginning with the first.

Could not this man who opened the eyes of the blind, have caused that even this man should not have died?

Has not he himself, have not all the martyrs after him, poured forth their blood in the conflict?

Are despots alone, to be reproached for unfeeling indifference, to the tears and blood of their subjects; are not republican rulers equally responsible?

Have the principles on which you ground the reproach on cabinets and kings, no practical influence or binding force on cabinets and presidents?

Shall we acquire the means of effectual resistance by lying supinely on our backs, and hugging the delusive phantom of hope, until our enemies shall have bound us hand and foot?

Can we ever hope to witness on earth a pure and holy generation, while even parents utter their polluting levities in the hearing of their own children; and vice and humor and gaiety are all indiscriminately blended into one conversation; and a loud laugh is ever ready to regale the man who can prostitute his powers of entertainment to the lowest species of profligacy and lasciviousness?

64.

Note. If a circumstance follows an interrogative, the same slide is continued through the circumstance.

EXAMPLES FOR DRILL.

Did you arrive in town this morning? said the teacher to James.

"Will you examine my work on Gymnastics?" shouted Mr. Smith to a group of boys—who seemed adepts in the science already.

65.

Exception 1. A definite interrogative used as an exclamation, may take the falling slide.

EXAMPLES FOR DRILL.

Was it not terrible! Can it be possible! Is it possible that my son should do such a thing as that! Could he think of returning under such circumstances!

John. Did you come from Cincinnati, yesterday?

Has the gentleman done? *Has he completely done?*

67.

Exception 3. In a series of definite interrogative sentences, the last may take the falling slide.

Note. If the answers are given in a series of definite questions, they may be delivered with the rising slide, and lower circumflex on the emphatic word, except the last, which requires the perfect close.

EXAMPLES FOR DRILL.

Do you know me, sir? Am I Dromio?
Am I your man? *Am I myself?*

Am I not an apostle? Am I not free? Have I not seen Jesus Christ our Lord? *Are not ye my work in the Lord?*

Are they Hebrews? So am I. Are they Israelites? So am I. Are they the seed of Abraham? So am I. *Are they the ministers of Christ?* I am more.

Are you poor, and likely to want for necessary food? The followers of Christ are, surely, more liberal than mere worldlings. Are you exposed to sickness and bodily pain? True Christians have ever manifested their love to Christ by ministering to him in the persons of the afflicted and distressed. Are you mourning over the sins and follies of a misspent life? Jesus is ready to receive, even to the uttermost, all that come to him in penitence and faith. Are you writhing under the anguish of blighted affections, and disappointed hopes? In Jesus you find an object worthy of your heart's best affections, and in his promises you may entertain such hopes as the wealth and power of this world can never realize. *Do you desire eternal life?* He alone has this boon to bestow.

68.

RULE IV.

Indefinite interrogative sentences are delivered with the falling slide; or with the rising slide to the emphatic word, and this taking the upper circumflex, with the falling slide to the end of the sentence.

EXAMPLES FOR DRILL.

What stranger came into our school this morning? Where did he come from? When will he visit us again?

Why! What evil hath he done?

Who hath warned you to flee from the wrath to come?

69.

Note. When the indefinite interrogative is succeeded by a circumstance in the same sentence, the latter is delivered with the continuation of the same slide with the former.

EXAMPLES FOR DRILL.

Who will come to our relief? said the terrified woman, as the flames approached the place where she stood with her babe in her arms.

When shall I be set free? said the dying man, with hope lighting up his countenance, to the physician who stood at his bedside.

70.

Note. In a compound indefinite interrogative sentence, the successive simple or complex interrogatives are delivered each with a falling slide, commencing and ending somewhat lower than that of the preceding.

EXAMPLES FOR DRILL.

By what title do you, Naso, sit on that chair and preside in judgment? by what right, Attius, do you accuse, or I defend? whence all this solemnity and pomp of judges, and clerks, and officers, of which this house is full?

Who is this that darkeneth words without knowledge? Where wast thou when I laid the foundations of the earth? Who hath laid the measure thereof, if thou knowest? or who hath stretched the line upon it? Whereupon are the foundations thereof fastened? or who hath laid the corner stone thereof?

How shall I attempt to follow them through the succession of great events, which a rare and kind Providence crowded into their lives? how shall I attempt to count all the links of that bright chain which binds the perilous hour of their first efforts for freedom, with the rich enjoyment of its consummation? how shall I attempt to enumerate the posts they filled, and the trusts they discharged, at home and abroad?

71.

RULE V.

Indirect interrogative sentences are delivered with the circumflex inflections on the emphatic words.

Note 1. The circumflexes in this class of sentences require a greater flexibility of the voice than elsewhere. When two are given in one sentence, the first is generally the upper, and the second the lower, rising above the key.

Note 2. The same indirect interrogative may be *correctly* delivered in two or more different ways, by varying the application and use of the circumflexes.

72.

EXAMPLES FOR DRILL

You *came* to town *yesterday?* did you not?

Your *brother* wrote that article in the Tribune respecting the *eleventh commandment?*

Mr. Smith's speculations in *western lands* have nearly *ruined* him, have they not?

Surely, you will not think that I was guilty of such an indiscretion as that?

You will grant him that small favor, I hope; even, though he has injured you?

Only *one* failed of obtaining a first grade certificate, eh? Who was he?

John Turpin.

John Turpin? Why, he was the best scholar in his class. He, surely, didn't fail on any of the questions proposed?

Oh, no, but John has a mind of his own, you know, and the examiners were incapable of distinguishing between independence and ignorance.

Then John, you think, could have given the examiners some valuable instruction?

Oh, no, they are too wise for that; they say, they are there to examine the candidates; and not to be examined or taught *by* the candidates.

73.

Note. Interrogative exclamations and words repeated as an echo to the thought, are delivered with one or the other of the circumflexes, according to the feeling designed to be expressed.

Remark. In many reading books, expressions of this class are marked for the rising inflection. This delivery does not agree with usage.

EXAMPLES FOR DRILL.

Prince Henry. What's the matter?

Falstaff. *What's the matter?* Here be four of us have taken a thousand pounds this morning.

Prince H. Where is it, Jack? Where is it?

Fals. *Where is it?* Taken from us, it is.

And you call that fellow a poet, do you? A poet! He could never even make the rhymes jingle in his doggerel. A poet! Ha! ha! ha! that's the last thing I ever should think of calling him.

74.

RULE VI.

Double interrogative sentences are delivered with the rising slide to the disjunctive *or*, and with the falling slide from it.

Note. The word *or* is generally delivered in the same pitch as the commencement of the sentence.

EXAMPLES FOR DRILL.

Did you arrive last evening, or this morning?

Art thou he that should come, or do we look for another?

Is there nothing that whispers to that right honorable gentleman, that the crisis is too big, that the times are too gigantic, to be ruled by the little hackneyed and every-day means of ordinary corruption; or are we to believe that he has within himself a conscious feeling, that disqualifies him for rebuking the ill-timed selfishness of his new allies?

75.

RULE VII.

Compellatives in familar discourse are delivered with the rising slide, but in earnest or respectful discourse, may be delivered with the falling slide.

EXAMPLES FOR DRILL.

John, what are you about there?

Sammy, my fine fellow, you are just the one I wanted to see.

Mary, I should hardly have thought that of you.

Friends, countrymen and lovers, hear me for my cause, and be silent that you may hear.

Remark. If the compellatives in the two last and similar examples are given with the falling slide, and with the pitch much depressed on each succeeding word, the delivery will be much more impressive than with the rising slide on each; or than with the rising slide on all but the last, and the falling slide on that.

Mr. President, Ladies, Gentlemen, and Friends This is surely no ordinary occasion.

Ye hypocrites! ye vipers! who shall deliver you from the wrath to come?

76.

RULE VIII.

Parentheses are delivered with inflections according to preceding rules; but with increased rate, depressed pitch, and diminished force.

EXAMPLES FOR DRILL.

Know ye not, brethren, (for I speak to them that know the law,) that the law hath dominion over a man as long as he liveth?

She had managed this matter so well (oh! she was the most artful of women!) that my father's heart was gone before I even suspected it was in danger.

77

RULE IX.

Mixed sentences are delivered according to the rules applicable to each of their parts.

EXAMPLES FOR DRILL.

He kept repeating in an under tone: Gone? Gone? is it possible that she has gone with some one else?

My friends often asked: What are you going to do with yourself when you get an education? Are you going to come out a poet or a ninny?

78.

RULE X

Poetry is delivered with the same inflections and emphasis as the same class of sentences requires in prose.

Nota Bene. Let there be no recognition of the metrical construction in the delivery of poetry, unless it is the design to sing it.

Remark. Poetry, properly constructed, will yield, really, the most pleasure to the ear, when these directions are carefully complied with.

METHOD OF DRILL FOR POETRY.

Let the teacher select such easy, flowing, melodious pieces as are most likely to be *sung* by scholars, rather than read; and let him contrast the faulty methods of delivery with the correct, before he shall call on the scholars to read them. If still any pupil shall be governed by the measure more than by the sense in his delivery, let the teacher deliver the same passage—and caricature the fault, saying when he has done: "You did not read half as badly as that, but somewhat in that manner. I wish you to try and avoid it altogether. You may read that passage again, if you are willing."

79.

EMPHASIS.

Emphasis. Any means by which a word, phrase, or sentence, is rendered more impressive than the words, phrases, or sentences with which it stands connected.

Ordinary Emphasis. That placed on a word or phrase, without relation to any other emphasized word, phrase, or sentence.

Antithetic Emphasis. That placed on two or more related words or phrases in different members of a sentence, to exhibit the relation more clearly.

Explanation. As antithesis is the most common relation thus exhibited, it gives its name to this class of emphasis.

Cumulative Emphasis. That placed on successive words or phrases in the same member of a sentence, to make them increasingly impressive.

Deferred Emphasis. That which is retained in the delivery of a succession of particulars of increasing importance, till the utterance of the last.

Conventional Emphasis. That given in some common expressions by general usage, without regard to the sense.

80.

METHODS OF GIVING EMPHASIS.

Remark. These are so various and complicated, that it will require too much space to give a complete analysis of them. The more common methods are given in the outline on page 365. It will be my purpose, only, to give such examples here, as will illustrate, in as brief a space as possible, the different CLASSES of Emphasis, and as will afford the teacher the means of drilling his class in most of the METHODS comprised in the outline, and in any other that may occur to him.

81.

METHOD OF DRILL IN EMPHASIS.

1. Let the teacher select such passages from this book, or any other, as shall illustrate the different CLASSES of emphasis, and give the proper delivery of one example; then call on the class to give in concert the same passage; then let him call on individuals to give the same or other similar passages, till every one is able to *distinguish* the different classes of emphasis and to deliver them properly.

2. Let the teacher select such passages as shall illustrate the different METHODS of emphasis, and pursue a similar course as with the CLASSES, and dwell on each METHOD long enough, and with a sufficient variety of examples, so that its propriety and force shall be acknowledged and felt by the class, and the majority of the class shall be able to avail themselves of the different methods, in a measure, spontaneously, in the delivery of selected or original pieces.

Remark. No department of vocal culture affords so appropriate a field for the cultivation of good taste, and judicious management of the voice and expression of the countenance as that of emphasis. If never before, here is the place to remove all sing-song tones, to extinguish all boarding school affectation, to infuse so much vivacity, feeling and soul into the pupil, that all tendency to a mechanical delivery shall be lost, in his appreciation of his subject, and in his effort to arouse suitable sympathy in his audience.

82.

EXAMPLES FOR DRILL IN CLASSES OF EMPHASIS.

ORDINARY EMPHASIS.

Did you say that I was not in school yesterday?

Remark. Ordinary Emphasis may, in different readings of this question, be placed on any word in it; and the drill requires that every scholar shall be able to read this or any similar sentence, and place the emphasis as he is directed by the trainer.

No man may put off the Law of God. Evil communications corrupt good manners. Do you think you will walk to town to-day?

83.

ANTITHETIC EMPHASIS.

Single Antithesis.

It is better to *mend* our faults than to *hide* them.

He who cannot *bear* a joke should never *give* one.

I come to *bury* Cæsar, not to *praise* him.

It is *sown* in weakness; it is *raised* in power. It is *sown* a natural body; it is *raised* a spiritual body.

Double Antithesis.

It is *sown* in *weakness;* it is *raised* in *power.*

It is *sown* a *natural* body; it is *raised* a *spiritual* body.

It is better to *trust* in the *Lord* than to *put confidence* in *Princes.*

Although the *fig-tree* shall not *blossom*, neither shall *fruit* be found on the *vines*, the *labor* of the *olive* shall *fail*, and the *fields* shall *yield no meat*, the *flock* shall be cut off from the *fold*, and there shall be no *herd* in the *stalls*; yet *I* will rejoice in the *Lord*. I will *joy* in the God of my salvation.

Remark. This passage admits of a great variety of emphasis. It may be read with the ordinary, rather than with the antithetic, or with the single antithesis rather than with the double. It may be read also with the triple antithesis.

Triple Antithesis.

She always called the *misfortunes* of *others*, *judgments;* while she considered the *calamities* that befell *herself*, *afflictions*.

A *friend* cannot be *known* in *prosperity*, an *enemy* cannot be *hidden* in *adversity*.

84.

CUMULATIVE EMPHASIS.

I tell you, though *you*, though the WHOLE WORLD, though an ANGEL FROM HEAVEN, were to declare the truth of it, I would not believe it.

Were I an American, as I am an Englishman, while a single foreign troop remained in my country, I would never lay down my arms. *Never!* NEVER!! NEVER!!!

We have petitioned, we have *remonstrated*, we have SUPPLICATED, we have PROSTRATED ourselves at the foot of the throne.

Sink or swim, live or die, survive or perish, I am for the declaration.

85.

DEFERRED EMPHASIS.

The knowledge, power, wisdom, holiness, and *goodness* of God are all unbounded.

Remark. Any of the examples given under cumulative, may be used as examples for deferred emphasis.

86.

CONVENTIONAL EMPHASIS.

Dry Goods, Groceries, Yankee Notions, and *so* forth.

From *day* to *day;* from *man* to *man.*

Remark. To show that the emphasis is *conventional*, and not *ordinary*, in these examples, I will give others in which the ordinary emphasis may be given under similar circumstances.

Dry Goods, Groceries, Yankee Notions, and so *on* to the end of the list.

From everlasting *to* everlasting, He is the same.

87.

EXAMPLES FOR DRILL ON THE METHODS OF EMPHASIS.

Remark. Almost any of the preceding examples may be used for illustrating emphasis as effected by elevation of pitch, and increase of force.

DEPRESSION OF PITCH AND DIMINUTION OF FORCE.

You know that you are Brutus, that speak this,
Or, *by the gods*, this speech were else your last.

Yet half I hear the parting spirit sigh,
"*It is a dread and awful thing to die.*"

DEPRESSION OF PITCH AND INCREASE OF FORCE.

I scorn your proffered treaty; the pale face I defy,
Revenge is stamped upon my spear, and *blood* my battle cry.

If influenced by local pride, or gangrened by State jealousy, I get up here to abate a tithe of a hair from his just character, and just fame—*may my tongue cleave to the roof of my mouth.*

88.

WHISPER.

And the deep thunder peal on peal afar,
And near the beat of the alarming drum,
Roused up the soldier, ere the morning star,
While thronged the citizens with terror dumb,
Or whispering, with white lips, "*The foe, they come, they come.*"

INCREASE OR DIMINUTION OF RATE.

Remark. A sufficient variety of examples to illustrate these methods may be found in connection with other methods.

CHANGE OF ACCENT.

He shall *in*crease, but I shall *de*crease.

There is a difference between giving and *for*giving.

In this species of composition *plau*sibility is much more desirable than *prob*ability.

89.

EMPHATIC SWEEP.

Are not you, sir, who sit in that chair, is not he, our venerable colleague near you, are you not both the predestined objects of punishment and vengeance? Cut off from all hope of royal clemency, what are you, what can you be, while the power of England yet remains, but out-laws?

90.

EMPHATIC PAUSE.

Woe,—woe,—woe,—to the inhabitants of the earth.

Strike—till the last armed foe expires,
Strike—for your altars and your fires,

Strike—for the green graves of your sires,
God—and your native land.

O, woman!—in our hours of ease
Uncertain,—coy,—and hard to please,
And—variable—as the shade,
By the light quivering aspen made;
When pain and anguish wring the brow,
A ministering angel—thou.

The war that for a space did fail,
Now trebly thundering, swelled the gale,
And—Stanley—was the cry.

I know there is not a man here,—who would not rather see a general conflagration—sweep over the land,—or an earthquake—sink it,—than one jot or tittle of that plighted faith fall to the ground. For myself, having twelve months ago, in this place, moved you, that George Washington be appointed commander of the forces raised, or to be raised, for the defense of American liberty; may my right hand forget her cunning—and my tongue cleave to the roof of my mouth—if I hesitate—or waver—in the support I give him.

91.

TONE.

Tone. That quality of the voice which depends on the proper, or improper use of the articulatory and vocal organs; also, on their healthy or diseased condition.

Pure Tone. That clear, ringing, bell-like sound which can result only from a proper arrangement and healthy condition of the vocal and articulatory organs.

Remark 1. If the trainer has been competent and faithful thus far, his pupils will by this time not only understand the nature of PURE TONE, but they will possess the ability and the desire to use it.

Remark 2. The nasal, guttural, aspirated and husky tones should all be avoided—scrupulously avoided—in ordinary and protracted delivery; but each may be used with good effect to give expression to some passion or emotion, as will be illustrated in the following examples.

92.

EXAMPLES FOR DRILL IN IMPURE TONES.

NASAL TONE.

And this *Cæsar* has become a *god*, and Cassius a *wretched creature.*

How like a fawning publican he looks,
I hate him, for he is a Christian.

GUTTURAL TONE.

Thou slave! thou wretch! thou coward!
Thou little valiant, great in villainy!
Thou ever strong upon the stronger side!

ASPIRATED TONE.

Oh! mercy! mercy on us! What is that? Didn't you hear it? Don't you see it? Oh! Mercy! Mercy! The Lord have mercy on us!

TREMULOUS TONE.

Pity the sorrows of a poor old man,
Whose trembling limbs have borne him to your door
Whose days are dwindled to the shortest span,
Oh! give relief, and Heaven will bless your store.

93.

STYLES OF DELIVERY.

STYLE OF DELIVERY. That peculiar adaptation of Key, Force, Rate, Inflections, Emphasis, Tone and Personation, required to impress any given style of thought and feeling; to awaken any particular kind of emotion, or to represent any passion, habit, or usage, whether individual, provincial, or national.

Remark. Instead of definitions one or two brief examples will be given for drill, under each style of delivery. It is expected here, as elsewhere, that each scholar will be drilled on each example given. It is found to serve a better purpose to drill all the pupils of a class on one or two appropriate examples, than each one on a different example. It is well to require the whole class to memorize one or more of the examples every day, that they may give them without the book.

METHOD OF DRILL.

1. Let the pupil who is called on, for reading or speaking, take his place in a proper manner on the rostrum. Let his position, bow, and manner of holding the book receive due attention. If he shall not succeed in complying with the directions given by the teacher, let him be excused, while the teacher gives an example on the rostrum of the manner in which he would have the pupil perform his part. If necessary, the teacher can caricature the errors of the pupil, and awkwardness in general, always encouraging the pupil, by assuring him that his errors are not as gross as those of the caricature.

2. The class *may* be called on for criticism in the case of each pupil under drill, before the teacher shall offer any corrections.

3. The exercise may be varied by concert reading, or concert speaking of any one of the examples given; the teacher having first read or spoken the piece alone, then in concert with the class; the class will then read or speak the piece without the teacher; while he gives his special attention to the most faulty.

4. Gesticulation may be introduced into these concert exercises with good effect; the teacher always leading the way by first giving the example with appropriate gestures, before he shall require them of the class.

94.

EXAMPLES FOR DRILL.

Narrative Style.

The late Rev. Mr. W. relates the following circumstance in one of his journals: Wednesday, 9th. I rode over to a neighboring town to wait on a Justice of the Peace, a man of candor and understanding, before whom, I was informed, their angry neighbors had carried a whole load of these new heretics, (the Methodists.) But when he asked them what they had done, there was a deep silence, for that was a point the persecutors had forgot. At length, one said: "Why, they pretend to be better than other people; and besides, they pray from morning to night." The Justice asked, "But have they done nothing else?" "Yes sir," said an old man, "an't please your worship, they have *convarted* my wife. Till she went among them, she had such a tongue! and now she is as quiet as a lamb." "Carry them back! carry them back!" said the Justice, "and let them convert all the scolds in the town."

95.

Didactic Style.

There is nothing more characteristic of a true Christian than humility. It is the first lesson that he learns in the school of Christ, and is the source of contentment and solid peace of mind. If he hears that any one has reviled him, he is ready to say, with the philosopher, "Had he known me better, he would have said worse things of me than that." The fiercest storms of adversity blow *over* him. Humility gives a pliancy to his mind, which saves it by yielding to the force it cannot resist; like the weak and bending reed, that weathers out the tempest, which fells the tall and sturdy oak.

In the evening of the day on which Sir Eadly Wilmot was appointed Chief Justice of England, one of his sons, a youth of seventeen, attended him to his bedside. "Now," said he, "my son, I will tell you a secret worth knowing, and remembering. The elevation I have met with in life, particularly the last instance of it, has not been owing to my superior merit or abilities, but to my *humility*, to my not having set myself up above others; and to a uniform endeavor to pass through life void of offence toward God and man." Thus humility is the way to honor.

96.

Persuasive Style.

Whatever plans of liberality you may have before you, it is well not to procrastinate, but to improve the first opportunity of executing them. How much more satisfaction does the truly beneficent man derive from his daily appropriation of his wealth than did Stephen Girard in hoarding property for some other person to appropriate it. None can so well use property as he who earns it. Suppose Girard had himself established the Asylum for Orphans. How much satisfaction he must have derived from the comfort, improvement, and promise of the thousands that his vast wealth might have rescued from penury and crime. Could he now witness the gross misapplication in lavish expenditure of that which he gathered so carefully, and guarded so scrupulously, how keen and continuous the pangs would be, that he had not given the money its just direction by his own administration while living.

I repeat it, then, my friends, enjoy your own means by applying them to such objects of charity and usefulness as may seem most worthy of them, and as will yield you the greater amount of pleasure in the appropriate and economical disposition of them.

97.

Argumentative Style.

Sink or swim, live or die, survive or perish, I give my hand and my heart to this vote. It is true, indeed, that in the beginning, we aimed not at independence. But there is a divinity which shapes our ends. The injustice of England has driven us to arms; and blinded to her own interest, she has obstinately persisted, till independence is now within our grasp. We have but to reach forth to it, and it is ours. Why then should we defer the declaration? Is any man so weak, as now to hope for a reconciliation with England, which shall leave either safety to the country and its liberties, or security to his own life, and his own honor? Are not you, sir, who sit in that chair, is not he, our venerable colleague, near you, are you not both, already the proscribed and predestined objects of punishment and of vengeance? Cut off from all hope of royal clemency, what are you, what can you be, while the power of England remains, but *outlaws?*

If we postpone independence, do we mean to carry on, or to give up the war? Do we mean to submit, and consent that we shall be ground to powder, and our country and its rights trodden down in the dust? I *know* we do not mean to submit. We NEVER *shall submit!* Do we intend to violate that most solemn obligation ever entered into by men, that plighting, before God, of our sacred honor to Washington, when, putting him forth to incur the dangers of war, as well as the political hazards of the times, we promised to adhere to him in every extremity, with our fortunes and our lives? I know there is not a man here, who would not rather see a general conflagration sweep over the land, or an earthquake sink it, than one jot or tittle of that plighted faith fall to the ground. For myself, having twelve months ago, in this place, moved you, that George Washington be appointed commander of the forces raised, or to be raised for the defense of American liberty, may my right hand forget her cunning, and my tongue cleave to the roof of my mouth, if I hesitate or waver in the support I give him.

98.

Colloquial Style.

(*Scene.—Dr. Gregory's Study. Enter a plump Glasgow merchant.*)

Patient. Good morning, Dr. Gregory! I'm just come into Edinburgh about some law business, and I thought when I was here, at any rate, I might just as weel take your advice, sir, about my trouble.

Dr. Pray, sir, sit down. And now, my good sir, what may your trouble be?

Pa. Indeed, doctor, I 'm not very sure; but I 'm thinking it 's a kind of weakness that makes me dizzy at times, and a kind of pinkling about my stomach;—I 'm just na right.

Dr. You are from the west-country, I should suppose, sir?

Pa. Yes, sir, from Glasgow.

Dr. Ay; pray, sir, are you a glutton?

Pa. God forbid, sir; I 'm one of the plainest men living in all the west-country.

Dr. Then, perhaps, you are a drunkard?

Pa. No, Dr. Gregory; thank God, no one can accuse me of that. I 'm of the dissenting persuasion, doctor, and an elder; so you may suppose I 'm na drunkard.

Dr. I 'll suppose no such thing till you tell me your mode of life. I 'm so much puzzled with your symptoms, sir, that I should wish to hear in detail what you *do* eat and drink. When do you breakfast, and what do you take at it?

Pa. I breakfast at nine o'clock; take a cup of coffee, and one or two cups of tea, a couple of eggs, and a bit of ham or kippered salmon, or, may be, both, if they 're good, and two or three rolls and butter.

Dr. Do you eat no honey, or jelly, or jam, at breakfast?

Pa. Oh, yes, sir! but I do n't count that as anything.

Dr. Come, this is a very moderate breakfast. What kind of a dinner do you make?

Pa. Oh, sir, I eat a very plain dinner indeed. Some soup, and some fish, and a little plain roast or boiled; for I dinna care for made dishes: I think, some way, they never satisfy the appetite.

Dr. You take a little pudding then, and afterwards some cheese?

Pa. Oh, yes! though I do n't care much about them.

Dr. You take a glass of ale or porter with your cheese?

Pa. Yes, one or the other; but seldom both.

Dr. You west-country people generally take a glass of Highland whisky after dinner?

Pa. Yes, we do; it 's good for digestion.

Dr. Do you take any wine during dinner?

Pa. Yes, a glass or two of sherry; but I 'm indifferent as to wine during dinner. I drink a good deal of beer.

Dr. What quantity of port do you drink?

Pa. Oh, very little; not above half a dozen glasses or so.

Dr. In the west-country, it is impossible, I hear, to dine without punch?

Pa. Yes, sir; indeed, 't is punch we drink chiefly; but for myself, unless I happen to have a friend with me, I never take more than a couple of tumblers or so, and that 's moderate.

Dr. Oh, exceedingly moderate indeed! You then, after this slight repast, take some tea and bread and butter?

Pa. Yes, before I go to the counting-house to read the evening letters.

Dr. And on your return you take supper, I suppose?

Pa. No, sir, I canna be said to take supper; just something before going to bed; — a rizzered haddock, or a bit of toasted cheese, or a half-hundred of oysters, or the like o' that, and may be, two-thirds of a bottle of ale; but I take no *regular* supper.

99.

Remark 1. It will be well at this stage, in the progress of a class, to take up the reading and speaking of poetry. Suitable pieces in the various styles can be selected from almost any reading book in use. For want of room, such pieces cannot be given here.

Remark 2. Scholars may be requested to select favorite pieces, in prose or verse, for class or individual drill.

Humorous Style.

Remark. The varieties of the humorous style are numerous. One of the most common, only, will be given.

Remark. Almost any piece may be rendered humorous, or ludicrous, by assuming some style in its delivery, other than that adapted to it; for example: apply the ministerial style, somewhat exaggerated, to any of the preceding examples; again, apply the argumentative style of delivery to any narrative piece, or *vice versa;* the pathetic style to a denunciatory piece, or *vice versa.* Let it be tried.

100.

Bah! that's the third umbrella gone since Christmas. What were you to do? Why, let him go home in the rain, to be sure. I am very certain there was nothing about him that could spoil. Take cold, indeed! He does n't look like one of the sort to take cold. Besides, he'd have better taken cold than taken our umbrella.—Do you hear the rain, Mr. Caudle?

I say, do you hear the rain? And as I am alive, if it is n't St. Swithin's day! Do you hear it against the windows? Nonsense; you don't impose upon me; you can't be asleep with such a shower as that! Do you hear it, I say? Oh! you *do* hear it!—Well, that's a pretty flood, I think, to last for six weeks; and no stirring all the time out of the house. Pooh! don't think me a fool, Mr. Caudle; don't insult me; *he* return the umbrella! Anybody would think you were born yesterday. As if anybody ever did return an umbrella! There; do you hear it? Worse and worse. Cats and *dogs*, and for six weeks; and no umbrella.

I should like to know how the children are to go to school to-morrow. They sha n't go through such weather; I am determined. No; they shall stop at home and never learn anything, (the blessed creatures!) sooner than go and get wet! And when they grow up, I wonder who they'll have to thank for knowing nothing; who, indeed, but their father. People who can't feel for their own children ought never to be fathers.

101.

Plaintive.

"Oh! cease not yet to beat, thou vital urn!
Wait, gushing life, oh, wait my love's return!
Hoarse barks the wolf, the vulture screams from far,
The angel, pity, shuns the walks of war;
Oh! spare, ye war hounds, spare their tender age,
On me, on me," she cried, "exhaust your rage."
Then, with weak arms her weeping babes caressed,
And, sighing, hid them in her blood-stained vest.

102.

Denunciatory.

I ask now, Verres, what thou hast to advance against this charge? Will you pretend to deny it? Will you pretend that anything false, that even anything exaggerated is alleged against you? Had any prince, or any State committed the same outrage against the privileges of Roman citizens, should we not think we had reason for declaring immediate war against them? What punishment, then, ought to be inflicted on a tyrannical and wicked prætor, who dared, at no greater distance than Sicily, within sight of the Italian coast, to put to the infamous death of crucifixion that unfortunate and innocent citizen, Publius Gavius Cosanus, only for having asserted his privilege of citizenship? The unhappy man, arrested as he was going to embark for his native country, is brought before the wicked prætor. With eyes darting fury, and a countenance distorted with cruelty, he orders the helpless victim of his rage to be stripped, and rods to be brought, and the infamous punishment to be inflicted.

103.

Contemptuous.

Banished from Rome! What's banished but set free?
"Tried and convicted traitor!" Who says this?
Who'll prove it at his peril on my head?
Banished! I thank you for it. It breaks my chain
I held some slack allegiance till this hour,
But now my sword's my own. Smile on, my lords!
I scorn to count what feelings, withered hopes,
Strong provocations, bitter, burning wrongs,
I have within my heart's core shut up,
To leave you in your lazy dignities;
But here I stand and scoff you! Here I fling
Hatred and full defiance in your face!
Your Consul's merciful—for this, all thanks;
He dares not touch one hair of Cataline.

104.

Ironical.

"But, Mr. Speaker, we have a right to tax America." Oh, inestimable right! Oh, wonderful, transcendent right! the assertion which has cost this country thirteen provinces, six islands, one hundred thousand lives, and seventy millions of money. Oh! invaluable right! for the sake of which we have sacrificed our rank among nations, our importance abroad, and our happiness at home! Oh, right, more dear to us than our existence! which has already cost us so much, and which seems likely to cost us our all. Infatuated man! miserable and undone country! not to know that the claim of right, without the power of enforcing it, is nugatory, idle. We have a right to tax America. This is the profound logic which comprises the whole chain of his reasoning.

Not inferior to this was the wisdom of him who resolved to shear the wolf What, shear a wolf! have you considered the resistance, the difficulty, the danger of the attempt? No, says the mad man, I have considered nothing but the right. Man has a right of dominion over the beasts of the forest, and therefore I will shear the wolf.

105.

Angry.

Ye dark, designing knaves! ye murderers! parricides! how dare you tread upon the earth, which has drank the blood of slaughtered innocents, shed by your hands; how dare you breathe the air which wafted to the ear of heaven the groans of those who fell a sacrifice to your accursed ambition! But if the laboring earth doth not expand her jaws, if the air you breathe is not commissioned to be the minister of death, yet hear it and tremble! The eye of heaven penetrates the darkest chambers of the soul; traces the leading clue through all the labyrinths which your industrious folly has devised; and you, however you may have screened yourselves from human eyes, must be arraigned, must lift your hands, red with the blood of those whose death you have procurod, at the tremendous bar of God.

106.

PERSONATING STYLE OF DELIVERY.

Remark. The personation of the passions is somewhat different from the delivery of passages when really under the influence of such passions, as has been supposed in the preceding sections. For instance, the personation of Love, presupposes that the individual is under no restraint from any observer; that he is alone, or only in the presence of the object of his affection. It is farther taken for granted by the audience, that every such personation is somewhat over-acted, whereas in the former styles of delivery, directed really to the audience, no such overaction is tolerated.

The Personating Style, therefore, may, perhaps, more properly be called the *Caricaturing* style, though not designed, in all instances, to provoke humor by any means.

107.

Love.

Strange! that one lightly-whispered tone
Is far, far sweeter unto me,
Than all the sounds that kiss the earth
Or breathe along the sea;
But, lady, when thy voice I greet,
Not heavenly music sounds so sweet.

108.

Fear.

Ah! what sound was that?—
The trap-door fallen? and the spring-lock caught—
Well, have I not the key?—Of course I have!
'Tis in this pocket—No. In this?—No. Then
I left it at the bottom of the ladder—
Ha! 'tis not there. Where then?—Ah mercy, Heaven!
'Tis in the lock outside?
What's to be done?
Help, help! Will no one hear? O! would that I
Had not discharged old Simeon!—but he begged
Each week for wages—would not give me credit.
I'll try my strength upon the door—Despair!
I might as soon root up the eternal rocks
As force it open. Am I here a prisoner,
And no one in the house?—Horrible fate!
I sink—I faint beneath the bare conception.

109.

Hate.

How like a fawning publican he looks!
I hate him, for he is a Christian;
But more, for that, in low simplicity,
He lends out money gratis, and brings down
The rate of usance with us in Venice.
If I can catch him once upon the hip,
I will feed fat the ancient grudge I bear him!
He hates our sacred nation; and he rails,
Even there where merchants most do congregate,
On me, my bargains, and my well-won thrift,
Which he calls interest.—Cursed be my tribe,
If I forgive him.

110.

Anger.

Thou slave! thou wretch! thou coward!
Thou little valiant, great in villainy!
Thou ever strong upon the stronger side,
Thou fortune's champion, thou dost never fight
But when her humorous lady's hiss is by
To teach thee safety! Thou art perjured too,
And soothest up greatness! What a fool art thou,
A ramping fool, to brag, and stamp, and sweat,
Upon my party. Thou coldblooded slave,
Hast thou not spoke like thunder on my side?
Been sworn my soldier? bidding me depend
Upon my stars, thy fortune and thy strength?
And dost thou now fall over to my foes?
Thou wear a lion's hide? Doff it for shame,
And hang a calfskin on those recreant limbs.

111.

PERSONIFICATION OF NATIONAL PECULIARITIES.

Irish.

O'Mulligan. 'Pon me sowl, if it's not yourself that I see.

Sobersense. How now, Pat, what news?

O'M. News! it's meself that's afther telling ye that! Ye see I'm jist like a letther rite out of the mail, that's come by tiligraph, walking over the thrack like a staim taekittle; and sure as me name is Pat O'Mulligan, that owld boy of a stbudent has made a diskivery in chimistry that'll make a great man of him all his days. And has not he been offered a dale of money for it, and a chance to be a teacher in the siminary?

Sob. Why surely, Pat, you must be dreaming, for he was here but a short time since, and he said nothing about it.

O'M. The divil a bit am I a dhraming. It's like the likes o' him to say niver a word at all, at all. Did he iver till how he supported the poor mither of his all the time he was afther studying the books? Shure and was n't he the dacentest boy this side of the ould counthry? Sure and it's meself that's just from the post office with news.

112.

Dutch.

Mr. Foreman and Toder Jurymens:—Hans peen dried for Murder pefore you, and you must pring in te verdict; put it must pe 'cordin' to law.

Der man he killed vash n't killed at all, as vash broved; he is in ter jail in Morristown, for sheep stealing. Put dat ish no matter; te law say ven ter ish a doubt you give him to ter brisoner; put here ter ish no doubt. Zo you see ter brisoner is guilty.

Pesides, he is a great loafer. I have known him fifty years, and he has not done any work in all dat times; and dere ish no one depending upon him for dere living, for he ish no use for nopody.

I dinks, derefore, Mr. Foreman, he petter pe hung next Fourth of July, as der militia is going to drain in anoder county, and dere will pe noting going on here.

113.

TRANSITION.

Transition. A sudden change in the manner of delivery.

Explanation. In commencing new paragraphs, or in personating several characters in the delivery of one piece, we find the most common and important use for *Transition.* There are many other forms of transition, however, some of which I shall exemplify.

114.

TRANSITION IN PARAGRAPHS.

Remark. Most of our reading books being as absurdly divided into verses as is the Bible, this kind of transition is precluded. Appropriate examples may be found on pages 419—20; others should be found by the teacher in *some* book, and all the pupils should be trained in this form of delivery.

Rule. The transition from one paragraph to another, or from one topic of a discourse to another, generally requires a *lower pitch, slower rate,* and *subdued force;* also, a slight change in the position on the stage.

115.

TRANSITION IN STYLE.

Remark. Dialogue and colloquy afford the best examples of this form of transition; though narrative pieces, having conversations interspersed, are often more difficult to deliver, requiring also a frequent transition from the narrative to the colloquial style. Examples of both kinds will be given.

116.

Transitions in Colloquial Style.

[*Sir Robert Bramble and Humphrey Dobbins.*]

Sir R. I'll tell you what, Humphrey Dobbins, there is not a syllable of sense in all you have been saying. But I suppose you will maintain there is.

Hum. Yes.

Sir R. Yes! is that the way you talk to me, you old boor? What's my name?

Hum. Robert Bramble.

Sir R. An't I a baronet? Sir Robert Bramble of Blackberry Hall, in the county of Kent? 'Tis time you should know it, for you have been my clumsy, two-fisted valet these thirty years: can you deny that?

Hum. Hem!

Sir R. Hem? what do you mean by hem? Open that rusty door of your mouth, and make your ugly voice walk out of it. Why don't you answer my question?

Hum. Because, if I contradict you, I shall tell you a lie, and when I agree with you, you are sure to fall out.

Sir R. Humphrey Dobbins, I have been so long endeavoring to beat a few brains into your pate, that all your hair has tumbled off before my point is carried.

Hum. What then? Our parson says my head is an emblem of both our honors.

Sir R. Ay; because honors like your head are apt to be empty.

Hum. No; but if a servant has grown bald under his master's nose, it looks as if there was honesty on one side, and regard for it on the other.

Sir R. Why, to be sure, old Humphrey, you are as honest as a—pshaw! the parson means to palaver us; but, to return to my position, I tell you, I don't like your flat contradiction.

Hum. Yes you do.

Sir R. I tell you I don't. I only love to hear men's arguments. I hate their flummery.

Hum. What do you call flummery?

Sir R. Flattery, blockhead! a dish too often served up by paltry poor men to paltry rich ones.

117.

Transition from Narrative to Colloquial.

[*The Gouty Merchant and the Stranger*]

IN Broadstreet building, (on a winter night)
Snug by his parlor-fire, a gouty wight
Sat all alone, with *one* hand rubbing
His feet, rolled up in fleecy hose,
With *t'other* he'd beneath his nose

The Public Ledger, in whose columns grubbing,
He noted all the sales of hops,
Ships, shops, and slops;
Gums, galls, and groceries; ginger, gin,
Tar, tallow, tumeric, turpentine, and tin;
When lo! a decent personage in black,
Entered and most politely said,—
"Your *footman*, sir, has gone his nightly track
To the King's Head,
And left your *door ajar*, which I
Observed in passing by;
And thought it *neighborly* to give you *notice*."
"*Ten thousand thanks;* how *very few* do get,
In times of danger,
Such *kind attentions* from a *stranger!*
Assurdly that fellow's throat is
Doomed to a final drop at Newgate:
He *knows*, too, (the unconscionable elf,)
That there's *no soul* at home except *myself*."
"*Indeed*," replied the stranger (looking grave),
"Then he's a *double* knave,
He knows that *rogues* and *thieves* by scores
Nightly beset unguarded doors:
And see, how *easily* might one
Of these domestic foes,
Even beneath your *very nose*,
Perform his knavish tricks;
Enter your room as I have done,
Blow out your *candles—thus*—and *thus*—
Pocket your *silver candlesticks*,
And—*walk off—thus*,"—
So said, so done; he made no more remark,
Nor waited for replies,
But marched off with his prize,
Leaving the gouty merchant in the dark.

118.

TRANSITION IN PARENTHESIS.

Examples have before been given of ordinary parenthesis,—I shall here add one of rather extraordinary character. It affords the material for an excellent drill.

119.

Example of Transition in Parenthesis.

[*Ode to an Infant Son.*]

Thou happy, happy elf!
(But stop, first let me kiss away that tear,)
Thou tiny image of myself!
(My love, he's poking peas into his ear,)
Thou merry, laughing sprite,
With spirits, feather light,
Untouched by sorrow, and unsoiled by sin,
(My dear, the child is swallowing a pin!)

Thou little tricksy Puck!
With antic toys so funnily bestruck,
Light as the singing bird that wings the air,
(The door! the door! he'll tumble down the stair!)
Thou darling of thy sire!
(Why, Jane, he'll set his pin-afore afire!)
Thou imp of mirth and joy!
In love's dear chain so bright a link,
Thou idol of thy parents;—(Hang the boy!
There goes my ink!)

120.

Transition from Male to Female Voice.

MISTER Socrates Snooks, a lord of creation,
The second time entered the married relation;
Xantippe Caloric accepted his hand,
And thought him the happiest man in the land.
But scarce had the honeymoon passed o'er his head,
When, one morning, to Xantippe, Socrates said,
"I think, for a man of my standing in life,
This house is too small, as I now have a wife:
So, as early as possible, carpenter Carey
Shall be sent for to widen my house and my dairy
"Now, Socrates, dearest," Xantippe replied,
"I hate to hear everything vulgarly *my'd;*
Now, whenever you speak of your chattles again,
Say, *our* cow house, *our* barn yard, *our* pig pen."
"By your leave, Mrs. Snooks, I will say what I please
Of *my* houses, *my* lands, *my* gardens, *my* trees."
"Say *Our,*" Xantippe exclaimed in a rage.
I won't Mrs. Snooks, though you ask it an age!"

Oh, woman! though only a part of man's rib,
If the story in Genesis don't tell a fib,
Should your naughty companion e'er quarrel with you,
You are certain to prove the best man of the two.
In the following case this was certainly true;
For the lovely Xantippe just pulled off her shoe,
And laying about her, all sides at random,
The adage was verified—"Nil desperandum."
Mister Socrates Snooks, after trying in vain,
To ward off the blows which descended like rain,—
Concluding that valor's best part was discretion—
Crept under the bed like a terrified Hessian:
But the dauntless Xantippe, not one whit afraid,
Converted the siege into a blockade.
At last, after reasoning the thing in his pate,
He concluded 't was useless to strive against fate;
And so, like a tortoise protruding his head,
Said, "My dear, may we come out from under *our* bed?'
"Hah! hah!" she exclaimed, "Mr. Socrates Snooks,
I perceive you agree to my terms, by your looks:
Now, Socrates,—hear me,—from this happy hour,
If you'll only obey me, I'll never look sour."
Tis said the next Sabbath, ere going to church,
He chanced for a clean pair of trowsers to search:
Having found them, he asked, with a few nervous twitches
"My dear, may we put on our new Sunday breeches?"

[*From Kidd's Elocution.*

GESTICULATION.

CLASSES.

As to Origin,
Natural, Artificial.

As to Style,
Colloquial, Oratorical, Dramatic.

As to Order,
Principal, Subordinate.

As to Combination,
Simple, Complex, Compound.

As to Use,

Introductory,	To an Audience, Of a Speech, a Paragraph, etc.
Demonstrative,	of Places, Persons, Things, Extent, Limitation, of Antithesis, etc.
Significant,	Of Assent, Denial, Approbation, Disapprobation, Request, Command, Prohibition, Threatening, Silencing, Directing, etc.
Emphatic,	Earnest, Rhetorical.
Impassioned,	Of Joy, Grief, Love, Hate, Contempt Fear, Horror, Despair, Surprise, Astonishment, Fright, Pride, Arrogance, Humility. Servility, Shame, Bashfulness, etc.
Imitative,	Of Personal Peculiarities. Of National Peculiarities. Of Feminine or Masculine Peculiarities. Of Cockney Peculiarities. Of Clownish Peculiarities.
Concluding,	Departure from Individual. Retreat from the Stage.

USE OF THE PARTS.

- **Feet,**
  - Right.
  - Left.
    - Positions.
      - 1st, 2d, 3d, 4th.
      - Contracted.
      - Extended.
      - Parallel.
      - Introverted.
    - Changes of Position.
      - Advancing.
      - Retiring.
      - Traversing.
      - Starting.
      - Stamping.
      - Kicking.
    - Errors—1, 2, 3.

- **Lower Limbs,**
  - Conditions. — Firm, Rigid, Feeble, Trembling. Straight, Bent, Kneeling.
  - Motions. — Bending, Kneeling, Shaking Staggering.
  - Errors—1, 2, 3.

- **Trunk,**
  - Conditions, — Erect, Rigid, Stooping, Leaning, Reclining, Square. Oblique.
  - Motions, — Bending, Stooping, Turning, Strutting, Reclining, Swaggering, Quivering.
  - Errors, 1, 2, 3.

- **Shoulders,**
  - Positions, — Thrown back, Drawn forward, Elevated, Depressed, Contracted.
  - Motions, — Throwing back, Drawing forward. Elevating, Depressing, Shrugging.

- **Arms,**
  - Positions,
    - As to vertical direction,
      - Horizontal,
      - Downward,
      - Upward,
      - Zenith,
      - Rest.
    - As to Transverse direction,
      - Forwards, Oblique,
      - Across, Extended,
      - Backwards.
  - Positions in Combination, — Folded, Kimbo, Reposed, Arrogant.
  - Motions,
    - As to Direction,
      - Downward, Horizontal, Upward,
        - Front, Cross, Oblique, Extended, Backward,
          - Direct, Inwards, Outwards, Revolving,
    - As to Force, — Violent, Medium, Moderate, Feeble.
    - Divisions, — Preparatory, Commencing, Stroke, Conclusion.

Hands,
- Position of the palm, — prone, supine, inwards, outwards, vertical, forwards, backwards.
- Position of the fingers, — natural, clinched, extended, index, collected, holding, hollow, thumb extended, grasping.
- Position of hands and fingers with regard to each other, — applied, clasped, crossed, folded, inclosed, wringing, touching, enumerating.
- Positions with regard to other parts of the body, — on the forehead, over the eyes, over the chin, over the mouth, pinching the chin, on the breast, finger on the lips, on the nose.
- Motions of hands, — pointing, noting, beckoning, repressing, advancing, springing, striking, pressing, retracting, rejecting, bending, recoiling, shaking, throwing, clinching, collecting.

Head,
- Positions, —erect, inclined, elevated, aside.
- Motions,—assenting, denying, shaking, tossing, aside.

Eyes,
- Direction, — forwards, averted, downwards, upwards, around, on vacancy, fixed.
- Conditions, — smiling, glistening, winking, frowning, weeping, closing, distended, starting, staring, wild, phrensied, bloodshot, etc.

Mouth and Lips,
- Condition, — closed, gaping, grinning, pouting, down in the mouth, with stiff upper lip.
- Actions, — laughing, hissing, yawning, sneering, flouting, hooting, chuckling, spitting, whistling.

QUALITIES.

Magnificent,	Just,	Constrained,
Bold,	Appropriate,	Tame,
Energetic,	Forcible,	Feeble,
Varied,	Select,	Monotonous,
Simple,	Adequate,	Theatrical,
Few,	Sufficient,	Excessive,
Graceful,	Suitable,	Awkward,
Precise,	Well-timed,	Ill-timed.

METHODS OF DRILL.

1. In gestures alone,	Simple,	Oratorical.
	Complex,	
2. In gestures with voice,	Compound.	Dramatic.

DEFINITIONS, REMARKS AND EXPLANATIONS.

Remark 1. Most of the text books on Elocution, virtually ignore the subject of Gesticulation, by saying that it cannot be taught by pictures; or by referring it to teachers, who, for the most part, are unacquainted even with its nomenclature.

Remark 2. Having given an outline of Gesticulation, embracing its nomenclature, I shall have room only for the definitions of such terms and explanations of such parts of it as seem most to require them.

Remark 3. Almost any teacher, by going over this classification and familiarizing himself with its terms and details, and by practicing them in his private room, will be able to introduce the following drills on Gesture into his school with good effect. They *can* take the place of other gymnastic exercises during recesses or intermissions.

Remark 4. An abridged notation may be secured by using capital initial letters for the positions and motions of the head, eyes, mouth, also for the lower extremeties; and small initial letters for the motions, positions, and conditions of all other parts. In case the initial letters are alike in two terms, the first two letters must be used; and when the first two are alike, the first three can be used. The letter added to an initial capital should be small. This notation is convenient in guiding drills; also, for noting the errors or defects of pupils under drill in order for efficient criticism.

Remark 5. All that has been gained by the drill in the Management of the Person, as treated of on pages 357—365, will be valuable as introductory to Drills in Gesticulation.

GESTICULATION. See page 55, section 7.

CLASSES.

NATURAL GESTICULATION. See page 43, section 6.

ARTIFICIAL GESTICULATION. See page 44, section 6.

COLLOQUIAL GESTURE. That which occurs in ordinary conversation.

Explanation. This often consists in motions of the head only; not unfrequently, however, the motions of the hand and forearm are used; seldom the motions of the arm.

ORATORICAL GESTURE. That used in the pulpit, and in legislative assemblies.

Explanation. This consists of the positions and motions of all parts of the system, except such attitudes and highly wrought displays, as are necessary to exhibit the stronger emotions, as of fright, horror, despair, etc. It forbids the use of the forearm, by itself, entirely.

DRAMATIC GESTURE. That which is suitable for the drama or theater.

Explanation. It includes all oratorical gesture; also, the appropriate portrayal of the strongest passions and emotions of the soul.

SIMPLE GESTURE. That made by one member or equally by a pair of members, when designed to give expression to only one gush of thought or feeling.

COMPLEX GESTURE. That which involves the motions of two or more members, a part of which motions are subordinate to others.

COMPOUND GESTURE. Gesture continued from one thought or feeling to another, with, or without change.

PRINCIPAL GESTURE. That which in a complex gesture is the most prominent.

INTRODUCTORY GESTURE. That which is designed to accompany the introduction of a speaker to an audience, or to prepare the minds of an audience for a new speech or a new paragraph.

Explanation. The bow is commonly addressed to the audience, when a speaker is introduced both by the speaker and the person introducing him; also, a downward oblique outward gesture with the right hand, by the latter.

Remark. For want of room, I shall be compelled to omit the definitions and explanations of other classes of Gesture. They will, for the most part, explain themselves to any intelligent teacher.

POSITIONS AND MOTIONS OF THE FEET.

1st Position. Body on the left foot, right foot forward, head erect, hands down.

2d Position. Body forward on the right foot; the left foot behind, resting on the toe.

2d Position. Body on the right foot, the left in front.

4th Position. Body on the left foot, the right behind, resting on the toe.

Contracted. Feet nearly touching.

Extended. Feet far apart.

Parallel. Both feet in the same direction.

Introverted. Feet with toes turned inward.

Remark. The motions of the feet will explain themselves; and for want of room, I shall leave the Outline on the Trunk and Shoulders for the ingenuity of the teacher and pupil to master.

POSITIONS OF THE ARM.

Horizontal. Extended in a straight line from the shoulder, neither elevated nor depressed.

Downward. Depressed 45° from the horizontal position.

Upward. Elevated 45° from the horizontal position.

Zenith. Pointing vertically upward.

Rest. Hanging by the force of gravity only.

Forward. Extending in a straight line, neither inclining to right or left.

Oblique. The right arm inclined 45° towards the left; the left arm extended 45° towards the right.

Both arms are in the right oblique position, when inclined 45° towards the right; and in the left oblique position, when inclined 45° towards the left.

Across. The right arm directed towards the left, or the left arm directed towards the right, in contact with the breast.

Extended. Directed outward, 90° from *forward.*

Backward. Making an obtuse angle with *forward.*

Folded. Wrapped across the breast, and enclosing each other.

Kimbo. With the elbow extended, and the hand placed on the hip.

Arrogant. The elbows in contact with the person, and the thumbs in the arm-holes of the vest.

Reposed. With one hand covering the other over the stomach. A feminine position.

Remark. Outline of Motions must explain itself. It gives at least 96 different gestures with each arm, without including any changes of the hand or fingers.

DIVISIONS OF GESTURE WITH THE UPPER EXTREMITY.

Preparation. This consists in such elevation of the hand and arm from the position of Rest as is necessary to perform the gesture.

Commencement. The first part of the motion which is given with less force than the *Stroke.*

Stroke. Climax or telling point of the gesture which must be given with greater energy than that of the motion preceding it.

Conclusion. The falling back of the hand and arm to the state of Rest.

POSITIONS OF THE HAND.

Prone. Palm downward.

Supine Palm upward.

Inward Palm toward the body

Outward Palm away from the body

Vertical. Pointing directly upward.

Forward. Palm turned forward, the arm being at rest, or in one of the extended or backward positions.

Backward. Palm turned backward, the arm being at rest, or in one of the extended or backward positions.

DISPOSITION OF THE FINGERS.

Natural The fingers all a little bent in towards the palm, and the extremity of the thumb a little bent outward; the same arrangement as when offered for shaking hands.

Clinched. The fingers firmly closed, and thumb pressing over them.

Extended. The fingers separated from according to the excitement of the speaker.

Index. The fore finger extended, the other fingers being closed.

Collected. The ends of the fingers inclined towards, or touching the end of the thumb.

Holding. The fore and middle fingers pressed at their middle against the thumb, the other fingers being more or less contracted.

Hollow. The hand supine, and the fingers curved without touching.

Thumb. The fingers closed, the thumb being used as an index.

COMBINED POSITION OF THE HANDS.

Applied. The palms, fingers and thumbs mutually pressed against each other.

Clasped. All the fingers inserted between each other, and closed, as far as possible.

Folded. The fingers of the right hand laid between the thumb and forefinger of the left, the right thumb crossing the left.

Crossed. One hand laid on the breast and the other laid over it.

Inclosed. One hand so laid within the other that one thumb lies over the other.

GESTURES WITH HAND AND ARM.

Pointing. Indicating the direction of any object.

Noting. The right hand as an index descending gently and repeatedly; often towards the palm of the other hand, *hollow*.

Repelling. The arms first retracted, being pushed forward with the hand *vertical* and *outward*.

Waving. The fingers first downward, being raised quickly by extending the joints of the hands and arms.

BECKONING. The hand *inward*, and brought repeatedly towards the breast.

REPRESSING. The hand *outward*, being carried repeatedly *forward.* It is the opposite of the preceding.

ADVANCING. The hand first moved downward and backward, then regularly *forward* to the *horizontal;* a step being made forward to aid in the gesture.

SPRINGING. The hand having nearly arrived at its limit in a gesture, being suddenly thrown forward making the *stroke* of the gesture. This must be simultaneous with the enunciation of the accented syllable in the emphatic word.

STRIKING. The arm being thrown towards the person addressed, as it were, by the force of the gesture.

THREATENING. The hand suddenly clinched, is raised into a posture of offence.

PRESSING. The hand already laid on some part, the elbow being raised and the fingers pressed more forcibly on that part, denoting greater violence of the emotion.

RETRACTING. Withdrawing the arm preparatory to gesture.

REJECTING. Pushing the hand forward toward an object, at the same time averting the face.

METHOD OF DRILL WITHOUT VOICE.

Remark 1. A few minutes spent in these or similar drills of gesticulation, every day, in connection with reading lessons, or at recesses or intermissions, will be sufficient to give propriety, force and beauty to the *expression* of gesture, where otherwise there is the greatest backwardness. or the most repulsive awkwardness in gesticulation.

Remark 2. It is not to be supposed that these drills as laid down here are the only drills by which a class ought to be trained. They are only given as specimens for the *commencement* of the training in Oratorical Gesticulation; for want of room, drills in Dramatic Gesture are omitted.

Remark 3. The constrained and feeble action of Colloquial Gesticulation calls for no training otherwise than to break it up in Reading, Declamation and Oratory

ORATORICAL GESTICULATION.

DIRECTIONS TO THE TEACHER.

Direction 1. Arrange the members of the class on the floor, at such distances that their hands cannot meet. Let them stand as many as possible so that their feet can be seen.

Direction 2. Having cleared off your table, take your stand on it, in order that your entire figure may be seen by every pupil in the class.

Direction 3. Illustrate every new position and motion to the class by examples, cautioning them against the various awkward errors to which they will be liable, illustrating such errors also by example.

Direction 4. Let the class take the same position and go through with the same evolutions, *many times*, in concert with yourself; then by themselves in compliance with your directions, while your attention is given to the faults of individuals, so that you can correct them in the repetition of the exercise. If simply describing the error does not enable the pupil to correct it, you will illustrate it, or caricature it, till he will be glad to abandon it.

Direction 5. When the class shall have become familiar with the meaning of the words used describing positions and motions, either by practice in the drills or by study of the Outline and Definitions, you can introduce a random exercise; firstly, requiring the class to follow your lead as closely as possible; secondly, requiring them to comply with your random verbal directions.

TEACHER'S DIRECTIONS TO PUPILS.

Explanation 1. Words in italics in the following directions are technical; they will be found in the Outline on Gesticulation in their proper places, and their definitions are given so far as has been thought necessary among the Definitions following the Outline.

Explanation 2. The word Position, when commencing with a capital, will refer to the position of the feet; and the word *Rest*, to the hands and arms.

INTRODUCTORY AND CONCLUDING GESTURE.

Series 1. Take your places. First Position Second Position with the bow, First Position, Second Position with the *Introductory*. (*Explanation*. This is given by raising the right hand from *Rest*, gracefully and in the *natural* position, as if to shake hands. It is used to introduce a speech or a new paragraph.) First Position with *Rest*. Third Position, Fourth Position, and *Introductory* with the left hand. Third Position and *Rest*, concluding bow. First Position, with a step backward.

Series 2. First Position. Second Position with a bow and *sweep* of the right hand towards the right. Second Position with a bow and *sweep* of the left hand towards the left. First Position, *Introductory* and Second Position. First Position and *sweeping* bow, *retiring* one or two steps to the First Position.

POSITIONS AND MOTIONS OF THE HANDS AND ARMS.

Series 1. First Position, arms *horizontal forward*, hands *natural*, *prone*, *supine*, *forward*, *clinched*, *Rest*.

Hands *natural*, arms *forward*, with second Position; *downward*, *horizontal*, *upward*, *zenith*, *Rest*.

Right hand *index*, arm north. Right arm *Rest*, with the left hand *index*, arm south. Left arm *Rest*, with the right hand *index*, arm east; Right arm *Rest*, with the left hand *index*, arm west, *Rest*. With the right *index*, point to me, to the clock, to the zenith, etc.

Remark. These gestures must be given with vivacity, in graceful curves, rather than with awkward, angular motions; also with the *spring*, making the *stroke*.

First Position, arms *horizontal oblique*, with hands *supine;* arms *folded*, *kimbo*, *horizontal extended* with hand *forward*, arms *arrogant*, with trunk *swaggering;* hands *applied;* arms *upward*, *extended*, with hands *natural;* hands *wringing*. *Rest*.

Remark to the Teacher. By studying the Outline and Definitions you will be able to carry on such exercises, varying them, and bringing in new positions, motions, and combinations, until your class shall become familiar with the nomenclature of Gesticulation, and are able to gesticulate with freedom, grace and effect.

DRILL IN GESTICULATION WITH VOICE.

Several authors on Gesticulation have given a variety of pieces with the appropriate gestures of all the different parts of the system marked, either with figures or letters. I have found it difficult to make any good use of either kind of notation, without devoting more time to learn them than a teacher can well afford, who is fully occupied in teaching the various branches of a common school. Neither have I found the cuts representing the various *positions* of any real service; and if they were, it would amount to little, as *motions* cannot be represented, which of course are the most difficult to acquire and to teach. The method of drill which I have found most serviceable is the declamation of short pieces, in concert, with the pupils, after they have had opportunity to memorize them: giving one or two such pieces at each reading lesson, to be memorized for recital and practice in gesticulation, a few moments, at the next reading exercise.

I shall leave it to the judgment and taste of the trainer to select examples from these following, or from other books, and to give appropriate gestures in their delivery.

EXAMPLES FOR DRILL IN GESTICULATION AND VOCAL DELIVERY.

Demonstrative Gesture.

Though you, though all the world, though an angel from heaven were to declare the truth of it, I could not believe it.

From North to South, from East to West, in all its wide extent, our country calls on heaven for blessings this day. Oh that they may descend without measure, and sweep crime and oppression from all the land.

Are not you, sir, is not your honorable colleague sitting near you, are you not both the proscribed and predestined objects of punishment and of vengeance?

Is there not rain enough in the sweet heavens to wash this crimson hand as white as snow?

O thou that rollest above, round as the shield of my fathers! Whence are thy beams, O Sun, thy everlasting light? Thou comest forth in thy awful beauty; the stars hide themselves in the sky, the moon cold and pale sinks in the western wave. But thou, thyself movest alone; who can be a companion of thy course?

Know ye this, my friends, that he who reigneth in Heaven, whose footstool is the solid globe, who at a glance taketh in all things, whose essence filleth all space, the immensity of the universe, regardeth us, the creatures of his wisdom and his bounty, not as objects to be cast away or repelled from his presence, but as beings to whom his heart is ever open, his hand ever extended. He will take us to his arms, as a mother taketh her child!—[*From Fitzgerald's Exhibition Speaker.*

Ye crags and peaks, I'm with you once again
I hold to you the hands you first beheld
To show they still are free. Methinks
I hear a spirit in your echoes answer me
And bid your tenant welcome to his home
Again! O sacred forms, how proud you look!
How high you lift your heads into the sky!
How huge you are! how mighty and how free!
Ye are things that tower, that shine—whose smile
Makes glad, whose frown is terrible, whose forms,
Robed or unrobed, do all the impress wear
Of awe divine. Ye guards of liberty,
I'm with you once again. I call to you
With all my voice. I hold my hands to you
To show they still are free. I rush to you
As though I could embrace you!

Demonstrative, Emphatic, Significant and Impassioned Gesture.

HOHENLINDEN.

On Linden, when the sun was low,
All bloodless lay the untrodd'n snow,
And dark as winter was the flow
Of Iser rolling rapidly.

But Linden saw another sight,
When the drum beat at dead of night,
Commanding fires of death to light
  The darkness of her scenery.

By torch and trumpet fast array'd,
Each horseman drew his battle blade;
And furious every charger neigh'd,
  To join the dreadful revelry.

Then shook the hills with thunder riv'n,
Then rush'd the steeds to battle driv'n,
And louder than the bolts of heav'n,
  Far flashed the red artillery.

And redder yet those fires shall glow
On Linden's hills of bloodstained snow;
And darker yet, shall be the flow
  Of Iser rolling rapidly.

'Tis morn—but scarce yon lurid sun
Can pierce the war clouds, rolling dun,
Where furious Frank, and fiery Hun
  Shout in their sulph'rous canopy.

The combat deepens—On, ye brave,
Who rush to glory, or the grave!
Wave, Munich, all thy banners wave!
  And charge with all thy chivalry!

Few, few shall part where many meet!
The snow shall be their winding sheet,
And every turf beneath their feet,
  Shall be a soldier's sepulchre.

THE SEMINOLE'S DEFIANCE.

I've scared ye in the city,
  I scalped ye on the plains;
Go, count your chosen, where they fell
  Beneath my leaden rain!
I scorn your proffered treaty!
  The pale-face I defy!
Revenge is stamped upon my spear,
  And blood my battle cry.

Ye've trailed me through the forest,
  Ye've tracked me o'er the stream;

And struggling through the everglades,
  Your bristling bayonets gleam;
But I stand as should the warrior,
  With his rifle and his spear;
The scalp of vengeance still is red,
  And warns ye—Come not here!

I loathe ye in my bosom,
  I scorn ye with mine eye,
And I'll taunt ye with my latest breath,
  And fight ye till I die!
I ne'er will ask ye quarter,
  And I ne'er will be your slave;
But I'll swim the sea of slaughter,
  Till I sink beneath its wave!

THE MISER.

The wind was high—the window shakes;
With sudden start the miser wakes!
Along the silent room he stalks;
Looks back, and trembles as he walks!
Each lock, and every bolt he tries,
In every creek, and corner pries;
Then opes his chest with treasure stor'd,
And stands in rapture o'er his hoard.
But now with sudden qualms possess'd,
He wrings his hands, and beats his breast—
By conscience stung, he wildly stares;
And thus his guilty soul declares:
Had the deep earth her stores confined,
This heart had known sweet peace of mind.
But virtue's sold! Good gods! what price
Can recompense the pangs of vice?
Oh, bane of good! seducing cheat,
Can man, weak man, thy power defeat?
Gold banish'd honor from the mind,
And only left the name behind;
Gold sowed the world with every ill;
Gold taught the murd'rers sword to kill;
'T was gold instructed coward hearts
In treach'ry's more pernicious arts.
Who can recount the mischiefs o'er?
Virtue resides on earth no more.

ELIZA.

Now stood Eliza on the wood-crowned height,
O'er Minden's plain spectatress of the fight.
Sought with bold eye, amid the bloody strife,
Her dearer self, the partner of her life;
From hill to hill the rushing host pursued,
And viewed his banner, or believed she viewed.
Pleased with the distant roar, with quicker tread,
Fast by her hand one lisping boy she led;
And one fair girl, amid the loud alarm,
Slept on her kerchief, cradled by her arm;
While around her brows bright beams of honor dart,
And love's warm eddies circle round her heart.
Near and more near the intrepid beauty press'd,
Saw through the driving smoke his dancing crest;
Saw on his helm, her virgin hands inwove,
Bright stars of gold, and mystic knots of love;
Heard the exulting shout, "They run, they run!
Great heav'n," she cried, "he's safe! the battle's won!"
A ball now hisses through the airy tides,
(Some fury winged it, and some demon guides!)
Parts the fine locks her graceful head that deck,
Wounds her fair ear and sinks into her neck;
The red stream issuing from her azure veins,
Dyes her white veil, her ivory bosom stains.
"Ah me!" she cried, and sinking on the ground,
Kiss'd her dear babes, regardless of the wound;
"Oh! cease not to beat, thou vital urn!
Wait, gushing, oh, wait my love's return!"
Hoarse barks the wolf, the vulture screams from far,
The angel, Pity, shuns the ranks of war!
"Oh! spare, ye war-hounds, spare their tender age;
On me, on me," she cried, "exhaust your rage!"
Then with weak arms her weeping babes caressed,
And, sighing, hid them in her bloodstained vest.
From tent to tent the impatient warrior flies,
Fear in his heart, and frenzy in his eyes;
Eliza's name along the camp he calls,—
"Eliza" echoes through the canvas walls.
Quick through the murmuring gloom his footsteps tread,
O'er groaning heaps, the dying and the dead;
Vault o'er the plain, and in the tangled wood
Lo! dead Eliza, weltering in her blood.
Soon hears his listening son the welcome sounds,

With open arms and sparkling eyes he bounds;
"Speak low," he cries, and gives his little hand,
"Eliza sleeps upon the dew cold sand:"
Poor weeping babe, with bloody fingers press'd
And tried with pouting lips, her milkless breast,
"Alas we both with cold and hunger quake—
Why do you weep? Mamma will soon awake."—
"She'll wake no more!" the hapless mourner cried,
Upturn'd his eyes, and clasped his hand and sigh'd;
Stretched on the ground awhile entranced he lay,
And pressed warm kisses on the lifeless clay:
And then upsprung, with wild convulsive start,
And all the father kindled in his heart.
"Oh, heavens," he cried, "my first rash vow forgive;
These bind to earth, for these I pray to live!"
Round his chill babes he wrapt his crimson vest,
And clasped them, sobbing, to his aching breast.

ROLLA TO HIS SOLDIERS.

They follow an adventurer whom they fear, and obey a power which they hate. We serve a monarch whom we love, a God whom we adore! Whene'er they move in anger, desolation tracks their progress; whene'er they pause in amity, affliction mourns their friendship!—They boast they come but to enlarge our minds, and free us from the yoke of error. Yes; they will give enlightened freedom to our minds, who are themselves the slaves of passion, avarice and pride! They offer us their protection. Yes; such protection as vultures give to lambs,—covering and devouring them! They call on us to barter all the good we have inherited and proved, for the desperate chance of something better which they promise. Be our plain answer this:—The throne we honor is the people's choice: the laws we reverence are our brave forefather's legacy; the faith we follow teaches us to live in peace with all mankind, and die with hopes of bliss beyond the grave!

RIENZI TO THE ROMANS.

Friends!
I came not here to talk. Ye know too well
The story of our thraldom. We are slaves!
The bright sun rises to his course, and lights
A race of slaves! He sets, and his last beam

Falls on a slave! not such as, swept along
By the full tide of power, the conqueror leads
To glory and undying fame,—
But base, ignoble slaves!—slaves to a horde
Of petty tyrants, feudal despots; lords,
Rich in some dozen paltry villages;
Strong in some hundred spearmen; only great
In that strange spell, a name! Each hour, dark fraud
Or open rapine, or protected murder,
Cry out against them. But this very day
An honest man, my neighbor,—there he stands—
Was struck—struck like a dog, by one who wore
The badge of Ursini! because, forsooth,
He tossed not high the ready cap in air,
Nor lifted up his voice in servile shouts,
At sight of that great ruffian. Be we men
And suffer such dishonor? Men, and wash not
The stain away in blood? Such shames are common.
I have known deeper wrongs. I that speak to ye—
I had a brother once, a gracious boy,
Full of all gentleness, of calmest hope,
Of sweet and quiet joy. There was the look
Of heaven on his face, which limners give
To the belov'd disciple. How I loved
That gracious boy! Younger by fifteen years,
Brother at once and son! He left my side,
A summer bloom on his fair cheeks—a smile
Parting his innocent lips. In one short hour
The pretty, harmless boy was slain. I saw
The corpse, the mangled corpse, and then I [slaves!
Cried for vengeance! Rouse, ye Romans! Rouse ye
Have ye brave sons? Look in the next fierce brawl
To see them die. Have ye fair daughters? Look
To see them live, torn from your arms, distained,
Dishonored; and if ye dare call for justice
Be answered by the lash! Yet this is Rome,
That sat on her seven hills, and from her throne
Of beauty ruled the world! Yet, we are Romans
Why, in that elder day, to be a Roman
Was greater than to be a king. And once again—
Hear me, ye walls, that echoed to the tread
Of either Brutus—once again I swear
The Eternal City shall be free.

CONTENTS.

PART I. CLASSIFICATION OF KNOWLEDGE.

PART II. ORTHOEPY AND ORTHOGRAPHY.

ORTHOEPY.

ORTHOGRAPHY.

PART III. GRAMMAR.

PART IV. GEOGRAPHY.

PART V. ARITHMETIC.

PART VI. ELOCUTION.

GESTICULATION.

PARKER & WATSON'S NATIONAL READERS.

The salient features of these works which have combined to render them so popular may be briefly recapitulated as follows:

1. **THE WORD-BUILDING SYSTEM.**—This famous progressive method for young children originated and was copyrighted with these books. It constitutes a process with which the beginner with *words* of one letter is gradually introduced to additional lists formed by prefixing or affixing single letters, and is thus led almost insensibly to the mastery of the more difficult constructions. This is one of the most striking modern improvements in methods of teaching.

2. **TREATMENT OF PRONUNCIATION.**—The wants of the youngest scholars in this department are not overlooked. It may be said that from the first lesson the student by this method need never be at a loss for a prompt and accurate rendering of every word encountered.

3. **ARTICULATION AND ORTHOEPY** are considered of primary importance.

4. **PUNCTUATION** is inculcated by a series of interesting *reading lessons*, the simple perusal of which suffices to fix its principles indelibly upon the mind.

5. **ELOCUTION.** Each of the higher Readers (3d, 4th and 5th) contains elaborate, scholarly, and thoroughly practical treatises on elocution. This feature alone has secured for the series many of its warmest friends.

6. **THE SELECTIONS** are the crowning glory of the series. Without exception it may be said that no volumes of the same size and character contain a collection so diversified, judicious, and artistic as this. It embraces the choicest gems of English literature, so arranged as to afford the reader ample exercise in every department of style. So acceptable has the taste of the authors in this department proved, not only to the educational public but to the reading community at large, that thousands of copies of the Fourth and Fifth Readers have found their way into public and private libraries throughout the country, where they are in constant use as manuals of literature, for reference as well as perusal.

7. **ARRANGEMENT.** The exercises are so arranged as to present constantly alternating practice in the different styles of composition, while observing a definite plan of progression or gradation throughout the whole. In the higher books the articles are placed in formal sections and classified topically, thus concentrating the interest and inculcating a principle of association likely to prove valuable in subsequent general reading.

8. **NOTES AND BIOGRAPHICAL SKETCHES.** These are full and adequate to every want. The biographical sketches present in pleasing style the history of every author laid under contribution.

9. **ILLUSTRATIONS.** These are plentiful, almost profuse, and of the highest character of art. They are found in every volume of the series as far as and including the Third Reader.

10. **THE GRADATION** is perfect. Each volume overlaps its companion preceding or following in the series, so that the scholar, in passing from one to another, is only conscious, by the presence of the new book, of the transition.

11. **THE PRICE** is reasonable. The National Readers contain more matter than any other series in the same number of volumes published. Considering their completeness and thoroughness they are much the cheapest in the market.

12. **BINDING.** By the use of a material and process known only to themselves, in common with all the publications of this house, the National Readers are warranted to outlast any with which they may be compared—**the ratio of relative durability being in their favor as two to one.**

WATSON'S INDEPENDENT READERS.

This Series is designed to meet a general demand for smaller and cheaper books than the National Series proper, and to serve as well for intermediate volumes of the National Readers in large graded schools requiring more books than one ordinary series will supply.

Beauty. The most casual observer is at once impressed with the unparalleled mechanical beauty of the Independent Readers. The Publishers believe that the æsthetic tastes of children may receive no small degree of cultivation from their very earliest school books, to say nothing of the importance of making study attractive by all such artificial aids that are legitimate. In accordance with this view, not less than $25,000 was expended in their preparation before publishing, with a result which entitles them to be considered "The Perfection of Common School Books."

Selections. They contain, of course, none but entirely new selections. These are arranged according to a strictly progressive and novel method of developing the elementary sounds in order in the lower numbers, and in all, with a view to topics and general literary style. The mind is thus led in fixed channels to proficiency in every branch of good reading, and the evil results of 'scattering' as practised by most school-book authors, avoided.

The Illustrations, as may be inferred from what has been said, are elegant beyond comparison. They are profuse in every number of the series from the lowest to the highest. This is the only series published of which this is true.

The Type is semi-phonetic, the invention of Prof. Watson. By it every letter having more than one sound is clearly distinguished in all its variations without in any way mutilating or disguising the normal form of the letter.

Elocution is taught by prefatory treatises of constantly advancing grade and completeness in each volume, which are illustrated by wood-cuts in the lower books, and by black-board diagrams in the higher. Prof. Watson is the first to introduce Practical Illustrations and Black-board Diagrams for teaching this branch.

Foot Notes on every page afford all the incidental instruction which the teacher is usually required to impart. Indices of words refer the pupil to the place of their first use and definition. The Biographies of Authors and others are in every sense excellent.

Economy. Although the number of pages in each volume is fixed at the minimum, for the purpose recited above, the utmost amount of matter available without overcrowding is obtained in the space. The pages are much wider and larger than those of any competitor and contain *twenty per cent* more matter than any other series of the same type and number of pages.

All the Great Features. Besides the above all the popular features of the National Readers are retained except the Word-Building system. The latter gives place to an entirely new method of progressive development, based upon some of the best features of the Word System, Phonetics and Object Lessons.

NATIONAL READERS.

ORIGINAL AND "INDEPENDENT" SERIES.

SPECIMEN TESTIMONIALS.

From D. H. HARRIS, *Supt. Public Schools, Hannibal, Mo.*

The National Series of Readers are now in use in our public schools, and I regard them *the best* that I have ever examined or used.

From HON. J. K. JILLSON, *Supt. of Education, State of South Carolina.*

I have carefully examined your new and beautiful Series of Readers known as "The Independent Readers," and do not hesitate to recommend it as the finest and most excellent ever presented to the public.

From D. N. ROOK, *Sec. of School Board, Williamsport, Pa.*

I would say that Parker & Watson's Series of Readers and Spellers give the best satisfaction in our schools of any Series of Readers and Spellers that have ever been used. There is nothing published for which we would exchange them

From PROF. H. SEELE, *New Braunfels Academy, Texas.*

I recommend the National Readers for four good reasons: (1.) The printing, engraving, and binding is excellent. (2.) They contain choice selections from English Literature. (3.) They inculcate good morals without any sectarian bias. (4.) They are truly *National*, because they teach pure patriotism and not sectional prejudice.

From S. FINDLEY, *Supt. Akron Schools, Ohio.*

We use no others, and have no desire to. They give entire satisfaction. We like the freshness and excellence of the selections. We like the biographical notes and the definitions at the foot of the page. We also like the white paper and clear and beautiful type. In short, we do not know where to look for books which would be so satisfactory both to teachers and pupils.

From PRES. ROBERT ALLYN, *McKendree College, Ill.*

Since my connection with this college, we have used in our preparatory department the Series of Readers known as the "National Readers," compiled by Parker & Watson, and published by Messrs. A. S. Barnes & Co. They are *excellent;* afford choice selections; contain the right system of elocutionary instruction, and are well printed and bound so as to be serviceable as well as interesting. I can commend them as among the excellent means used by teachers to make their pupils proficient in that noblest of school arts, GOOD READING.

From W. T. HARRIS, *Supt. Public Schools, St. Louis, Mo.*

I have to admire these excellent selections in prose and verse, and the careful arrangement which places first what is easy of comprehension, and proceeds gradually to what is difficult. I find the lessons so arranged as to bring together different treatments of the same topic, thereby throwing much light on the pupil's path, and I doubt not adding greatly to his progress. The proper variety of subjects chosen, the concise treatise on elocution, the beautiful typography and substantial binding—all these I find still more admirable than in the former series of National Readers, which I considered *models* in these respects.

From H. T. PHILLIPS, Esq., *of the Board of Education, Atlanta, Ga.*

The Board of Education of this city have selected for use in the public schools of Atlanta the entire series of your Independent Readers, together with Steele's Chemistry and Philosophy. As a member of the Board, and of the Committee of Text-books, the subject of Readers was referred to me for examination. I gave a pretty thorough examination to ten (10) different series of Readers, and in endeavoring to arrive at a decision upon the sole question of merit, and entirely independent of any extraneous influence, I very cordially recommended the Independent Series. This verdict was approved by the Committee and adopted by the Board.

From Report of REV. W. T. BRANTLY, D.D., *late Professor of Belles Lettres, University of Georgia, on "Text-Books in Reading," before the Teachers' Convention of Georgia, May 4, 1870.*

The *National Series*, by Parker & Watson, is deserving of its high reputation. The Primary Books are suited to the weakest capacity; whilst those more advanced supply instructive illustration on all that is needed to be known in connection with the art.

WATSON'S CHILD'S SPELLER.

THE INDEPENDENT CHILD'S SPELLER.

This unique book, published in 1872, is the first to be consistently printed in imitation of writing; that is, it teaches orthography as we use it. It is for the smallest class of learners, who soon become familiarized with words by their forms, and learn to read writing while they spell.

EXTRACT FROM THE PREFACE.

Success in teaching English orthography is still exceptional, and it must so continue until the principles involved are recognized in practice. Form is foremost: the eye and the hand must be trained to the formation of words; and since spelling is a part of writing, the written form only should be used. The laws of mental association, also—especially those of resemblance, contrast, and contiguity in time and place—should receive such recognition in the construction of the text-book as shall insure, whether consciously or not, their appropriate use and legitimate results. Hence, the spelling-book, properly arranged, is a necessity from the first; and, though primers, readers, and dictionaries may serve as aids, it can have no competent substitute.

Consistently with these views, the words used in the Independent Child's Speller have such original classifications and arrangements in columns—in reference to location, number of letters, vowel sounds, alphabetic equivalents, and consonant terminations—as exhibit most effectively their formation and pronunciation. The vocabulary is strictly confined to the simple and significant monosyllables in common use. He who has mastered these may easily learn how to spell and pronounce words of more than one syllable.

The introduction is an illustrated alphabet in script, containing twenty-six pictures of objects, and their names, commencing both with capitals and small letters. Part First embraces the words of one, two, and three letters; Part Second, the words of four letters; and Part Third, other monosyllables. They are divided into short lists and arranged in columns, the vowels usually in line, so as to exhibit individual characteristics and similarity of formation. The division of words into paragraphs is shown by figures in the columns. Each list is immediately followed by sentences for reading and writing, in which the same words are again presented with irregularities of form and sound. Association is thus employed, memory tested, and definition most satisfactorily taught.

Among the novel and valuable features of the lessons and exercises, probably the most prominent are their adaptedness for young children and their being printed in exact imitation of writing. The author believes that hands large enough to spin a top, drive a hoop, or catch a ball, are not too small to use a crayon, or a slate and pencil; that the child's natural desire to draw and write should not be thwarted, but gratified, encouraged, and wisely directed; and that since the written form is the one actually used in connection with spelling in after-life, the eye and the hand of the child should be trained to that form from the first. He hopes that this little work, designed to precede all other spelling-books and conflict with none, may satisfy the need so universally recognized of a fit introduction to orthography, penmanship, and English composition.

The National Readers and Spellers.

THEIR RECORD.

These books have been adopted by the School Boards, or official authority, of the following important States, cities, and towns—in most cases for exclusive use

The State of Missouri. **The State of Kentucky.**
The State of Alabama.
The State of Florida. **The State of North Carolina.**
The State of Delaware. **The State of Louisiana.**

New York.
New York City.
Brooklyn.
Buffalo.
Albany.
Rochester.
Troy.
Syracuse.
Elmira.
&c., &c.

Pennsylvania.
Reading.
Lancaster.
Erie.
Scranton.
Carlisle.
Carbondale.
Westchester.
Schuylkill Haven.
Williamsport.
Norristown.
Bellefonte.
Wilkesbarre.
&c., &c.

New Jersey.
Newark.
Jersey City.
Paterson.
Trenton.
Camden.
Elizabeth.
New Brunswick.
Phillipsburg.
Orange.
&c., &c.

Delaware.
Wilmington.

D. C.
Washington.

Illinois.
Chicago.
Peoria.
Alton.
Springfield.
Aurora.
Galesburg.
Rockford.
Rock Island.
&c., &c.

Wisconsin.
Milwaukee.
Fond du Lac.
Oshkosh.
Janesville.
Racine.
Watertown.
Sheboygan.
La Crosse.
Waukesha.
Kenosha.
&c., &c.

Michigan.
Grand Rapids.
Kalamazoo.
Adrian.
Jackson.
Monroe.
Lansing.
&c., &c.

Ohio.
Toledo.
Sandusky.
Conneaut.
Chardon.
Hudson.
Canton.
Salem.
&c., &c.

Indiana.
New Albany.
Fort Wayne.
Lafayette.
Madison.
Logansport.
Indianapolis.

Iowa.
Davenport.
Burlington.
Muscatine.
Mount Pleasant.
&c.

Nebraska.
Brownsville.
Lincoln.
&c.

Oregon.
Portland.
Salem.
&c.

Virginia.
Richmond.
Norfolk.
Petersburg.
Lynchburg.
&c.

South Carolina.
Columbia.
Charleston.

Georgia.
Savannah.

Louisiana.
New Orleans.

Tennessee.
Memphis

The *Educational Bulletin* records periodically all new points gained

SCHOOL-ROOM CARDS.

Baade's Reading Case,

A frame containing movable cards, with arrangement for showing one sentence at a time, capable of 28,000 transpositions.

Eureka Alphabet Tablet

Presents the alphabet upon the Word Method System, by which the child will learn the alphabet in nine days, and make no small progress in reading and spelling in the same time.

National School Tablets, 10 Nos.

Embrace reading and conversational exercises, object and moral lessons, form, color, &c. A complete set of these large and elegantly illustrated Cards will embellish the school-room more than any other article of furniture.

READING.

Fowle's Bible Reader

The narrative portions of the Bible, chronologically and topically arranged, judiciously combined with selections from the Psalms, Proverbs, and other portions which inculcate important moral lessons or the great truths of Christianity. The embarrassment and difficulty of reading the Bible itself, by course, as a class exercise, are obviated, and its use made feasible, by this means.

North Carolina First Reader
North Carolina Second Reader
North Carolina Third Reader

Prepared expressly for the schools of this State, by C. H. Wiley, Superintendent of Common Schools, and F. M. Hubbard, Professor of Literature in the State University.

Parker's Rhetorical Reader

Designed to familiarize Readers with the pauses and other marks in general use, and lead them to the practice of modulation and inflection of the voice.

Introductory Lessons in Reading and Elocution

Of similar character to the foregoing, for less advanced classes.

High School Literature

Admirable selections from a long list of the world's best writers, for exercise in reading, oratory, and composition. Speeches, dialogues, and model letters represent the latter department.

ORTHOGRAPHY.

SMITH'S SERIES

Supplies a speller for every class in graded schools, and comprises the most complete and excellent treatise on English Orthography and its companion branches extant.

1. Smith's Little Speller

First Round in the Ladder of Learning.

2. Smith's Juvenile Definer

Lessons composed of familiar words grouped with reference to similar signification or use, and correctly spelled, accented, and defined.

3. Smith's Grammar-School Speller

Familiar words, grouped with reference to the sameness of sound of syllables differently spelled. Also definitions, complete rules for spelling and formation of derivatives, and exercises in false orthography.

4. Smith's Speller and Definer's Manual

A complete *School Dictionary* containing 14,000 words, with various other useful matter in the way of Rules and Exercises.

5. Smith's Etymology—Small, and Complete Ed's.

The first and only Etymology to recognize the *Anglo-Saxon* our *mother tongue;* containing also full lists of derivatives from the Latin, Greek, Gaelic, Swedish, Norman, &c., &c; being, in fact, a complete etymology of the language for schools.

Sherwood's Writing Speller
Sherwood's Speller and Definer
Sherwood's Speller and Pronouncer

The Writing Speller consists of properly ruled and numbered blanks to receive the words dictated by the teacher, with space for remarks and corrections. The other volumes may be used for the dictation or ordinary class exercises.

Price's English Speller

A complete spelling-book for all grades, containing more matter than "Webster," manufactured in superior style, and sold at a lower price—consequently the cheapest speller extant.

Northend's Dictation Exercises

Embracing valuable information on a thousand topics, communicated in such a manner as at once to relieve the exercise of spelling of its usual tedium, and combine it with instruction of a general character calculated to profit and amuse.

Wright's Analytical Orthography

This standard work is popular, because it teaches the elementary sounds in a plain and philosophical manner, and presents orthography and orthoepy in an easy, uniform system of analysis or parsing.

Fowle's False Orthography

Exercises for correction.

Page's Normal Chart

The elementary sounds of the language for the school-room walls.

ORTHOGRAPHY—Continued.

Barber's Complete Writing Speller

"The Student's Own Hand-Book of Orthography, Definitions, and Sentences, consisting of Written Exercises in the Proper Spelling, Meaning, and Use of Words." (Published 1873.) This differs from Sherwood's and other Writing Spellers in its more comprehensive character. Its blanks are adapted to writing whole sentences instead of detached words, with the proper divisions for numbering, corrections, etc. Such aids as this, like Watson's Child's Speller and Sherwood's Writing Speller, find their *raison d'être* in the postulate that the art of correct spelling is dependent upon written, and not upon spoken language, for its utility, if not for its very existence. Hence the indirectness of purely oral instruction.

Pooler's Test Speller

The best collection of "hard words" yet made. The more uncommon ones are fully defined, and the whole are *arranged alphabetically* for convenient reference. The book is designed for Teachers' Institutes and "Spelling Schools," and is prepared by an experienced and well-known conductor of Institutes.

ETYMOLOGY.

Smith's Complete Etymology,
Smith's Condensed Etymology,

Containing the Anglo-Saxon, French, Dutch, German, Welsh, Danish, Gothic, Swedish, Gaelic, Italian, Latin, and Greek Roots, and the English words derived therefrom accurately spelled, accented, and defined.

From HON. JNO. G. MCMYNN, *late State Superintendent of Wisconsin.*

I wish every teacher in the country had a copy of this work.

From PRIN. WM. F. PHELPS, *Minn. State Normal.*

The book is superb—just what is needed in the department of etymology and spelling.

From PROF. C. H. VERRILL, *Pa. State Normal School.*

The Etymology (Smith's) which we procured of you we like much. It is the best work for the class-room we have seen.

From HON. EDWARD BALLARD, *Supt. of Common Schools, State of Maine.*

The author has furnished a manual of singular utility for its purpose.

DICTIONARY.

The Topical Lexicon,

This work is a School Dictionary, an Etymology, a compilation of synonyms, and a manual of general information. It differs from the ordinary lexicon in being arranged by topics instead of the letters of the alphabet, thus realizing the apparent paradox of a "Readable Dictionary." An unusually valuable school book.

ENGLISH GRAMMAR.

CLARK'S DIAGRAM SYSTEM.

Clark's Easy Lessons in Language,

Published 1874. Contains illustrated object lessons of the most attractive character, and is couched in language freed as much as possible from the dry technicalities of the science.

Clark's Brief English Grammar,

Published 1872. Part I. is adapted to youngest learners, and the whole forms a complete "brief course" in one volume, adequate to the wants of the common school.

Clark's Normal Grammar,

Published 1870, and designed to take the place of Prof. Clark's veteran "Practical" Grammar, though the latter is still furnished upon order. The Normal is an entirely new treatise. It is a full exposition of the system as described below, with all the most recent improvements. Some of its peculiarities are—A happy blending of SYNTHESES with ANALYSES; thorough Criticisms of common errors in the use of our Language; and important improvements in the Syntax of Sentences and of Phrases.

Clark's Key to the Diagrams,

Clark's Analysis of the English Language,

Clark's Grammatical Chart,

The theory and practice of teaching grammar in American schools is meeting with a thorough revolution from the use of this system. While the old methods offer proficiency to the pupil only after much weary plodding and dull memorizing, this affords from the inception the advantage of *practical Object Teaching*, addressing the eye by means of illustrative figures; furnishes association to the memory, its most powerful aid, and diverts the pupil by taxing his ingenuity. Teachers who are using Clark's Grammar uniformly testify that they and their pupils find it the most interesting study of the school course.

Like all great and radical improvements, the system naturally met at first with much unreasonable opposition. It has not only outlived the greater part of this opposition, but finds many of its warmest admirers among those who could not at first tolerate so radical an innovation. All it wants is an impartial trial to convince the most skeptical of its merit. No one who has fairly and intelligently tested it in the school-room has ever been known to go back to the old method. A great success is already established, and it is easy to prophecy that the day is not far distant when it will be the *only system of teaching English Grammar.* As the SYSTEM is copyrighted, no other text-books can appropriate this obvious and great improvement.

Welch's Analysis of the English Sentence,

Remarkable for its new and simple classification, its method of treating connectives, its explanations of the idioms and constructive laws of the language, etc.

Clark's Diagram English Grammar.

TESTIMONIALS.

From J. A. T. DURNIN, *Principal Dubuque R. C. Academy, Iowa.*

In my opinion, it is well calculated by its system of analysis to develop those rational faculties which in the old systems were rather left to develop themselves, while the memory was overtaxed, and the pupils discouraged.

From B. A. COX, *School Commissioner, Warren County, Illinois.*

I have examined 150 teachers in the last year, and those having studied or taught Clark's System have universally stood fifty per cent. better examinations than those having studied other authors.

From M. H. B. BURKET, *Principal Masonic Institute, Georgetown, Tennessee.*

I traveled two years amusing myself in instructing (exclusively) Grammar classes with Clark's system. The first class I instructed fifty days, but found that this was more time than was required to impart a theoretical knowledge of the science. During the two years thereafter I instructed classes only *thirty* days each. Invariably I proposed that unless I prepared my classes for a more thorough, minute, and accurate knowledge of English Grammar than that obtained from the ordinary books and in the ordinary way in from one to two years, I would make no charge. I never failed in a solitary case to far exceed the hopes of my classes, and made money and character rapidly as an instructor.

From A. B. DOUGLASS, *School Commissioner, Delaware County, New York.*

I have never known a class pursue the study of it under a *live* teacher, that has not succeeded; I have never known it to have an opponent in an educated teacher who had *thoroughly* investigated it; I have never known an *ignorant* teacher to examine it; I have never known a teacher who has used it, to try any other.

From J. A. DODGE, *Teacher and Lecturer on English Grammar, Kentucky.*

We are tempted to assert that it foretells the dawn of a brighter age to our mother-tongue. Both pupil and teacher can fare sumptuously upon its contents, however highly they may have prized the manuals into which they may have been initiated, and by which their expressions have been moulded.

From W. T. CHAPMAN, *Superintendent Public Schools, Wellington, Ohio.*

I regard Clark's System of Grammar the best published. For teaching the analysis of the English Language, it surpasses any I ever used.

From F. S. LYON, *Principal South Norwalk Union School, Connecticut.*

During ten years' experience in teaching, I have used six different authors on the subject of English Grammar. I am fully convinced that Clark's Grammar is better calculated to make thorough grammarians than any other that I have seen.

From CATALOGUE OF ROHRER'S COMMERCIAL COLLEGE, *St. Louis, Missouri.*

We do not hesitate to assert, without fear of successful contradiction, that a better knowledge of the English language can be obtained by this system in six weeks than by the old methods in as many months.

From A. PICKETT, *President of the State Teachers' Association, Wisconsin.*

A thorough experiment in the use of many approved authors upon the subject of English Grammar has convinced me of the superiority of Clark. When the pupil has completed the course, he is left upon a foundation of *principle*, and not upon the *dictum* of the author.

From GEO. F. MCFARLAND, *Prin. McAllisterville Academy, Juniata Co., Penn.*

At the first examination of public-school teachers by the county superintendent, when one of our student teachers commenced analyzing a sentence according to Clark, the superintendent listened in mute astonishment until he had finished, then asked what that meant, and finally, with a very knowing look, said such work wouldn't do here, and asked the applicant to parse the sentence right, and gave the lowest certificates to all who barely mentioned Clark. Afterwards, I presented him with a copy, and the next fall he permitted it to be partially used, while the third of last fall, he openly commended the system, and appointed three of my best teachers to explain it at the two Institutes and one County Convention held since September.

☞ **For further testimony of equal force, see the Publishers' Special Circular, or current numbers of the Educational Bulletin.**

GEOGRAPHY.

NATIONAL GEOGRAPHICAL SYSTEM.

THE SERIES.

I. Monteith's First Lessons in Geography,
II. Monteith's New Manual of Geography,
II. McNally's System of Geography,

INTERMEDIATE OR ALTERNATE VOLUMES.

1*. Monteith's Introduction to Geography,
2*. Monteith's Physical and Political Geography,

ACCESSORIES.

Monteith's Wall Maps 2 sets (see page 15),
Monteith's Manual of Map-Drawing (Allen's System)
Monteith's Map-Drawing and Object-Lessons,
Monteith's Map-Drawing Scale,

1. PRACTICAL OBJECT TEACHING. The infant scholar is first introduced to *a picture* whence he may derive notions of the shape of the earth, the phenomena of day and night, the distribution of land and water, and the great natural divisions, which mere words would fail entirely to convey to the untutored mind. Other pictures follow on the same plan, and the child's mind is called upon to grasp no idea without the aid of a pictorial illustration. Carried on to the higher books, this system culminates in Physical Geography, where such matters as climates, ocean currents, the winds, peculiarities of the earth's crust, clouds and rain, are pictorially explained and rendered apparent to the most obtuse. The illustrations used for this purpose belong to the highest grade of art.

2. CLEAR, BEAUTIFUL, AND CORRECT MAPS. In the lower numbers the maps avoid unnecessary detail, while respectively progressive, and affording the pupil new matter for acquisition each time he approaches in the constantly enlarging circle the point of coincidence with previous lessons in the more elementary books. In the Physical and Political Geography the maps embrace many new and striking features. One of the most effective of these is the new plan for displaying on each map the relative sizes of countries not represented, thus obviating much confusion which has arisen from the necessity of presenting maps in the same atlas drawn on different scales. The maps of "McNally" have long been celebrated for their superior beauty and completeness. This is the only school-book in which the attempt to make a *complete* atlas *also clear and distinct*, has been successful. The map *coloring* throughout the series is also noticeable. Delicate and subdued tints take the place of the startling glare of inharmonious colors which too frequently in such treatises dazzle the eyes, distract the attention, and serve to overwhelm the names of towns and the natural features of the landscape.

GEOGRAPHY—Continued.

3. **THE VARIETY OF MAP-EXERCISE.** Starting each time from a different basis, the pupil in many instances approaches the same fact no less than *six times*, thus indelibly impressing it upon his memory. At the same time, this system is not allowed to become wearisome—the extent of exercise on each subject being graduated by its relative importance or difficulty of acquisition.

4. **THE CHARACTER AND ARRANGEMENT OF THE DESCRIPTIVE TEXT.** The cream of the science has been carefully culled, unimportant matter rejected, elaboration avoided, and a brief and concise manner of presentation cultivated. The orderly consideration of topics has contributed greatly to simplicity. Due attention is paid to the facts in history and astronomy which are inseparably connected with, and important to the proper understanding of geography—and *such only* are admitted on any terms. In a word, the National System teaches geography as a science, pure, simple, and exhaustive.

5. **ALWAYS UP TO THE TIMES.** The authors of these books, editorially speaking, never sleep. No change occurs in the boundaries of countries, or of counties, no new discovery is made, or railroad built, that is not at once noted and recorded, and the next edition of each volume carries to every school-room the new order of things.

6. **SUPERIOR GRADATION.** This is the only series which furnishes an available volume for every possible class in graded schools. It is not contemplated that a pupil must necessarily go through every volume in succession to attain proficiency. On the contrary, *two* will suffice, but *three* are advised; and, if the course will admit, the whole series should be pursued. At all events, the books are at hand for selection, and every teacher, of every grade, can find among them one *exactly suited* to his class. The best combination for those who wish to abridge the course consists of Nos. 1, 2, and 3, or where children are somewhat advanced in other studies when they commence geography, Nos. 1*, 2, and 3. Where but *two* books are admissible, Nos. 1* and 2*, or Nos. 2 and 3, are recommended.

7. **FORM OF THE VOLUMES AND MECHANICAL EXECUTION.** The maps and text are no longer unnaturally divorced in accordance with the time-honored practice of making text-books on this subject as inconvenient and expensive as possible. On the contrary, all map questions are to be found on the page opposite the map itself, and each book is complete in one volume. The mechanical execution is unrivalled. Paper and printing are everything that could be desired, and the binding is—A. S. Barnes & Company's.

8. **MAP-DRAWING.** In 1869 the system of Map-Drawing devised by Professor Jerome Allen was secured *exclusively* for this series. It derives its claim to originality and usefulness from the introduction of a *fixed unit of measurement* applicable to every Map. The principles being so few, simple and comprehensive, the subject of Map-Drawing is relieved of all practical difficulty. (In Nos. 2, 2*, and 3, and published separately.)

9. **ANALOGOUS OUTLINES.** At the same time with Map-Drawing was also introduced (in No. 2) a new and ingenious variety of Object Lessons, consisting of a comparison of the outlines of countries with familiar objects pictorially represented.

GEOGRAPHY—Continued.

MONTEITH'S INDEPENDENT COURSE.

Elementary Geography

Comprehensive Geography (with 103 Maps)

☞ These volumes are not revisions of old works—not an addition to any series—but are entirely new productions—each by itself complete, independent, comprehensive, yet simple, brief, cheap, and popular; or, taken together, the most admirable "series" ever offered for a common-school course. They present the following features, skillfully interwoven—the student learning all about one country at a time.

LOCAL GEOGRAPHY, or the Use of Maps. Important features of the Maps are the coloring of States as objects, and the ingenious system for laying down a much larger number of names for reference than are found on any other Maps of same size—and without crowding.

PHYSICAL GEOGRAPHY, or the Natural Features of the Earth, illustrated by the original and striking ***Relief Maps,*** being bird's-eye views or photographic pictures of the Earth's surface.

DESCRIPTIVE GEOGRAPHY, including the Physical; with some account of Governments, and Races, Animals, etc.

HISTORICAL GEOGRAPHY, or a brief summary of the salient points of history, explaining the present distribution of nations, origin of geographical names, etc.

MATHEMATICAL GEOGRAPHY, including ASTRONOMICAL, which describes the Earth's position and character among planets; also the Zones, Parallels, etc.

COMPARATIVE GEOGRAPHY, or a system of analogy, connecting new lessons with the previous ones. Comparative sizes and latitudes are shown on the margin of each Map, and all countries are measured in the "*frame of Kansas.*"

TOPICAL GEOGRAPHY, consisting of questions for review, and testing the student's general and specific knowledge of the subject, with suggestions for *Geographical Compositions.*

ANCIENT GEOGRAPHY. A section devoted to this subject, with Maps, will be appreciated by teachers. It is seldom taught in our common schools, because it has heretofore required the purchase of a separate book.

GRAPHIC GEOGRAPHY, or MAP-DRAWING by Allen's "Unit of Measurement" system (now almost universally recognized as without a rival) is introduced throughout the lessons, and not as an appendix.

CONSTRUCTIVE GEOGRAPHY, or GLOBE-MAKING. With each book a set of Map Segments is furnished, with which each student may make his own Globe by following the directions given.

RAILROAD GEOGRAPHY, with a grand Map illustrating routes of travel in the United States. Also, a "Tour in Europe."

MAP DRAWING.

Monteith's Map-Drawing Made Easy.

A neat little book of outlines and instructions, giving the "corners of States" in suitable blanks, so that Maps can be drawn by unskillful hands from any atlas; with instructions for written exercises or compositions on geographical subjects, and Comparative Geography.

Monteith's Manual of Map-Drawing (Allen's System).

The only consistent plan, by which all Maps are drawn on one scale. By its use much time may be saved, and much interest and accurate knowledge gained.

Monteith's Map-Drawing and Object Lessons.

The last-named treatise, bound with Mr. Monteith's ingenious system for committing outlines to memory by means of pictures of living creatures and familiar objects. Thus, South America resembles a dog's head; Cuba, a lizard; Italy, a boot; France, a coffee-pot; Turkey, a turkey, etc., etc.

Monteith's Map-Drawing Scale.

A ruler of wood, graduated to the "Allen fixed unit of measurement."

WALL MAPS.

Monteith's Pictorial Chart of Geography.

The original drawing for this beautiful and instructive chart was greatly admired in the publisher's "exhibit" at the Centennial Exhibition of 1876. It is *a picture* of the Earth's surface with every natural feature displayed, teaching also physical geography, and especially the mutations of water. The uses to which man puts the earth and its treasures and forces, as Agriculture, Mining, Manufacturing, Commerce, and Transportation are also graphically portrayed so that the young learner gets a realistic idea of "the world we live in," which weeks of book-study might fail to convey.

Monteith's School Maps, 8 Numbers.

The "School Series" includes the Hemispheres (2 Maps), United States, North America, South America, Europe, Asia, Africa.—Price, $2.50 each.

Each map is 28 × 34 inches, beautifully colored, has the names all laid down, and is substantially mounted on canvas with rollers.

Monteith's Grand Maps, 8 Numbers.

The "Grand Series" includes the Hemispheres (1 Map), United States, South America, Europe, Asia, Africa, The World on Mercator's Projection, and Physical Map of the World.—Price, $5.00 each. Size 42 × 52 inches, names laid down, colored, mounted, &c.

Monteith's Sunday School Maps,

Including a Map of Paul's Travels ($5.00), one of Ancient Canaan ($3.00), and Modern Palestine ($3.00), or Palestine and Canaan together ($5.00).

MONTEITH'S GEOGRAPHIES

Have been adopted, by official authority, for the schools of the following States and Cities—in most cases for *exclusive* and uniform use.

California,	Tennessee,	Iowa,	Arkansas,	North Carolina,
Missouri,	Texas,	Louisiana,	Florida,	Kansas,
Alabama,	Vermont,	Oregon,	Minnesota,	Mississippi.

Cities.—New York City, Brooklyn, Chicago, New Orleans, Buffalo, Richmond, Jersey City, Hartford, Worcester, San Francisco, Louisville, Newark, Milwaukee, Charleston, Rochester, Mobile, Syracuse, Memphis, Salt Lake City, Nashville, Utica, Wilmington, Trenton, Norfolk, Norwich, Lockport, Dubuque, Galveston, Portland, Savannah, Indianapolis, Springfield, Wheeling, Toledo, Bridgeport, St. Paul, Vicksburg, &c.

Monteith & McNally's National Geographies.

CRITICAL OPINIONS.

From R. A. ADAMS, *Member of Board of Education, New York.*

I have found, by examination of the Book of Supply of our Board, that considerably the largest number of any series now used in our public schools is the National, by Monteith and McNally.

From BRO. PATRICK, *Chief Provincial of the Vast Educational Society of the* CHRISTIAN BROTHERS *in the United States.*

Having been convinced for some time past that the series of Geographies in use in our schools were not giving satisfaction, and came far short of meeting our most reasonable expectations, I have felt it my imperative duty to examine into this matter, and see if a remedy could not be found.

Copies of the different Geographies published in this country have been placed at our command for examination. On account of other pressing duties we have not been able to give as much time to the investigation of all these different series as we could have desired; yet we have found enough to convince us that there are many others better than those we are now using; but we cheerfully give our most decided preference, above all others, to the National Series, by Monteith & McNally.

Their easy gradation, their thoroughly practical and independent character, their comprehensive completeness as a full and accurate system, the wise discrimination shown in the selection of the subject matter, the beautiful and copious illustrations, the neat cut type, the general execution of the works, and *other excellencies*, will commend them to the friends of education everywhere.

From the "HOME MONTHLY," *Nashville, Tenn.*

MONTEITH'S AND MCNALLY'S GEOGRAPHIES.—Geography is so closely connected with Astronomy, History, Ethnology, and Geology, that it is difficult to define its limits in the construction of a text-book. If the author confines himself strictly to a description of the earth's surface, his book will be dry, meager, and unintelligible to a child. If, on the other hand, he attempts to give information on the cognate sciences, he enters a boundless field, and may wander too far. It seems to us that the authors of the series before us have hit on the happy medium between too much and too little. *The First Lessons*, by applying the system of object-teaching, renders the subject so attractive that a child, just able to read, may become deeply interested in it. The second book of the course enlarges the view, but still keeps to the maps and simple descriptions. Then, in the third book, we have Geography combined with History and Astronomy. A general view of the solar system is presented, so that the pupil may understand the earth's position on the map of the heavens. The first part of the fourth book treats of Physical Geography, and contains a vast amount of knowledge compressed into a small space. It is made bright and attractive by beautiful pictures and suggestive illustrations, on the principle of object-teaching. The maps in the second part of this volume are remarkably clear, and the map exercises are copious and judicious. In the fifth and last volume of the series, the whole subject is reviewed and systematized. This is strictly a Geography. Its maps are beautifully engraved and clearly printed. The map exercises are full and comprehensive. In all these books the maps, questions and descriptions are given in the same volume. In most geographies there are too many details and minute descriptions—more than any child out of purgatory ought to be required to learn. The power of memory is overstrained; there is confusion—no clearly defined idea is formed in the child's mind. But in these books, in brief, pointed descriptions, and constant use of bright, accurate maps, the whole subject is photographed on the mind.

MATHEMATICS.

DAVIES' NATIONAL COURSE.

ARITHMETIC.

1. **Davies' Primary Arithmetic,**
2. **Davies' Intellectual Arithmetic,**
3. **Davies' Elements of Written Arithmetic,.**
4. **Davies' Practical Arithmetic,**
5. **Davies' University Arithmetic.**

TWO BOOK SERIES.

1. **First Book in Arithmetic,** Primary and Mental.
2. **Complete Arithmetic.**

ALGEBRA.

1. **Davies' New Elementary Algebra,**
2. **Davies' University Algebra,**
3. **Davies' New Bourdon's Algebra.**

GEOMETRY.

1. **Davies' Elementary Geometry and Trigonometry,**
2. **Davies' Legendre's Geometry,**
3. **Davies' Analytical Geometry and Calculus,**
4. **Davies' Descriptive Geometry,**
5. **Davies' New Calculus,**

MENSURATION.

1. **Davies' Practical Mathematics and Mensuration,**
2. **Davies' Elements of Surveying,**
3. **Davies' Shades, Shadows, and Perspective,**

MATHEMATICAL SCIENCE.

Davies' Grammar of Arithmetic,
Davies' Outlines of Mathematical Science,
Davies' Nature and Utility of Mathematics,
Davies' Metric System,
Davies & Peck's Dictionary of Mathematics,

DAVIES' NATIONAL COURSE of MATHEMATICS.

ITS RECORD.

In claiming for this series the first place among American text-books, of what ever class, the Publishers appeal to the magnificent record which its volumes have earned during the *thirty-five years* of Dr. Charles Davies' mathematical labors. The unremitting exertions of a life-time have placed *the modern series* on the same proud eminence among competitors that each of its predecessors has successively enjoyed in a course of constantly improved editions, now rounded to their perfect fruition—for it seems almost that this science is susceptible of no further demonstration.

During the period alluded to, many authors and editors in this department have started into public notice, and by borrowing ideas and processes original with Dr. Davies, have enjoyed a brief popularity, but are now almost unknown. Many of the series of to-day, built upon a similar basis, and described as "modern books," are destined to a similar fate; while the most far-seeing eye will find it difficult to fix the time, on the basis of any data afforded by their past history, when these books will cease to increase and prosper, and fix a still firmer hold on the affection of every educated American.

One cause of this unparalleled popularity is found in the fact that the enterprise of the author did not cease with the original completion of his books. Always a practical teacher, he has incorporated in his text-books from time to time the advantages of every improvement in methods of teaching, and every advance in science. During all the years in which he has been laboring, he constantly submitted his own theories and those of others to the practical test of the class-room —approving, rejecting, or modifying them as the experience thus obtained might suggest. In this way he has been able to produce an almost perfect series of class-books, in which every department of mathematics has received minute and exhaustive attention.

Upon the death of Dr. Davies, which took place in 1876; his work was immediately taken up by his former pupil and mathematical associate of many years, Prof. W. G. PECK, LL.D., of Columbia College. By him the original Series is kept carefully revised and not allowed in any way to fall behind the times.

DAVIES' SYSTEM IS THE ACKNOWLEDGED NATIONAL STANDARD FOR THE UNITED STATES, for the following reasons :—

1st. It is the basis of instruction in the great national schools at West Point and Annapolis.

2d. It has received the *quasi* endorsement of the National Congress.

3d. It is exclusively used in the public schools of the National Capital.

4th. The officials of the Government use it as authority in all cases involving mathematical questions.

5th. Our great soldiers and sailors commanding the national armies and navies were educated in this system. So have been a majority of eminent scientists in this country. All these refer to "Davies" as authority.

6th. A larger number of American citizens have received their education from this than from any other series.

7th. The series has a larger circulation throughout the whole country than any other, being *extensively used in every State in the Union.*

Davies' National Course of Mathematics.

TESTIMONIALS.

From L. VAN BOKKELEN, *State Superintendent Public Instruction, Maryland.*

The series of Arithmetics edited by Prof. Davies, and published by your firm, have been used for many years in the schools of several counties, and the city of Baltimore, and have been approved by teachers and commissioners.

Under the law of 1865, establishing a uniform system of Free Public Schools, these Arithmetics were unanimously adopted by the State Board of Education, after a careful examination, and are now used in all the Public Schools of Maryland.

These facts evidence the high opinion entertained by the School Authorities of the value of the series theoretically and practically.

From HORACE WEBSTER, *President of the College of New York.*

The undersigned has examined, with care and thought, several volumes of Davies' Mathematics, and is of the opinion that, as a whole, it is the most complete and best course for Academic and Collegiate instruction, with which he is acquainted.

From DAVID N. CAMP, *State Superintendent of Common Schools, Connecticut.*

I have examined Davies' Series of Arithmetics with some care. The language is clear and precise; each principle is thoroughly analyzed, and the whole so arranged as to facilitate the work of instruction. Having observed the satisfaction and success with which the different books have been used by eminent teachers, it gives me pleasure to commend them to others.

From J. O. WILSON, *Chairman Committee on Text-Books, Washington, D. C.*

I consider Davies' Arithmetics decidedly superior to any other series, and in this opinion I am sustained, I believe, by the entire Board of Education and Corps of Teachers in this city, where they have been used for several years past.

From JOHN L. CAMPBELL, *Professor of Mathematics, Wabash College, Indiana.*

A proper combination of abstract reasoning and practical illustration is the chief excellence in Prof. Davies' Mathematical works. I prefer his Arithmetics, Algebras, Geometry and Trigonometry to all others now in use, and cordially recommend them to all who desire the advancement of sound learning.

From MAJOR J. H. WHITTLESEY, *Government Inspector of Military Schools.*

Be assured, I regard the works of Prof. Davies, with which I am acquainted, as by far the best text-books in print on the subjects which they treat. I shall certainly encourage their adoption wherever a word from me may be of any avail.

From T. MCC. BALLANTINE, *Prof. Mathematics Cumberland College, Kentucky.*

I have long taught Prof. Davies' Course of Mathematics, and I continue to like their working.

From JOHN MCLEAN BELL, B. A., *Prin. of Lower Canada College.*

I have used Davies' Arithmetical and Mathematical Series as text-books in the schools under my charge for the last six years. These I have found of great efficacy in exciting, invigorating, and concentrating the intellectual faculties of the young.

Each treatise serves as an introduction to the next higher, by the similarity of its reasonings and methods; and the student is carried forward, by easy and gradual steps, over the whole field of mathematical inquiry, and that, too, in a *shorter* time than is usually occupied in mastering a single department. I sincerely and heartily recommend them to the attention of my fellow-teachers in Canada.

From D. W. STEELE, *Prin. Philekoian Academy, Cold Springs, Texas.*

I have used Davies' Arithmetics till I know them nearly by heart. A better series of school-books never were published. I have recommended them until they are now used in all this region of country.

A large mass of similar "Opinions" may be obtained by addressing the publishers for special circular for Davies' Mathematics. New recommendations are published in current numbers of the *Educational Bulletin.*

MATHEMATICS—Continued.

PECK'S ARITHMETICS.

By the Prof. of Mathematics at Columbia College, New York.

1. Peck's First Lessons in Numbers,

Embracing all that is usually included in what are called Primary and Intellectual Arithmetics; proceeding gradually from object lessons to abstract numbers; developing Addition and Subtraction simultaneously: with other attractive novelties.

2. Peck's Manual of Practical Arithmetic,

An excellent "Brief" course, conveying a sufficient knowledge of Arithmetic for ordinary business purposes.

It is thoroughly "practical," because the author believes the Theory cannot be studied with advantage until the pupil has acquired a certain facility in combining numbers, which can only be had by practice.

3. Peck's Complete Arithmetic,

The whole subject—theory and practice—presented within very moderate limits. This author's most remarkable faculty of mathematical treatment is comprehended in three words: System, Conciseness, Lucidity. The directness and simplicity of this work cannot be better expressed than in the words of a correspondent who adopted the book at once, because, as he said, it is "free from that *juggling with numbers*" practiced by many authors.

From the "Galaxy," New York.

In the "Complete Arithmetic" each part of the subject is logically developed. First are given the necessary definitions; second, the explanations of such signs (if any) as are used; third, the principles on which the operation depends; fourth, an exemplification of the manner in which the operation is performed, which is so conducted that the reason of the rule which is immediately thereafter deduced is made perfectly plain; after which follow numerous graded examples and corresponding practical problems. All the parts taken together are arranged in logical order. The subject is treated as a whole, and not as if made up of segregated parts. It may seem a simple remark to make that (for example) addition is in principle one and the same everywhere, whether employed upon simple or compound numbers, fractions, etc., the only difference being in the *unit* involved; but the number of persons who understand this practically, compared to the number who have studied arithmetic, is not very great. The student of the "Complete Arithmetic" cannot fail to understand it. All the principles of the science are presented within moderate limits. Superfluity of matter—to supplement defective definitions, to make clear faulty demonstrations and rules expressed either inaccurately or obscurely, to make provision for a multiplicity of cases for which no provision is requisite—has been carefully avoided. The definitions are plain and concise; the principles are stated clearly and accurately; the demonstrations are full and complete; the rules are perspicuous and comprehensive; the illustrative examples are abundant and well fitted to familiarize the student with the application of principles to the problems of science and of every-day life.

☞ The Definitions constitute the power of the book. We have never seen them excelled for clearness and exactness.—*Iowa School Journal.*

MATHEMATICS—Continued.

PECK'S HIGHER COURSE.

Peck's Manual of Algebra,

Bringing the methods of Bourdon within the range of the Academic Course.

Peck's Manual of Geometry,

By a method purely practical, and unembarrassed by the details which rather confuse than simplify science.

Peck's Practical Calculus,

Peck's Analytical Geometry,

Peck's Elementary Mechanics,

Peck's Mechanics, with Calculus,

The briefest treatises on these subjects now published. Adopted by the great Universities; Yale, Harvard, Columbia, Princeton, Cornell, &c.

ARITHMETICAL EXAMPLES.

Reuck's Examples in Denominate Numbers,

Reuck's Examples in Arithmetic,

These volumes differ from the ordinary arithmetic in their peculiarly *practical* character. They are composed mainly of examples, and afford the most severe and thorough discipline for the mind. While a book which should contain a complete treatise of theory and practice would be too cumbersome for every-day use, the insufficiency of *practical* examples has been a source of complaint.

HIGHER MATHEMATICS.

Macnie's Algebraical Equations,

Serving as a complement to the more advanced treatises on Algebra, giving special attention to the analysis and solution of equations with numerical coefficients.

Church's Elements of Calculus,

Church's Analytical Geometry,

Church's Descriptive Geometry, 2 vols.,

These volumes constitute the "West Point Course" in their several departments.

Courtenay's Elements of Calculus,

A standard work of the very highest grade.

Hackley's Trigonometry,

With applications to navigation and surveying, nautical and practical geometry and geodesy.

PENMANSHIP.

Beers' System of Progressive Penmanship. Per dozen

This "round hand" system of Penmanship in twelve numbers, commends itself by its simplicity and thoroughness. The first four numbers are primary books. Nos. 5 to 7, advanced books for boys. Nos. 8 to 10, advanced books for girls. Nos. 11 and 12, ornamental penmanship. These books are printed from steel plates (engraved by McLees), and are unexcelled in mechanical execution. Large quantities are annually sold.

Beers' Slated Copy Slips, per set

All beginners should practice, for a few weeks, slate exercises, familiarizing them with the form of the letters, the motions of the hand and arm, &c., &c. These copy slips, 32 in number, supply all the copies found in a complete series of writing-books, at a trifling cost.

Payson, Dunton & Scribner's Copy-B'ks. P. doz.,

The National System of Penmanship, in three distinct series—(1) Common School Series, comprising the first six numbers; (2) Business Series, Nos. 8, 11, and 12; (3) Ladies' Series, Nos. 7, 9, and 10.

Fulton & Eastman's Chirographic Charts,

To embellish the school room walls, and furnish class exercise in the elements of Penmanship.

Payson's Copy-Book Cover, per hundred

Protects every page except the one in use, and furnishes "lines" with proper slope for the penman, under. Patented.

National Steel Pens, Card with all kinds

Pronounced by competent judges the perfection of American-made pens, and superior to any foreign article.

SCHOOL SERIES.		Index Pen, per gross . . .	75
School Pen, per gross, . . $	60	BUSINESS SERIES.	
Academic Pen, do . .	63	Albata Pen, per gross, . .	40
Fine Pointed Pen, per gross	70	Bank Pen, do . .	70
POPULAR SERIES.		Empire Pen, do . .	70
Capitol Pen, per gross, . . 1	00	Commercial Pen, per gross .	60
do do pr. box of 2 doz.	25	Express Pen, do .	75
Bullion Pen (imit. gold) pr. gr.	75	Falcon Pen, do .	70
Ladies' Pen do	63	Elastic Pen, do .	75

Stimpson's Scientific Steel Pen, per gross $1 50.

One forward and two backward arches, ensuring great strength, well-balanced elasticity, evenness of point, and smoothness of execution. One gross in twelve contains a Scientific Gold Pen.

Stimpson's Ink-Retaining Holder, per doz. 1 50

A simple apparatus, which does not get out of order, withholds at a single dip as much ink as the pen would otherwise realize from a dozen trips to the inkstand, which it supplies with moderate and easy flow.

Stimpson's Gold Pen, $3 00; with Ink Retainer 4 50

Stimpson's Penman's Card, $0 25

One dozen Steel Pens (assorted points) and Patent Ink-retaining Pen holder.

HISTORY.

Monteith's Youth's History.

A History of the United States for beginners. It is arranged upon the catechetical plan, with illustrative maps and engravings, review questions, dates in parentheses (that their study may be optional with the younger class of learners), and interesting Biographical Sketches of all persons who have been prominently identified with the history of our country.

Willard's United States, School and University Editions.

The plan of this standard work is chronologically exhibited in front of the title-page; the Maps and Sketches are found useful assistants to the memory, and dates, usually so difficult to remember, are so systematically arranged as in a great degree to obviate the difficulty. Candor, impartiality, and accuracy, are the distinguishing features of the narrative portion.

Willard's Universal History.

The most valuable features of the "United States" are reproduced in this. The peculiarities of the work are its great conciseness and the prominence given to the chronological order of events. The margin marks each successive era with great distinctness, so that the pupil retains not only the event but its time, and thus fixes the order of history firmly and usefully in his mind. Mrs. Willard's books are constantly revised, and at all times written up to embrace important historical events of recent date.

Lancaster's English History,

By the Master of the Stoughton Grammar School, Boston. The most practical of the "brief books." Though short, it is not a bare and uninteresting outline, but contains enough of explanation and detail to make intelligible the *cause and effect* of events. Their relations to the history and development of the American people is made specially prominent.

Willis' Historical Reader,

Being Collier's Great Events of History adapted to American schools. This rare epitome of general history, remarkable for its charming style and judicious selection of events on which the destinies of nations have turned, has been skillfully manipulated by Prof. Willis, with as few changes as would bring the United States into its proper position in the historical perspective. As reader or text-book it has few equals and no superiors.

Berard's History of England,

By an authoress well known for the success of her History of the United States. The social life of the English people is felicitously interwoven, as in fact, with the civil and military transactions of the realm.

Ricord's History of Rome

Possesses the charm of an attractive romance. The Fables with which this history abounds are introduced in such a way as not to deceive the inexperienced, while adding materially to the value of the work as a reliable index to the character and institutions, as well as the history of the Roman people.

Hanna's Bible History.

The only compendium of Bible narrative which affords a connected and chronological view of the important events there recorded, divested of all superfluous detail.

Summary of History; American, French and English.

A well-proportioned outline of leading events, condensing the substance of the more extensive text-book in common use into a series of statements so brief, that every word may be committed to memory, and yet so comprehensive that it presents an accurate though general view of the whole continuous life of nations.

Marsh's Ecclesiastical History.

Affording the History of the Church in all ages, with accounts of the pagan world during Biblical periods, and the character, rise, and progress of all Religions, as well as the various sects of the worshipers of Christ. The work is entirely non-sectarian, though strictly catholic. A separate volume contains carefully prepared QUESTIONS for class use.

HISTORY—Continued.

BARNES' ONE-TERM HISTORY.

A Brief History of the United States,

This is probably the MOST ORIGINAL SCHOOL-BOOK published for many years, in any department. A few of its claims are the following:

1. **Brevity.**—The text is complete for Grammar School or intermediate classes, in 290 12mo pages, large type. It may readily be completed, if desired, in one term of study.

2. **Comprehensiveness.**—Though so brief, this book contains the pith of all the wearying contents of the larger manuals, and a great deal more than the memory usually retains from the latter.

3. **Interest** has been a prime consideration. Small books have heretofore been bare, full of dry statistics, unattractive. This one is charmingly written, replete with anecdote, and brilliant with illustration.

4. **Proportion of Events.**—It is remarkable for the discrimination with which the different portions of our history are presented according to their importance. Thus the older works being already large books when the civil war took place, give it less space than that accorded to the Revolution.

5. **Arrangement.**—In six epochs, entitled respectively, Discovery and Settlement, the Colonies, the Revolution, Growth of States, the Civil War, and Current Events.

6. **Catch Words.**—Each paragraph is preceded by its leading thought in prominent type, standing in the student's mind for the whole paragraph.

7. **Key Notes.**—Analogous with this is the idea of grouping battles, etc. about some central event, which relieves the sameness so common in such descriptions, and renders each distinct by some striking peculiarity of its own.

8. **Foot Notes.**—These are crowded with interesting matter that is not strictly a part of history proper. They may be learned or not, at pleasure. They are certain in any event to be read.

9. **Biographies** of all the leading characters are given in full in foot-notes.

10. **Maps.**—Elegant and distinct Maps from engravings on copper-plate, and beautifully colored, precede each epoch, and contain all the places named.

11. **Questions** are at the back of the book, to compel a more independent use of the text. Both text and questions are so worded that the pupil must give intelligent answers IN HIS OWN WORDS. "Yes" and "No" will not do.

12. **Historical Recreations.**—These are additional questions to test the student's knowledge, in review, as: "What trees are celebrated in our history?" "When did a fog save our army?" "What Presidents died in office?" "When was the Mississippi our western boundary?" "Who said, 'I would rather be right than President?'" etc.

13. **The Illustrations,** about seventy in number, are the work of our best artists and engravers, produced at great expense. They are vivid and interesting, and mostly upon subjects never before illustrated in a school-book.

14. **Dates.**—Only the leading dates are given in the text, and these are so associated as to assist the memory, but at the head of each page is the date of the event first mentioned, and at the close of each epoch a summary of events and dates.

15. **The Philosophy of History** is studiously exhibited—the causes and effects of events being distinctly traced and their interconnection shown.

16. **Impartiality.** — All sectional, partisan, or denominational views are avoided. Facts are stated after a careful comparison of all authorities without the least prejudice or favor.

17. **Index.**—A verbal index at the close of the book perfects it as a work of reference.

It will be observed that the above are all particulars in which School Histories have been signally defective, or altogether wanting. Many other claims to favor it shares in common with its predecessors.

BARNES' ONE-TERM HISTORY—Continued.

From PROF. WM. F. ALLEN, *State Univ. of Wisconsin.*

I think the author of the new "Brief History of the United States" has been very successful in combining brevity with sufficient fullness and interest. *Particularly*, he has avoided the excessive number of names and dates that most histories contain. Two features that I like *very much* are the *anecdotes* at the foot of the page and the "*Historical Recreations*" in the Appendix. The latter, I think, is quite a *new* feature, and the other is *very* well executed.

From S. G. WRIGHT, *Assist.-Supt. Pub. Inst., Kansas.*

It is with extreme pleasure we submit our recommendation of the "Brief History of the United States." It meets the needs of young and older children, combining concision with perspicuity, and if "brevity is the soul of wit," this "Brief History" contains not only that well-chosen ingredient, but wisdom sufficient to enlighten those students who are wearily longing for a "new departure" from certain old and uninteresting presentations of fossilized writers. We congratulate a progressive public upon a progressive book.

From HON. NEWTON BATEMAN, *Supt. Pub. Inst., Illinois.*

Barnes' One-Term History of the United States is an exceedingly attractive and spirited little book. Its claim to several new and valuable features seems well founded. Under the form of six well-defined Epochs, the History of the United States is traced tersely, yet pithily, from the earliest times to the present day. A good map precedes each epoch, whereby the history and geography of the period may be studied together, *as they always should be.* The syllabus of each paragraph is made to stand in such bold relief, by the use of large, heavy type, as to be of much *mnemonic* value to the student. The book is written in a sprightly and piquant style, the interest never flagging from beginning to end—a rare and difficult achievement in works of this kind.

From the "Chicago Schoolmaster" (Editorial).

A thorough examination of Barnes' Brief History of the United States brings the examiner to the conclusion that it is a superior book in almost every respect. The book is neat in form, and of good material. The type is clear, large, and distinct. The facts and dates are correct. The arrangement of topics is just the thing needed in a history text-book. By this arrangement the pupil can see at once what he is expected to do. The topics are well selected, embracing the leading ideas or principal events of American history. . . . The book as a whole is much superior to any I have examined. So much do I think this, that I have ordered it for my class, and shall use it in my school. (Signed) B. W. BAKER.

A Brief History of France,

By the author of the "Brief United States," with all the attractive features of that popular work (which see), and new ones of its own.

It is believed that the history of France has never before been presented in such brief compass, and this is effected without sacrificing one particle of interest. The book reads like a romance, and, while drawing the student by an irresistible fascination to his task, impresses the great outlines indelibly upon the memory.

Gilman's First Steps in General History,

A "suggestive outline" of rare compactness. Each country is treated by itself, and the United States receive special attention. Frequent Maps, contemporary events in Tables, References to Standard Works for fuller details, and a minute Index constitute the "Illustrative Apparatus." From no other work that we know of can so succinct a view of the world's history be obtained. Considering the necessary limitation of space, the style is surprisingly vivid, and at times even ornate. In all respects a charming, though not the less practical, text-book.

Gilman's "Seven Historic Ages,"

This book is written in the style used by a father talking with his children on the progress of history. As one Age after another is taken up, the author brings before the young reader the prominent men and characteristic events by which it is to be remembered. The object is to stimulate the pupil in school or the child at home to study history, to think of it as a lively picture of the doings of men, and not as a dead list of uninteresting dates.

Baker's Brief History of Texas,

On the plan of "Barnes' Brief Histories," with Constitution of the State, for schools.

DRAWING.

Chapman's American Drawing Book,

The standard American text-book and authority in all branches of art. A compilation of art principles. A manual for the amateur, and basis of study for the professional artist. Adapted for schools and private instruction.

CONTENTS.—"Any one who can Learn to Write can Learn to Draw."—Primary Instruction in Drawing.—Rudiments of Drawing the Human Head.—Rudiments in Drawing the Human Figure.—Rudiments of Drawing.—The Elements of Geometry.—Perspective.—Of Studying and Sketching from Nature.—Of Painting.—Etching and Engraving.—Of Modeling.—Of Composition.—Advice to the American Art-Student. The work is of course magnificently illustrated with all the original designs.

Chapman's Elementary Drawing Book,

A Progressive Course of Practical Exercises, or a text-book for the training of the eye and hand. It contains the elements from the larger work, and a copy should be in the hands of every pupil; while a copy of the "American Drawing Book," named above, should be at hand for reference by the class.

The Little Artist's Portfolio,

25 Drawing Cards (progressive patterns), 25 Blanks, and a fine Artist's Pencil, all in one neat envelope.

Clark's Elements of Drawing,

A complete course in this graceful art, from the first rudiments of outline to the finished sketches of landscape and scenery.

Fowle's Linear and Perspective Drawing,

For the cultivation of the eye and hand, with copious illustrations and directions for the guidance of the unskilled teacher.

Monk's Drawing Books—Six Numbers, per set,

Each book contains *eleven* large patterns, with opposing blanks. No. 1. Elementary Studies. No. 2. Studies of Foliage. No. 3. Landscapes. No. 4. Animals, I. No. 5. Animals, II. No. 6. Marine Views, etc.

Allen's Map-Drawing, Scale,

This method introduces a new era in Map-Drawing, for the following reasons:—1. It is a system. This is its greatest merit.—2. It is easily understood and taught. —3. The eye is trained to exact measurement by the use of a scale.—4. By no special effort of the memory, distance and comparative size are fixed in the mind.—5. It discards useless construction of lines.—6. It can be taught by any teacher, even though there may have been no previous practice in Map-Drawing.—7. Any pupil old enough to study Geography can learn by this System, in a short time, to draw accurate maps.—8. The System is not the result of theory, but comes directly from the school-room. It has been thoroughly and successfully tested there, with all grades of pupils.—9. It is economical, as it requires no mapping plates. It gives the pupil the ability of rapidly drawing accurate maps.

Ripley's Map-Drawing,

Based on the Circle. One of the most efficient aids to the acquirement of a knowledge of Geography is the practice of map-drawing. It is useful for the same reason that the best exercise in orthography is the *writing* of difficult words. Sight comes to the aid of hearing, and a double impression is produced upon the memory. Knowledge becomes less mechanical and more intuitive. The student who has sketched the outlines of a country, and dotted the important places, is little likely to forget either. The impression produced may be compared to that of a traveller who has been over the ground, while more comprehensive and accurate in detail.

BOOK-KEEPING.

Folsom's Logical Book-keeping,
Folsom's Blanks to Book-keeping,

This treatise embraces the interesting and important discoveries of Prof. Folsom (of the Albany "Bryant & Stratton College"), the partial enunciation of which in lectures and otherwise has attracted so much attention in circles interested in commercial education.

After studying business phenomena for many years, he has arrived at the positive laws and principles that underlie the whole subject of Accounts; finds that the science is based in *Value* as a generic term; that value divides into *two classes* with varied species; that all the exchanges of values are reducible to nine equations; and that all the results of all these exchanges are limited to *thirteen* in number.

As accounts have been universally taught hitherto, without setting out from a radical analysis or definition of values, the science has been kept in great obscurity, and been made as difficult to impart as to acquire. On the new theory, however, these obstacles are chiefly removed. In reading over the first part of it, in which the governing laws and principles are discussed, a person with ordinary intelligence will obtain a fair conception of the *double entry* process of accounts. But when he comes to study thoroughly these laws and principles as there enunciated, and works out the examples and memoranda which elucidate the *thirteen results* of business, the student will neither fail in readily acquiring the science as it is, nor in becoming able intelligently to apply it in the interpretation of business.

Smith & Martin's Book-keeping,
Smith & Martin's Blanks,

This work is by a practical teacher and a practical book-keeper. It is of a thoroughly popular class, and will be welcomed by every one who loves to see theory and practice combined in an easy, concise, and methodical form.

The Single Entry portion is well adapted to supply a want felt in nearly all other treatises, which seem to be prepared mainly for the use of wholesale merchants, leaving retailers, mechanics, farmers, etc., who transact the greater portion of the business of the country, without a guide. The work is also commended, on this account, for general use in Young Ladies' Seminaries, where a thorough grounding in the simpler form of accounts will be invaluable to the future housekeepers of the nation.

The treatise on Double Entry Book-keeping combines all the advantages of the most recent methods, with the utmost simplicity of application, thus affording the pupil all the advantages of actual experience in the counting-house, and giving a clear comprehension of the entire subject through a judicious course of mercantile transactions.

The shape of the book is such that the transactions can be presented as in actual practice; and the simplified form of Blanks—three in number—adds greatly to the ease experienced in acquiring the science.

NATURAL SCIENCE.

FAMILIAR SCIENCE.

Norton & Porter's First Book of Science,

By eminent Professors of Yale College. Contains the principles of Natural Philosophy, Astronomy, Chemistry, Physiology, and Geology. Arranged on the Catechetical plan for primary classes and beginners.

Chambers' Treasury of Knowledge,

Progressive lessons upon—*first*, common things which lie most immediately around us, and first attract the attention of the young mind; *second*, common objects from the Mineral, Animal, and Vegetable kingdoms, manufactured articles, and miscellaneous substances; *third*, a systematic view of Nature under the various sciences. May be used as a Reader or Text-book.

NATURAL PHILOSOPHY.

Norton's First Book in Natural Philosophy,

By Prof. NORTON, of Yale College. Designed for beginners. Profusely illustrated and arranged on the Catechetical plan.

Peck's Ganot's Course of Nat. Philosophy,

The standard text-book of France, Americanized and popularized by Prof. PECK, of Columbia College. The most magnificent system of illustration ever adopted in an American school-book is here found. For intermediate classes.

Peck's Elements of Mechanics,

A suitable introduction to Bartlett's higher treatises on Mechanical Philosophy, and adequate in itself for a complete academical course.

Bartlett's SYNTHETIC, AND ANALYTIC, Mechanics,

Bartlett's Acoustics and Optics,

A system of Collegiate Philosophy, by Prof. BARTLETT, of West Point Military Academy.

Steele's 14 Weeks Course in Philos. (see p. 34)

Steele's Philosophical Apparatus,

Adequate to performing the experiments in the ordinary text-books. The articles will be sold separately, if desired. See special circular for details.

GEOLOGY.

Page's Elements of Geology,

A volume of Chambers' Educational Course. Practical, simple, and eminently calculated to make the study interesting.

Emmons' Manual of Geology,

The first Geologist of the country has here produced a work worthy of his reputation.

Steele's 14 Weeks Course (see p. 34)

Steele's Geological Cabinet,

Containing 125 carefully selected specimens. In four parts. Sold separately, if desired. See circular for details.

Peck's Ganot's Popular Physics.

TESTIMONIALS.

From PROF. ALONZO COLLIN, *Cornell College, Iowa.*

I am pleased with it. I have decided to introduce it as a text-book.

From H. F. JOHNSON, *President Madison College, Sharon, Miss.*

I am pleased with Peck's Ganot, and think it a magnificent book.

From PROF. EDWARD BROOKS, *Pennsylvania State Normal School.*

So eminent are its merits, that it will be introduced as the text-book upon elementary physics in this institution.

From H. H. LOCKWOOD, *Professor Natural Philosophy U. S. Naval Academy.*

I am so pleased with it that I will probably add it to a course of lectures given to the midshipmen of this school on physics.

From GEO. S. MACKIE, *Professor Natural History University of Nashville, Tenn.*

I have decided on the introduction of Peck's Ganot's Philosophy, as I am satisfied that it is the best book for the purposes of my pupils that I have seen, combining simplicity of explanation with elegance of illustration.

From W. S. MCRAE, *Superintendent Vevay Public Schools, Indiana.*

Having carefully examined a number of text-books on natural philosophy, I do not hesitate to express my decided opinion in favor of Peck's Ganot. The matter, style, and illustration eminently adapt the work to the popular wants.

From REV. SAMUEL MCKINNEY, D.D., *Pres't Austin College, Huntsville, Texas.*

It gives me pleasure to commend it to teachers. I have taught some classes with it as our text, and must say, for simplicity of style and clearness of illustration, I have found nothing as yet published of equal value to the teacher and pupil.

From C. V. SPEAR, *Principal Maplewood Institute, Pittsfield, Mass.*

I am much pleased with its ample illustrations by plates, and its clearness and simplicity of statement. It covers the ground usually gone over by our higher classes, and contains many fresh illustrations from life or daily occurrence, and new applications of scientific principles to such.

From J. A. BANFIELD, *Superintendent Marshall Public Schools, Michigan.*

I have used Peck's Ganot since 1863, and with increasing pleasure and satisfaction each term. I consider it superior to any other work on physics in its adaptation to our high schools and academies. Its illustrations are superb— better than three times their number of pages of fine print.

From A. SCHUYLER, *Prof. of Mathematics in Baldwin University, Berea, Ohio.*

After a careful examination of Peck's Ganot's Natural Philosophy, and an actual test of its merits as a text-book, I can heartily recommend it as admirably adapted to meet the wants of the grade of students for which it is intended. Its diagrams and illustrations are *unrivaled.* We use it in the Baldwin University.

From D. C. VAN NORMAN, *Principal Van Norman Institute, New York.*

The Natural Philosophy of M. Ganot, edited by Prof. Peck, is, in my opinion, the best work of its kind, for the use intended, ever published in this country. Whether regarded in relation to the natural order of the topics, the precision and clearness of its definitions, or the fullness and beauty of its illustrations, it is certainly, I think, an advance.

☞ For many similar testimonials, see current numbers of the Illustrated Educational Bulletin.

NATURAL SCIENCE—Continued.

CHEMISTRY.

Porter's First Book of Chemistry,

Porter's Principles of Chemistry,

The above are widely known as the productions of one of the most eminent scientific men of America. The extreme simplicity in the method of presenting the science, while exhaustively treated, has excited universal commendation.

Darby's Text-Book of Chemistry,

Purely a Chemistry, divesting the subject of matters comparatively foreign to it (such as heat, light, electricity, etc.), but usually allowed to engross too much attention in ordinary school-books.

Gregory's Chemistry, (Organic and Inorganic, each)

The science exhaustively treated. For colleges and medical students.

Steele's Fourteen Weeks Course,

A successful effort to reduce the study to the limits of a *single term*. **(See page 34.)**

Steele's Chemical Apparatus,

Adequate to the performance of all the important experiments.

BOTANY.

Thinker's First Lessons in Botany,

For children. The technical terms are largely dispensed with in favor of an easy and familiar style adapted to the smallest learner.

Wood's Object-Lessons in Botany,

Wood's American Botanist and Florist,

Wood's New Class-Book of Botany,

The standard text-books of the United States in this department. In style they are simple, popular, and lively; in arrangement, easy and natural; in description, graphic and strictly exact. The Tables for Analysis are reduced to a perfect system. More are annually sold than of all others combined.

Wood's Plant Record,

A simple form of Blanks for recording observations in the field.

Wood's Botanical Apparatus,

A portable Trunk, containing Drying Press, Knife, Trowel, Microscope, and Tweezers, and a copy of Wood's Plant Record—composing a complete outfit for the collector.

Willis's Flora of New Jersey,

"*Catalogus Plantarum in Nova Cæsarea repertarum.*" This remarkable flora is of great interest to all botanists, and the Jersey Pines have been termed "the Mecca to which every young botanist hopes some day to make a pilgrimage." This work is indispensable to those botanizing on the ground, and is the most useful book of reference ever published for collectors in all parts of the country. It contains also a Botanical Directory, with addresses of living American botanists.

Young's Familiar Lessons,

Combining simplicity of diction with some degree of technical and scientific knowledge for intermediate classes. Specially adapted for Texas and the Southwest.

Darby's Southern Botany,

Embracing general Structural and Physiological Botany, with vegetable products, and descriptions of Southern plants, and a complete Flora of the Southern States.

NATURAL SCIENCE—Continued.

WOOD'S BOTANIES.

TESTIMONIALS.

From PROF. RICHARD OWEN, *University of Indiana.*

I am well pleased with the evidence of philosophical method exhibited in the general arrangement, as well as with the clearness of the explanations, the ready intelligibility of the analytical tables, and the illustrative aid furnished by the numerous and excellent wood-cuts. I design using the work as a text-book with my next class.

From PRIN. B. R. ANDERSON, *Columbus Union School, Wisconsin.*

I have examined several works with a view to recommending some good text-book on Botany, but I lay them all aside for "Wood's Botanist and Florist." The arrangement of the book is in my opinion excellent, its style fascinating and attractive, its treatment of the various departments of the science is thorough, and last, but far from unimportant, I like the topical form of the questions to each chapter. It seems to embrace the entire science. In fact, I consider it a complete, attractive, and exhaustive work.

From M. A. MARSHALL, *New Haven High School, Conn.*

It has all the excellencies of the well-known Class-Book of Botany by the same author in a smaller book. By a judicious system of condensation, the size of the Flora is reduced one-half, while no species are omitted, and many new ones are added. The descriptions of species are very brief, yet sufficient to identify the plant, and, when taken in connection with the generic description, form a complete description of the plant. The book as a whole will suit the wants of classes better than anything I have yet seen. The adoption of the Botanist and Florist would not require the exclusion of the Class-Book of Botany, as they are so arranged that both might be used by the same class.

From PROF. G. H. PERKINS, *University of Vermont and State Agricultural College.*

I can truly say that the more I examine Wood's Class-Book, the better pleased I am with it. In its illustrations, especially of particulars not easily observed by the student, and the clearness and compactness of its statements, as well as in the territory its flora embraces, it appears to me to surpass any other work I know of. The whole science, so far as it can be taught in a college course, is well presented and rendered unusually easy of comprehension. The mode of analysis is excellent, avoiding as it does to a great extent those microscopic characters which puzzle the beginner, and using those that are obvious as far as possible. I regard the work as a most admirable one, and shall adopt it as a text-book another year.

AGRICULTURE.

Pendleton's Scientific Agriculture,

A text-book for colleges and schools; treats of the following topics: Anatomy and Physiology of Plants; Agricultural Meteorology; Soils as related to Physics: Chemistry of the Atmosphere; of Plants; of Soils; Fertilizers and Natural Manures; Animal Nutrition, etc. By E. M. PENDLETON, M. D., Prof. of Agriculture in the University of Georgia.

From President A. D. WHITE, *Cornell University.*

Dear Sir: I have examined your "Text-book of Agricultural Science," and it seems to me excellent in view of the purpose it is intended to serve. Many of your chapters interested me especially, and all parts of the work seem to combine scientific instruction with practical information in proportions dictated by sound common sense.

From President ROBINSON, *of Brown University.*

It is scientific in method as well as in matter, comprehensive in plan, natural and logical in order, compact and lucid in its statements, and must be useful both as a text-book in Agricultural colleges, and as a hand-book for intelligent planters and farmers.

NATURAL SCIENCE—Continued.

PHYSIOLOGY.

Jarvis' Elements of Physiology,

Jarvis' Physiology and Laws of Health,

The only books extant which approach this subject with a proper view of the true object of teaching Physiology in schools, viz., that scholars may know how to take care of their own health. In bold contrast with the abstract *Anatomies*, which children learn as they would Greek or Latin (and forget as soon), to *discipline the mind*, are these text-books, using the *science* as a secondary consideration, and only so far as is necessary for the comprehension of the *laws of health*.

Hamilton's Vegetable and Animal Physiology,

The two branches of the science combined in one volume lead the student to a proper comprehension of the Analogies of Nature.

Steele's Fourteen Weeks Course,

In the popular style, avoiding technical and purely scientific formulas. It contains beautiful and vivid illustrations, some of them colored, and a blackboard analysis of the skeleton. The sections on diseases and accidents, and their prompt home treatment, give the book great practical value (see p. 34).

ASTRONOMY.

Willard's School Astronomy,

By means of clear and attractive illustrations, addressing the eye in many cases by analogies, careful definitions of all necessary technical terms, a careful avoidance of verbiage and unimportant matter, particular attention to analysis, and a general adoption of the simplest methods. Mrs. Willard has made the best and most attractive *elementary* Astronomy extant.

McIntyre's Astronomy and the Globes,

A complete treatise for intermediate classes. Highly approved.

Bartlett's Spherical Astronomy,

The West Point course, for advanced classes, with applications to the current wants of Navigation, Geography, and Chronology.

Steele's Fourteen Weeks Course,

Reduced to a single term, and better adapted to school use than any work heretofore published. Not written for the information of scientific men, but for the inspiration of youth, the pages are not burdened with a multitude of figures which no memory could possibly retain. The whole subject is presented in a clear and concise form. (See p. 34.)

NATURAL HISTORY.

Carll's Child's Book of Natural History,

Illustrating the Animal, Vegetable, and Mineral Kingdoms, with application to the Arts. For beginners. Beautifully and copiously illustrated.

ZOOLOGY.

Chambers' Elements of Zoology,

A complete and comprehensive system of Zoology, adapted for academic instruction, presenting a systematic view of the Animal Kingdom as a portion of external Nature.

Steele's Fourteen Weeks Course,

Notable for its superb and entertaining illustrations, which include every animal named; blackboard tables of classification and tabular review of the whole animal kingdom; interesting and characteristic facts and anecdotes; directions for collecting and preserving specimens, etc., etc. (See p. 34.)

Jarvis' Physiology and Laws of Health.

TESTIMONIALS.

From SAMUEL B. MCLANE, *Superintendent Public Schools, Keokuk, Iowa.*

I am glad to see a really good text-book on this much neglected branch. This is clear, concise, accurate, and eminently adapted to the *class-room.*

From WILLIAM F. WYERS, *Principal of Academy, West Chester, Pennsylvania.*

A thorough examination has satisfied me of its superior claims as a text-book to the attention of teacher and taught. I shall introduce it at once.

From H. R. SANFORD, *Principal of East Genesee Conference Seminary, N. Y.*

"Jarvis' Physiology" is received, and fully met our expectations. We immediately adopted it.

From ISAAC T. GOODNOW, *State Superintendent of Kansas—published in connection with the "School Law."*

"Jarvis' Physiology," a common-sense, practical work, with just enough of anatomy to understand the physiological portions. The last six pages, on Man's Responsibility for his own health, are worth the price of the book.

From D. W. STEVENS, *Superintendent Public Schools, Fall River, Mass.*

I have examined Jarvis' "Physiology and Laws of Health," which you had the kindness to send to me a short time ago. In my judgment it is far the best work of the kind within my knowledge. It has been adopted as a text-book in our public schools.

From HENRY G. DENNY, *Chairman Book Committee, Boston, Mass.*

The very excellent "Physiology" of Dr. Jarvis I had introduced into our High School, where the study had been temporarily dropped, believing it to be by far the best work of the kind that had come under my observation; indeed, the reintroduction of the study was delayed for some months, because Dr. Jarvis' book could not be had, and we were unwilling to take any other.

From PROF. A. P. PEABODY, D.D., LL.D., *Harvard University.*

* * I have been in the habit of examining school-books with great care, and I hesitate not to say that, of all the text-books on Physiology which have been given to the public, Dr. Jarvis' deserves the first place on the score of accuracy, thoroughness, method, simplicity of statement, and constant reference to topics of practical interest and utility.

From JAMES N. TOWNSEND, *Superintendent Public Schools, Hudson, N. Y.*

Every human being is appointed to take charge of his own body; and of all books written upon this subject, I know of none which will so well prepare one to do this as "Jarvis' Physiology"—that is, in so small a compass of matter. It considers the pure, simple *laws of health* paramount to science; and though the work is thoroughly scientific, it is divested of all cumbrous technicalities, and presents the subject of physical life in a manner and style really charming. It is unquestionably the best text-book on physiology I have ever seen. It is giving great satisfaction in the schools of this city, where it has been adopted as the standard.

From L. J. SANFORD, M.D., *Prof. Anatomy and Physiology in Yale College*

Books on human physiology, designed for the use of schools, are more generally a failure perhaps than are school-books on most other subjects.

The great want in this department is met, we think, in the well-written treatise of Dr. Jarvis, entitled "Physiology and Laws of Health." * * The work is not too detailed nor too expansive in any department, and is clear and concise in all. It is not burdened with an excess of anatomical description, nor rendered discursive by many zoological references. Anatomical statements are made to the extent of qualifying the student to attend, understandingly, to an exposition of those functional processes which, collectively, make up health; thus the laws of health are enunciated, and many suggestions are given which, if heeded, will tend to its preservation.

☞ For further testimony of similar character, see current numbers of the Illustrated Educational Bulletin.

NATURAL SCIENCE.

"FOURTEEN WEEKS" IN EACH BRANCH.

By J. DORMAN STEELE, A. M.

Steele's 14 Weeks Course in Chemistry (New Ed.)
Steele's 14 Weeks Course in Astronomy
Steele's 14 Weeks Course in Philosophy
Steele's 14 Weeks Course in Geology
Steele's 14 Weeks Course in Physiology
Steele's 14 Weeks Course in Zoology

Our Text-Books in these studies are, as a general thing, dull and uninteresting. They contain from 400 to 600 pages of dry facts and unconnected details. They abound in that which the student cannot learn, much less remember. The pupil commences the study, is confused by the fine print and coarse print, and neither knowing exactly what to learn nor what to hasten over, is crowded through the single term generally assigned to each branch, and frequently comes to the close without a definite and exact idea of a single scientific principle.

Steele's Fourteen Weeks Courses contain only that which every well-informed person should know, while all that which concerns only the professional scientist is omitted. The language is clear, simple, and interesting, and the illustrations bring the subject within the range of home life and daily experience. They give such of the general principles and the prominent facts as a pupil can make familiar as household words within a single term. The type is large and open; there is no fine print to annoy; the cuts are copies of genuine experiments or natural phenomena, and are of fine execution.

In fine, by a system of condensation peculiarly his own, the author reduces each branch to the limits of a single term of study, while sacrificing nothing that is essential, and nothing that is usually retained from the study of the larger manuals in common use. Thus the student has rare opportunity to *economize his time*, or rather to employ that which he has to the best advantage.

A notable feature is the author's charming "style," fortified by an enthusiasm over his subject in which the student will not fail to partake. Believing that Natural Science is full of fascination, he has moulded it into a form that attracts the attention and kindles the enthusiasm of the pupil.

The recent editions contain the author's "Practical Questions" on a plan never before attempted in scientific text-books. These are questions as to the nature and cause of common phenomena, and are not directly answered in the text, the design being to test and promote an intelligent use of the student's knowledge of the foregoing principles.

Steele's General Key to his Works.

This work is mainly composed of Answers to the Practical Questions and Solutions of the Problems in the author's celebrated "Fourteen Weeks Courses" in the several sciences, with many hints to teachers, minor Tables, &c. Should be on every teacher's desk.

Steele's 14 Weeks in each Science.

TESTIMONIALS.

From L. A. Bikle, *President N. C. College.*

I have not been disappointed. Shall take pleasure in introducing this series.

From J. F. Cox, *Prest. Southern Female College, Ga.*

I am much pleased with these books, and expect to introduce them.

From J. R. Branham, *Prin. Brownsville Female College, Tenn.*

They are capital little books, and are now in use in our institution.

From W. H. Goodale, *Professor Readville Seminary, La.*

We are using your 14 Weeks Course, and are much pleased with them.

From W. A. Boles, *Supt. Shelbyville Graded School, Ind.*

They are as entertaining as a story book, and much more improving to the mind.

From S. A. Snow, *Principal of High School, Uxbridge, Mass.*

Steele's 14 Weeks Courses in the Sciences are a perfect success.

From John W. Doughty, *Newburg Free Academy, N. Y.*

I was prepared to find Prof. Steele's Course both attractive and instructive. My highest expectations have been fully realized.

From J. S. Blackwell, *Prest. Ghent College, Ky.*

Prof. Steele's unexampled success in providing for the wants of academic classes, has led me to look forward with high anticipations to his forthcoming issue.

From J. F. Cook, *Prest. La Grange College, Mo.*

I am pleased with the neatness of these books and the delightful diction. I have been teaching for years, and have never seen a lovelier little volume than the Astronomy.

From M. W. Smith, *Prin. of High School, Morrison, Ill.*

They seem to me to be admirably adapted to the wants of a public school, containing, as they do, a sufficiently comprehensive arrangement of elementary principles to excite a healthy thirst for a more thorough knowledge of those sciences.

From J. D. Bartley, *Prin. of High School, Concord, N. H.*

They are just such books as I have looked for, viz., those of interesting style, not cumbersome and filled up with things to be omitted by the pupil, and yet sufficiently full of facts for the purpose of most scholars in these sciences in our high schools; there is nothing but what a pupil of average ability can thoroughly master.

From Alonzo Norton Lewis, *Principal of Parker Academy, Conn.*

I consider Steele's Fourteen Weeks Courses in Philosophy, Chemistry, &c., the *best* school-books that have been issued in this country.

As an introduction to the various branches of which they treat, and especially for that numerous class of pupils who have not the time for a more extended course, I consider them *invaluable.*

From Edward Brooks, *Prin. State Normal School, Millersville, Pa.*

At the meeting of Normal School Principals, I presented the following resolution, which was unanimously adopted: "*Resolved,* That Steele's 14 Weeks' Courses in Natural Philosophy and Astronomy, or an amount equivalent to what is contained in them, be adopted for use in the State Normal Schools of Pennsylvania." The works themselves will be adopted by at least three of the schools and, I presume, by them all.

LITERATURE.

Gilman's First Steps in English Literature,

The character and plan of this exquisite little text-book may be best understood from an analysis of its contents:

INTRODUCTION. Chapter I, Historical; II, Definition of Terms; III, Languages of Europe, with Chart.

PERIOD OF IMMATURE ENGLISH, with Chart. Chapter IV, Original English; V, Broken English; VI, Dead English; VII, Reviving English.

PERIOD OF MATURE ENGLISH, with Chart. Chapter VIII, The Italian Influence; IX, Puritan Influence; X, French Influence; XI, Age of Pope; XII, Age of Johnson; XIII, Age of Poetical Romance; XIV, Age of Prose Romance.

The volume concludes with a Chart of Bible Translations, a Bibliography or Guide to General Reading, and other aids to the student.

Cleveland's Compendiums,

ENGLISH LITERATURE. AMERICAN LITERATURE.
ENGLISH LITERATURE OF THE XIXTH CENTURY.

In these volumes are gathered the cream of the literature of the English-speaking people for the school-room and the general reader. Their reputation is national. More than 125,000 copies have been sold.

Boyd's English Classics,

MILTON'S PARADISE LOST. THOMSON'S SEASONS.
YOUNG'S NIGHT THOUGHTS. POLLOK'S COURSE OF TIME.
COWPER'S TASK, TABLE TALK, &C. LORD BACON'S ESSAYS.

This series of annotated editions of great English writers, in prose and poetry, is designed for critical reading and parsing in schools. Prof. J. R. Boyd proves himself an editor of high capacity, and the works themselves need no encomium. As auxiliary to the study of Belles Lettres, etc., these works have no equal.

Pope's Essay on Man,

Pope's Homer's Iliad,

The metrical translation of the great poet of antiquity, and the matchless "Essay on the Nature and State of Man," by ALEXANDER POPE, afford superior exercise in literature and parsing.

ÆSTHETICS.

Huntington's Manual of the Fine Arts,

A view of the rise and progress of Art in different countries, a brief account of the most eminent masters of Art, and an analysis of the principles of Art. It is complete in itself, or may precede to advantage the critical work of Lord Kames.

Boyd's Kames' Elements of Criticism,

The best edition of this standard work; without the study of which none may be considered proficient in the science of the Perceptions. No other study can be pursued with so marked an effect upon the taste and refinement of the pupil.

CLEVELAND'S COMPENDIUMS.

TESTIMONIALS.

From the New Englander.

This is the very best book of the kind we have ever examined.

From George B. Emerson, Esq., *Boston.*

The Biographical Sketches are just and discriminating; the selections are admirable, and I have adopted the work as a text-book for my first class.

From Prof. Moses Coit Tyler, *of the Michigan University.*

I have given your book a thorough examination, and am greatly delighted with it; and shall have great pleasure in directing the attention of my classes to a work which affords so admirable a bird's-eye view of recent "English Literature."

From the Saturday Review.

It acquaints the reader with the characteristic method, tone, and quality of all the chief notabilities of the period, and will give the careful student a better idea of the recent history of English Literature than nine educated Englishmen in ten possess.

From the Methodist Quarterly Review, New York.

This work is a transcript of the best American mind; a vehicle of the noblest American spirit. No parent who would introduce his child to a knowledge of our country's literature, and at the same time indoctrinate his heart in the purest principles, need fear to put this manual in the youthful hand.

From Rev. C. Peirce, *Principal, West Newton, Mass.*

I do not believe the work is to be found from which, within the same limits, so much interesting and valuable information in regard to English writers and English literature of every age, can be obtained; and it deserves to find a place in all our high schools and academies, as well as in every private library.

From the Independent.

The work of selection and compilation—requiring a perfect familiarity with the whole range of English literature, a judgment clear and impartial, a taste at once delicate and severe, and a most sensitive regard to purity of thought or feeling—has been better accomplished in this than in any kindred volume with which we are acquainted.

POLITICAL ECONOMY.

Champlin's Lessons on Political Economy,

An improvement on previous treatises, being shorter, yet containing everything essential, with a view of recent questions in finance, etc., which is not elsewhere found.

From J. L. Bothwell, *Prin. Public School No. 14, Albany, N. Y.*

I have examined Champlin's Political Economy with much pleasure, and shall be pleased to put it into the hands of my pupils. In quantity and quality I think it superior to anything that I have examined.

From Pres. N. E. Cobleigh, *East Tennessee Wesleyan University.*

An examination of Champlin's Political Economy has satisfied me that it is the book I want. For brevity and compactness, division of the subject, and clear statement, and for appropriateness of treatment, I consider it a better text-book than any other in the market.

From the Evening Mail, New York.

A new interest has been imparted to the science of political economy since we have been necessitated to raise such vast sums of money for the support of the government. The time, therefore, is favorable for the introduction of works like the above. This little volume of two hundred pages is intended for beginners, for the common school and academy. It is intended as a basis upon which to rear a more elaborate superstructure. There is nothing in the principles of political economy above the comprehension of average scholars, when they are clearly set forth. This seems to have been done by President Champlin in an easy and graceful manner.

ELOCUTION.

Thwing's Vocal Culture.

A Drill-Book for voice and gesture, by Rev. Prof. Thwing, of Brooklyn Tabernacle Lay College. Price 50 cts.

Taverner Graham's Reasonable Elocution,

Based upon the belief that true Elocution is the right interpretation of THOUGHT, and guiding the student to an intelligent appreciation, instead of a merely mechanical knowledge, of its rules.

Zachos' Analytic Elocution.

All departments of elocution—such as the analysis of the voice and the sentence, phonology, rhythm, expression, gesture, etc.—are here arranged for instruction in classes, illustrated by copious examples.

Sherwood's Self Culture.

Self-culture in reading, speaking, and conversation—a very valuable treatise to those who would perfect themselves in these accomplishments.

SPEAKERS.

Northend's Little Orator—Child's Speaker.

Two little works of the same grade but different selections, containing simple and attractive pieces for children under twelve years of age.

Northend's Young Declaimer.

Northend's National Orator.

Two volumes of Prose, Poetry, and Dialogue, adapted to intermediate and grammar classes respectively.

Northend's Entertaining Dialogues.

Extracts eminently adapted to cultivate the dramatic faculties, as well as entertain an audience.

Swett's Common School Speaker.

Selections from recent literature.

Raymond's Patriotic Speaker,

A superb compilation of modern eloquence and poetry, with original dramatic exercises. Nearly every eminent *living* orator is represented, without distinction of place or party.

COMPOSITION AND RHETORIC.

Brookfield's First Book in Composition,

Making the cultivation of this important art feasible for the smallest child. By a new method, to induce and stimulate thought.

Boyd's Composition and Rhetoric.

This work furnishes all the aid that is needful or can be desired in the various departments and styles of composition, both in prose and verse.

Day's Art of Rhetoric,

Noted for exactness of definition, clear limitation, and philosophical development of subject; the large share of attention given to Invention, as a branch of Rhetoric, and the unequalled analysis of style.

MIND AND MORALS.

Mahan's Intellectual Philosophy.

The subject exhaustively considered. The author has evinced learning, candor, and independent thinking.

Mahan's Science of Logic

A profound analysis of the laws of thought. The system possesses the merit of being intelligible and self consistent. In addition to the author's carefully elaborated views, it embraces results attained by the ablest minds of Great Britain, Germany, and France, in this department.

Boyd's Elements of Logic

A systematic and philosophic condensation of the subject, fortified with additions from Watts, Abercrombie, Whately, &c.

Watts on the Mind

The Improvement of the Mind, by Isaac Watts, is designed as a guide for the attainment of useful knowledge. As a text-book it is unparalleled; and the discipline it affords cannot be too highly esteemed by the educator.

Peabody's Moral Philosophy

A short course; by the Professor of Christian Morals, Harvard University—for the Freshman Class and for High Schools.

Fletcher's Practical Ethics

A topical analysis of each of the Virtues and Graces, furnishing outlines for the pupil to illustrate from his own experience or reading.

Alden's Text-Book of Ethics

For young pupils. To aid in systematizing the ethical teachings of the Bible, and point out the coincidences between the instructions of the sacred volume and the sound conclusions of reason.

Willard's Morals for the Young

Lessons in conversational style to indicate the elements of moral philosophy. The study is made attractive by narratives and engravings.

GOVERNMENT.

Howe's Young Citizen's Catechism

Explaining the duties of District, Town, City, County, State, and United States Officers, with rules for parliamentary and commercial business.

Young's Lessons in Civil Government

A comprehensive view of Government, and abstract of the laws showing the rights, duties, and responsibilities of citizens.

Mansfield's Political Manual.

This is a complete view of the theory and practice of the General and State Governments, designed as a text-book. The author is an esteemed and able professor of constitutional law, widely known for his sagacious utterances in the public press.

Martin's Civil Government

Emanating from Massachusetts State Normal School. Historical and statistical. Each chapter summarized by a succinct statement of underlying principles on which good government is based.

MODERN LANGUAGE.

Illustrated Language Primers,

FRENCH AND ENGLISH. GERMAN AND ENGLISH.
SPANISH AND ENGLISH.

The names of common objects properly illustrated and arranged in easy lessons.

Ledru's French Fables,

Ledru's French Grammar,

Ledru's French Reader,

The author's long experience has enabled him to present the most thoroughly practical text-books extant, in this branch. The system of pronunciation (by phonetic illustration) is original with this author, and will commend itself to all American teachers, as it enables their pupils to secure an absolutely correct pronunciation without the assistance of a native master. This feature is peculiarly valuable also to "self-taught" students. The directions for ascertaining the gender of French nouns—also a great stumbling-block—are peculiar to this work, and will be found remarkably competent to the end proposed. The criticism of teachers and the test of the school-room is invited to this excellent series, with confidence.

Worman's French Echo,

To teach conversational French by actual practice, on an entirely new plan, which recognizes the importance of the student learning *to think* in the language which he speaks. It furnishes an extensive vocabulary of words and expressions in common use, and suffices to free the learner from the embarrassments which the peculiarities of his own tongue are likely to be to him, and to make him thoroughly familiar with the use of proper idioms.

Worman's German Echo,

On the same plan. See Worman's German Series, page 42.

Pujol's Complete French Class-Book,

Offers, in one volume, methodically arranged, a complete French course—usually embraced in series of from five to twelve books, including the bulky and expensive Lexicon. Here are Grammar, Conversation, and choice Literature—selected from the best French authors. Each branch is thoroughly handled; and the student, having diligently completed the course as prescribed, may consider himself, without further application, *au fait* in the most polite and elegant language of modern times.

Pujol's French Grammar, Exercises, Reader,

These volumes contain Part I, Parts II and III, and Part IV of the Complete Class-Book respectively, for the convenience of scholars and teachers. The Lexicon is bound with each part.

Maurice-Poitevin's Grammaire Francaise,

American schools are at last supplied with an American edition of this famous text-book. Many of our best institutions have for years been procuring it from abroad rather than forego the advantages it offers. The policy of putting students who have acquired some proficiency from the ordinary text-books, into a Grammar written in the vernacular, cannot be too highly commended. It affords an opportunity for finish and review at once; while embodying abundant practice of its own rules.

Joynes' French Pronunciation,

Willard's Historia de los Estados Unidos,

The History of the United States, translated by Professors TOLON and DE TORNOS, will be found a valuable, instructive, and entertaining reading-book for Spanish classes.

Pujol's Complete French Class-Book.

TESTIMONIALS.

From PROF. ELIAS PEISSNER, *Union College.*

I take great pleasure in recommending Pujol and Van Norman's French Class-Book, as there is no French grammar or class-book which can be compared with it in completeness, system, clearness, and general utility.

From EDWARD NORTH, *President of Hamilton College.*

I have carefully examined Pujol and Van Norman's French Class-Book, and am satisfied of its superiority, for college purposes, over any other heretofore used. We shall not fail to use it with our next class in French.

From A. CURTIS, *Pres't of Cincinnati Literary and Scientific Institute.*

I am confident that it may be made an instrument in conveying to the student, in from six months to a year, the art of speaking and writing the French with almost native fluency and propriety.

From HIRAM ORCUTT, A. M., *Prin. Glenwood and Tilden Ladies' Seminaries.*

I have used Pujol's French Grammar in my two seminaries, exclusively, for more than a year, and have no hesitation in saying that I regard it the best text-book in this department extant. And my opinion is confirmed by the testimony of Prof. F. De Launay and Mademoiselle Marindin. They assure me that the book is eminently accurate and practical, as tested in the school-room.

From PROF. THEO. F. DE FUMAT, *Hebrew Educational Institute, Memphis, Tenn.*

M. Pujol's French Grammar is one of the best and most practical works. The French language is chosen and elegant in style—modern and easy. It is far superior to the other French class-books in this country. The selection of the conversational part is very good, and will interest pupils; and being all completed in only one volume, it is especially desirable to have it introduced in our schools.

From PROF. JAMES H. WORMAN, *Bordentown Female College, N. J.*

The work is upon the same plan as the text-books for the study of French and English published in Berlin, for the study of those who have not the aid of a teacher, and these books are considered, by the first authorities, the best books. In most of our institutions, Americans teach the modern languages, and heretofore the trouble has been to give them a text-book that would dispose of the difficulties of the French pronunciation. This difficulty is successfully removed by P. and Van N., and I have every reason to believe it will soon make its way into most of our best schools.

From PROF. CHARLES S. DOD, *Ann Smith Academy, Lexington, Va.*

I cannot do better than to recommend "Pujol and Van Norman." For comprehensive and systematic arrangement, progressive and thorough development of all grammatical principles and idioms, with a due admixture of theoretical knowledge and practical exercise, I regard it as superior to any (other) book of the kind.

From A. A. FORSTER, *Prin. Pinehurst School, Toronto, C. W.*

I have great satisfaction in bearing testimony to M. Pujol's System of French Instruction, as given in his complete class-book. For clearness and comprehensiveness, adapted for all classes of pupils, I have found it superior to any other work of the kind, and have now used it for some years in my establishment with great success.

From PROF. OTTO FEDDER, *Maplewood Institute, Pittsfield, Mass.*

The conversational exercises will prove an immense saving of the hardest kind of labor to teachers. There is scarcely any thing more trying in the way of teaching language, than to rack your brain for short and easily intelligible bits of conversation, and to repeat them time and again with no better result than extorting at long intervals a doubting "oui," or a hesitating "non, monsieur"

☞ For further testimony of a similar character, see special circular, and current numbers of the Educational Bulletin.

GERMAN.

A COMPLETE COURSE IN THE GERMAN.

By JAMES H. WORMAN, A.M.

Worman's Elementary German Grammar
Worman's Complete German Grammar

These volumes are designed for intermediate and advanced classes respectively.

Though following the same general method with "Otto" (that of 'Gaspey'), our author differs essentially in its application. He is more practical, more systematic, more accurate, and besides introduces a number of invaluable features which have never before been combined in a German grammar.

Among other things, it may be claimed for Prof. Worman that he has been *the first* to introduce in an American text-book for learning German, a system of analogy and comparison with other languages. Our best teachers are also enthusiastic about his methods of inculcating the art of speaking, of understanding the spoken language, of correct pronunciation; the sensible and convenient original classification of nouns (in four declensions), and of irregular verbs, also deserves much praise. We also note the use of heavy type to indicate etymological changes in the paradigms, and, in the exercises, the parts which specially illustrate preceding rules.

Worman's Elementary German Reader
Worman's Collegiate German Reader

The finest and most judicious compilation of classical and standard German Literature. These works embrace, progressively arranged, selections from the masterpieces of Goethe, Schiller, Korner, Seume, Uhland, Freiligrath, Heine, Schlegel, Holty, Lenau, Wieland, Herder, Lessing, Kant, Fichte, Schelling, Winkelmann, Humboldt, Ranke, Raumer, Menzel, Gervinus, &c., and contains complete Goethe's "Iphigenie," Schiller's "Jungfrau;" also, for instruction in modern conversational German, Benedix's "Eigensinn."

There are besides, Biographical Sketches of each author contributing, Notes, explanatory and philological (after the text), Grammatical References to all leading grammars, as well as the editor's own, and an adequate Vocabulary.

Worman's German Echo

Consists of exercises in colloquial style entirely in the German, with an adequate vocabulary, not only of words but of idioms. The object of the system developed in this work (and its companion volume in the French) is to break up the laborious and tedious habit of *translating the thoughts*, which is the student's most effectual bar to fluent conversation, and to lead him to *think in the language in which he speaks.* As the exercises illustrate scenes in actual life, a considerable knowledge of the manners and customs of the German people is also acquired from the use of this manual.

Worman's German Copy-Books, 3 Numbers,

On the same plan as the most approved systems for English penmanship, with progressive copies.

Worman's German Grammars.

TESTIMONIALS.

From Prof. R. W. Jones, *Petersburg Female College, Va.*

From what I have seen of the work it is almost certain *I shall introduce it into* this institution.

From Prof. G. Campbell, *University of Minnesota.*

A valuable addition to our school-books, and will find many friends, and do great good.

From Prof. O. H P. Corprew, *Mary Military Inst., Md.*

I am better pleased with them than any I have ever taught. I have already ordered through our booksellers.

From Prof. R. S. Kendall, *Vernon Academy, Conn.*

I at once put the Elementary Grammar into the hands of a class of beginners, and have used it *with great satisfaction.*

From Prof. D. E. Holmes, *Berlin Academy, Wis.*

Worman's German works are *superior.* I shall use them hereafter in my German classes.

From Prof. Magnus Buchholtz, *Hiram College, Ohio.*

I have examined the Complete Grammar, and find it *excellent.* You may rely that it will be used here.

From Prin. Thos. W. Tobey, *Paducah Female Seminary, Ky.*

The Complete German Grammar is worthy of an extensive circulation. It is *admirably adapted* to the class-room. I shall use it.

From Prof. Alex. Rosenspitz, *Houston Academy, Texas.*

Bearer will take and pay for 3 dozen copies. Mr. Worman deserves the approbation and esteem of the teacher and the thanks of the student.

From Prof. G. Malmene, *Augusta Seminary, Maine.*

The Complete Grammar cannot fail to *give great satisfaction* by the simplicity of its arrangement, and by its completeness.

From Prin. Oval Pirkey, *Christian University, Mo.*

Just such a series as is positively necessary. I do hope the author will succeed as well in the French, &c., as he has in the German.

From Prof. S. D. Hillman, *Dickinson College, Pa.*

The class have lately commenced, and my examination thus far warrants me in saying that I regard it as *the best* grammar for instruction in the German.

From Prin. Silas Livermore, *Bloomfield Seminary, Mo.*

I have found a classically and scientifically educated Prussian gentleman whom I propose to make German instructor. I have shown him both your German grammars. He has expressed *his approbation* of them generally.

From Prof. Z. Test, *Howland School for Young Ladies, N. Y.*

I shall introduce the books. From a cursory examination I have no hesitation in pronouncing the Complete Grammar *a decided improvement* on the text-books at present in use in this country.

From Prof. Lewis Kistler, *Northwestern University, Ill.*

Having looked through the Complete Grammar with some care I must say that you have produced *a good book;* you may be awarded with this gratification—that your grammar promotes the facility of learning the German language, and of becoming acquainted with its rich literature.

From Pres. J. P. Rous, *Stockwell Collegiate Inst., Ind.*

I supplied a class with the Elementary Grammar, and it gives *complete satisfaction.* The conversational and reading exercises are well calculated to illustrate the principles, and lead the student on an easy yet thorough course. I think the Complete Grammar equally attractive.

THE CLASSICS.

LATIN.

Silber's Latin Course,

The book contains an Epitome of Latin Grammar, followed by Reading Exercises, with explanatory Notes and copious References to the leading Latin Grammars, and also to the Epitome which precedes the work. Then follow a Latin-English Vocabulary and Exercises in Latin Prose Composition, being thus complete in itself, and a very suitable work to put in the hands of one about to study the language.

Searing's Virgil's Æneid,

It contains only the first six books of the Æneid. 2. A very carefully constructed Dictionary. 3. Sufficiently copious Notes. 4. Grammatical references to four leading Grammars. 5. Numerous Illustrations of the highest order. 6. A superb Map of the Mediterranean and adjacent countries. 7. Dr. S. H. Taylor's "Questions on the Æneid." 8. A Metrical Index, and an Essay on the Poetical Style. 9. A photographic *fac simile* of an early Latin M.S. 10. The text according to Jahn, but paragraphed according to Ladewig. 11. Superior mechanical execution.

"Have examined it with great pleasure and can safely say it is the best edition of Virgil with which I am acquainted."—PROF. LESLIE WAGGENER, *Bethel College, Ky.*

"Am *very* much pleased. In following points think it surpasses: instructive illustrations, pointed and sensible notes where they are convenient to use, and a vocabulary that gives the *derivation of Latin words.*"—PRIN. E. L. RICHARDSON, *Addison Union School, N. Y.*

"A fine specimen of art, and edited in a *masterly manner.*"—SUPT. W. C. ROTE, *Lawrence Public Schools, Kansas.*

"Of Searing's Virgil I cannot speak in too high terms. While as a text-book it contains as many excellences as any I have ever seen, the fineness of the paper and the beauty of typography and exceeding neatness make it an ornament for the centre-table."—PRIN. E. C. SPALDING, *Nunda Academy, N. Y.*

☞ *For further testimonials, see page 45.*

Blair's Latin Pronunciation,

An inquiry into the proper sounds of the Language during the Classical Period. By Prof. Blair, of Hampden Sidney College, Va.

GREEK.

Crosby's Greek Grammar,
Crosby's Xenophon's Anabasis,

MYTHOLOGY.

Dwight's Grecian and Roman Mythology.

School edition, University edition,

A knowledge of the fables of antiquity, thus presented in a systematic form, is as indispensable to the student of general literature as to him who would peruse intelligently the classical authors. The mythological allusions so frequent in literature are readily understood with such a Key as this.

SEARING'S VIRGIL.

SPECIMEN FRAGMENTS OF LETTERS.

"I adopt it gladly."—PRIN. V. DABNEY, *Loudoun School, Va.*

"I like Searing's Virgil."—PROF. BRISTOL, *Ripon College, Wis.*

"Meets my desires very thoroughly."—PROF. CLARK, *Berea College, Ohio.*

"Superior to any other edition of Virgil."—PRES. HALL, *Macon College, Mo.*

"Shall adopt it at once."—PRIN. B. P. BAKER, *Searcy Female Institute, Ark.*

"Your Virgil is a *beauty*."—PROF. W. H. DE MOTTE, *Illinois Female College.*

"After use, I regard it the best."—PRIN. G. H. BARTON, *Rome Academy, N. Y.*

"We like it better every day."—PRIN. R. K. BUEHRLE, *Allentown Academy, Pa.*

"I am delighted with your Virgil."—PRIN. W. T. LEONARD, *Pierce Academy, Mass.*

"Stands well the test of class-room."—PRIN. F. A. CHASE, *Lyons Col. Inst., Iowa.*

"I do not see how it can be improved."—PRIN. N. F. D. BROWNE, *Charl. Hall, Md.*

"The most complete that I have seen."—PRIN. A. BROWN, *Columbus High School, Ohio.*

"Our Professor of Language very highly approves."—SUPT. J. G. JAMES, *Texas Military Institute.*

"It responds to a want long felt by teachers. It is beautiful and complete."—PROF. BROOKS, *University of Minnesota.*

"The ideal edition. We want a few more classics of the same sort."—PRIN. C. F. P. BANCROFT, *Lookout Mountain Institute, Tenn.*

"I certainly have never seen an edition so complete with important requisites for a student, nor with such fine text and general mechanical execution."—PRES. J. R. PARK, *University of Deseret, Utah.*

"It is charming both in its design and execution. And, on the whole, I think it is the best thing of the kind that I have seen."—PROF. J. DE F. RICHARDS, *Pres. pro tem. of University of Alabama.*

"In beauty of execution, in judicious notes, and in an adequate vocabulary, it merits all praise. I shall recommend its introduction."—PRES. J. K. PATTERSON, *Kentucky Agricultural and Mechanical College.*

"Containing a good vocabulary and judicious notes, it will enable the industrious student to acquire an accurate knowledge of the most interesting part of Virgil's works."—PROF. J. T. DUNKLIN, *East Alabama College.*

"It wants no element of completeness. It is by far the best classical text-book with which I am acquainted. The notes are just right. They help the student when he most needs help."—PRIN. C. A. BUNKER, *Caledonia Grammar School, Vt.*

"I have examined Searing's Virgil with interest, and find that it more nearly meets the wants of students than that of any other edition with which I am acquainted. I am able to introduce it to some extent at once."—PRIN. J. EASTER, *East Genesee Conference Seminary.*

"I have been wishing to get a sight of it, and it exceeds my expectations. It is a beautiful book in every respect, and bears evidence of careful and critical study. The engravings add instruction as well as interest to the work. I shall recommend it to my classes."—PRIN. CHAS. H. CHANDLER, *Glenwood Ladies' Seminary.*

"A. S. Barnes & Co. have published an edition of the first six books of Virgil's Æneid, which is superior to its predecessors in several respects. The publishers have done a good service to the cause of classical education, and the book deserves a large circulation."—PROF. GEORGE W. COLLORD, *Brooklyn Polytechnic, N. Y.*

"My attention was called to Searing's Virgil by the fact of its containing a vocabulary which would obviate the necessity of procuring a lexicon. But use in the class-room has impressed me most favorably with the accuracy and just proportion of its notes, and the general excellence of its grammatical suggestions. The general character of the book in its paper, its typography, and its engravings is highly commendable, and the fac-simile manuscript is a valuable feature. I take great pleasure in commending the book to all who do not wish a complete edition of Virgil. It suits our short school courses admirably."—HENRY L. BOLTWOOD, *Master of Princeton High School, Ill.*

RECORDS.

Cole's Self-Reporting Class-Book,

For saving the Teacher's labor in averaging. At each opening are a full set of Tables showing any scholar's standing at a glance and entirely obviating the necessity of computation.

Tracy's School-Record, Pocket edition,

For keeping a simple but exact record of Attendance, Deportment, and Scholarship. The larger edition contains also a Calendar, an extensive list of Topics for Compositions and Colloquies, Themes for Short Lectures, Suggestions to Young Teachers, etc.

Brooks' Teacher's Register,

Presents at one view a record of Attendance, Recitations, and Deportment for the whole term.

Carter's Record and Roll-Book,

This is the most complete and convenient Record offered to the public. Besides the usual spaces for General Scholarship, Deportment, Attendance, etc., for each name and day, there is a space in red lines enclosing six minor spaces in blue for recording Recitations.

National School Diary,

A little book of blank forms for weekly report of the standing of each scholar, from teacher to parent. A great convenience.

REWARDS.

National School Currency,

A little box containing certificates in the form of Money. The most entertaining and stimulating system of school rewards. The scholar is paid for his merits and fined for his shortcomings. Of course the most faithful are the most successful in business. In this way the use and value of money and the method of keeping accounts are also taught. One box of Currency will supply a school of fifty pupils.

TACTICS.

The Boy Soldier,

Complete Infantry Tactics for Schools, with illustrations, for the use of those who would introduce this pleasing relaxation from the confining duties of the desk.

CHARTS.

McKenzie's Elocutionary Chart,

Baade's Reading Case,

This remarkable piece of school-room furniture is a receptacle containing a number of primary cards. By an arrangement of slides on the front, one sentence at a time is shown to the class. Twenty-eight thousand transpositions may be made, affording a variety of progressive exercises which no other piece of apparatus offers. One of its best features is, that it is so exceedingly simple as not to get out of order, while it may be operated with one finger.

Marcy's Eureka Tablet,

A new system for the Alphabet, by which it may be taught without fail in nine lessons.

Scofield's School Tablets,

On Five Cards, exhibiting Ten Surfaces. These Tablets teach Orthography, Reading, Object-Lessons, Color, Form, etc.

Watson's Phonetic Tablets,

Four Cards, and Eight Surfaces; teaching Pronunciation and Elocution phonetically—for class exercises.

Page's Normal Chart,

The whole science of Elementary Sounds tabulated. By the author of Page's Theory and Practice of Teaching.

Clark's Grammatical Chart,

Exhibits the whole Science of Language in one comprehensive diagram.

Davies' Mathematical Chart,

Mathematics made simple to the eye.

Monteith's Reference Maps, School series, Grand series,

Eight Numbers. Mounted on Rollers. Names all laid down in small type, so that to the pupil at a short distance they are Outline Maps, while they serve as *their own key* to the teacher.

Willard's Chronographers,

Historical. Four Numbers. Ancient Chronographer; English Chronographer; American Chronographer; Temple of Time (general). Dates and Events represented to the eye.

APPARATUS.

Harrington's Geometrical Blocks,

These patented blocks are *hinged*, so that each form can be dissected.

Harrington's Fractional Blocks,

Steele's Chemical Apparatus,

Steele's Philosophical Apparatus, (see p.28)

Steele's Geological Cabinet, (see p.28)

Wood's Botanical Apparatus, (see p.30)

Bock's Physiological Apparatus,

MUSIC.

The National School Singer,

Bright, new music for the day school, embracing Song Lessons, Exercise Songs, Songs of Study, Order, Promptness and Obedience, of Industry and Nature, Patriotic and Temperance Songs, Opening and Closing Songs; in fact, everything needed in the school-room. By an eminent Musician and Composer.

Jepson's Music Readers. 3 vols.

These are not books from which children simply learn songs, parrot-like, but teach the subject progressively—the scholar learning to read music by methods similar to those employed in teaching him to read printed language. Any teacher, however ignorant of music, provided he can, upon trial, simply sound the scale, may teach it without assistance, and will end by being a good singer himself. The "Elementary Music Reader," or first volume, fully develops the system. The two companion volumes carry the same method into the higher grades, but their use is not essential.

The First Reader is also published in three parts, at 30 cents each, for those who prefer them in that form.

Bartley's Songs for the School.

A selection of appropriate Hymns of an unsectarian character, carefully classified and set to popular and "singable" Tunes, for opening and closing exercises. The Secular Department is full of bright and well selected music.

Nash & Bristow's Cantara,

The first volume is a complete musical text-book for schools of every grade. No. 2 is a choice selection of Solos and Part Songs. The authors are Directors of Music in the public schools of New York City, in which these books are the standard of instruction.

The Polytechnic

Collection of Part Songs for High and Normal Schools and Clubs. This work contains a quantity of exceedingly valuable material, heretofore accessible only in sheet form or scattered in numerous and costly works. The collection of "College Songs" is a very attractive feature.

Curtis' Little Singer,—School Vocalist,

Kingsley's School-Room Choir,—Young Ladies' Harp,

Hager's Echo (A Cantata).

DEVOTION.

Brooks' School Manual of Devotion,

This volume contains daily devotional exercises, consisting of a hymn, selections of Scripture for alternate reading by teacher and pupils, and a prayer. Its value for opening and closing school is apparent.

Brooks' School Harmonist,

Contains appropriate *tunes* for each hymn in the "Manual of Devotion" described above.

A. S. BARNES & CO.'S CATALOGUE.

DEPARTMENT OF GENERAL LITERATURE.

PRICES INCLUDING POSTAGE.

THE TEACHERS' LIBRARY.

Object Lessons—Welch, - - - - - - $1 00

This is a complete exposition of the popular modern system of "object-teaching," for teachers of primary classes.

Theory and Practice of Teaching—Page, - - 1 50

This volume has, without doubt, been read by two hundred thousand teachers, and its popularity remains undiminished—large editions being exhausted yearly. It was the pioneer, as it is now the patriarch, of professional works for teachers.

The Graded School—Wells, - - - - - - 1 25

The proper way to organize graded schools is here illustrated. The author has availed himself of the best elements of the several systems prevalent in Boston, New York, Philadelphia, Cincinnati, St. Louis, and other cities.

The Normal—Holbrook, - - - - - - 1 50

Carries a working school on its visit to teachers, showing the most approved methods of teaching all the common branches, including the technicalities, explanations, demonstrations, and definitions introductory and peculiar to each branch.

School Management—Holbrook, - - - - - 1 50

Treating of the Teacher's Qualifications: How to overcome Difficulties in Self and Others; Organization; Discipline; Methods of inciting Diligence and Order; Strategy in Management; Object Teaching.

The Teachers' Institute—Fowle, - - - - - 1 25

This is a volume of suggestions inspired by the author's experience at institutes, in the instruction of young teachers. A thousand points of interest to this class are most satisfactorily dealt with.

Schools and Schoolmasters—Dickens, - - - - 1 25

Appropriate selections from the writings of the great novelist.

The Metric System—Davies, - - - - - 1 50

Considered with reference to its general introduction, and embracing the views of John Quincy Adams and Sir John Herschel.

The Student; The Educator—Phelps, - - each, 1 50

The Discipline of Life—Phelps, - - - - - 1 75

The authoress of these works is one of the most distinguished writers on education, and they cannot fail to prove a valuable addition to the School and Teachers' Libraries, being in a high degree both interesting and instructive.

A Scientific Basis of Education—Hecker, - - 2 50

Adaptation of study and classification by temperaments.

Teachers' Hand-Book — Phelps - - - - $1 50

By Wm. F. Phelps, Principal of Minnesota State Normal School. Embracing the objects, history, organization and management of Teachers' Institutes, followed by Methods of Teaching, in detail, for all the fundamental branches. Every young teacher, every practical teacher, every experienced teacher even, needs this book.

From the New York Tribune.

"The discipline of the school should prepare the child for the discipline of life. The country schoolmaster, accordingly, holds a position of vital interest to the destiny of the republic, and should neglect no means for the wise and efficient discharge of his significant functions. This is the key-note of the present excellent volume. In view of the supreme importance of the teacher's calling, Mr. Phelps has presented an elaborate system of instruction in the elements of learning, with a complete detail of methods and processes, illustrated with an abundance of practical examples and enforced by judicious counsels, which may serve as an aid to the teacher in the performance of his arduous duties, and in the attainment of the highest excellence in his profession. The author's directions may not always be accepted without challenge by experienced instructors, who, however, are encouraged to think for themselves; but they are always suggestive, and cannot fail to be of signal value to those who are just entering upon their profession and beginning to comprehend its difficulties, as well as to discover its secrets."

American Education — Mansfield - - - - - 1 50

A treatise on the principles and elements of education, as practised in this country, with ideas towards distinctive republican and Christian education.

American Institutions — De Tocqueville - - - 1 50

A valuable index to the genius of our Government.

Universal Education — Mayhew - - - - - 1 75

The subject is approached with the clear, keen perception of one who has observed its necessity, and realized its feasibility and expediency alike. The redeeming and elevating power of improved common schools constitutes the inspiration of the volume.

Higher Christian Education — Dwight - - - - 1 50

A treatise on the principles and spirit, the modes, directions and results of all true teaching; showing that right education should appeal to every element of enthusiasm in the teacher's nature.

Oral Training Lessons — Barnard - - - - - 1 00

The object of this very useful work is to furnish material for instructors to impart orally to their classes, in branches not usually taught in common schools, embracing all departments of Natural Science and much general knowledge.

Lectures on Natural History — Chadbourne - - 75

Affording many themes for oral instruction in this interesting science—especially in schools where it is not pursued as a class exercise.

Outlines of Mathematical Science — Davies - - 1 00

A manual suggesting the best methods of presenting mathematical instruction on the part of the teacher, with that comprehensive view of the whole which is necessary to the intelligent treatment of a part, in science.

Nature and Utility of Mathematics — Davies - - 1 50

An elaborate and lucid exposition of the principles which lie at the foundation of pure mathematics, with a highly ingenious application of their results to the development of the essential idea of the different branches of the science.

Mathematical Dictionary — Davies and Peck - - 4 00

This cyclopædia of mathematical science defines, with completeness, precision, and accuracy, every technical term; thus constituting a popular treatise on each branch, and a general view of the whole subject.

Liberal Education of Women—Orton . . *$1 50

Treats of "the demand and the method;" being a compilation of the best and most advanced thought on this subject, by the leading writers and educators in England and America. Edited by a Professor in Vassar College.

Education Abroad—Northrop *1 50

A thorough discussion of the advantages and disadvantages of sending American children to Europe to be educated; also, Papers on Legal Prevention of Illiteracy, Study and Health, Labor as an Educator, and other kindred subjects. By the Hon. Secretary of Education for Connecticut.

The Teacher and the Parent—Northend . . *1 50

A treatise upon common-school education, designed to lead teachers to view their calling in its true light, and to stimulate them to fidelity.

The Teachers' Assistant—Northend *1 50

A natural continuation of the author's previous work, more directly calculated for daily use in the administration of school discipline and instruction.

School Government—Jewell *1 50

Full of advanced ideas on the subject which its title indicates. The criticisms upon current theories of punishment and schemes of administration have excited general attention and comment.

Grammatical Diagrams—Jewell *1 00

The diagram system of teaching grammar explained, defended, and improved. The curious in literature, the searcher for truth, those interested in new inventions, as well as the disciples of Prof. Clark, who would see their favorite theory fairly treated, all want this book. There are many who would like to be made familiar with this system before risking its use in a class. The opportunity is here afforded.

The Complete Examiner—Stone *1 25

Consists of a series of questions on every English branch of school and academic instruction, with reference to a given page or article of leading text-books where the answer may be found in full. Prepared to aid teachers in securing certificates, pupils in preparing for promotion, and teachers in selecting review questions.

School Amusements—Root *1 50

To assist teachers in making the school interesting, with hints upon the management of the school-room. Rules for military and gymnastic exercises are included. Illustrated by diagrams.

Institute Lectures—Bates *1 50

These lectures, originally delivered before institutes, are based upon various topics in the departments of mental and moral culture. The volume is calculated to prepare the will, awaken the inquiry, and stimulate the thought of the zealous teacher.

Method of Teachers' Institutes—Bates . . . *75

Sets forth the best method of conducting institutes, with a detailed account of the object, organization, plan of instruction, and true theory of education on which such instruction should be based.

History and Progress of Education *1 50

The systems of education prevailing in all nations and ages, the gradual advance to the present time, and the bearing of the past upon the present in this regard, are worthy of the careful investigation of all concerned in education.

THE SCHOOL LIBRARY.

The two elements of instruction and entertainment were never more happily combined than in this collection of standard books. Children and adults alike will here find ample food for the mind, of the sort that is easily *digested*, while not degenerating to the level of modern romance.

LIBRARY OF LITERATURE.

Milton's Paradise Lost. Boyd's Illustrated Ed., $1 60

Young's Night Thoughts . . . . do. . . 1 60

Cowper's Task, Table Talk, &c. . do. . . 1 60

Thomson's Seasons . . . . do. . . 1 60

Pollok's Course of Time . . . . do. . . 1 60

These works, models of the best and purest literature, are beautifully illustrated, and notes explain all doubtful meanings.

Lord Bacon's Essays (Boyd's Edition) . . . 1 60

Another grand English classic, affording the highest example of purity in language and style.

The Iliad of Homer. Translated by POPE. . . 80

Those who are unable to read this greatest of ancient writers in the original, should not fail to avail themselves of this metrical version.

Compendium of Eng. Literature—Cleveland, 2 25

English Literature of XIXth Century do. 2 25

Compendium of American Literature do. 2 25

Nearly one hundred and fifty thousand volumes of Prof. CLEVELAND's inimitable compendiums have been sold. Taken together they present a complete view of literature. To the man who can afford but a few books these will supply the place of an extensive library. From commendations of the very highest authorities the following extracts will give some idea of the enthusiasm with which the works are regarded by scholars:

With the Bible and your volumes one might leave libraries without very painful regret.—The work cannot be found from which in the same limits so much interesting and valuable information may be obtained.—Good taste, fine scholarship, familiar acquaintance with literature, unwearied industry, tact acquired by practice, an interest in the culture of the young, and regard for truth, purity, philanthropy and religion are united in Mr. Cleveland.—A judgment clear and impartial, a taste at once delicate and severe.—The biographies are just and discriminating.—An admirable bird's-eye view.—Acquaints the reader with the characteristic method, tone, and quality of each writer.—Succinct, carefully written, and wonderfully comprehensive in detail, etc., etc.

Milton's Poetical Works—CLEVELAND . . . 2 25

This is the very best edition of the great Poet. It includes a life of the author, notes, dissertations on each poem, a faultless text, and is *the only* edition of Milton with a complete verbal Index.

LIBRARY OF HISTORY.

Seven Historic Ages—Gilman, - - - - - $1 00

Or, Talks about Kings, Queens, and Barbarians. These delightful sketches of notable events stir the imagination of the young reader, and give him a taste for further historical reading. Illustrated.

Outlines of General History—Gilman, - - - - 1 25

The number of facts which the author has compressed into these outline sketches is really surprising; the chapters on the Middle Ages and Feudalism afford striking examples of his power of succinct but comprehensive statement. In his choice of representative periods and events in the histories of Nations he shows very sound judgment, and his characterization of conspicuous historical figures is accurate and impartial.

Great Events of History—Collier, - - - - - 1 50

This celebrated work, edited for American readers by Prof. O. R. Willis, gives, in a series of pictures, a pleasantly readable and easily remembered view of the Christian era. Each chapter is headed by its central point of interest to afford association for the mind. Delineations of life and manners at different periods are interwoven. A geographical appendix of great value is added.

History of England—Lancaster, - - - - - 1 50

An arrangement of the essential facts of English History in the briefest manner consistent with clearness. With a fine Map.

History of Liberty—Aiken, - - - - - - 1 00

Explaining the growth of the "fair consummate flower" of freedom in America as the result of centuries of trial and experience in the Old World.

Critical History of the Civil War—Mahan, - - 3 00

A logical analysis of campaigns and battles, and the causes of victory and defeat. By Dr. Asa Mahan, first President of Oberlin College. Dr. Mahan never forgets that history is "philosophy teaching by examples," and his work should be a text-book for American youth.

History of Europe—Alison, - - - - - - 2 50

A reliable and standard work, which covers with clear, connected, and complete narrative the eventful occurrences of the years A. D. 1789 to 1815, being mainly a history of the career of Napoleon Bonaparte.

History of Rome—Ricord, - - - - - - 1 75

An entertaining narrative for the young. Illustrated. Embracing successively, The Kings; The Republic; The Empire.

Ecclesiastical History—Marsh, - - - - - - 2 00

A history of the Church in all ages, with a comprehensive review of all forms of religion from the creation of the world. No other source affords, in the same compass, the information here conveyed.

History of the Ancient Hebrews—Mills, - - - 1 75

The record of "God's people" from the call of Abraham to the destruction of Jerusalem; gathered from sources sacred and profane.

The Mexican War—Mansfield, - - - - - 1 50

A history of its origin, and a detailed account of its victories; with official despatches, the treaty of peace, and valuable tables. Illustrated.

Early History of Michigan—Sheldon, - - - - 2 50

A work of value and deep interest to the people of the West. Compiled under the supervision of Hon. Lewis Cass. Portraits.

History of Texas—Baker, - - - - - - 1 25

A pithy and interesting resumé. Copiously illustrated. The State constitution and extracts from the speeches and writings of eminent Texans are appended.

NEW LIBRARY OF HISTORY.

Barnes' Centenary History, - - - - - - *$6 00

"*One Hundred Years of American Independence.*" This superbly illustrated work, by the author of "Barnes' Brief Histories" (for schools), is appropriately issued in the "centennial year" (1876). An extended Introduction brings down the history from the earliest times. The leading idea is to make American History *popular* for the masses, and especially with the young. The style is therefore life-like and vivid, carrying the reader along by the sweep of the story as in a novel, so that when he begins an account of an important event he cannot very well lay down the book until he finishes.

Lamb's History of New York City.

One of the most important works ever issued. It opens with a brief outline of the condition of the old world prior to the settlement of the new, and proceeds to give a careful analysis of the two great Dutch Commercial Corporations to which New York owes its origin. It sketches the rise and growth of the little colony on Manhattan Island; describes the Indian Wars with which it was afflicted; gives color and life to its Dutch rulers; paints its subjugation by the English, its after vicissitudes, the Revolution of 1689; in short, it leads the reader through one continuous chain of events down to the American Revolution. Then, gathering up the threads, the author gives an artistic and comprehensive account of the progress of the City, in extent, education, culture, literature, art, and political and commercial importance, during the last century. Prominent persons are introduced in all the different periods, with choice bits of family history, and glimpses of social life. The work contains maps of the City in the different decades, and several rare portraits from original paintings, which have never before been engraved. The illustrations, about 250 in number, are all of an interesting and highly artistic character.

The work is now being published, by subscription only, in about 30 parts, at 50 cents each.

Carrington's Battles of the Revolution, - - - - $6 00

A careful description and analysis of every engagement of the War for Independence, with topographical charts prepared from personal surveys by the author, a veteran officer of the U. S. Army, and Professor of Military Science in Wabash College.

Baker's Texas Scrap-Book, - - - - - - $5 00

Comprising the History, Biography, Literature, and Miscellany of Texas and its people. A valuable collection of material, anecdotical and statistical, which is not to be found in any other form. The work is handsomely illustrated. (Sheep, $6.00.)

LIBRARY OF REFERENCE.

Home Cyclopædia of Literature and Fine Arts, - $3 00

A complete index to all terms employed in belles lettres, philosophy, theology, law, mythology, painting, music, sculpture, architecture, and all kindred arts.

The Rhyming Dictionary—Walker, - - - - 1 25

A serviceable manual to composers, being a complete index of allowable rhymes.

The Topical Lexicon—Williams, - - - - - 1 75

The useful terms of the English language *classified by subjects* and arranged according to their affinities of meaning, with etymologies, definitions, and illustrations. A very entertaining and instructive work.

Mathematical Dictionary—Davies and Peck, - - 4 00

A thorough compendium of the science, with illustrations and definitions.

LIBRARY OF BIOGRAPHY.

Autobiography of President Finney, - - - $2 00

The "Memoirs of Rev. Charles G. Finney, written by himself," with Portrait on steel. The work presents the experience, labors, and thoughts of the eminent Evangelist, Preacher, and Teacher. It gives the history of the great revivals in which he labored, and also his work in connection with Oberlin College.

The book is full of personal incidents illustrating the power of the Gospel upon the hearts and lives of men, and of practical suggestions for the promotion of revivals. It is also rich in its exhibition of personal religious experience, and of the nature and the efficacy of prayer.

Life of P. P. Bliss—Whittle, Moody & Sankey, - - 2 00

The memorials of the lamented singer and evangelist which have here been gathered by the hands of loving friends will commend themselves to a great multitude of interested readers. Ten thousand copies of the book were sold within thirty days after publication. It contains steel-plate engravings of the Bliss family, and a number of new songs with music not before published.

Life of Dr. Sam Johnson—Boswell, - - - 2 25

This work has been before the public for seventy years, with increasing approbation. Boswell is known as "the prince of biographers."

Henry Clay's Life and Speeches—Mallory. 2 vols., 4 50

This great American statesman commands the admiration, and his character and deeds solicit the study of every patriot.

Life and Services of General Scott—Mansfield, - 1 75

The hero of the Mexican war, who was for many years the most prominent figure in American military circles, should not be forgotten in the whirl of more recent events than those by which he signalized himself. Illustrated.

Garibaldi's Autobiography, - - - - - - 1 50

The Italian patriot's record of his own life, translated and edited by his friend and admirer. A thrilling narrative of a romantic career. With portrait.

Lives of the Signers—Dwight, - - - - 1 50

The memory of the noble men who declared our country free at the peril of their own "lives, fortunes, and sacred honor," should be embalmed in every American's heart.

Life of Sir Joshua Reynolds—Cunningham, - - 1 50

A candid, truthful, and appreciative memoir of the great painter, with a compilation of his discourses. The volume is a text-book for artists, as well as those who would acquire the rudiments of art. With a portrait.

Prison Life, - - - - - - - - - - 75

Interesting biographies of celebrated prisoners and martyrs, designed especially for the instruction and cultivation of youth.

LIBRARY OF TRAVEL.

Texas; the Coming Empire—McDaniel and Taylor, $1 50

Narrative of a two thousand mile trip on horseback through the Lone Star State; with lively descriptions of people, scenery, and resources.

Life in the Sandwich Islands—Cheever, - - 1 50

The "Heart of the Pacific, as it was and is," shows most vividly the contrast between the depth of degradation and barbarism and the light and liberty of civilization, so rapidly realized in these islands under the humanizing influence of the Christian religion. Illustrated.

The Republic of Liberia—Stockwell, - - - - 1 25

This volume treats of the geography, climate, soil and productions of this interesting country on the coast of Africa, with a History of its early settlement. Our colored citizens especially, from whom the founders of the new State went forth, should read Mr. Stockwell's account of it. It is so arranged as to be available for a School Reader, and in colored schools is peculiarly appropriate as an instrument of education for the young. Liberia is likely to bear an important part in the future of their race.

Ancient Monasteries of the East—Curzon, - - 1 50

The exploration of these ancient seats of learning has thrown much light upon the researches of the historian, the philologist, and the theologian, as well as the general student of antiquity. Illustrated.

Discoveries in Babylon and Nineveh—Layard, - - 1 75

Valuable alike for the information imparted with regard to these most interesting ruins and the pleasant adventures and observations of the author in regions that to most men seem like Fairyland. Illustrated.

A Run Through Europe—Benedict, - - - - 2 00

A work replete with instruction and interest—an admirable guide-book.

St. Petersburgh—Jermann, - - - - - - 1 00

Americans are less familiar with the history and social customs of the Russian people than those of any other modern civilized nation. Opportunities such as this book affords are not, therefore, to be neglected.

The Polar Regions—Osborn, - - - - - - 1 25

A thrilling and intensely interesting narrative of one of the famous expeditions in search of Sir John Franklin—unsuccessful in its main object, but adding many facts to the repertoire of science.

Thirteen Months in the Confederate Army, - - 75

The author, a northern man conscripted into the Confederate service, and rising from the ranks by soldierly conduct to positions of responsibility, had remarkable opportunities for the acquisition of facts respecting the conduct of the Southern armies, and the policy and deeds of their leaders. He participated in many engagements, and his book is one of the most exciting narratives of adventure ever published. Mr. Stevenson takes no ground as a partisan, but views the whole subject as with the eye of a neutral—only interested in subserving the ends of history by the contribution of impartial facts. Illustrated.

RELIGIOUS LIBRARY.

Abbott's Commentaries—MATTHEW AND MARK, $2 50

With Notes, Comments, Maps, and Illustrations; also, an Introduction to the study of the New Testament, a condensed Life of Christ, and a Tabular Harmony of the Gospels. Trade edition, $2.50; subscription edition, royal 8vo, $3.50.

THE GOSPEL OF LUKE, $1 75. ACTS OF THE APOSTLES, $2 00

With Notes, etc., as above; also, an Introduction to the study, a Gazetteer, Chronological Table, etc.

Ray Palmer's Poetical Works, ... 4 00

An exquisite edition of the complete hymns and other poetical writings of the most eminent of American sacred poets—author of "My faith looks up to Thee."

Dale on the Atonement, ... 2 00

The theory and fact of Christ's atonement profoundly considered.

The Service of Song—Stacy 1 50

A treatise on Singing, in public and private devotion. Its history, office, and importance considered.

True Success in Life—Palmer 1 50

Earnest words for the young who are just about to meet the responsibilities and temptations of mature life.

"Remember Me."—Palmer 1 50

Preparation for the Holy Communion.

Chrysostom, or the Mouth of Gold—Johnson 1 00

An entertaining dramatic sketch, by Rev. Edwin Johnson, illustrating the life and times of St. Chrysostom.

The Memorial Pulpit—Robinson. 2 vols., each 1 50

A series of wide-awake sermons by the popular pastor of the Memorial Presbyterian Church, New York.

Responsive Worship—Budington 60

An argument in favor of alternate Scripture reading by Pastor and Congregation.

Lady Willoughby 1 00

The diary of a wife and mother. An historical romance of the seventeenth century. At once beautiful and pathetic, entertaining and instructive.

Favorite Hymns Restored—Gage 1 25

Most of the standard hymns have undergone modification or abridgment by compilers, but this volume contains them exactly as written by the authors.

Poets' Gift of Consolation 1 50

A beautiful selection of poems referring to the death of children.

The Mosaic Account of Creation 1 50

The Miracle of To-day; or New Witnesses of the Oneness of Genesis and Science. With Essays on the Cause and Epoch of the present Inclination of the Earth's Axis, and on Cosmology. By Charles B. Warring.

VALUABLE LIBRARY BOOKS.

Principles and Acts of the Revolution, . . 3 00

Compiled from "Niles's Register." Being "a collection of Speeches, Orations, and Proceedings, with Sketches and Remarks on Men and Things." This work has long been standard, though for many years out of print, and the eager demand for its republication induces the publishers to offer this new edition.

American Institutions—De Tocqueville . . 1 50

Democracy in America—De Tocqueville . . 2 50

The views of this distinguished foreigner on the genius of our political institutions are of unquestionable value, as proceeding from a standpoint whence we seldom have an opportunity to hear.

Constitutions of the United States 2 25

Contains the Constitution of the General Government, and of the several State Governments, the Declaration of Independence, and other important documents relating to American history. Indispensable as a work of reference.

Public Economy of the United States . . . 2 25

A full discussion of the relations of the United States with other nations, especially the feasibility of a free-trade policy.

Grecian and Roman Mythology—Dwight . 3 00

The presentation, in a systematic form, of the Fables of Antiquity, affords most entertaining reading, and is valuable to all as an index to the mythological allusions so frequent in literature, as well as to students of the classics who would peruse intelligently the classical authors. Illustrated.

General View of the Fine Arts—Huntington 1 75

The preparation of this work was suggested by the interested inquiries of a group of young people concerning the productions and styles of the great masters of art, whose names only were familiar. This statement is sufficient index of its character.

The Poets of Connecticut—Everest 1 75

With the biographical sketches, this volume forms a complete history of the poetical literature of the State.

The Son of a Genius—Hofland 75

A juvenile classic which never wears out, and finds many interested readers in every generation of youth.

Sunny Hours of Childhood 75

Interesting and moral stories for children.

Morals for the Young—Willard 75

A series of moral stories, by one of the most experienced of American educators. Illustrated.

Improvement of the Mind—Isaac Watts . . 50

A classical standard. No young person should grow up without having perused it.

PUBLIC WORSHIP.

Songs for the Sanctuary,

By REV. S. C. ROBINSON. 1344 Hymns, with Tunes. The most successful modern hymn and tune book, for congregations and choirs. More than 200,000 copies have been sold. Separate editions for Presbyterian, Congregational, and Baptist Churches. Editions without Tunes, $1.75; in large type, $2.50. Abridged edition ("Songs for Christian Worship"), 859 Hymns, with Tunes, $1.50. Chapel edition, 607 Hymns, with Tunes, $1.40.

Psalms and Hymns and Spiritual Songs,

Also by Dr. ROBINSON. Differs from "Songs for the Sanctuary" in having *all the hymns* set to music, for pure congregational singing. 1294 Psalms and Hymns, with Tunes. Cheap edition, $1.75; edition without Tunes, 75 cents.

Baptist Praise Book,

By REV. DRS. FULLER, LEVY, PHELPS, FISH, ARMITAGE, WINKLER, EVARTS, LORIMER and MANLY, and J. P. HOLBROOK, Esq. 1311 Hymns, with Tunes. Edition without Tunes, $1.75. Chapel edition, 550 Hymns, with Tunes, $1.25.

Plymouth Collection,

(Congregational.) By REV. HENRY WARD BEECHER. 1374 Hymns, with Tunes. Separate edition for Baptist Churches. Editions without Tunes, $1.25 and $1.75.

Hymns of the Church,

(Undenominational.) By REV. DRS. THOMPSON, VERMILYE, and EDDY. 1007 Hymns, with Tunes. The use of this book is required in all congregations of the Reformed Church in America. Edition without Tunes, $1.75. Chapel edition ("Hymns of Prayer and Praise"), 320 Hymns, with Tunes, 75 cts.

Episcopal Common Praise,

The Service set to appropriate Music, with Tunes for all the Hymns in the Book of Common Prayer.

Hymnal, with Tunes,

(Episcopal.) By HALL & WHITELEY. The new Hymnal, set to Music. Edition with Chants, $1.50. Edition of Hymns only ("Companion" Hymnal), 60 cts.

Metrical Tune Book. By PHILIP PHILLIPS.

Quartet and Chorus Choir. By J. P. HOLBROOK.

Containing Music for the Unadapted Hymns in Songs for the Sanctuary.

Pilgrim Melodies. By J. E. SWEETSER.

Christian Melodies. By GEO. B. CHEEVER. Hymns and Tunes.

Mount Zion Collection. By T. E. PERKINS. For the Choir.

Selah. By THOS. HASTINGS. For the Choir.

Public Worship (Partly Responsive)

Containing complete services (not Episcopal) for five Sabbaths; for use in schools, public institutions, summer resorts, churches without a settled pastor; in short, wherever Christians desire to worship—no clergyman being present.

The Union Prayer Book,

A Manual for Public and Private Worship. With those features which are objectionable to other denominations of Christians than Episcopal eliminated or modified. Contains a Service for Sunday Schools and Family Prayers.

The Psalter,

Selections from the Psalms, for responsive reading.

LATEST PUBLICATIONS.

The Commonwealth Reconstructed—Clark, - - $1 50

Setting forth why our democracy is a partial failure, with a remedial method.

Nine Lectures on Preaching—Dale, - - - - 1 50

By Rev. R. W. Dale, of England. Delivered at Yale College, October 1877. Contents: Perils of Young Preachers; The Intellect in Relation to Preaching; Reading; Preparation of Sermons; Extemporaneous Preaching; Evangelistic Preaching; Pastoral Preaching; Conduct of Public Worship.

The Working Classes in Europe—Hughes, - - 1 00

Choice Articles from the "International Review" on Labor, Republican Government, and kindred topics. By Thomas Hughes, M.P., and other competent writers.

Our National Currency—Amasa Walker, - - - 0 50

The money problem in all its bearings.

The World's Fair in 1876—F. A. Walker, - - 0 75

An historical and critical account by the distinguished chief of the Bureau of Awards, Gen. Francis A. Walker.

Student's Common-Place Book—Fox, - - - $4 50

The result of over thirty years effective reading by a clergyman and teacher, forming a Cyclopedia of Illustration and Fact. Interleaved for Additions by the owner; thus combining a printed Manual of Literature with the Blanks of an Index Rerum. Its double value will make it the favorite book of the library.

Biographical and Critical Essays—Atlas Series, - - 1 50

Choice articles from the International Review on Macaulay, Ticknor, Ernst Curtius, Hamerton, Longfellow, Bryant, Poe, Chas. Tennyson, Freeman, Sumner, John Stuart Mill. By Edward A. Freeman, and other eminent writers.

Formation of Religious Opinions—Palmer, - - 1 25

Hints for the benefit of young people who have found themselves disturbed by inward questionings or doubts concerning the Christian faith.

Outlines of English Literature—Gilman, - - - 1 00

Gives, within the compass of two hundred pages, a suggestive outline sketch of the history of English Literature, grouping authors in accordance with the development of the language and literature.

PERIODICALS.

The International Review, - - - - - - $5 00

As its title indicates, presents "the ripest and best thought of the age" in all countries. Its contributors are the leading thinkers and writers of both Continents. Published bi-monthly, $5.00 per year. Bound volumes for 1874 and succeeding years, each, $6.00.

Magazine of American History, - - - - 5 00

For the collection and preservation of all material relating to our country. Edited by John Austin Stevens, Librarian of the New York Historical Society. Monthly, $5.00 per year.

FURNITURE.

(SUPPLIED BY THE NATIONAL SCHOOL FURNITURE CO.)

PEARD'S PATENT FOLDING DESK AND SETTEE.

This great improvement for the school-room has come already into such astonishing demand as to tax the utmost resources of the company's two factories to supply it. By a simple movement the desk-lid is folded away over the back of the settee attached in front, making a false back, and at once converting the school-room into a lecture or assembly-room. When the seat also is folded, the whole occupies *only ten inches of space*, leaving room for gymnastic exercises, marching, etc., or for the janitor to clean the room effectively.

NATIONAL STUDY DESK AND SETTEE.

When not in use for writing, the desk-lid slides back vertically into a chamber, leaving in front an "easel," with clamps, upon which the student places his book and studies in an erect posture. As a folding-desk this offers many of the same advantages as the "Peard."

THE GEM DESK AND SETTEE.

Fixed top, and folding seat. This is the *neatest* pattern of the Standard School Desk, and the *strongest* in use.

THE ECONOMIC DESK AND SETTEE.

This is the *cheapest* good desk, with stationary lid and folding seat.

All descriptions of

HIGH SCHOOL DESKS,
TEACHERS' DESKS,
BLACKBOARDS,
CHAIRS,
SCHOOL SETTEES,
CHURCH SETTEES,
PEW ENDS,
LECTERNS, Etc.

Also,

TAYLOR'S PATENT CLASS AND LECTURE CHAIR.

The difficulty of reconciling furniture appropriate for the Lecture-room or Church with that convenient for the Sunday-school is an old one. This article effectually remedies it. It consists simply of a plan by which chairs of a somewhat peculiar shape are connected with a coupling. The rows of chairs thus adjusted may at pleasure and with ease be spread out straight in one line, forming pews or benches; or they may be bent in an instant into a semi-circular form to accomodate classes of any size to receive instruction from teachers seated in their midst.

For further particulars, consult catalogues of the National School Furniture Co. and the Taylor Patent Chair Co., which may be obtained of A. S. Barnes & Co.

GENERAL INDEX TO
A. S. BARNES & CO.'S DESCRIPTIVE CATALOGUE

The Peabody Correspondence.

NEW YORK, April 29, 1867.

TO THE BOARD OF TRUSTEES OF THE PEABODY EDUCATIONAL FUND:

GENTLEMEN—Having been for many years intimately connected with the educational interests of the South, we are desirous of expressing our appreciation of the noble charity which you represent. The Peabody Fund, to encourage and aid common schools in these war-desolated States, cannot fail of accomplishing a great and good work, the beneficent results of which, as they will be exhibited in the future, not only of the stricken population of the South, but of the nation at large, seem almost incalculable.

It is probable that the use of meritorious text-books will prove a most effective agency toward the thorough accomplishment of Mr. Peabody's benevolent design. As we publish many which are considered such, we have selected from our list some of the most valuable, and ask the privilege of placing them in your hands for gratuitous distribution in connection with the fund of which you have charge, among the teachers and in the schools of the destitute South.

Observing that the training of teachers (through the agency of Normal Schools and otherwise) is to be a prominent feature of your undertaking, we offer you for this purpose 5,000 volumes of the "Teacher's Library"—a series of professional works designed for the efficient self-education of those who are in their turn to teach others—as follows:—

500 Page's Theory and Practice of Teaching.
500 Welch's Manual of Object-Lessons.
500 Davies' Outlines of Mathematical Science.
250 Holbrook's Normal Methods of Teaching.
250 Wells on Graded Schools.
250 Jewell on School Government.
250 Fowle's Teachers' Institute.
250 Bates' Method of Teachers' Institutes
250 De Tocqueville's American Instit'ns.
250 Dwight's Higher Christian Educat'n.
250 History of Education.
250 Mansfield on American Education.
250 Mayhew on Universal Education.
250 Northend's Teacher's Assistant.
250 Northend's Teacher and Parent.
250 Root on School Amusement.
250 Stone's Teachers' Examiner.

In addition to these we also ask that you will accept 25,000 volumes of school books for intermediate classes, embracing—

5,000 The National Second Reader.
5,000 Davies' Written Arithmetic.
5,000 Monteith's Second Book in Geography.
3,000 Monteith's United States History.
5,000 Beers' Penmanship.
500 First Book of Science.
500 Jarvis' Physiology and Health.
500 Peck's Ganot's Natural Philosophy.
500 Smith & Martin's Book-keeping.

Should your Board consent to undertake the distribution of these volumes, we shall hold ourselves in readiness to pack and ship the same in such quantities and to such points as you may designate.

We further propose that, should you find it advisable to use a greater quantity of our publications in the prosecution of your plans, we will donate, for the benefit of this cause, *twenty-five per cent.* of the usual wholesale price of the books needed.

Hoping that our request will meet with your approval, and that we may have the pleasure of contributing in this way to wants with which we deeply sympathize, we are, gentlemen, very respectfully yours, A. S. BARNES & CO.

MESSRS. A. S. BARNES & CO., PUBLISHERS, NEW YORK: BOSTON, May 7, 1867.

GENTLEMEN—Your communication of the 29th ult., addressed to the Trustees of the Peabody Education Fund, has been handed to me by our general agent, the Rev. Dr. Sears. I shall take the greatest pleasure in laying it before the board at their earliest meeting. I am unwilling, however, to postpone its acknowledgment so long, and hasten to assure you of the high value which I place upon your gift. Five thousand volumes of your "Teachers' Library," and twenty-five thousand volumes of "School-books for intermediate classes," make up a most munificent contribution to the cause of Southern education in which we are engaged. Dr. Sears is well acquainted with the books you have so generously offered us, and unites with me in the highest appreciation of the gift. You will be glad to know, too, that your letter reached us in season to be communicated to Mr. Peabody, before he embarked for England on the 1st inst., and that he expressed the greatest gratification and gratitude on hearing what you had offered.

Believe me, gentlemen, with the highest respect and regard, your obliged and obedient servant, ROBT. C. WINTHROP, Chairman.

www.ingramcontent.com/pod-product-compliance
Lightning Source LLC
LaVergne TN
LVHW021313110826
845150LV00003B/562
* 9 7 8 1 4 2 5 5 5 7 8 7 4 *